AGS

Life Skills
Health

AGS®

American Guidance Service, Inc.
Circle Pines, Minnesota 55014-1796
800-328-2560

Acknowledgment

The publisher gratefully acknowledges the students of Dr. Robert Wandberg, John F. Kennedy High School, Bloomington, Minnesota, for writing the self-assessments for each unit.

Photos:

Front cover: upper right—©Rob Gage; lower left and background—©Jess Stock/Tony Stone Images; Back cover: background—©Jess Stock/Tony Stone Images; lower left—©Cameron Hervet; pp. xi, 8—(Dugald Bremmer/Tony Stone Images; pp. 4, 256—(David Young-Wolff/Tony Stone Images; pp. 10, 72, 162, 204, 258, 304, 370—©Joe McBride/Tony Stone Images; pp. 11, 28, 52—©Manfred Kage/Peter Arnold, Inc.; pp. 14, 249—©Myrleen Ferguson/PhotoEdit; pp. 23, 380—©Gary Conner/PhotoEdit; pp. 30, 37, 45, 54, 226, 238, 295, 353—David Young-Wolff/ PhotoEdit; p. 38—©Jess Stock/Tony Stone Images; pp. 41, 70, 423, 427—©Skjold Photographs; pp. 62, 109, 309, 402—©Michael Newman/PhotoEdit; pp. 73, 98, 116, 140—©Runk/Schoenberger/Grant

Heilman Photography, Inc.; p. 119—©SuperStock International; p. 126—Dana Shetter; p. 134—©Tom McCarthy/PhotoEdit; pp. 143, 213, 222, 394—©Robert Brenner/PhotoEdit; pp. 148, 273, 180, 329, 332, 349, 409 right—©Tony Freeman/PhotoEdit; pp. 160, 287, 400—©Mary Kate Denny/PhotoEdit; pp. 163, 186—©Howard L. Garrett/Rainbow; pp. 169, 175, 177, 182—©Felicia Martinez/PhotoEdit; pp. 172—©Steven Needham/Envision; p. 173—©Richard Hutchings/PhotoEdit; p. 178—©Shaun Egan/Tony Stone Images; p. 189—©Jeff Greenberg/PhotoEdit; p. 202—©UPI/Corbis; pp. 205, 218, 232—©NIBSC/Science Photo Library/Photo Researchers, Inc.; p. 235—©John Bavosi/Science Photo Library/Photo Researchers, Inc.; p. 242—©Mark Douet/Tony Stone

Images; p. 246—©American Diabetes Association; pp. vii, 259, 284—©Uniphoto; pp. 260, 261, 267, 268, 274, 279—©Michael Crousek; p. 302— ©Rudy VonBriel/PhotoEdit; pp. 305, 328, 346—©William James Warren/Westlight; p. 312—©Vince Streano/Tony Stone Images; p. 316—©Eric R. Berndt/Unicorn Stock Photos; p. 320—©Charles Doswell III/Tony Stone Images; p. 321—©Billy Barnes/PhotoEdit; pp. 322, 384—©A. Ramey/PhotoEdit; p. 360—©Zigy Kaluzny/Tony Stone Images; p. 362—©David K. Crow/PhotoEdit; p. 368—©Spencer Grant/ PhotoEdit; pp. 371, 392, 434—©Craig Aurness/Westlight; p. 374—©Stan Fellerman/Tony Stone Images; p. 380—©Gary A. Conner/PhotoEdit; pp. 409 left, 417—©Anne Heller; p. 447—Custom Medical Stock Photo

Printed in the United States of America

ISBN 0-7854-1859-8

Product Number 92000

A 0 9 8 7 6 5 4 3

Contents

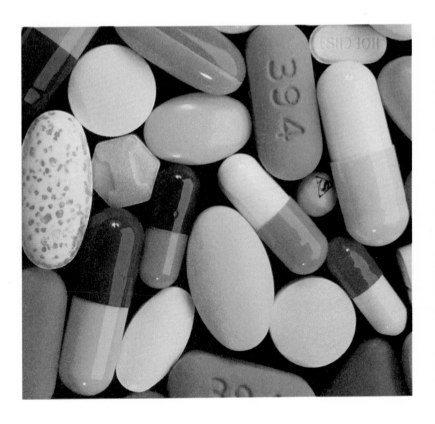

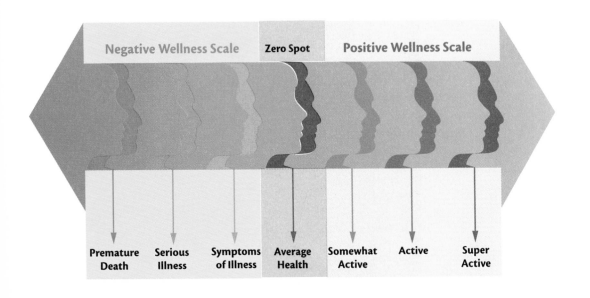

How to Use This Book: A Study Guide

Welcome to the study of health. Everyone wants to have good health and wellness. Studying health helps to learn ways to promote wellness. It helps identify causes of health problems and ways to prevent them.

As you read the units, chapters, and lessons of this book, you will learn about promoting emotional, physical, and social health.

How to Study

- Plan a regular time to study.

- Choose a quiet desk or table where you will not be distracted. Find a spot that has good lighting.

- Gather all the books, pencils, and paper you need to complete your assignments.

- Decide on a goal. For example: "I will finish reading and taking notes on Chapter 1, Lesson 1, by 8:00."

- Take a five- to ten-minute break every hour to keep alert.

- If you start to feel sleepy, take a short break and get some fresh air.

Before Beginning Each Unit

- ■ Read the title and the opening paragraph.

- ■ Study the photograph. What does the photo say to you about health?

- ■ What does the quotation say to you?

- ■ Read the titles of the chapters in the unit.

- ■ Take the Self-Assessment to rate your knowledge of that health topic.

- ■ Look at the headings of the lessons and paragraphs to help you locate main ideas.

- ■ Read the chapter and unit summaries to help you identify key issues.

- ■ Read the Deciding for Yourself page at the end of each unit.

It is in your power to withdraw into yourself whenever you desire. Perfect tranquillity within consists in the good ordering of the mind—the realm of your own.
—Marcus Aurelius

Unit 1

Mental and Emotional Health

Who are you? When you meet someone new, how do you answer this question? A simple answer would include your name, age, and year in school. Would these answers really describe you? Think about who you are. Who do you want to be in the future? How do these compare?

The way you view yourself has a big impact on your life. Your beliefs about yourself affect what you do, and how healthy you are. These beliefs also play a major role in how you handle relationships. In this unit, you will learn about mental and emotional health. Applying these ideas to your own experiences will help you attain your goals and become the person you want to be.

▶ Chapter 1 Emotions
▶ Chapter 2 Maintaining Mental Health
▶ Chapter 3 Mental Health Problems

Each unit covers a different health topic.

Before Beginning Each Chapter

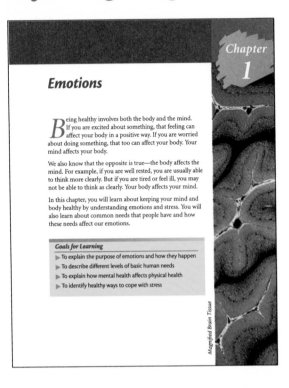

■ Read the chapter title.

■ Study the goals for learning. The chapter review and tests will ask questions related to these goals.

■ Read the caption for the long narrow photograph on the edge of the page.

Before Beginning Each Lesson

Read the lesson title and restate it in the form of a question. For example:

Lesson 1

A Healthy Diet

Write: *What is a healthy diet?*

Look over the entire lesson, noting . . .

- pictures
- tables
- charts
- figures
- bold words
- text organization
- questions in the margins
- lesson review

Also note these features . . .

■ Action for Health—An action you can take

■ Careers—A health career and its requirements

■ Healthy Subjects—A subject such as math or literature related to the chapter topic

■ Technology—A technologic advance related to the chapter topic

■ Then and Now—An explanation of how health was approached in earlier years compared with today

■ Tips—A short, easy-to-use tip on health, fitness, or nutrition

■ Writing About Health—Write about how a topic applies to your health and life

As You Read the Lesson

■ Read the major headings. Each subhead is a question.

■ Read the paragraphs that follow to answer the question.

■ Before moving on to the next heading, see if you can answer the question. If you cannot, reread the section to look for the answers. If you are still unsure, ask for help.

■ Answering the questions in the lesson will help you determine if you know the lesson's key ideas.

Using the Bold Words

Knowing the meaning of all the boxed words in the left column will help you understand what you read.

These words appear in **bold type** the first time they appear in the text and are defined in the paragraph.

> **glucose**, the main sugar in blood

All of the words in the left column are also defined in the **glossary.**

> **Glucose**—The main sugar in blood; the major energy source of the body (p. 171)

Bold type
Words seen for the first time will appear in bold type

Glossary
Words listed in this column are also found in the glossary

Taking Notes in Class

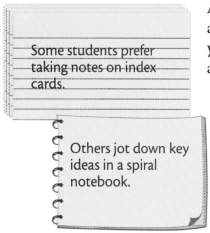

Some students prefer taking notes on index cards.

Others jot down key ideas in a spiral notebook.

As you read, you will be learning many new facts and ideas. Your notes will be useful and will help you remember when preparing for class discussions and studying for tests.

- Always write the main ideas and supporting details.
- Use an outline format to help save time.
- Keep your notes brief. You may want to set up some abbreviations to speed up your note-taking. For example: *with = w/ and = + dollars = $*
- Use the same method all the time. Then when you study for a test, you will know where to find the information you need to review.

Here are some tips for taking notes during class discussion:

- Use your own words.
- Do not try to write everything the teacher says.
- Write down important information only.
- Don't be concerned about writing in complete sentences. Use phrases.
- Be brief.
- Rewrite your notes to fill in possible gaps as soon as you can after class.

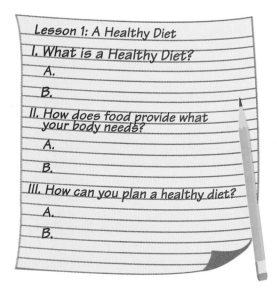

Lesson 1: A Healthy Diet

I. What is a Healthy Diet?

  A.

  B.

II. How does food provide what your body needs?

  A.

  B.

III. How can you plan a healthy diet?

  A.

  B.

Using an Outline

You may want to outline the section using the subheads as your main points. An outline will help you remember the major points of the section. An example of an outline is shown in the left margin. Your teacher may have you use the Student Study Guide for this book.

Getting Ready to Take a Test

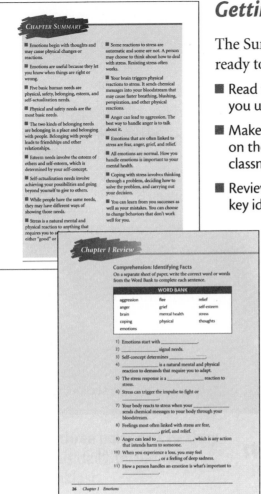

The Summaries and Reviews can help you get ready to take tests.

- Read the summaries from your text to make sure you understand the chapter's main ideas.

- Make up a sample test of items you think may be on the test. You may want to do this with a classmate and share your questions.

- Review your notes and test yourself on words and key ideas.

- Practice writing about some of the main ideas from the chapter.

- Answer the questions under Identifying Facts.

- Answer the questions under Understanding the Main Ideas.

- Write what you think about the questions under Write Your Opinion.

Use the Test Taking Tip

- Read the Test Taking Tip with each Chapter Review of the text.

Test Taking Tip | Avoid waiting until the night before a test to study. Plan your study time so that you can get a good night's sleep the night before a test.

The Wellness Scale

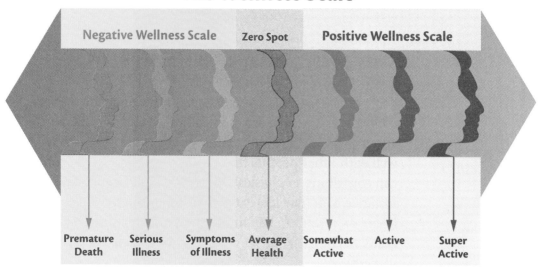

| Negative Wellness Scale | | | Zero Spot | Positive Wellness Scale | | |

| Premature Death | Serious Illness | Symptoms of Illness | Average Health | Somewhat Active | Active | Super Active |

What Is Wellness?

Wellness is an active state of health in which an individual moves toward balancing physical, social, and emotional health. The Wellness Scale shows how to chart a person's level of wellness. At one end of the scale is a high state of physical, social, and emotional health. People in the middle of the scale have average health. At the other end of the scale is serious illness and early death.

As you read this textbook, you will learn more about what is involved in achieving good health and wellness. But before you begin the text, think about your present health and its three parts. Think about where you are on the Wellness Scale. To help you rate your health and wellness, use the Health Self-Rating Chart to rate some behaviors and choices that may affect your health. The chart may help you define areas of your health that you'd like to improve.

HEALTH SELF-RATING CHART

Directions: Number a sheet of paper to correspond to each chart section. Read each statement. If the statement is mostly true for you, write *yes*. If it is mostly false, write *no*.

You do not need to share your results with anyone. Score each section as the instructions tell you. To score your overall health level, add your scores on all sections.

30–35 = top 10 percent
25–29 = above average
20–24 = average
19 and lower = below average

PHYSICAL HEALTH

1. I eat a healthy breakfast every day.
2. I eat a balanced diet that is different every day.
3. I avoid unhealthy snacks.
4. I avoid foods high in sugar, salt, and fats.
5. I do not use tobacco or alcohol or take drugs that a doctor hasn't directed me to use.
6. I get eight hours of sleep each night.
7. I seldom feel tired or run-down.
8. I take part in exercises and sports I like.
9. Whenever possible, I use stairs instead of elevators or escalators.
10. I work at developing muscle tone and fitness three times a week.
11. I stretch in some way to promote flexibility several times a week.
12. I bike, swim, run, or walk for at least 30 minutes three or more times a week.
13. I relax at least ten minutes a day.
14. I get regular medical and dental checkups.

Score one point for each *yes* answer.
13–14 = top 10 percent
11–12 = above average
9–10 = average
8 or lower = below average

SOCIAL HEALTH

1. I meet people and make friends often.
2. I have one or two close friends.
3. I can say no to my friends if they want me to do something I don't want to do.
4. I balance having my way with letting others have their way.
5. I respect other people's right to be different from me.
6. I am able to work cooperatively with others.
7. If I have a problem with other people, I face the problem and try to work it out with them.
8. I am comfortable communicating with adults.
9. I am comfortable talking with females and males my age.
10. I practice good citizenship.
11. I am fair and trustworthy with others.

Score one point for each *yes* answer.
10–11 = top 10 percent
8–9 = above average
6–7 = average
5 or lower = below average

EMOTIONAL HEALTH

1. I try to accept my feelings of love, fear, anger, and sadness.
2. I can tell when I am under pressure.
3. I try to find ways to deal with pressure and control it.
4. I try to have a positive outlook.
5. I ask for help when I need it.
6. I have friends and relatives with whom I discuss problems.
7. I can accept compliments.
8. I give compliments.
9. I can accept and use constructive comments.
10. I take responsibility for my actions.
11. I am honest with myself and others.

Score one point for each *yes* answer.
10–11 = top 10 percent
8–9 = above average
6–7 = average
5 or lower = below average

It is in your power to withdraw into yourself whenever you desire. Perfect tranquillity within consists in the good ordering of the mind—the realm of your own.

—Marcus Aurelius

Mental and Emotional Health

Who are you? When you meet someone new, how do you answer this question? A simple answer would include your name, age, and year in school. Would these answers really describe you? Think about who you are. Who do you want to be in the future? How do these compare?

The way you view yourself has a big impact on your life. Your beliefs about yourself affect what you do, and how healthy you are. These beliefs also play a major role in how you handle relationships. In this unit, you will learn about mental and emotional health. Applying these ideas to your own experiences will help you attain your goals and become the person you want to be.

Self-Assessment

1. How much do you know about emotional health?

2. How much do you know about depression?

3. How much knowledge do you have on suicide?

4. How much knowledge do you have on mental illness?

5. If you noticed a friend being abused, but the friend denies it, who would you tell?

6. In your opinion, is getting struck or being verbally harassed a sign of abuse?

7. I have friends and get along with others.

8. I know how to reduce my stress.

9. I have adults and friends that I can talk to.

10. I know how to relax.

Emotions

Being healthy involves both the body and the mind. If you are excited about something, that feeling can affect your body in a positive way. If you are worried about doing something, that too can affect your body. Your mind affects your body.

We also know that the opposite is true—the body affects the mind. For example, if you are well rested, you are usually able to think more clearly. But if you are tired or feel ill, you may not be able to think as clearly. Your body affects your mind.

In this chapter, you will learn about keeping your mind and body healthy by understanding emotions and stress. You will also learn about common needs that people have and how these needs affect our emotions.

Goals for Learning

▶ To explain the purpose of emotions and how they happen

▶ To describe different levels of basic human needs

▶ To explain how mental health affects physical health

▶ To identify healthy ways to cope with stress

Magnified Brain Tissue

Your Emotions

Emotions
Feelings
Hierarchy
Order from most to least important
Reaction
Response

The same experience can cause different people to react, or respond, in different ways. Why? It happens because every human being has **emotions**, or feelings. Emotions are a person's individual **reactions** to an experience. A reaction is a response. Your emotions make you different from every other person.

Emotions can be difficult to understand. Emotions start with thoughts. When we think about something that happens, we may feel a certain way about that event. Our thinking triggers an emotion. This emotion may then cause the body to react. It may cause a physical change. For example, if you think about an upcoming test and feel worried, your stomach may begin to hurt. Or, if you think about going to a party, you may feel excited when it's time to leave. Then your heart may beat faster. Your thoughts about these events triggered emotions that caused physical changes in your body.

What Do Emotions Do?

Emotions are natural—they serve a purpose. Emotions signal reactions to events and experiences. They let us know when something is right as well as when things are wrong. Learning about your feelings can help you to understand yourself better.

All people have needs, including emotional needs. Most people have similar needs even though they lead very different lives. Understanding these needs can help you to understand yourself and your emotions.

What Basic Needs Do People Have?

Abraham Maslow is someone who studied what humans need. He observed that people have five basic needs. They are physical, safety, belonging, esteem, and self-actualization needs. Maslow put the needs in a **hierarchy**, or order, beginning with the most basic needs. Physical needs are at the bottom of the hierarchy. Safety needs come next, and so on.

Maslow's hierarchy is usually represented as a pyramid, or triangle, as shown in Figure 1.1.

Once you satisfy one level of needs, you can usually work on meeting the next level of needs. For example, a person must first satisfy the physical need to eat—that need is basic to survival. Once that need is met, a person can satisfy the need to find a safe place to live. Later, that person can satisfy the need to be with others and to belong to groups.

Maslow said that most of us spend our lives working on the first three needs. Many people never get to the last two. Also, most people work on meeting the basic needs throughout their life even though they are also working on the higher needs. As you read these explanations of needs, think about where you are in the hierarchy.

Physical Needs

Physical needs are everything necessary to stay alive—water, food, and oxygen. Regularly eating the right foods meets many of your physical needs.

Safety Needs

Safety needs are protection needs. That means protecting yourself from danger and the conditions around you. Being sheltered from harm meets your basic safety needs.

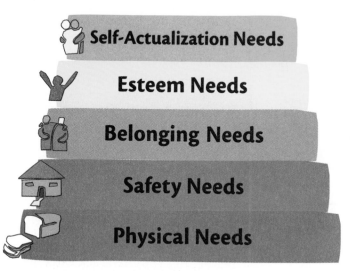

Figure 1.1. Maslow's hierarchy of needs

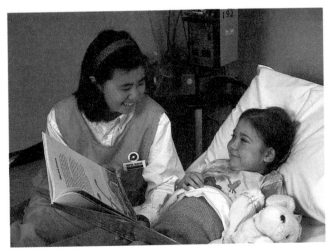

Volunteering to help others is a way to meet belonging needs.

Belonging Needs

Belonging needs are more involved than physical needs. There are two kinds of belonging—belonging in a place and belonging with people. When you belong in a place, you may feel loyal to that place. It may be your home, school, town, or country. Belonging in a place helps you to feel secure and to meet other needs such as safety. Needing to belong with people leads you to form friendships or join groups. Some relationships may be very important to you. Everyone needs them to feel healthy and secure. A relationship based on need is called an **attachment**, or bond or tie to others.

People experience different kinds of love in their need to belong with people. **Family love** is based on attachment and support. Family members often feel safe when they are in contact with one another and support each other.

Friendship is a type of love based on choice. You are born into your family, but you can choose your friends. You usually choose friends because you have common interests and goals. The more similar you are to someone, the easier it is to be friends. You can have many friends. Usually, however, you have only a few friends to whom you feel especially close.

Romantic love is a strong physical and emotional attraction between two people. When it is part of belonging, romantic love is based on need. Two people may feel they are in love because they want to be together and are unhappy when they are apart.

Esteem Needs

If you are able to meet your needs for survival, safety, and belonging, you then seek **esteem**. Esteem is the value or worth you place on yourself. People need two kinds of esteem—the

Attachment
Bond or tie to others

Esteem
Value or worth; how one sees oneself or others

Family love
Love based on attachment and support

Friendship
Love based on choice

Romantic love
Strong physical and emotional attraction between two people

Self-actualization
Achieving one's possibilities

Self-concept
Ideas one has about oneself

Self-esteem
Self-respect, how one feels about oneself

esteem of others and **self-esteem**. You feel the esteem of others when family members express their love for you. You feel it when friends tell you that you've done a good job.

Self-esteem, or self-respect, is your sense of being valuable and worthwhile. Feeling happy and content is usually part of high self-esteem. Feeling unimportant and unsatisfied is usually part of low self-esteem. Your **self-concept**, or your ideas about who you are, determines your self-esteem. Good self-concept usually leads to high self-esteem. Poor self-concept usually leads to low self-esteem. Anything that affects your self-concept, or how you see yourself, can influence your self-esteem. Your self-concept and self-esteem develop throughout life.

Self-Actualization Needs

If you are able to satisfy all the other needs, you can begin to work on **self-actualization**. Self-actualization means achieving your possibilities. In a way, it means going beyond yourself. People who have satisfied their other needs can feel joy and happiness. They have reached a goal and can go beyond themselves to give to others. For example, you might feel good about yourself when you spend time volunteering at a hospital.

Then and Now

ANCIENT EMPHASIS

Around 400 B.C., the Spartans of ancient Greece believed in physically strong people. Young boys were trained in athletics. They were forced to exercise so they became strong soldiers. They learned only how to fight and farm. No other attempts were made to develop the mind.

At the same time, the Greek people of ancient Athens believed in strong minds and bodies. They wanted their people to learn traditions, science, and the arts.

Most cultures have followed the Athenians. They believe that the mind and body work together. Developing both helps a person be healthier.

Writing About Health

You have read about the five basic human needs. Write about the needs that take up most of your time and attention.

People who reach the level of self-actualization may find that they experience a different kind of love. The types of belonging love are based on need, while self-actualized love is based on giving. It is a less selfish and more giving kind of love. Like all the other needs, people continually work to meet self-actualization needs.

How Do Needs Lead to Different Emotions?

Emotions help you to realize what you need. For example, if you often feel frightened, your need for safety is not being met. Your feelings or emotions are closely connected to your needs. Sometimes you may feel unpleasant emotions such as **guilt** or shame. Guilt is the feeling of having done something wrong. Shame is an emotion coming from a strong sense of guilt, embarrassment, or unworthiness. If you make a mistake in front of friends, you may feel ashamed or embarrassed. Your need to belong is what leads to your feeling of embarrassment.

Guilt
A feeling of having done something wrong

While people have the same needs, they may have different ways of showing those needs. For example, you may want a certain style of clothing to feel that you belong to a group. Another person may not want that style of clothing. However, that person may want more friends to feel secure or socially accepted. You both have a need to belong, but you each show that need in a different way. If you recognize this, you can understand yourself and other people better.

LESSON 1 REVIEW On a separate sheet of paper, write *True* if the statement is true or *False* if it is not true.

1) Emotions involve both thoughts and physical changes.

2) The need for food and safety are physical needs.

3) People experience different kinds of love in meeting belonging needs.

4) Your self-concept determines your self-esteem.

5) Self-actualization needs are the most basic needs.

Stress and Your Body

Stress
A state of physical or emotional pressure

Stress response
Automatic physical reactions to stress

*E*motions begin with thoughts and may cause physical changes or reactions. The more basic a need is, the more people experience the emotions that signal that need. When basic needs are threatened, people experience **stress**. Stress is a state of physical or emotional pressure. It is a reaction to anything that places demands on the body or mind to which people must adapt. Understanding how stress affects your mind and your body is important.

Stress is normal, and it can be either "good" or "bad." For example, if you are excited about a project and do a good job on it, you benefit from "good" stress. Happy events such as graduations, dates, and weddings can all be sources of "good" stress. "Good" stress helps people to accomplish goals and to change. Usually we hear about "bad" stress because its effects are harmful. Examples of "bad" stress are changing schools or the death of a loved one. "Bad" stress can interfere with healthy living. Usually too much stress causes problems for people.

How Do People React to Stress?

When you face stress, you try to find out what is wrong and whether it is dangerous. For example, if your teacher seems unhappy and says she wants to talk with you, you may feel stress. You think you may hear bad news. First, you ask yourself what might be wrong and if it could be serious. Then, you react. You may decide what your reactions will be. For example, you may react by simply asking your teacher if something is wrong. Most of your reaction may be automatic and physical. For example, you may feel worried and notice that your heart is beating faster. This is called the **stress response**. The stress response affects your body in ways you may not be able to control. Your heart beats faster, you perspire, and your breathing quickens. These are automatic physical reactions to stress. Other examples are blushing, gasping in surprise, and crying out. Stronger reactions to stress are headaches, stomach pain, sleeping problems, and feeling nervous.

Take time to eat well when you're under stress.

BIOFEEDBACK

When you hear *biofeedback*, do you think of science fiction? While biofeedback isn't science fiction, it does help treat illness. Technicians place electronic sensors on a person's head or muscles and then use computers to track and measure muscle activity. Changes in muscle activity appear on an attached computer monitor that shows stress. By using positive thoughts, people can control—or stop—pain and stress. In addition, biofeedback is used to treat long-term pain and many disorders. These include migraine headaches, epilepsy, sleeplessness, hyperactivity, attention deficit disorders, and chemical dependency. Athletes use it to control anxiety before games. Biofeedback is not a sure cure, but for some people, it seems to work.

Fitness Tip

Get regular exercise to reduce stress and make coping with difficult situations easier.

Is it possible to avoid stress? Why?

A person's response to stress often takes one of two forms: fight or flight. When something threatens or angers you, you may feel an impulse to fight it. If you fight, you attack what threatens you. Fighting may simply be using words to stand up for what you believe. The other response is to flee. If you flee, you leave the situation but nothing changes. The fight-or-flight impulse is natural and happens without thinking.

We can also react to stress by thinking about what to do. After you react to a stressful event, your body becomes calmer. Then you can decide what to do to resist stress. For example, if you enter a dark room and hear a noise, you may jump back. Then you decide to turn on a light to see what is making the noise. You find the noise was nothing to worry about. The stress was imagined, and you were able to resist it. Resisting stress often works. When people get rid of or avoid stress, they feel relief.

What Physical Reactions Does Stress Cause?

When you interpret something as a threat, your thought processes trigger your brain into action. The brain triggers the body into action to fight or flee. The brain also sends a chemical message to the body system that controls bodily processes. The chemicals go directly into the bloodstream. Some chemical messages cause faster breathing and a rush of blood to the arms, legs, and head. This is what causes people to blush, feel warm, and perspire when they are worried or excited. Other chemical messages from the brain strengthen the muscles for endurance in case the stress lasts a long time.

Normally, physical reactions to stress help people resist stress. The chemicals that the body produces help people react quickly. They help us remain alert while we choose the best way to respond to the threat. Good stress can have a positive effect on the body, and bad stress can have a harmful effect.

What Life Events Cause Stress?

A number of events can cause stress. Chart 1.1 lists a few events that commonly cause stress for teens.

Chart 1.1. Common Stressful Life Events for Teens

• Death of a parent	• An outstanding personal achievement
• A visible deformity	• Being accepted to college
• Parents' divorce or separation	• Being a senior in high school
• Being involved with alcohol or other drugs	• A change in acceptance by peers
• Death of a brother or sister	• A change in parents' financial status
• Beginning to date	

LESSON 2 REVIEW Write the answers to these questions on a separate sheet of paper, using complete sentences.

1) What is stress?

2) How can good stress help people?

3) What are some automatic physical reactions to stress?

4) What does it mean to respond to stress by fighting? by fleeing?

5) Where do the chemicals go when the brain sends messages to the body system controlling bodily processes?

Managing Stress

Aggression
Any action that intends harm to someone

Anger
Strong feeling of displeasure

Anxiety
A feeling of uneasiness or fearful concern

Fear
A strong feeling of fright; awareness of danger

Frustration
Being blocked from something

Well-being
State of being physically and emotionally healthy

Several emotions are related to stress. It helps to understand these emotions and how the body reacts to some of them.

What Emotions Are Linked to Stress?

The emotions most commonly linked with stress are fear, anger, grief, and relief.

Fear

Fear is a feeling that causes a person to want to escape. When something important to your survival and **well-being** is threatened, you feel fear. For example, you would be frightened if a car were to turn in front of you just as you cross a street. Anything that might cause you physical or emotional pain can be frightening.

Your body reacts to fear. You may notice muscle tightness, especially in your legs. Your hands may shake nervously. You may bite your fingernails or feel like crying. To deal with fear, you can try to change the situation causing the fear or talk about the fear. Talking with a trusted person is a healthy way to keep from bottling up fears.

An emotion related to fear is **anxiety**, or fearful concern. For example, when you are nervous about a test, you may feel anxious. You do not really feel fear because the test cannot hurt you, but you may worry about getting a low grade. Anxiety is very unpleasant. The best way to deal with anxiety is to identify its source and take effective action. For example, if you are anxious about giving a speech, you can plan plenty of time to practice it. If you feel well prepared, you will be more relaxed and self-confident when giving your speech.

Anger

Anger is a strong feeling of displeasure. Everyone feels angry at times. Strong anger, however, can lead to the desire to attack or be **aggressive**. Aggression is any action that intends harm to someone. **Frustration**, or being blocked from something you want, often causes aggression. When frustrated, you may feel aggressive. You might push someone who blocked your way. You might hit the machine that kept your money. Aggression is a common impulse, but it's not an effective response to frustration. Aggression is likely to cause more problems than it solves.

When you are angry, you have a complaint about someone or something. The best way to express your anger is to say why you are angry and what you want to happen. You can do that without accusing or blaming another person by using "I" messages. For example, you could try saying, "I feel hurt when you tease me." Sometimes this alone solves the problem. Other times you may need to bargain to work out a solution. Talking about your complaint is a more successful way to handle anger than aggression is.

Uncontrolled anger keeps you from thinking through your decisions clearly. Working out a solution and talking about feelings helps manage anger. Staying calm is another way to control anger. Self-talk also helps. For example, it can calm your body to tell yourself, "Stay calm. Relax. Stay in control." Taking deep breaths and breathing in and out slowly will relax your muscles. You can redirect the anger by doing something physical such as taking a walk, exercising, or listening to music.

Careers

MENTAL HEALTH ASSISTANT

Do you think of yourself as caring and trustworthy? Then why not become a mental health assistant? Mental health assistants work closely with mental health counselors to help people solve problems. Counselors help people to handle different problems, whether mental or emotional. Some people have family or marriage problems. Sometimes they have job-related problems. They may feel stress, have low self-esteem, or even want to commit suicide. Mental health assistants need to be caring and able to gain the people's trust. Good communication skills are important. Most employers prefer mental health assistants who have had college courses that emphasize people skills.

Depression
A state of deep sadness

Grief
A feeling of sorrow; feelings after a loss

Relief
A light, pleasant feeling after something painful or distressing is gone

All of these actions can help you to think more clearly and consider what to do when you feel angry.

Grief

Loss is a common source of stress that you cannot fight or escape. You experience loss when a relationship breaks up, a good friend moves away, or someone dies. The feelings you experience after a loss are part of **grief**, or sorrow. Grief can be a mixture of several emotions, including fear, anger, anxiety, and guilt.

Grief is a natural healing process. Usually a person goes through these reactions to grief:

- Denial—pretending a loss has not occurred
- Anger—feeling angry about the loss
- Bargaining—wishing for a second chance
- **Depression**—feeling deep sadness
- Acceptance—accepting something over which you had no power

Each reaction to grief can take a long time. The length of time is different for each person. Also each person may go through the reactions in any order or may go back and forth among them. Talking about the painful emotions felt from the loss helps. Depression is the most common of these reactions. A depressed person sometimes needs professional help to feel good again. You can help a grieving person by listening and offering support.

Relief

Relief is a light, pleasant feeling people experience when stress is gone. Sometimes stress returns. Then you only feel relief for a little while. You may be nervous because you know the stress can return. For example, you feel relief because your math test was put off until tomorrow. But the relief doesn't last long, since you still have to take the test. Learning to deal with stress brings relief that lasts. Relief is an emotion you can work to achieve.

Cope
To deal with or overcome problems and difficulties

How Can Stressful Emotions Be Handled?

All emotions are normal. Emotions are neither "good" nor "bad." How you handle an emotion is what's important to your mental health. To be mentally healthy, it helps to pay attention to emotional signals and take positive action. When you identify your needs, you can determine how best to meet them. Sometimes all you need to do is ask. If you need help with your homework, simply ask a friend.

Being direct works best. Dropping hints and hoping others will "guess" what you need usually doesn't work. You may need to work harder to get what you need. If you need high grades to get a job, you may have to study hard.

What Are Some Ways to Relieve Stress?

Coping is finding a way to deal with or overcome stress or other problems. Coping with a situation relieves the stress for the time being and brings relief. You will always have to deal with problems and emergencies. Coping with one threat will not solve all your problems. But it can reduce the number of problems with which you have to deal.

C Calm down

O Outline options

P Pick a plan

E Evaluate your plan

When an emotion signals a need, the healthiest response is to cope. To cope with a problem, you can do three things:

1. Identify what causes the problem.

2. Decide on a way to solve the problem.

3. Carry out your plan as a way to cope.

Studying is a way to handle school-related stress and improve your outlook for the future.

Coping helps you feel better and relieves anxiety. For example, you feel anxious about getting a job. To cope with the problem, plan ways to get help, including checking the newspaper and asking trusted adults for suggestions. Find and read a book about how to apply for a job. Set a plan and act on it. Your chance for success in finding a job is better because you are able to cope with the problem.

What is something you have learned from a success? What is something positive you have learned from a failure?

When you succeed in solving a problem, you relieve stress. Learning to cope with one problem may help you in dealing with other problems. You can learn from your successes as well as your mistakes.

Experience and time also help to relieve stress. Often when people try something new, they find it stressful. The more you do things and gain experience, the less stress will be associated with those things. For example, a first date can be stressful. The more you date an individual or a variety of people, the more experience you have in dating. While the first date with a new person may still be stressful, the stress may be less powerful with experience.

Here are some other actions that can relieve stress and promote mental health:

- Pay attention to your emotional signals.
- Identify what you need—make sure your expectations are reasonable.
- Be willing to take responsibility for meeting your needs without waiting for others to try to please you.
- Ask for what you need.
- Determine how to get the rest of what you need honestly and fairly.
- Seek help through talking with trusted individuals.
- Use positive self-talk—encourage yourself and keep an "I can" attitude.
- Engage in physical activity.
- Plan ahead.

WORD BANK

Anger
Coping
Fear
Grief
Relief

LESSON 3 REVIEW On a separate sheet of paper, write the word from the Word Bank that matches each description.

1) Feeling that causes a person to want to escape

2) Dealing with or overcoming problems

3) Feelings after a loss

4) Strong feeling of displeasure

5) Feeling after stress is gone

■ Emotions begin with thoughts and may cause physical changes or reactions.

■ Emotions are useful because they let you know when things are right or wrong.

■ Five basic human needs are physical, safety, belonging, esteem, and self-actualization needs.

■ Physical and safety needs are the most basic needs.

■ The two kinds of belonging needs are belonging in a place and belonging with people. Belonging with people leads to friendships and other relationships.

■ Esteem needs involve the esteem of others and self-esteem, which is determined by your self-concept.

■ Self-actualization needs involve achieving your possibilities and going beyond yourself to give to others.

■ While people have the same needs, they may have different ways of showing those needs.

■ Stress is a natural mental and physical reaction to anything that requires you to adapt. Stress can be either "good" or "bad."

■ Some reactions to stress are automatic and some are not. A person may choose to think about how to deal with stress. Resisting stress often works.

■ Your brain triggers physical reactions to stress. It sends chemical messages into your bloodstream that may cause faster breathing, blushing, perspiration, and other physical reactions.

■ Anger can lead to aggression. The best way to handle anger is to talk about it.

■ Emotions that are often linked to stress are fear, anger, grief, and relief.

■ All emotions are normal. How you handle emotions is important to your mental health.

■ Coping with stress involves thinking through a problem, deciding how to solve the problem, and carrying out your decision.

■ You can learn from you successes as well as your mistakes. You can choose to change behaviors that don't work well for you.

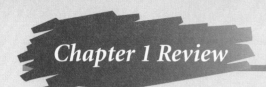

Comprehension: Identifying Facts

On a separate sheet of paper, write the correct word or words from the Word Bank to complete each sentence.

WORD BANK		
aggression	flee	relief
anger	grief	self-esteem
brain	mental health	stress
coping	physical	thoughts
emotions		

1) Emotions start with _____.

2) _____ signal needs.

3) Self-concept determines _____.

4) _____ is a natural mental and physical reaction to demands that require you to adapt.

5) The stress response is a _____ reaction to stress.

6) Stress can trigger the impulse to fight or _____.

7) Your body reacts to stress when your _____ sends chemical messages to your body through your bloodstream.

8) Feelings most often linked with stress are fear, _____, grief, and relief.

9) Anger can lead to _____, which is any action that intends harm to someone.

10) When you experience a loss, you may feel _____, or a feeling of deep sadness.

11) How a person handles an emotion is what's important to _____.

12) A good way to handle stress and other problems is

_____.

13) _____ is a light, pleasant feeling that comes after stress is gone.

Comprehension: Understanding Main Ideas

On a separate sheet of paper, write the answers to the following questions using complete sentences.

14) How are emotions useful?

15) What are the levels of human needs, beginning with the most basic needs?

16) What is the stress response?

17) What are some ways your body reacts to fear?

18) What are the three main steps involved in coping?

Critical Thinking: Write Your Opinion

19) Why do you think coping with stress and other emotions is important to your physical and mental health?

20) What could you do to help a friend who feels sad and upset?

Test Taking Tip | If you know you will have to define certain terms on a test, write the term on one side of a card. Write its definition on the other side. Use the cards to test yourself, or work with a partner.

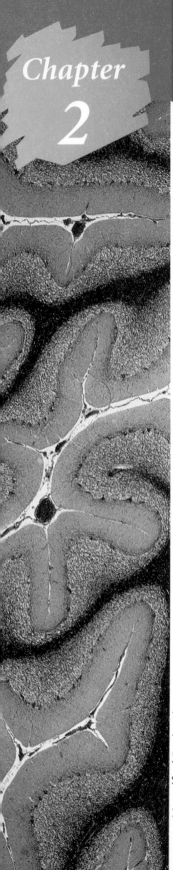

Magnified Brain Tissue

Maintaining Mental Health

Many things can affect or influence your mental and emotional health. Your personal well-being has many sources. Getting to know yourself and becoming aware of your values and beliefs can make a difference in your emotional well-being. That can make a difference in your outlook on life and the quality of your relationships, too. You can do many things to improve and maintain good mental and emotional health.

In this chapter, you will learn about influences on mental health. You will learn about the characteristics of mentally healthy people and healthy relationships. You will also learn some ways that you can become more emotionally healthy.

Goals for Learning

▶ To explain how personality develops

▶ To identify four sources of well-being

▶ To explain the characteristics of emotionally healthy people

▶ To describe what makes relationships healthy

Influences on Mental Health

Personality
All of one's behavioral, mental, and emotional characteristics

Temperament
A person's emotional makeup

What kind of person are you? Friendly, helpful, cooperative? Moody, fearful, selfish? You may at different times be all of these things. Thoughts, feelings, and behavior, no matter what they are, form **personality**. Personality changes as we grow older, because thoughts and behaviors change as a result of experiences and opportunities.

How Does Personality Develop?

As a baby, you had a limited range of behaviors. Even though you had not yet developed your personality, you had a certain temperament. **Temperament** is a person's emotional makeup. A baby's temperament shows soon after birth. Some babies cry often while others are calmer and sleep more. As children grow, they become aware of new thoughts and feelings. They learn new behaviors. Their temperament remains the same, but they begin to develop their personality.

Early experiences may strongly influence a child's personality. For example, a baby needs close contact or attachment with a parent or caregiver to feel secure. If that need is met, the baby is content. If that need is not met, the baby may become distressed. Attachment patterns formed early in life may influence how a person relates to people later on.

Early experiences, along with many other experiences, play a part in determining personality.

What Is Self-Concept?

How can a person who gets teased a lot develop a good self-concept?

Self-concept is our ideas about who we are and what our personality is like. We all have natural positive esteem within us. In addition to this natural esteem, what other people tell us about ourselves shapes our self-concept. For example, your music teacher says you have a good sense of rhythm. That may shape an idea you have about your musical talent.

The actions of others may also help shape self-concept. For example, team captains always try to choose a certain girl for their team. She learns that others think she is a good athlete.

These messages from others are called social messages. Social messages about you may not always match your self-concept. For example, you may think of yourself as shy and not very interesting. Your friends, however, think you are quiet and sincere. They tell you you have a good sense of humor. In this case, the social message you heard did not match your own belief. Sometimes, you may decide to change your belief about yourself.

Sometimes you won't want to change a belief about yourself. For example, you dropped the ball during a baseball game. Your friend tells you you aren't very good and should quit the sport. You know that you made four other very good plays in that game. You believe you really are good at baseball, so you decide not to change your belief.

No matter what message you receive from others, these social messages all play a part in forming your self-concept. They reflect your **social esteem**. Social esteem is how others value you. If others have a good opinion of you, you are more likely to have high self-esteem. Unfortunately, this also works the other way. If others do not seem to value you, you are more likely to have low self-esteem.

Others give us social messages that help to form our social esteem.

What Is Well-Being?

Well-being is feeling happy, healthy, and content. Well-being involves balancing many different needs and behaviors. If a person feels healthy and content, it means that many forms of well-being are working together. These include physical, emotional, social, and personal well-being.

Think about what you want to find out when you get to know a person. List the things you think are important.

Physical well-being is your body's ability to meet the demands of daily living. It involves being physically healthy and free from pain and illness.

Emotional well-being is the ability to handle problems and stress in daily life. Emotional well-being means you have a positive outlook and that you are in control of your emotions.

Social well-being is the ability to get along well with others. Since people interact with others many times every day, social well-being is important.

Your satisfaction with your own values and beliefs contributes to your sense of personal well-being. Your values and personal beliefs develop and change over time. Your values may be very much like your friends' values, or they may be very different. Whatever your values and beliefs are, if they are right for you and respectful of others, they increase your well-being. Your system of beliefs can guide you when you feel confused. Your beliefs can also help you make decisions that are right for you.

How Are the Forms of Well-Being Related?

Your overall well-being depends on how all these forms of well-being work together. One form of well-being supports another. For example, when you are physically healthy, you may be able to handle emotional stress better. A good mental attitude can promote physical health.

It is also true that problems in one area of well-being can affect another area. For example, if you don't feel well physically, you may feel sad or depressed. If you feel fine physically but you are worried about something, you may not like being with others. This lack of well-being may hurt your relationships with others for a while.

You can promote your overall well-being when you pay attention to how its different parts interact. Problems in one area may actually cause problems in another. Establishing support for all four forms of your well-being is the key to mental health.

CREATE YOUR OWN SUPPORT SYSTEM

An important part of mental health is being able to provide your own support. You can assemble some resources for times when you feel down.

Make a list of things you can do to solve problems. For example, write down ideas such as "talk it over," "get another opinion," or "ask for help." Include the names of your closest friends and their phone numbers on your list. Review your list whenever you have been hurt or disappointed. Call one of the friends on your list if you need to talk about it.

What Actions Promote Well-Being?

In many cases, you can promote your physical and mental health and well-being through your own actions. The rest of the lesson gives some suggestions.

Physical well-being requires being healthy. This includes eating right, resting, and exercising. Understanding illnesses and what to do about them helps people stay healthy. For example, when you understand that rest speeds recovery from the flu, you may sleep more to get well quickly.

For your emotional well-being, you need to learn how to handle stress. Many times physical activity—even taking a brisk walk—helps to relieve stress. Understanding and dealing with many different emotions also helps relieve stress.

To promote your social well-being, you need to improve your understanding of others. You can learn about what others need. Some social skills that you can learn are:

• Communication skills—listen, pay attention when others speak, ask questions, be honest in what you say

• Friendship skills—be a friend, ask others' advice, show respect and loyalty, keep promises and confidences

- Citizenship skills—follow the rules of society, respect others, do your part, volunteer to help

To promote personal well-being involves forming beliefs about what is important to you and what you believe is right. Is it right to help a friend? Is it right to copy answers on a test? Is it right to stay up too late and oversleep the next day? You face many similar issues every day. Your sense of personal well-being can help you find the answers.

Working on all these forms of well-being helps to promote your mental health. Sometimes you will be more successful than at other times. But maintaining your mental health, even though it can be difficult, is important to your well-being.

LESSON 1 REVIEW Write the answers to these questions on a separate sheet of paper, using complete sentences.

1) What is one important early influence on personality development?

2) What helps shape a person's self-concept?

3) What are the four major forms of well-being?

4) How do the forms of well-being influence one another?

5) What are some skills that promote social well-being?

Emotional Health

*E*motionally healthy people learn to solve problems and adjust to their world. Emotional well-being is an ongoing process rather than an unchanging state of mind. Everyone has occasional setbacks and problems. Abilities and behaviors that make people emotionally healthy can be learned.

How Can a Person Learn and Change?

People learn most things through experience. They change their behavior when they discover a better way to act.

When you make a mistake, you may feel upset or embarrassed. Learning from the mistake helps you to avoid repeating it. By acting differently another time, you can figure out what works and make a change. Sometimes change is hard because you might be afraid to admit you were wrong. Breaking habits is also hard. However, you can overcome feeling embarrassed and make the changes that are right for you.

How Can Relationships Be Maintained?

Relationship problems are common. After all, relationships can be tangled and difficult to understand. People have to learn how to communicate and interact with others. Emotionally healthy people usually can balance their own wishes with those of others. They learn to get along. When they have problems with others, they are able to work through them. They respond to the needs of friends or family members.

Relationships change as you mature, or grow older. When you were young, you depended completely on others for love, care, and survival. As you mature, you form attachments to other people. Emotionally healthy people value these attachments to others, and at the same time they remain independent. They find a balance between their attachments to or dependence on others and their independence. For example, you may ask your friends for advice about an important decision. You do that because you are attached

Compromise
To come to an agreement by both sides giving a little

Optimism
Tending to expect the best possible outcome

Pessimism
Tending to expect the worst possible outcome

What is a reasonable goal you can set for yourself this week?

to them and value their opinions. In the end, however, you must decide on your own what is right for you.

People need each other in many ways. Emotionally healthy people are able to form bonds with others and still remain independent.

How Can Goals Be Set and Reached?

It is important for emotional health to be able to set realistic, or reasonable, goals. Realistic goals are balanced between **pessimism** and unrealistic **optimism**. Pessimism means tending to expect the worst possible outcome. Optimism means tending to expect the best possible outcome. If a goal is too high, or too optimistic, you may spend all your time and effort trying to reach it. You may overlook other things that are important to you and still not reach your goal. If you feel pessimistic about a goal you set, you may give up without trying. You may give up because you believe you won't make it anyway. It may be difficult to set reasonable goals. However, you are more likely to feel good about and reach reasonable goals.

How Can Problems Be Solved?

Frustration is a common feeling when people are blocked from reaching a goal. If another person seems to cause the frustration, two people may experience conflict or strife. Rather than dwell on these conflicts, it is important for emotional health to be able to find solutions to them. It is important to be able to think about a problem and try to solve it. If the conflict is difficult to solve, people may **compromise**. To compromise means that both people involved in the conflict agree to give in a little. That way, no one feels they "lost," and the conflict is resolved.

Another emotionally healthy way to solve a problem is to suggest working together to solve a conflict. For example, two people might argue about how to raise money for the school. They each can agree to find out about several plans. Then they can work together to decide which plan is best.

Rational
Being realistic or reasonable

Rational thinking is important in solving problems. Rational means being reasonable. For example, you want to buy a new music system. However, your parents think it is more than you can afford. You have to think rationally. You have to consider your resources. Do you have enough money, or can you earn the amount you need? If you borrow the money, will you be willing and able to pay it back? After careful thought, you may decide that your plan is workable. Or, you may decide that the item is too expensive to buy.

How Can Emotions Be Managed?

Remember that emotions signal needs. However, these signals are not always adjusted to the correct "volume." For example, when you are tired, you may react too strongly, or overreact, to a situation. If you were rested, you might react with more control.

All of us have certain impulses. If someone bumps into you, your impulse may be to strike back. Your impulse may even cause you to overreact. But you can stop yourself from giving in to that impulse. Emotional health depends on learning to control impulses and express feelings appropriately.

People often are able to predict the consequences, or results, of actions ahead of time. To do this, they consider what might happen if they react a certain way. They can change their actions to avoid a negative consequence. For example, you notice a friend has a new hairstyle. You think the haircut is too short. Your impulse is to say "I think your hair is too short!" Then you realize that statement might hurt your friend's feelings. You decide to say instead, "I see you have a new hair style." You were able to think ahead to make a comment that wouldn't hurt your friend's feelings.

What Are Some Healthy Ways of Thinking

Most actions and emotions begin with thoughts. For example, if you think someone has insulted you, you may feel angry. However, if you believe the person did not mean to insult you, you may not feel angry.

Try to think of as many ways as possible to solve a problem.

Emotionally healthy people think in ways that help them to adjust and reach their goals. They have four helpful thinking styles—realistic optimism, coping, healthy explanations, and meaningful values.

Realistic Optimism

When emotionally healthy people think with realistic optimism, they:

- Set and work toward goals that are challenging but reachable.

- Recognize what can and cannot be controlled in their life.

- Have faith in themselves and hope that events will work out for the best.

Coping

People respond in two ways to stress—coping or avoidance. Coping deals with and removes stress. In some situations, avoidance is the best way to cope. For example, it is best to avoid a possibly harmful situation in which someone is being aggressive. In other situations, avoidance treats the **symptoms** of stress but doesn't deal with the real problem. A symptom is a bodily reaction that indicates a disease or physical problem. For example, you may feel anxious about a long assignment.

Disadvantages can be overcome.

You could escape by taking a break with friends to try to forget about it. Or, you could cope by beginning to work on it. Avoidance or escaping puts off your anxiety until it is time to turn in the work you haven't completed. Coping deals with your anxiety. You have worked hard and completed the assignment, so your anxiety is removed.

Emotionally healthy people cope by:

- Learning from experiences, mistakes, and successes.
- Knowing when to change behaviors that aren't working.
- Using resources to help with difficult situations.
- Trying again after a failure.

Healthy Explanations

Emotionally healthy people use a positive thinking style to explain events. With effort, people can learn to replace negative, or pessimistic, thinking with realistic, positive thinking. When surprising or unpleasant events occur, you may automatically wonder why they happened. The answers you come up with can influence the quality of your life. For example, a student receives a poor grade on a test. He could react by thinking, "This isn't fair! Why is it happening to me?" But a more positive reaction would be "That was a difficult test! I think I can do better next time."

Meaningful Values

Emotionally healthy people make sure their actions blend with the ideas and values they think are important. Emotionally healthy people:

- Develop values that become part of them and guide their thinking and behavior.
- Reflect on their own feelings and thoughts instead of worrying about how others might judge them.
- Face and overcome disadvantages.
- Find meaning in their work or play.

LESSON 2 REVIEW On a separate sheet of paper, write *True* if the statement is true or *False* if it is not true.

1) Emotionally healthy people control everything in their world.

2) Mentally healthy people learn from their experiences.

3) Complete independence from others promotes personal well-being.

4) Realistic goals are set between pessimism and unrealistic optimism.

5) Emotionally healthy people learn to control their impulses.

Healthy Relationships

*E*veryone has a need to belong with people. The most basic, common way people meet that need is to form and maintain close relationships. Some relationships, such as connections with family members, are chosen for you. You choose other relationships such as friendships and love. Healthy relationships can make your life happier and more fulfilling.

What Makes a Relationship Healthy?

A healthy, close relationship has these important characteristics:

- Emotional attachment

- Mutual, or common, dependence between partners

- Satisfaction of both partners' needs

The needs that a close relationship satisfies include **intimate** communication and the need to **nurture**. Intimate means something very personal or private. Intimate communication is being able to confide in someone you trust. To nurture means to help someone or something grow or develop.

What Is the Basis of Friendships?

The most common close relationship is friendship. Most friendships are based on something people have in common. You make friends because you share interests and activities or have similar backgrounds. You can more easily plan time doing things with someone who enjoys what you do. Sharing common values and goals can strengthen your self-concept and lift your self-esteem.

How Can Relationships Be Maintained?

As close as two people may seem to be, they are still individuals with separate lives and experiences. Staying friends can be difficult when one or both persons grow and change. Since everyone changes throughout life, you can do some things to maintain relationships. One thing is to keep

Communication is necessary to maintain relationships.

Health Tip

Take time for yourself—it helps you to accept yourself.

communicating with each other. Writing or talking can help you avoid misunderstandings. You can keep learning about each other.

Another action is to continue to pursue personal interests and goals. Favorite subjects or hobbies can satisfy you even when you are alone.

Self-acceptance is also important. When you accept yourself, it is easier to accept and not feel threatened by others' differences. Healthy relationships allow people to be themselves. For example, your friends, who all have pierced ears, accept you for yourself even though you choose not to pierce your ears. Relationships that restrict people or that involve fear of being pushed away are unhealthy. For example, if a friend threatens you because you won't go along with a plan, that relationship is unhealthy.

What Makes Communication Successful?

Communication is a basic element in relationships. Communication can mean talking, writing, touching, listening, smiling, and even knowing when to be silent. For example, studying together may not involve talking, but it can still make a relationship stronger.

Every communication has a sender and a receiver. The sender *intends* a message for the receiver to get. The message the receiver gets affects him or her. Communication is effective, or successful, when the sender's intent matches the effect on the receiver. For example, you want to compliment your friend on her work. If she feels good because of the words you say, your communication is effective. Communication is not effective when the sender's intent does not match the effect on the receiver. For example, if you say something that sounds insincere, your friend may find your words cutting. She may feel insulted rather than complimented.

What Makes Communication Unsuccessful?

Ineffective, or unsuccessful, communication has three possible sources. They are twisted sending, twisted receiving, and a poor communication climate. Twisted sending can be poor word choices or not knowing what to say. It can mean your body language gives the opposite message from what you are saying. For example, if you say "congratulations" without smiling, you are sending a twisted message.

Twisted receiving usually results from bad listening— a common problem in poor communication. For example, you may think a teacher is boring or that you know what the person is going to say. You may pretend to listen while your attention is elsewhere. Later, you realize that you have no idea what the teacher really said.

A poor communication climate may include distractions, noise, interruptions, and lack of time. Such a climate makes sending and receiving messages difficult. For example, the phone rings while you talk with a friend. He answers the call, and you lose your train of thought. After the call, you can't remember what you were saying. Your friend has difficulty returning his attention to you. A better communication climate is one without distractions, noise, and interruptions.

Does Self-Esteem Affect Relationships?

Relationships meet some but not all needs. It is easy to expect too much from a friend or partner. Romantic fairy tales and movies make people hope friendship and true love can make them happy. Unfortunately, no other person can make you happy. Your own thoughts, feelings, and actions produce your happiness. Likewise, you will never be able to make another person happy.

Relationships are healthy when both people have good self-esteem. People who accept themselves and have meaningful goals are better able to give affection and help to others. One of the best things you can do to promote healthy relationships is to learn about and appreciate yourself. Continue to develop your interests and improve your skills. Feel good about yourself. The more you like yourself, the healthier your relationships will be.

LESSON 3 REVIEW Write the answers to these questions on a separate sheet of paper, using complete sentences.

1) Name one characteristic of a healthy relationship.

2) What is the basis of most friendships?

3) What are two things you can do to maintain a relationship?

4) When is communication effective?

5) How does someone's self-esteem affect the quality of his or her relationships?

Becoming More Emotionally Healthy

Self-awareness
Understanding oneself as an individual or personality

Social comparison
Observing other people to determine how to behave

You can perform better when you accept and feel good about yourself. Your mind can work better, too. Accepting yourself can help make your relationships healthier. Improving your self-acceptance and relationships with others can support your mental health. Two things that can help you improve your self-acceptance are **self-awareness** and **social comparison**.

What Is Self-Awareness?

Self-awareness is understanding yourself as an individual. It is understanding your feelings and goals from moment to moment. For example, what are you feeling right now as you read this text? Are you physically comfortable? Or, are you tired and unable to concentrate? Sometimes just realizing how you feel can help. If you are not physically comfortable, you may decide to find a better study location. Your awareness can help you make a good choice that will increase your chances for success.

Self-awareness is understanding many things about yourself. For example, you may understand how you feel about school, friends, parents, your abilities, and even your appearance and behavior. The more you understand yourself, the easier it is for you to understand others.

What Is Social Comparison?

Once you are more aware of your feelings and goals, you can use social comparison to improve your self-acceptance. Social comparison involves observing other people to help you decide how to behave. For example, you are taking a new computer class and don't know exactly what to do. You notice other students ask permission before using the computers. You copy their behavior and in that way learn for yourself.

How Does Self-Acceptance Improve Relationships?

You probably will find that as you become more self-accepting, others will be more comfortable with you. Spending time with people who have poor self-acceptance can be uncomfortable. They may constantly put themselves

Accepting yourself helps others to accept you.

down. You may try to help them see themselves differently, but they may not accept your help. If people feel good about themselves, they don't expect others to reassure or entertain them. People who accept themselves are more likely to accept individual differences, get to know a variety of people, and give and accept help.

Accept Individual Differences

No two people are exactly alike. Even identical twins think differently. By nature, people are different from one another. Some differences are on the surface, and some are not visible. Some differences include age, race, gender, height, and eye color. Some differences that are not on the surface are thoughts, feelings, and behavior. For example, some people are born with a more sensitive temperament than others. Some people are stronger than others. Some people have different personal beliefs than others. Everyone has different talents and abilities.

Unfortunately, people may form negative, or unfavorable, opinions about someone who is different from themselves. They may have little knowledge about this person, but still dislike him or her. This is called **prejudice**. Prejudiced people tend to **discriminate** against others who are different from themselves. To discriminate means to treat differently on the basis of something other than individual worth. Prejudice creates an unhealthy situation. For example, imagine learning that people you have never met dislike you. You are different from them in some way. You, in turn, may find it hard to like these people. You believe they are being unfair. This cycle becomes difficult to break. Prejudice can destroy the fairness, honesty, and goodwill of a community.

Discriminate
To treat differently on the basis of something other than individual worth

Prejudice
Negative, or unfavorable, opinions formed about something or someone without enough experience or knowledge

What is one thing teenagers can do to stop prejudice?

THE BLUEST EYE

Toni Morrison's novel *The Bluest Eye* focuses on two African American girls from different families. One girl, Pecola Breedlove, has angry parents who abuse her. Other children laugh at her. She feels ugly for being black. Pecola believes that she can be happy only if she becomes white. She prays for blue eyes. Pecola's sadness, however, simply makes her ill. As time passes, her health gets even worse.

The other girl, Claudia McTeer, feels very loved by her family. She likes the way she looks. Unlike Pecola, Claudia accepts herself and pursues her dreams. Her self-acceptance helps her stay healthy.

Empathy
Identifying and trying to understand others' feelings

You can learn to value differences in people. This means truly getting to know a person. Differences in people add richness to your relationships. For example, as you get to know someone from another country, you find you are developing new tastes in food and music.

Get to Know a Variety of People

People can overcome prejudices when members of different groups get to know each other. Working together toward a common goal is a way to learn cooperation and discover similarities. Through this, people begin to have **empathy** with one another. Empathy is identifying and trying to understand others' feelings. Close relationships are healthiest when they are based on empathy.

Here are some other ways you can get to know a variety of people:

- Get to know a person of the opposite sex as a friend rather than a possible date.
- Meet people from different ethnic backgrounds through some common interest such as music or sports.
- Establish relationships with older adults—grandparents, family friends, or others. They can offer practical advice for problem solving and decision making based on experience.

Give and Accept Help

Friends help you do things, solve problems, and deal with hard times. Helping those we care about is called social support. To improve your relationships with others, you can learn how to give and accept social support.

When a friend is in need, you may empathize and feel like helping. For example, your best friend has had a painful loss. But your friend may not be willing to ask you for help. You can still do many things to provide support. You can take notes in a class your friend had to miss. You can offer to take care of a pet or run an errand. If someone needs your help, it is better to offer something specific. For example, you can ask, "Can I help by taking care of your younger brother for you today?"

Sometimes you have to accept social support when you need help. Needing help isn't a sign of weakness or failure. Everyone needs help at times. By letting others give you social support, you can strengthen your friendships. Learning to give and accept social support is another way to improve your emotional health.

RESIDENTIAL COUNSELOR

Residential counselors help small groups of people to handle their problems. They live with these groups in halfway houses or crisis shelters. Halfway houses help people who are recovering from substance abuse. Crisis shelters aid those who are abused. By providing emotional support, counselors provide a "bridge" for residents to return to independent living. They also manage the shelter by keeping records, purchasing supplies, and assigning rooms. Counselors make sure the building is in good shape and has what it needs. Residential counselors also supervise other staff members. Training and certification for most positions includes two to four years of college.

LESSON 4 REVIEW Write the answers to these questions on a separate sheet of paper, using complete sentences.

1) What are two things that can help improve your self-acceptance?

2) What is self-awareness?

3) What is one way you can improve your relationships with others?

4) Why is prejudice harmful to relationships with others?

5) How is empathy important in maintaining relationships?

■ Personality is your individual pattern of thoughts, feelings, and behavior.

■ Personality development is affected by temperament, meaningful relationships formed early in life, and self-concept.

■ Well-being involves a balance of physical, social, emotional, and personal well-being. The four forms of well-being often influence one another.

■ You can promote your well-being by staying healthy and learning how to handle stress. You can also promote your well-being by improving your understanding of others and forming beliefs and values.

■ Emotional well-being is an ongoing process that you work on throughout life.

■ Characteristics of emotional health are the abilities to learn and change through experiences; balance personal needs with the needs of others; balance forming social bonds with independence; set and reach realistic goals; sort out and solve problems rationally; control impulses and express feelings appropriately; and think in healthy ways.

■ Healthy relationships involve emotional attachment, mutual dependence, and satisfaction of both partners.

■ Maintaining healthy relationships involves successful communication and good self-esteem.

■ You can become more emotionally healthy by improving your self-acceptance through self-awareness and social comparison.

■ Self-acceptance helps people improve relationships with others. They can learn about and value differences among people, increase contact with a variety of people, and give and accept social support.

Chapter 2 Review

Comprehension: Identifying Facts

On a separate sheet of paper, write the correct word or words from the Word Bank to complete each sentence.

WORD BANK		
compromise	intent	social
coping	optimism	social comparison
discriminate	personal	temperament
empathy	personality	
impulses	prejudice	
independence	self-esteem	

1) _____ is a person's emotional makeup.

2) Early experiences and temperament influence an adult's _____.

3) Learning communication, friendship, and citizenship skills promotes _____ well-being.

4) The forms of well-being are physical, emotional, social, and _____.

5) Even though people form attachments, they must still maintain their _____.

6) Realistic goals are balanced between pessimism and unrealistic _____.

7) _____ happens when both people work out a solution to a problem by giving a little.

8) People respond to stress by _____ or avoidance.

9) Emotionally healthy people learn to control their _____.

10) Communication is successful when the sender's _____ matches the effect on the receiver.

11) Relationships are healthy when both people have good
_____.

12) _____ is trying to identify and understand others' feelings.

13) Observing others to determine how to behave is called
_____.

14) _____ is a negative opinion formed without enough experience or knowledge.

15) Prejudiced people tend to _____ against people who are different from themselves.

Comprehension: Understanding Main Ideas

On a separate sheet of paper, write the answers to the following questions using complete sentences.

16) What are some influences on personality development?

17) How do the forms of well-being affect one another?

18) What is the difference between coping and avoidance as ways to deal with stress and other emotional problems?

Critical Thinking: Write Your Opinion

19) Why is it so difficult for people to accept others who are different? What can you do to teach someone to be less prejudiced?

20) In communicating with others, are you better at sending or at receiving? Explain how you could improve.

Test Taking Tip | When studying for a test, use a marker to highlight important facts and terms in your notes. For a final review, read over highlighted areas.

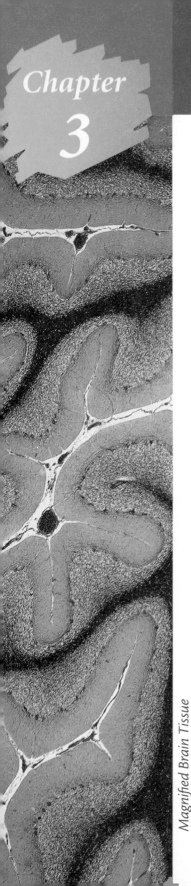

Magnified Brain Tissue

Chapter 3

Mental Health Problems

Have you ever heard someone called "crazy"? What did you think that meant? Have you wondered about the difference between mentally healthy and unhealthy behavior? Mental health spans a wide range of behaviors. The most helpful indication of mental health, however, is how well a person gets along in his or her world. Everyone has difficulties at different times. While it is never appropriate to call someone "crazy," a person whose behavior is often unhealthy may have mental health problems. The person may even have a mental disorder. Most mental health problems and disorders can be treated successfully.

In this chapter, you will learn about some of the symptoms of poor mental health and some self-defeating behaviors. You will learn about mental disorders and what can be done for them. You will learn some ways to improve your emotional well-being.

Goals for Learning

▶ To identify some characteristics of poor mental health

▶ To explain self-defeating behaviors

▶ To identify substance abuse disorders, anxiety disorders, affective disorders, and thought disorders, and how these disorders are treated

▶ To describe three kinds of eating disorders

Characteristics of Poor Mental Health

Abnormal
Unusual; different from normal

Psychologist
A person who studies mental and behavioral characteristics

Self-defeating behavior
Actions that block a person's efforts to reach goals

What are some adjustments you have had to make recently?

A person is usually neither completely healthy nor completely ill mentally. Healthy people may have problems, make mistakes, and behave in self-defeating ways. People with mental health problems still do many things well. The difference has to do with patterns of behavior that are either normal or not normal.

How Do Behaviors Indicate Mental Health?

A **psychologist** is someone who studies mental and behavioral characteristics. Most psychologists evaluate mental health by determining the level of normal (usual) behavior. If a person has many **abnormal** behaviors, that person may not be mentally healthy. Abnormal means unusual or not normal. The more abnormal a behavior or thinking pattern is, the greater the *possible* risk of mental illness.

Psychologists define normal and abnormal behavior in many ways. One way is to judge how well a person adjusts. People who meet their basic needs and personal goals show a normal pattern of behavior. They get along independently and maintain personal relationships. People who have difficulty getting along with others or who depend too much on others show abnormal behavior patterns. People who are defeated by repeated failure also show behavior that is considered abnormal.

What Are Self-Defeating Behaviors?

Self-defeating behaviors block a person from reaching his or her own goals. For example, you want to try out for the swim team. You know you must practice and increase your speed. The day before tryouts, you practice for a long time. Then you decide to practice even more that evening. You end up being tired and do not perform well at tryouts the next day. The decision to practice too much was self-defeating. It actually blocked you from reaching your goal.

Defense mechanism
A mental device one uses to protect oneself

Dysfunctional
Harmed; working abnormally

Phobia
An irrational or unreasonable fear of something

Sometimes self-defeating behavior is a sign of poor mental health. Such behavior can take many different forms. Three common forms of self-defeating behavior are anxiety, **defense mechanisms**, and **dysfunctional** relationships.

Anxiety

Anxiety is a feeling of uneasiness or fearful concern. You feel anxious when you have a sense that something bad will happen. You might feel anxious when you don't know what to expect in a certain situation. Anxiety may be so unpleasant that people do many things to escape it. Sometimes people use drugs to reduce anxiety, but the effects are only short-lived. Drugs do not get rid of the source of the anxiety. When the effect of the drugs wears off, the anxiety may be worse than before. Some people try to avoid the source of their anxiety. For example, someone who feels uncomfortable about meeting new people may avoid them. The person doesn't deal with the source of the anxiety but simply tries to avoid it by avoiding people. In this way, the person's behavior is self-defeating.

Feeling anxious can be unpleasant and uncomfortable.

One form of anxiety is a **phobia**, or an irrational fear of something. Claustrophobia, or fear of being in enclosed spaces, is a phobia you hear about often. This fear is irrational, or unreasonable, because enclosed spaces cannot really hurt a person. When people have a phobia, they create problems for themselves. For example, a man doesn't go into elevators because he has claustrophobia. He has to find ways to avoid elevators and other small spaces. This disrupts his normal behavior.

Denial
The conscious refusal to take a threat seriously

Displacement
Shifting an emotion from its real object to a safer or more immediate one

Projection
Accusing another person of having one's own attitudes, feelings, or purposes

Repression
The unconscious dismissal of painful impulses, desires, or fears from the conscious mind

Health Tip

Record your feelings in a journal to help deal with them.

Defense Mechanisms

People use various defense mechanisms to hide anxiety without solving their problems. A defense mechanism is a mental device that people use to protect themselves. An example of a defense mechanism is escaping or avoiding the anxiety. Defending against anxiety doesn't really deal with the problem. The most common defense mechanisms are repression, denial, projection, and displacement.

- **Repression** is refusing to think about something that upsets you. For example, you may "forget" about a dental appointment that you don't want to go to.

- **Denial** is a conscious refusal to take a threat seriously. For example, your pet is sick, but you tell yourself that it's fine and always acts that way.

- **Projection** is accusing someone of your attitudes, feelings, or purposes. For example, if you are angry with your brother, you may project your anger on him. You might say, "What are you so mad about?"

- **Displacement** is shifting an emotion from its real object to a "safer" or immediate one. For example, your supervisor made you stay late to fix a problem at work. You are angry but afraid to say anything to the supervisor. When your parent calls, you yell at her for asking a simple question. You displaced your anger from its real object to a safer one. You can probably identify many examples of these defense mechanisms in your own and others' behavior. Using defense mechanisms is often normal, but using them too much leads to self-defeating behavior.

You can watch your use of defense mechanisms by reviewing your behavior. For example, if you often "forget" important or unpleasant events, you may be using repression too much. If you often say "This isn't serious" when talking about difficulties, you may be overusing denial. Realizing that you use these defense mechanisms is the first step in changing your behavior.

Dysfunctional Relationships

Relationships that are full of conflict or are not satisfying are called dysfunctional. That means they do not function well. The most common form of dysfunction in a relationship is poor communication. For example, you are worried about something but refuse to confide in a trusted person about it. Therefore, the person can't offer help or understand what is wrong. If you continue to refuse someone's help, others may feel pushed away and may withdraw from you. Unfortunately, you may be cutting yourself off from others' support when you need it most.

Health Tip

Give "I" messages kindly and respectfully to maintain communication in relationships.

It is possible to avoid this self-defeating pattern of shutting others out. You do this by identifying the persons you trust. When you are troubled, you can talk with these people about your feelings. A helpful hint is to start your sentences with "I" statements. For example, "I feel nervous" or "I worry that you'll get frustrated with me." Starting a statement with "I" makes it easier for others to understand and respond to you.

Another common problem in dysfunctional relationships is low self-esteem and lack of confidence. When you feel unworthy, you may experience conflicting emotions. You may want someone to help you feel better. However, your low self-esteem makes you believe that no one would want to be close

Healthy Subjects
Geography

SEASONAL AFFECTIVE DISORDER

Scientists have found that Seasonal Affective Disorder (SAD) affects five million Americans. The condition causes depression, sleeplessness, and energy loss. Less daylight during winter months causes SAD. Northern areas of the United States have more cases of SAD. Alaska has the highest rate, at 20 percent. Florida's 1.4-percent rate is the lowest. Decreased daylight seems to reduce the amount of an important chemical in some people's brain. Recent tests show that treatment with light can restore the chemical. People sit in front of a "light box" for thirty minutes a day. When they do, they find their SAD symptoms are greatly reduced.

to you. Your conflict with your own feelings can make it difficult to have a good relationship with others.

When you have problems, you may make heavy demands on a friend or family member. You may want the person to reassure you or spend time with you. If you do this too much, the other person may become worn out and refuse to help you. Expecting any other person to make you happy is unreasonable. People who love you will give you help, but no one else can be responsible for your happiness.

If you feel you make too many demands on friends or family members, you can work on changing your behavior. You can try to help yourself. By learning to take care of yourself, you can help become more independent. You can also become less demanding and can improve your mental health.

LESSON 1 REVIEW On a separate sheet of paper, write *True* if the statement is true or *False* if it is not true.

1) Mentally healthy people never have problems or make mistakes.

2) One way to evaluate mental health is to judge how well a person adjusts.

3) Self-defeating patterns are signs of abnormal or unhealthy behavior.

4) A phobia is a sensible, rational fear.

5) Displacement means to shift an emotion from one object to another.

Mental Disorders and Their Treatment

Anxiety disorder
A mental problem that makes normal life difficult because of intense anxiety

Panic attack
A feeling of terror that comes without warning and includes chest pain, rapid heartbeat, sweating, shaking, or shortness of breath

Substance abuse disorder
An unhealthy dependence on alcohol or other drugs

While many mental health problems are not considered serious, some are quite severe. Trained mental health professionals are the best people to treat severe problems. Symptoms of these problems can be relieved so the person is better able to perform. Many disorders can be cured or people can learn to cope with them.

The more you know about the most common mental disorders, the less frightening they may seem. More knowledge can also help you promote your own and others' mental health.

How Are Substance Abuse Disorders Treated?

A **substance abuse disorder** is an unhealthy dependence on alcohol or other drugs. Most substance abuse begins as a defensive behavior pattern. For example, a person may drink because he thinks he will feel less shy and self-conscious. Someone else may use a drug because it makes her feel happy and confident. Alcohol and drugs never solve the real problem. Since the problem still exists, the user must rely on the drug more and more. Many substances are habit-forming. After a while, the individual can't stop using the drug.

People who abuse substances can get help. How well they respond to treatment depends on their determination to get well and regain control. They must decide never to use the drug again. The most important step is admitting a problem exists. For this reason, most treatment programs begin with self-awareness and admitting the need for help. Treatment may involve individual counseling, behavior change programs, or support groups.

How Are Anxiety Disorders Treated?

An **anxiety disorder** is a mental problem that makes normal life difficult because of intense anxiety. A phobia is one type of anxiety disorder. Another type is a **panic attack**. A panic attack is a feeling of terror that comes without warning. Its symptoms include chest pain, rapid heartbeat, sweating, shaking, or shortness of breath. It can be triggered by a particular place or situation or may result from increasing stress.

Anxiety disorders are really many different kinds of problems. Some are physical and some are psychological. Physical problems can be treated with medicine that a physician orders. Medicine can reduce the symptoms long enough for the person to learn how to prevent further problems. Psychological problems can be treated with **psychotherapy**, including **behavior modification**. Psychotherapy is psychological treatment for mental or emotional disorders. Behavior modification is a form of psychotherapy. It teaches a person to replace less effective behavior patterns with more effective ones. For example, through behavior modification, a person can learn to relax and avoid panic by using deep breathing.

How Are Affective Disorders Treated?

An **affective disorder** is a mental disorder characterized by disturbed or uncontrolled emotions. The most common affective disorder is **clinical depression**.

TREATMENT OF MENTAL ILLNESS

People have always been concerned about mental disorders. Ancient peoples thought "evil spirits" caused the problem. Holes were drilled in the person's head to let the spirits escape. Years later, healers performed "magic" to drive out "devils." During the Middle Ages, mentally ill people were often tortured or starved to get rid of "demons." At other times, people were locked up in insane asylums. These were prison-like buildings used to keep mentally disordered people apart from society. Society's safety was seen as more important than treating the ill.

Today mental disorders are better understood. Counseling and modern medicine are used to treat them more humanely.

Clinical depression is long-lasting, intense sadness. Many people have mild depression. For example, you may feel depressed if you break up with someone. Symptoms of mild depression may be sadness, anger, low energy, or pessimistic thinking. Changes in appearance or in eating and sleeping patterns also can be symptoms of mild depression. For most people, the level of depression is related to the loss. If it is not a serious loss, you will feel better and go back to normal activities in a few days.

In clinical depression, people stay sad for a long time. They have trouble handling normal activities. Clinically depressed people may experience new symptoms as a result of the depression. They may not eat and begin to lose weight. Then they feel even more tired and depressed. The problems begin to compound and the situation continues to get worse. Depressed people tend to have negative thoughts and to withdraw from social contact. Depression creates lack of energy. They need both social contact and energy to recover.

WATCH FOR THESE WARNING SIGNS OF SUICIDE

- Depression, lack of energy
- Change in sleeping patterns
- Change in appetite
- Withdrawal from social activities
- Drop in grades
- Personality changes— moody, withdrawn, doesn't care
- Increased risk taking
- Earlier suicide attempts

In its most dangerous extremes, depression may lead an individual to attempt **suicide**, or killing oneself. Unfortunately, depression and suicide affect many teens. In 1997, 2,000 teens committed suicide, which is the third leading cause of death among 15- to 24-year-olds.

Fortunately, clinical depression can be treated with help from professionals. Medical help includes antidepressant medicines. It also includes psychotherapy to help people see their problems and change behavior patterns so they can solve the problems.

One way to deal with depression—even mild depression—is to become involved in a goal-directed activity. Working to reach a reasonable goal helps set a new direction. The depressed person gains a sense of involvement in life and of being busy. Some examples are caring for a pet or taking up a hobby such as painting, photography, or writing stories. Physical activity also helps to relieve mild depression.

Bipolar disorder
A mental problem involving an uncontrolled shift from feeling too much energetic emotion to feeling very depressed

Delusion
A false belief

Hallucination
A twisted idea about an object or event that is not real

Thought disorder
A mental problem characterized by twisted or false ideas and beliefs

Another example of an affective disorder is **bipolar disorder**. This problem causes people to experience a wide shift in feeling. Their behavior changes from one extreme—of overly energetic emotion—to the other extreme—serious depression. As with clinical depression, bipolar disorder requires professional help for treatment.

How Are Thought Disorders Treated?

A **thought disorder** is the most serious kind of mental disorder. Symptoms of thought disorders are twisted or false ideas and beliefs. An example of a twisted idea is an **hallucination**—an idea about an object or event that is not real. For example, a person who has hallucinations might see things that don't exist. An example of a twisted or false belief is a **delusion**. A person who has delusions might falsely believe that he or she is an entirely different person.

The combination of twisted ideas and false beliefs keeps a person with thought disorders out of touch with reality. This loss of touch with reality may range from mild to severe. A person with thought disorders may have only a few unrealistic ideas or may seem to live in a dream world. The person may say things that make no sense and may do things that seem very odd. The behavior can be frightening and dangerous. This is the type of mental illness most people think of when they say someone is "crazy."

Only mental health professionals can treat thought disorders. Some medicines can reduce the symptoms. However, no cure has been found. Most individuals with thought disorders respond to treatment. Their symptoms may become fewer or may completely disappear. Some people do not respond to treatment and continue to have symptoms throughout their life.

How Are Eating Disorders Treated?

Eating disorders are attempts to cope with psychological problems through eating habits. People falsely believe that they don't look good and have to change their appearance. This focus on appearance often leads to an eating disorder. An eating disorder can be a way of avoiding the pain of regular life. Every feeling and struggle becomes a war between the individual and food. This problem often affects females. Look at Table 3.1 to learn about three eating disorders.

Eating disorders are serious and require professional help for treatment. However, people who have eating disorders often resist professional help. If you know someone who may have an eating disorder, encourage the person to get help. Let the person know you care about his or her well-being. Encourage the person to talk about his or her feelings. You can be a good role model by not criticizing your own body or appearance.

Treatment for mental health problems often involves professional counseling.

How Does Society Deal With Mental Illness?

Society has gradually changed the way it treats those who are mentally ill. Few people today believe that a person can "catch" mental illness from someone else. However, society still has great difficulty accepting mental illness without fear. People tend to fear what they do not understand. Other people's prejudices against mental illness can influence your attitudes. For example, you might find it hard to befriend a person whom others think is "sick" or "crazy."

Table 3.1. Eating Disorders

Disorder	Description	Characteristics	Consequences
Anorexia	Emotional problem characterized by severe weight loss	Affects more females than males Extreme dieting, food rituals, not eating Compulsive exercising Frequent weighing Intense fear of becoming fat when actually too thin Treatable with medicine, psychotherapy when found early	Malnutrition Menstruation stops Lowered metabolic rate Poor temperature regulation Heart problems Death
Bulimia	Emotional problem involving bingeing (eating large amounts of food in a short time) followed by purging (ridding one's body of the food) or severe dieting	Fear of or inability to stop eating Hard to detect vomiting or use of laxatives Constantly thinking about food Secretly storing up food Person wants help but won't ask Extreme concentration on appearance Feeling of being out of control Depression Treatable with medicine, psychotherapy	Enlarged or ruptured stomach Eroded tooth enamel Pneumonia from inhaling vomit Other physical problems Behavioral problems Psychological problems Danger of substance abuse
Compulsive overeating	Emotional problem involving bingeing but no purging	Continually snacking Large meals and frequent snacks while bingeing Great feelings of guilt and shame for feeling out of control Inability to stop eating during binges Possible family tendency to be overweight Treatable with medicine, psychotherapy	Obesity (condition of having extreme body fat) Heart disease Diabetes Some kinds of cancer Reduced life span

RESIDENT ASSISTANT

Resident assistants work with residents in mental health settings, hospitals, and nursing homes. When residents need help, assistants answer the call. They may check residents' temperature, blood pressure, pulse, and breathing rate. Sometimes they bathe residents or give massages. Resident assistants help people who must stay in bed or a wheelchair. They deliver and serve meals and help residents eat when necessary. They socialize with residents, make them comfortable, and lift their spirits. Sometimes resident assistants are called nurses' aides or nurse assistants. Training varies from on-the-job training to formal training programs. The training programs may take several weeks or more to complete.

Should mentally ill people be allowed to have jobs and children?

Fortunately, developments in psychology and medicine have helped to improve attitudes toward the mentally ill. Almost everyone knows or is related to someone who has had psychological problems. For most of these problems, people can get help that will lessen or solve the problem.

LESSON 2 REVIEW Write the answers to these questions on a separate sheet of paper, using complete sentences.

1) What does a substance abuse disorder involve?

2) What are two ways anxiety disorders can be treated?

3) What is clinical depression?

4) Give an example of an hallucination and a delusion.

5) Name one eating disorder and describe how it can be treated.

■ Mental health includes a broad range of behaviors. People are usually not completely mentally healthy nor completely mentally ill.

■ Normal or abnormal behavior is best judged by how well a person adjusts to meeting basic needs and goals.

■ Self-defeating behaviors block a person from achieving goals. Patterns of self-defeating behaviors may indicate abnormal behavior.

■ Three common self-defeating behavior patterns are anxiety, defense mechanisms, and dysfunctional relationships.

■ A phobia, or irrational fear of something, is one form of anxiety.

■ Defense mechanisms are mental devices people use to protect themselves. Some common defense mechanisms are repression, denial, projection, and displacement.

■ While most healthy people have some emotional problems, people with severe problems may need professional help.

■ Substance abuse disorders involve a dependence on alcohol and other drugs. This disorder can be treated if the individual is determined to get well and regain control.

■ Anxiety disorders can be treated with psychotherapy, including behavior modification.

■ One kind of affective disorder is clinical depression. People who are clinically depressed require medicine and help from professionals to get better.

■ Thought disorders, the most serious kind of mental disorder, involve twisted thoughts and false beliefs. Medicines and professional help can relieve the symptoms, but there is no cure for thought disorders.

■ Eating disorders are a type of mental problem involving overemphasis on appearance to avoid the pain of regular life. Three eating disorders are anorexia, bulimia, and compulsive overeating.

■ Society's attitudes toward mental illness have changed, but some people still fear it because it can be difficult to understand.

Comprehension: Identifying Facts

On a separate sheet of paper, write the correct word or words from the Word Bank to complete each sentence.

WORD BANK		
affective	dysfunctional	substance abuse
anorexia	phobia	
anxiety	psychologist	suicide
appearance	purging	thought
defense mechanisms	self-defeating behavior	

1) A _____ is someone who studies mental and behavior characteristics.

2) An irrational fear of something is a _____.

3) Anxiety is a form of _____.

4) _____ are mental devices people use to protect themselves.

5) A _____ relationship is one that works abnormally.

6) A _____ disorder is an unhealthy dependence on alcohol and other drugs.

7) A panic attack is a kind of _____ disorder.

8) Clinical depression and bipolar disorder are two kinds of _____ disorders.

9) Symptoms of _____ disorders are twisted ideas or false beliefs.

10) Extreme clinical depression may lead to _____.

11) Eating disorders involve unrealistic emphasis on _____.

12) Bulimia is an eating disorder characterized by bingeing and _____.

13) _____ is an eating disorder characterized by extreme weight loss.

Comprehension: Understanding Main Ideas

On a separate sheet of paper, write the answers to the following questions using complete sentences.

14) How do most psychologists evaluate mental health?

15) What are three forms of self-defeating behavior?

16) Why are some relationships called dysfunctional?

17) What is clinical depression and how is it treated?

18) Which eating disorder could result in death?

Critical Thinking: Write Your Opinion

19) Do you feel anxiety when you have to give a speech? How could you handle the anxiety?

20) If you believe a friend is feeling depressed, what could you do to help?

Test Taking Tip Avoid waiting until the night before a test to study. Plan your study time so that you can get a good night's sleep the night before a test.

Testimonial Ads for Health Products

Advertisers know that consumers pay attention to famous people. "Testimonials" are ads that use famous people to sell a product. Movie stars or TV stars may endorse brands of makeup, low-fat foods, or diet drinks. Famous businesspeople or politicians ask for donations to a cause. Older celebrities may promote products that promise to help people stay young.

Testimonial ads rarely give product facts. Instead, they appeal to people's emotions in two ways:

1. These ads trigger an emotional response to get you to buy the product.

   For example, an actress with beautiful, shining hair says she uses "X-Brand" shampoo. The message is that if you use the same shampoo, you will have hair like hers.

2. The ads sound as if the product is scientifically proved to be better than other products.

   For example, a singer recommends his brand of aspirin by saying, "My father is a doctor. He insists I use it." The message hints that doctors know which aspirin brand is best.

Often emotional appeal is more important in selling a product than the product's quality. Advertisers choose famous individuals whom they think people admire. The emotional appeal may be aimed at improving your self-image or at making you think you will be healthier or feel better.

Questions

1) When someone famous promotes a product, do you think the person uses the product and has compared it with similar products? Why or why not?

2) What are some health products that you have seen advertised? Have any of these ads used famous people to sell a health product?

3) What could be dangerous about advertising the health benefits of a certain product?

4) What are some questions you can ask yourself before deciding to buy a health product based on a testimonial ad?

■ Emotions begin with thoughts and may cause physical changes or reactions.

■ Five basic human needs are physical, safety, belonging, esteem, and self-actualization.

■ Stress is a natural mental and physical reaction to anything that requires a person to adapt. Stress can be either "good" or "bad," but continued "bad" stress can be harmful to a person's well-being.

■ In the stress response, the brain sends chemical messages into the bloodstream that cause faster breathing, blushing, perspiration, and other physical reactions.

■ All emotions are normal. How emotions are handled is important to mental health.

■ Coping, learning from mistakes, experience and time, and other actions help to relieve stress.

■ Personality development is affected by temperament, meaningful relationships formed early in life, and self-concept.

■ Well-being involves a balance of physical, social, emotional, and personal well-being. Some ways to promote well-being are staying healthy, learning how to handle stress, improving understanding of others, and forming beliefs and values.

■ Some characteristics of emotional health are learning and changing through experiences; balancing personal needs with others' needs; setting and reaching realistic goals; solving problems rationally; controlling impulses; and expressing feelings appropriately.

■ Maintaining healthy relationships involves successful communication, good self-esteem, and self-acceptance.

■ People are usually neither completely mentally healthy nor completely mentally ill.

■ Normal or abnormal behavior is best judged by how well a person adjusts to meeting basic needs and goals. Patterns of self-defeating behaviors may indicate abnormal behavior.

■ People use defense mechanisms such as repression, denial, projection, and displacement to protect themselves.

■ While most healthy people have some emotional problems, people with severe problems may need professional help. People can get help for substance abuse disorders, anxiety disorders, clinical depression, thought disorders, and eating disorders.

A family is a unit composed not only of children but of men, women, an occasional animal, and the common cold.

—Ogden Nash

Personal Health and Family Life

What do you think of when you hear the word *family?* Research tells us that today's families are made up differently from families in the past. Although the basic structures may have changed, many things have remained the same. It is within the family structure that you learn to relate to others and care for them.

What does it mean to be healthy? Decisions you make every day determine your physical, social, and mental well-being. In this unit, you will learn how your body systems are interrelated and how the parts affect the whole. You will learn about the life cycle from reproduction and birth through old age. You will learn about different family systems and family relationships.

▶ Chapter 4 The Body Systems

▶ Chapter 5 Hygiene and Fitness

▶ Chapter 6 The Life Cycle and Human Development

▶ Chapter 7 The Family

☑ Self-Assessment

1. Can you list five consequences of being sexually active?

2. Do you get at least eight hours of sleep each night?

3. Do you exercise at least three times a week for 20 minutes?

4. When outdoors, do you use anything to protect yourself from the sun's ultraviolet rays?

5. Do you know how to perform a self-examination on yourself to detect for melanoma?

6. Can you list and explain five STDs?

7. Can you list the seven warning signs of cancer?

8. Do you feel self-confident when it comes to your fitness level and the appearance of your body?

9. Do you feel as though you have an easy time developing relationships with others?

10. Can you use refusal techniques under pressure?

The Body Systems

Your body is amazing! All of your body systems work together as one unit to maintain your good health. For your body to work well, it must maintain set limits. For example, your body temperature must stay within certain limits. When your body maintains these limits, it is in a state of balance. All of your body systems work together constantly to maintain this balance.

In this chapter, you will learn about your body's systems and how they work together. You will learn about the skeletal and muscular systems, the nervous system and sense organs, and the endocrine system. You will learn about the respiratory and circulatory systems and the digestive and excretory systems. Finally, you will learn about the body's protective covering—the skin, hair, and nails.

Goals for Learning

▶ To describe the purpose of the muscular and skeletal systems

▶ To explain the parts of the nervous system and how information comes through the sense organs

▶ To explain how the endocrine glands work with the nervous system

▶ To describe respiration and how the body circulates blood

▶ To explain the digestive and excretory systems

▶ To describe the purpose and structure of the skin, hair, and nails

Magnified Red Blood Cells

The Skeletal and Muscular Systems

Nutrient
A food substance or ingredient

Two body systems that work together closely are the skeletal and muscular systems. The skeletal system is your body's system of connected bones, or your skeleton. It provides the frame for your body and protects your organs. The muscular system allows your body to move. Figure A.1 in Appendix A shows the skeletal system. Figure A.2 in Appendix A shows the muscular system.

What Is the Purpose of Bones?

Your body has more than 200 bones. Besides providing your body's structure, bones protect your organs, store important minerals, and produce certain blood cells.

Bones are living material. They are made of cells, the basic structure of life. Each cell has a certain job to do. The cells that perform the same job form tissues. Bone cells make up bone tissue. Because bones are living tissue, they need **nutrients** just as other parts of your body do. A nutrient is a food substance or ingredient. The nutrients come from the food you eat and are supplied to the bones through your blood.

The size of the bones in your body ranges from large to very small. There are three basic kinds of bones. Long bones are in the arms and legs. Short bones are in such places as the wrists and ankles. Flat bones are in such places as the ribs.

How Are Bones Joined?

Long bones have larger ends that form a joint with another bone. Joints allow for several kinds of movement. For example, the most flexible joint in your body is the ball-and-socket joint in your hips and shoulders. This joint allows you to move forward, backward, side to side, and in a circle.

Your knee joint is a hinge joint. It is similar to a hinge on a door. You can bend your knee back, but you can't bend it forward. Pivot joints are in your elbows and between your head and spinal column. They move in the same way hinge joints do but also can rotate.

Tough bands of tissue called **ligaments** hold joints together. Ligaments are elastic and move easily.

Long bones are somewhat hard on the outside. Inside, however, is a soft substance called **marrow**. Bone marrow makes both red and white blood cells. As these cells become worn out or damaged, the marrow replaces them. You will learn about blood cells in Lesson 4.

How Do the Muscular and Skeletal Systems Work Together?

Joints allow your body's framework to move. However, all body movements also depend on muscles. Your body has about 600 muscles that do many things. They move your bones, pump blood, carry nutrients, and move air in and out of your lungs.

A muscle consists of a mass of fibers grouped together. When muscles contract, or shorten, they produce movement. Muscles hold your skeleton in place, and they also produce body heat. They act on messages they receive from your body's nervous system. You will learn about the nervous system in Lesson 2.

Healthy Subjects
Consumer Science

BUYING THE RIGHT RUNNING SHOES

Many people choose running as a way to keep fit. Choosing the right shoes is important for healthy feet. For most runners, "stability shoes" offer good cushioning, center support, and durability. However, "motion-control shoes" are better for people who tend to "roll" their feet inward as they step. These shoes are heavier but provide much-needed support for runners. Other runners' feet may be less flexible in the center. These people need cushioned shoes without much middle support. Off-road runners should wear "trail shoes." The soles of trail shoes give extra traction. They also include toe "bumpers," durable tops, and stronger stitching. The next time you buy shoes, consider how to keep your feet happy.

Your body has three basic types of muscles—smooth, skeletal, and cardiac muscles. Smooth muscles are involuntary. That is, they work even though you don't think about making them work. Some of your body's smooth muscles are in the walls of your stomach and of your blood vessels. Smooth muscles move food, waste, and blood through your body.

Skeletal muscles are voluntary muscles. That is, they are under your control. You decide what they will do. For example, if you decide to stand, walk, jump, or run, your voluntary muscles react to your decision. Skeletal muscles are connected to the skeletal system. Tough tissues called **tendons** usually attach skeletal muscles to bones. A tendon is a strong set of fibers that joins muscle to bone or muscle to muscle.

Because a strong heart works more efficiently, what is the importance of exercise for having a strong heart?

Cardiac muscles are in the walls of your heart. They contract regularly to pump blood throughout your body. Cardiac muscles are similar to smooth muscles in that they are involuntary.

Careers

ORDERLY

Health care professionals rely on orderlies. Orderlies assist doctors and nurses in caring for residents in hospitals, nursing homes, and clinics. They take care of residents' emotional and physical needs. Orderlies check residents' health, help keep them clean, and socialize with them. Being an orderly is a great way to try the health care field and see many different situations in it. Job prospects are excellent. A nursing home association says there is a continued demand for entry-level positions. Some health care facilities offer on-the-job training or might pay for classes. With training, orderlies can move up to be case managers, nurses, therapists, or counselors.

How Do Muscles Work?

Muscles work by contracting and relaxing. When a muscle contracts, it pulls on the tendon. The tendon acts on the bone to produce a movement. Some muscles work in pairs. When one contracts, the other one relaxes. You can feel this happening when you bend your arm at the elbow. The muscle on the top of your upper arm contracts. At the same time, the muscle on the bottom of your upper arm relaxes. When you extend your arm, the opposite happens.

What Is Muscle Tone?

Some muscles never relax completely. They are somewhat contracted at all times. This is called muscle tone. When you are in good health, a constant flow of impulses from your nerves to your muscles maintains muscle tone. Exercise and healthy eating are important for good muscle tone.

LESSON 1 REVIEW On a separate sheet of paper, write *True* if the statement is true or *False* if it is not true.

1) The skeletal system works separately from the muscular system.

2) Bones get nutrients from the blood.

3) A hinge joint allows bones to rotate.

4) Cardiac muscles are found in the heart.

5) Muscles contract to produce movement.

The Nervous System and Sense Organs

Brain stem
Part of the brain that connects the cerebrum with the spinal cord

Cerebellum
Part of the brain that controls balance and muscular activities

Cerebrum
Part of the brain that permits a person to read, think, and remember

Medulla
Part of the brain stem that controls automatic activities

The nervous system is the body's communication network. It sends messages throughout your body. Figure A.3 in Appendix A shows the nervous system. The nervous system has two parts—the central nervous system and the peripheral nervous system. The central nervous system is made up of the brain and the spinal cord.

How Does the Brain Control the Body?

Your brain receives messages from your nerves and sends messages through the nerves to all parts of your body. Your brain is like a computer and a chemical factory combined. It produces and uses chemicals to send signals, and it is able to process and store information. The brain has three main parts that work together to control your body. Figure 4.1 shows the parts of the brain.

The **cerebrum** is the part of the brain that lets a person read, think, and remember. It is the largest part of your brain. The cerebrum is divided into two halves. The right half controls activities on the left side of your body, including artistic skills and instinctive thinking. The left half controls the right side of your body. It controls math and language skills and logical, or sensible, thinking.

The other two parts of your brain are much smaller than your cerebrum. They are the **cerebellum** and **brain stem**. The cerebellum lies between the cerebrum and brain stem. Your cerebellum controls balance and helps coordinate muscular activities like walking. The brain stem connects the cerebrum with the spinal cord.

One part of the brain stem—the **medulla**—controls the body's automatic activities. These include breathing, digesting food, circulating blood, swallowing, coughing, and sneezing.

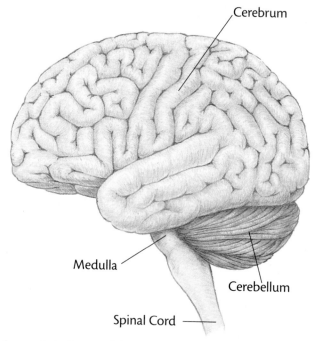

Cerebrum

Medulla

Cerebellum

Spinal Cord

Figure 4.1. Parts of the brain

How Does the Spinal Cord Assist the Brain?

The spinal cord is a major pathway that your brain uses to send messages to your body. Imagine your spinal cord as a thick telephone cable, or a bunch of wires wound together. Your spinal cord is a bunch of long nerve cells wound together. It connects to your brain stem and extends down to the lower part of your back. The spinal column is a series of small bones that surrounds and protects your spinal cord.

The nerves that make up the spinal cord act like telephone wires. They receive messages from the brain and relay them to another set of nerves.

Peripheral nerves
Nerves that carry all messages sent between the central nervous system and the rest of the body

What Does the Peripheral Nervous System Do?

The peripheral nervous system is a network of **peripheral nerves**. Peripheral nerves carry all the messages sent between your brain and spinal cord and the rest of your body. Peripheral means located away from the center.

One part of the peripheral nervous system helps control your body's automatic activities. It helps your body carry out all the processes necessary to remain stable, or under control. It also is what helps your body react in an emergency. For example, you are in a dangerous situation and need to react by running fast. This system signals your body to speed up your breathing and heartbeat so you are able to react. These are the body's reactions in the stress response. Afterward, this system will slow down the processes and return your body to normal.

Cornea
Part of the eye that light passes through

Iris
Colored part of the eye around the pupil

Optic nerve
Part of the eye that sends light information from the retina to the brain

Pupil
Dark center part of the eye that adjusts to let in the correct amount of light

Reflex
Automatic response

Retina
Part of the eye that receives and sends light information to the optic nerve

A special part of your peripheral nervous system controls your **reflexes**. Reflexes are automatic responses to something such as heat or pain. For example, when you touch something hot, you jerk your hand away without thinking about it. In this case, your nerves sent a message to the muscles in your hand. A person cannot stop reflex actions from happening.

How Do the Sense Organs Work?

Nerves throughout your body carry messages that reach your brain. Your brain receives messages and then sends signals to other parts of your body. When messages come from outside your body, your sense organs receive them. The sense organs are your eyes, ears, tongue, nose, and skin.

The Sense of Sight

Your eye is your organ of sight. Look at Figure 4.2 to see the parts of the eye. Your eye works like this. First, light enters your eye through the **cornea**. The cornea sends the light to the dark center of your eye called the **pupil**. Your pupil can adjust its size. It gets smaller in bright light and larger in low light. That way the pupil lets the right amount of light into your eye.

Behind your pupil is the soft, clear tissue called the lens. The lens helps focus the light energy onto the retina. The **retina** contains special cells that send the light information to the **optic nerve**. This is the nerve that sends the information to the brain, which translates the light information into understandable pictures. This entire process happens faster than you can blink!

Another part of your eye is the **iris**. The iris is the colored part surrounding the pupil that gives you your eye color.

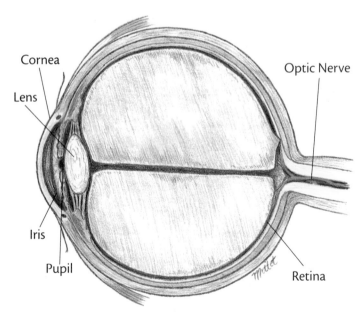

Cornea

Lens

Iris

Pupil

Optic Nerve

Retina

Figure 4.2. The eye

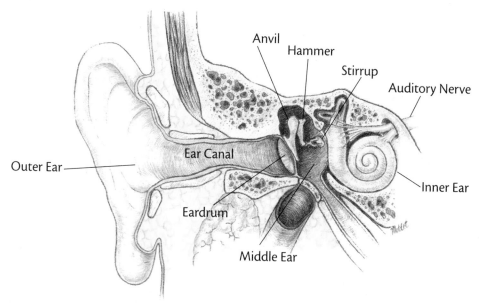

Figure 4.3. The ear

The Sense of Hearing

You may not notice that the air vibrates, or shakes, when a sound is made. But your ears notice. Figure 4.3 shows the parts of the ear. Your outer ear picks up the air vibrations and sends them through the ear canal to your eardrum. Your eardrum is a thin piece of tissue stretched across the ear canal. When your eardrum receives the vibrations, it also vibrates.

Eardrum vibrations cause three small bones in the middle ear to vibrate. These bones—the hammer, anvil, and stirrup—pass the vibrations to a snail-like organ in the inner ear. There, tiny cells transfer the vibrations to your **auditory nerve**. The auditory, or hearing, nerve sends information to your brain. Your brain interprets the message and tells you what kind of sound you heard. All of this happens in the time it takes for the sound to be made.

The Senses of Smell and Taste

Both your tongue and your nose contain **receptor cells**, or cells that receive information. The receptor cells in your nose send messages through nerves that are part of the **olfactory nerve**. Your olfactory nerve is connected to your brain. Your nose can detect thousands of different odors.

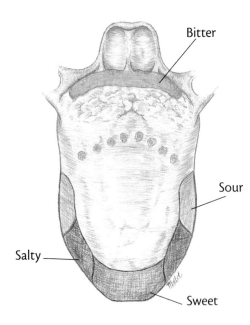

Bitter

Sour

Salty

Sweet

Figure 4.4. The taste centers of the tongue

Your tongue, however, can distinguish only four kinds of taste. The four tastes are sweet, salty, sour, and bitter. Taste buds, or receptors for each kind of taste, are located on different parts of your tongue. The taste buds send messages to your brain through nerves. That process tells you how something tastes. Figure 4.4 shows which part of your tongue detects the four tastes.

The Sense of Touch

Your skin, your sense organ for touch, is the largest organ your body has. Sense receptors all over your skin receive different sensations. You have receptors for touch, pressure, pain, heat, and cold. Your sense receptors send messages through the nerves to your spinal cord and brain. This is how you determine whether something is hot, cold, rough, or smooth. Your fingertips and lips are the most sensitive parts of your body because they have the most sense receptors.

LESSON 2 REVIEW Write the answers to these questions on a separate sheet of paper, using complete sentences.

1) Which half of the cerebrum controls artistic skills?

2) What is the main function of the peripheral nervous system?

3) What is a reflex?

4) Which part of the eye changes size to let in the correct amount of light?

5) What kinds of taste can the tongue detect?

The Endocrine System

Gland
A structure that secretes a special substance to help the body work

Hormone
A chemical messenger that helps control bodily functions

Metabolism
Rate at which cells produce energy

Pituitary gland
Part of the endocrine system that controls bodily functions such as growth and development

Thyroid gland
Part of the endocrine system that releases a hormone that affects metabolism

The endocrine system works closely with your nervous system to control certain activities in your body. The endocrine system is made up of tubeless **glands**. A gland is a group of cells or an organ that gives out, or secretes, a substance.

What Does the Endocrine System Do?

The endocrine system is made up of glands. Figure 4.5 on page 84 shows some of these glands. Endocrine glands produce **hormones** and secrete them directly into the bloodstream. Hormones are chemical messengers that help control bodily functions. You cannot control the secretion of hormones in your body.

How Do Glands Affect the Body's Growth?

One of the endocrine glands is the **pituitary gland**. It is a small gland at the base of the brain. The pituitary gland produces several hormones. One of these is a growth hormone. Too much or too little of this hormone can affect a person's size. For example, too much growth hormone produced during the growth years can make a person's bones unusually long. The person becomes much taller than other people.

What Does the Thyroid Gland Do?

Another endocrine gland is the **thyroid gland**. The thyroid is the largest endocrine gland and is located in the neck. The hormone it produces affects all tissues. Each cell in your body turns food into energy. The rate at which cells produce energy is called **metabolism**. The cells depend on the thyroid to change food into energy. Too much of the hormone can cause a person to feel overly energetic. This signals high metabolism. Too little of the hormone may result in low metabolism, causing a person to feel tired. The pituitary gland actually secretes a hormone that causes the thyroid to act.

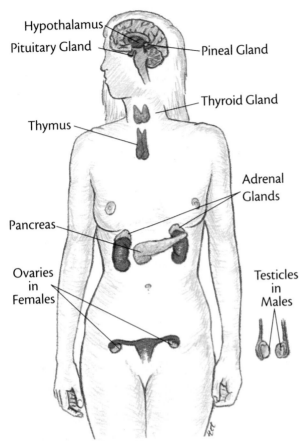

Hypothalamus

Pituitary Gland

Pineal Gland

Thyroid Gland

Thymus

Adrenal Glands

Pancreas

Ovaries in Females

Testicles in Males

Figure 4.5. The endocrine system

What Do the Adrenal Glands Do?

The system also contains two **adrenal glands** located on top of each kidney. These glands secrete a mixture of hormones that affect many body functions. They help the body maintain the proper water balance. One adrenal hormone helps a person to cope with stress.

The adrenal gland also secretes a hormone called **adrenaline**. Adrenaline causes your heart to beat faster and your blood pressure to rise in an emergency. Adrenaline is known as the emergency hormone. It is released into the blood in greater amounts when a person experiences fear.

Adrenal gland
Part of the endocrine system that releases several hormones

Adrenaline
Hormone released into the bloodstream that increases certain body functions

LESSON 3 REVIEW On a separate sheet of paper, write *True* if the statement is true or *False* if the statement is not true.

1) The endocrine system functions without help from other body systems.

2) The endocrine system has just three glands.

3) The thyroid is the largest gland in the endocrine system.

4) The adrenal glands are located in the neck.

5) Adrenaline is a hormone that is released when a person is afraid.

The Circulatory and Respiratory Systems

Platelet
Element in the blood that helps with clotting

*A*ll systems in your body work together. Just as all systems depend on your nervous system, they also depend on your circulatory and respiratory systems. The circulatory system includes your blood, heart, and three kinds of blood vessels. It is your body's transportation system. Look at Figure A.4 in Appendix A to see the circulatory system.

Why Does the Body Need Blood?

The circulatory system transports blood throughout your body. Blood carries food and oxygen to every cell in your body. Cells use the food and oxygen to do their work. The blood also carries waste products away from the cells.

Blood is made up of red blood cells, white blood cells, and **platelets**. Red blood cells carry oxygen to all parts of your body and remove carbon dioxide from these parts. White blood cells work to keep your body healthy by fighting disease and infection. Normally, your body has fewer white blood cells than red blood cells. However, white blood cells increase when your body is fighting infection. Platelets are the smallest elements in blood. They prevent the body from losing blood through a wound by a process called clotting, which stops bleeding.

How Does Blood Move Through the Body?

Your heart pumps blood to all parts of your body. Your heart has been beating every minute since before you were born. In fact, your heart beats about 72 times a minute. This regular beat is your pulse. Your heart is in the left side of your chest. It has four chambers—two on the left side and two on the right.

Blood from all parts of your body flows into the right side of your heart. This blood contains carbon dioxide, which the blood must get rid of. The right side of your heart pumps the blood to the lungs.

Artery
Vessel that carries blood away from the heart

Capillary
Tiny blood vessel that connects arteries and veins

Vein
Vessel that carries blood back to the heart

In your lungs, blood gets rid of carbon dioxide and picks up oxygen. Then the blood travels to the left side of your heart. From there, your heart pumps blood to all parts of your body to get oxygen to the cells.

Blood vessels distribute blood throughout your body. You have three kinds of blood vessels—**arteries**, **capillaries**, and **veins**. Arteries are the largest blood vessels and carry blood away from your heart. Arteries have thick, three-layered walls. Arteries branch into smaller vessels. These small branches regulate the flow of blood into the capillaries.

Capillaries are the smallest blood vessels, and they connect arteries and veins. They have thin walls that allow nutrients and oxygen to pass from the blood to the body cells. Capillaries also pick up waste products from the cells.

When blood leaves the capillaries, it travels to veins. Veins carry the blood back to your heart. Veins that receive blood from capillaries are small but become larger as they get closer to your heart.

This passage of the blood throughout your body happens quickly. It takes about one minute for blood to travel through your entire body.

What Is Blood Pressure?

Blood pressure is the force of blood on the walls of blood vessels. Pressure is created as your heart pumps blood to all parts of your body. Your body needs to maintain a certain level of blood pressure. Many things affect blood pressure, including age, tobacco use, diet, exercise, and heredity.

How Do the Respiratory and Circulatory Systems Work Together?

The circulatory system transports blood to all areas of your body. That blood carries oxygen to the cells. The cells need oxygen to break up nutrients, or food, in the cells. Energy is released from the food. Then the respiratory system gets the oxygen into your body. It also gets rid of carbon dioxide, a waste product. Together, the respiratory and circulatory

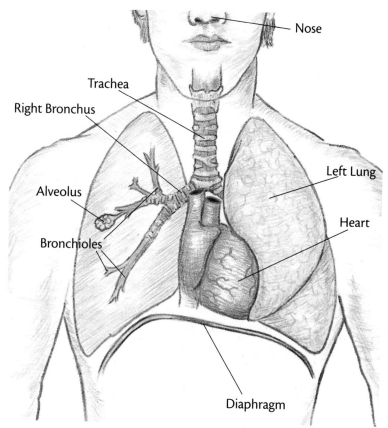

Figure 4.6. The respiratory system

Bronchi
Air tubes leading into the lungs

Bronchiole
Smallest division of the bronchi

Respiration
The process of breathing in oxygen and breathing out carbon dioxide

Trachea
Long tube running from the nose to the chest; windpipe

systems give the cells in all parts of your body the oxygen they need to survive.

Respiration is inhaling, or breathing in, oxygen and exhaling, or breathing out, carbon dioxide. The respiratory system is a system of tubes and organs that allows you to breathe. You need to breathe about 20 times every minute. Figure 4.6 shows the respiratory system.

How Does the Body Take in Oxygen?

When you breathe, you take in air through your nose or mouth. The air flows down through a long tube called the **trachea**, or windpipe. The trachea divides into two branches called **bronchi**, or bronchial tubes. Each bronchus leads into one of the lungs—the major breathing organs. In the lungs, each bronchus divides and divides again to form a network of tubes called **bronchioles**.

Then and Now

THE BENEFITS OF CINNAMON

Many "old-fashioned" treatments are now considered useless or even silly. However, some have proved to be useful. For instance, an ancient Chinese medical book suggested fighting germs with cinnamon. Cinnamon is a spice made from the bark of the cinnamon tree. Years later, Egyptians used cinnamon in perfumes. Europeans used it unsuccessfully to fight the plague. The people in Sri Lanka once used cinnamon in making good-smelling candles for their king.

Today, cinnamon is believed to increase blood flow. Many people who work with herbs mix cinnamon into remedies. The remedies are thought to help fight flu, chills, and several stomach illnesses.

Alveoli
Tiny air sacs at the ends of the bronchioles

Diaphragm
A band of muscles that lies beneath the lungs

At the end of each bronchiole is a cluster of air sacs with thin walls. These are called **alveoli**. You have about 300 million alveoli in your lungs. The alveoli are covered with a network of capillaries. The thin walls of the alveoli and capillaries allow the gases to change places. That is, the oxygen goes in and the carbon dioxide comes out.

Your lungs need help from your **diaphragm** and chest cavity. The diaphragm is a band of muscle tissue that lies beneath your respiratory organs. Your chest cavity includes ribs and muscles that surround your heart and lungs. When you inhale, your rib muscles and diaphragm contract. This enlarges your chest cavity and allows air to rush in. When you exhale, your rib muscles and diaphragm expand. This forces the air out.

LESSON 4 REVIEW Write the answers to these questions on a separate sheet of paper, using complete sentences.

1) What do white blood cells do?

2) What are the three kinds of blood vessels?

3) Why is clotting important?

4) What is carbon dioxide?

5) What happens when rib muscles and the diaphragm contract?

The Digestive and Excretory Systems

Enzyme
Substance that promotes a chemical reaction in the body

Esophagus
Long tube that connects the mouth and the stomach

Saliva
A liquid in the mouth containing an enzyme that breaks down food

Villi
Tiny fingerlike bulges in the walls of the small intestine that help to absorb nutrients

Your body needs food for energy, growth, and repair. Your body must break food down into substances that cells can use. Breaking down food into simpler substances is called digestion. The digestive system is the system that breaks down food for your body's use. Look at Figure 4.7 on page 90 to see the digestive organs.

How Does the Digestive System Break Down Food?

When your mouth waters at the sight, smell, or thought of food, it is producing **saliva**. Saliva is a liquid in your mouth. It contains an **enzyme**, a special chemical that breaks down food. Enzymes are in all your digestive organs. When you take a bite of a hamburger, your tongue pushes the food around. Your teeth help you chew the food into small pieces. As food is chewed, it is mixed with saliva. The enzyme in your saliva begins to break down the food.

Food next enters your **esophagus**, a long tube that connects your mouth and your stomach. Muscles in the walls of your esophagus push the food along to your stomach. Your stomach walls give off juices containing enzymes that break food down more. Your stomach also breaks down food by twisting and churning. Food remains in your stomach for three to four hours while the enzymes change solid food into partly liquid form.

From your stomach, food enters the small intestine. The small intestine is a curled-up tube that is just below your stomach. Most of the breakdown of food into chemicals takes place in your small intestine. The small intestine is lined with millions of tiny, fingerlike bulges called **villi**. Villi absorb the food that has been broken down into chemicals. Villi contain tiny blood vessels, which are connected with the rest of your bloodstream. The chemicals from digested food enter your blood vessels in the villi. Your bloodstream then sends them to all parts of your body.

Fitness Tip

Turn off the TV and do something physical—walk, bike, swim, run.

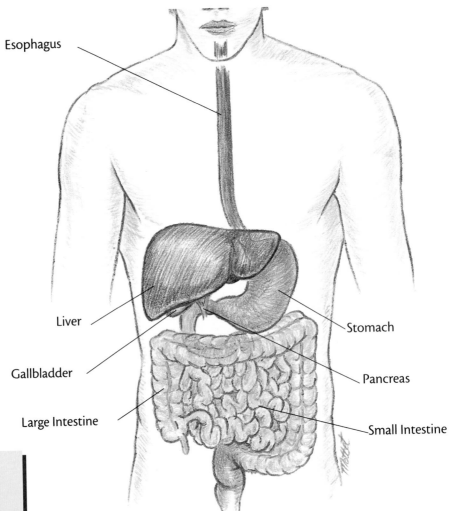

Esophagus

Liver

Gallbladder

Large Intestine

Stomach

Pancreas

Small Intestine

Figure 4.7. The digestive system

Your liver and **gallbladder** are also digestive organs. Your liver is a large organ that produces bile to help digest fats such as butter. Your gallbladder is a small pouch attached to the liver that stores **bile**. When bile is needed for digestion, it is pushed into the small intestine.

Your **pancreas** also helps in digestion. It produces a chemical called **insulin**, which helps cells use sugar. Your pancreas also gives off enzymes that break down certain foods.

Most food moves through your small intestine in one to four hours. Some foods are digested very quickly.

How Does the Body Get Rid of Solid Waste?

Any substances that the villi do not absorb in the small intestine move on to the large intestine. The large intestine is a tube connected to the small intestine. It helps your body by gathering and removing waste materials that are by-products of digestion. Through its walls, the large intestine absorbs water and nutrients from the waste material. The solid material remaining in the large intestine is **feces**. Feces are stored in the **rectum**, or lower part of the large intestine. Feces leave your body through an opening called the **anus**.

How Does the Body Get Rid of Liquid Waste?

Your body is efficient in using nutrients it needs and eliminating, or getting rid of, the rest. The system that allows the body to eliminate liquid and solid waste is the excretory system. Look at Figure 4.8 to see the excretory system. This system removes water and salts through your sweat glands.

Nutrition Tip

Drink at least six to eight 8-ounce glasses of water daily to help the kidneys function properly.

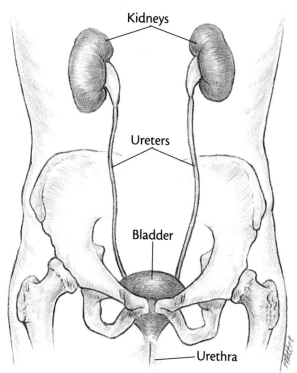

Figure 4.8. The excretory system

Kidney
Organ in the excretory system where urine forms

Ureter
Tube through which urine passes from a kidney to the urinary bladder

Urethra
Tube that takes urine out of the body

Urinary bladder
Bag that stores urine

Urine
Liquid waste product formed in the kidneys

It also takes waste products out of your blood. The main excretory organs that do this are your two **kidneys**. The kidneys are on either side of your spine in your lower back. After your kidneys take waste products out of your blood, they return substances like water to your blood.

As your blood supplies nutrients to your cells, the cells form waste products. These wastes flow through cells into your bloodstream. When blood circulates through your kidneys, wastes are filtered out. The blood then travels back to your heart through your veins.

Waste products travel out of your kidneys through tubes called **ureters** to your **urinary bladder**. The bladder can stretch to hold this liquid waste or **urine**. Urine passes out of your body through the **urethra**.

LESSON 5 REVIEW Write the answers to these questions on a separate sheet of paper, using complete sentences.

1) What happens when your mouth waters?

2) What is the esophagus?

3) What do enzymes do to solid food?

4) What are villi?

5) What organs filter out wastes from the blood?

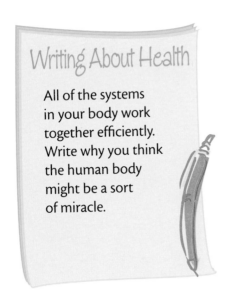

Writing About Health

All of the systems in your body work together efficiently. Write why you think the human body might be a sort of miracle.

Lesson 6

The Body's Protective Covering

Your skin is the largest organ in your body. It covers and protects your entire body. It is part of a system that protects and covers your body. The skin is one of your sense organs and is also part of the excretory system. It is also a separate system that includes your sweat glands, hair, and nails.

What Is the Structure of the Skin?

Figure 4.9 shows that the skin is made up of three layers. The **epidermis** is the outer layer of skin. The lower part of the epidermis creates new cells that are pushed up. The layer on the top of the epidermis is made up of dead cells. The dead cells flake off as the new ones replace them.

The **dermis** is the inner layer of skin that is made up of living cells. Nerves and blood vessels are in the dermis. Oil glands in the dermis help keep your hair and skin from cracking.

Below the dermis is the **subcutaneous layer**—the deepest layer of skin. It is mostly fatty tissue that protects your body from heat and cold. This layer also protects your body from injury.

How Does the Skin Protect the Body?

Skin protects your body in many ways. First, your skin prevents most **bacteria**, or germs, from entering your body. Bacteria are tiny structures that cause disease.

Skin also helps control your body's temperature. The epidermis has tiny openings called **pores**. Pores are connected with the sweat glands.

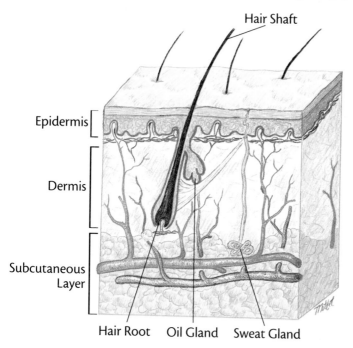

Figure 4.9. The structure of the skin

Hair Shaft

Epidermis

Dermis

Subcutaneous Layer

Hair Root   Oil Gland   Sweat Gland

Your body gets rid of perspiration through sweat glands. Perspiration helps to cool down your body.

The dermis helps protect your skin through cells that produce **melanin**. Melanin is the substance that gives skin its color. When you are in the sun, your skin produces more melanin to shield it from the sun's harmful rays. The increase in melanin is what makes skin look tanned. Freckles are actually small spots of melanin.

What Is the Structure of the Hair and Nails?

Hair and nails are two other parts of your body's protective covering. The roots of hair are made up of living cells and grow out of the dermis. A hair root grows out of a small pocket in the dermis that holds the root.

Hair is like the skin in that new cells are pushed up to replace the old cells. The hair on your head is made up of dead cells.

Nails are also dead cells. Nails grow out of the skin's epidermis. They contain a type of protein called **keratin**, which makes nails hard. Your nails protect the soft ends of your fingers and toes.

LESSON 6 REVIEW On a separate sheet of paper, write the word in parentheses that correctly completes each sentence.

1) The protective covering includes sweat (glands, pores, cells), hair, and nails.

2) The skin has (two, three, four) layers.

3) Skin protects the body from (bacteria, perspiration, melanin).

4) Melanin is the substance that gives the skin its (hardness, strength, color).

5) Hair grows out of the (epidermis, dermis, subcutaneous layer).

■ The skeletal system gives your body its shape. Bones provide a frame for your body and protect your organs. Bones are made of cells and also produce certain cells.

■ The muscular system allows your body to move. The body has smooth, skeletal, and cardiac muscles. Muscles act on messages they receive from the nervous system.

■ The nervous system controls your body's activities. The central nervous system includes your brain and spinal cord. Your brain has three parts. Your spinal cord is the pathway your brain uses to send messages.

■ Nerves in the spinal cord receive messages from your brain and relay them to peripheral nerves. Peripheral nerves send messages to the rest of your body.

■ Your sense organs let you know what is happening around you. Your sense organs are your eyes, ears, nose, tongue, and skin. They gather information to send to the brain.

■ The endocrine system is made up of glands. Glands secrete hormones, or chemical messages, that help to control bodily functions.

■ The circulatory system includes your blood, heart, and three kinds of blood vessels. Blood carries food and oxygen to every cell. Blood is made up of red blood cells, white blood cells, and platelets. Your heart pumps blood throughout your body.

■ The respiratory system allows you to breathe in oxygen and breathe out carbon dioxide. Cells need oxygen to break up nutrients.

■ The digestive system breaks down food for your body's use. All digestive organs contain enzymes. Enzymes promote chemical reactions that allow your body to break down food into substances that cells can use.

■ The excretory system rids your body of wastes in several ways.

■ Your skin has three layers that cover and protect your body. Your body's protective covering includes sweat glands, hair, and nails.

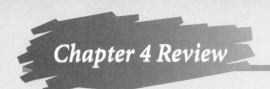

Chapter 4 Review

Comprehension: Identifying Facts

On a separate sheet of paper, write the correct word or words from the Word Bank to complete each sentence.

WORD BANK		
arteries	hormones	nervous
blood pressure	infection	pupil
bones	involuntary	reflexes
brain	medulla	small intestine
dermis	movement	vibrations

1) The skeletal system consists of more than 200 _____ and their joints.

2) Muscles are tissues that contract to produce _____.

3) Muscles are either voluntary, like skeletal muscles, or _____, like cardiac and smooth muscles.

4) The _____ system is the body's communication network.

5) The central nervous system is made up of the _____ and the spinal cord.

6) One part of the brain stem, the _____, controls automatic activities such as breathing.

7) _____ are automatic responses to heat or pain.

8) The _____ in the middle of the eye adjusts its size to let in the right amount of light.

9) The ear picks up _____ that are transferred to the auditory nerve and the brain.

10) The endocrine system includes glands that produce _____, which control the body's functions.

11) _____ carry blood away from the heart.

12) White blood cells increase to fight _____.

13) The force of blood on the walls of the blood vessels is _____.

14) The _____ is where most of the breakdown of food into chemicals takes place.

15) The three layers of the skin are the epidermis, _____, and the subcutaneous layer.

Comprehension: Understanding Main Ideas

On a separate sheet of paper, write the answers to the following questions using complete sentences.

16) How does the respiratory system work with the circulatory system?

17) What do the kidneys do?

18) How does the skin protect the body?

Critical Thinking: Write Your Opinion

19) Is one system of the body more important than the others? Explain your answer.

20) What do you think is the most amazing thing about how the human body works? Explain your answer.

| Test Taking Tip | Sometimes it is easier to learn new vocabulary words if you make them a part of your speaking and writing in other discussions and subject areas.

Magnified Red Blood Cells

Hygiene and Fitness

Taking care of yourself can be something you do for you. It can help you feel healthier. Taking care of yourself has other benefits as well. It can help you look better and feel better about yourself. How you feel about yourself affects how others feel about you. Taking time to care for your eyes, ears, skin, hair, nails, and teeth shows you value yourself. Exercising and getting enough sleep can also be ways you value yourself.

In this chapter, you will learn about ways to take care of yourself and stay healthy. You will also learn about the importance of fitness, exercise, and rest to your health and your social and emotional well-being.

Goals for Learning

▶ To explain the purpose of basic hygiene

▶ To describe ways to protect eyes, ears, skin, hair, nails, and teeth

▶ To explain three elements of health-related fitness

▶ To identify the benefits of regular exercise and the parts of an exercise program

▶ To identify why the body needs rest and sleep

Hygiene for Good Health

*H*ygiene refers to things that you do to promote good health. Protecting and caring for your eyes, ears, skin, hair, nails, and teeth are part of hygiene. These are all important parts of your body, so caring for them is important. For example, think what it might be like if you lost your sight or hearing.

How Can You Care for Your Eyes and Sight?

Your body protects your eyes and sight in many ways. The hard bones of your skull surround your eyes. Your eyelids, eyebrows, and eyelashes keep dirt, perspiration, and direct light out of your eyes. Blinking protects your eyes from dirt and direct light. Tears wash away tiny objects and help destroy harmful germs that may enter your eye.

Here are some things you can do to protect your eyes:

• Avoid touching your eyes with dirty hands and keep sharp objects away from them.

technology

LASER SURGERY

Spy movies may show lasers as a threat to world peace. In reality, lasers are used for many jobs, like surgery. Laser surgery uses a powerful beam of light that can be controlled accurately. This kind of surgery was first used in the mid-1960s. Different lasers are used for different medical procedures, most of which are safe and relatively painless. Lasers can seal blood vessels or break up kidney stones. They can cut skin tissue or whiten teeth. Lasers can gently remove scars, spots, and wrinkles or help to correct drooping upper eyelids. Some lasers help nearsighted people see without eyeglasses or contacts by changing the eyeball's shape and restoring normal vision. Lasers can even help people who snore.

Table 5.1. Some Vision Problems

Farsightedness	Difficulty seeing close objects
Nearsightedness	Difficulty seeing distant objects
Astigmatism	Blurred vision caused from uneven shape of cornea or lens
Strabismus	Crossed eyes; eye muscles do not work together; one or both eyes turn inward or outward
Color Blindness	Inherited lack of ability to see certain colors, usually in males

- Read and watch television in a well-lighted room to avoid eyestrain.
- Avoid being in bright sunlight for long periods.
- If you wear contact lenses, follow instructions for cleaning and wearing them.
- Wear safety glasses, goggles, or a helmet to shield your eyes from glare, damaging light, chemicals, dirt, and sport injuries.
- Wear sunglasses in the sun, but not indoors.

In addition, you need regular eye exams by an eye professional to check for eye and vision problems. Your vision is normal when you see a sharp, clear image. In an eye exam, you read rows of letters from a chart. Letters get smaller with each new row. If you stand 20 feet from the chart and can read the 20/20 row, you have normal vision. If your vision isn't normal, your eye professional can write an order for lenses to correct the problem. Table 5.1 lists some common vision problems.

How Can You Care for Your Ears and Hearing?

Your body also protects your ears. Your skull protects the most delicate parts of your ears. The wax in your outer ears keeps dirt from going into other parts of your ears. A certain amount of wax in your ears is normal. Sometimes, the wax

Allergy
Unusual response of the body to a food or substance in the air

Decibel
A unit that measures sound

Infection
A sickness caused by a germ in the body

may build up so you don't hear as well as normal. If that happens, a trained health professional can remove the wax.

Many things cause hearing loss. The most common reason for hearing loss is loud noise. If you are around loud noise a lot, you may be at risk for a hearing loss. The loss usually happens gradually and without pain. Sometimes it can happen instantly from a single loud noise such as a rock concert.

A hearing test will show what your hearing level is. If an ear exam shows you have hearing or ear problems, a doctor can recommend ways to help the problem. Hearing loss from noise is almost totally preventable.

Other things that can cause hearing loss are **infection**, heredity, **allergy**, wax buildup, or injury. Infection is a sickness caused by a germ in the body. An allergy is an unusual response of your body to a food or substance in the air.

Action for Health

PROTECT YOUR HEARING

Loud noises can cause hearing loss. Intensity, or strength, of sound is measured in **decibels** (db). Here are the decibel levels for some common sounds:

Normal breathing	10 db
Whisper	30 db
Normal conversation	60 db
Truck traffic	90 db
Rock concert	120 db
Jet engine at takeoff	140 db

Decibel levels higher than 85 can cause injury and hearing loss. In jobs where noise is greater than 85 db, workers must wear earplugs or earmuffs to protect their hearing.

You can protect your hearing from harmful noise levels. Be aware of the noise levels around you. Any sound that requires you to shout to be heard threatens your hearing. If your ears buzz or ring when you leave a noisy area, the noise level is too high. Be sure to keep the volume on radios, CD players, and TVs at safe levels, especially when wearing headphones. Get away from any sound that is too loud.

NOISE POLLUTION

Many industries and companies have taken steps to prevent hearing loss from loud noise. Airport ground crews wear head gear to protect their ears when jets take off. New offices have sound-absorbing walls and ceilings. These cut down noise. Some noisy machines in factories are put in sound-decreasing cases. Machines make fewer noisy vibrations when connected to floors and walls. If the walls and ceilings of a workspace are too hard, they echo and enlarge machine noises. When "sound-deadening" materials are added, noises decrease. Many industrial workers wear other noise-control devices that further protect them.

Here are some ways you can protect your hearing and your ears.

- Avoid loud noise and music or wear earplugs or earmuffs when near loud noise.

- Clean your ears only with a damp washcloth on your fingertip—never with a cotton swab.

- Avoid putting objects in your ears.

- Be careful to swim in clean water and to dry your ears after swimming.

- Wear a head guard when playing contact sports.

How Can You Protect Your Skin?

There are two basic rules for good skin care. The first rule is to keep your skin clean. The most effective way to keep your skin clean is to wash with soap and water. Your skin prevents bacteria, or germs, from entering your body. Buildup of dirt, bacteria, and dead skin lowers your skin's ability to keep bacteria out. Washing with soap and water prevents these buildups. How often you need to wash depends on your skin type and how active you are.

You may think perspiration has an odor, but it doesn't. Odor results when perspiration contacts bacteria on your skin. Washing with soap and water reduces body odor by removing bacteria. A **deodorant** is a product that can cover up the odor. An **antiperspirant** is a product that helps to control perspiration by closing the pores. Neither product, however, removes odor-causing bacteria.

The second basic rule for skin care is to protect your skin from severe winds, cold, and sun. High wind and severe cold can cause your skin's outer layer to lose moisture rapidly. Your skin can become chapped, or cracked and split. The sun provides us with warmth and at least one nutrient, but too much sun can be harmful. Long exposure to the sun can cause eye damage, sunburn, wrinkled skin, and skin cancer. Damage from the sun builds up over the years and cannot be reversed. Some sun rays can give you a sunburn even on cloudy days. Those rays also reflect off snow, sand, and water. That increases the chance of sunburn when you are skiing or at the beach.

Here are some other ways you can protect your skin from wind, cold, and sun.

- In windy, cold weather, dress warmly and cover your face and hands.

- Use a cream or lotion to keep the skin's natural moisture.

- Wear a sunscreen to protect from sunburn and block the harmful effects of the sun. A sunscreen with a sun protection factor (SPF) of 15 or more gives best protection.

How Can You Care for Skin Problems?

Acne is the most common skin problem for teenagers. Acne is clogged skin pores, or openings in the skin. Teenagers have a normal increase in hormones. Hormones cause oil glands to produce more oil. If the oil plugs your pores, you may get whiteheads, blackheads, or **pimples**. A whitehead results when oil gets trapped in a pore. A blackhead is an oil plug that darkens when exposed to air. A pimple forms if bacteria get into the clogged pore and inflame it. You have many oil glands in your face, neck, and back. Acne usually affects these areas. Acne has no cure; however, you can do some things to reduce the problem.

- Wash right after exercise to remove sweat and bacteria that can clog pores. Use a clean washcloth every day. Bacteria grow quickly on a damp washcloth.

- Shampoo your hair often to limit acne on your forehead, neck, and shoulders.

- Eat a well-balanced diet and get plenty of rest and exercise.

- Limit time in the sun and avoid tanning booths and sunlamps. Tanning booths and sunlamps damage skin in the same way the sun does.

- Avoid oil-based creams and lotions.

- Wash with soap and water every morning and evening. If your face is very oily, wash it once more during the day.

- Do not squeeze or pick pimples and blackheads. This can cause infection or leave a scar on your skin.

- Visit a skin doctor if you have severe acne.

Athlete's foot is itching and cracking between the toes. It is caused by a **fungus**. A fungus is an organism that grows in moist places such as a locker room. To prevent athlete's foot, keep your feet dry and avoid walking barefoot in locker rooms or showers. Mild athlete's foot can be treated with a special foot powder found at drugstores.

How Can You Care for Your Hair and Nails?

Shampooing and brushing your hair eliminate dirt and help distribute oils that make your hair shiny and soft. To protect your hair, avoid using hair dryers and curling irons too often. These heat sources can damage your hair.

Occasional flaking, or **dandruff**, from your scalp is normal. Your scalp is skin, and it sheds dead cells just as the rest of your skin does. Special shampoos can control dandruff. However, check with a doctor if you have an unusual amount of dandruff.

For good nail care, you can do two things regularly: 1) Keep your nails clean, especially underneath. 2) Cut your nails evenly and file ragged edges.

Writing About Health

The common saying "An ounce of prevention is worth a pound of cure" means that preventing a problem is easier than fixing it after it occurs. Write about how this saying might apply to caring for your teeth.

How Can You Care for Your Teeth?

Your teeth contribute to how you feel about yourself and how others see you. When your teeth are clean and healthy, you can smile with confidence. A bright smile with clean, strong teeth is one of the first things people notice about each other. Fortunately, with proper care, teeth can last a lifetime. You can do these things to protect your teeth:

- Brush and floss at least once a day to prevent tooth decay and gum disease.

- Use a toothpaste with fluoride—a chemical that helps prevent tooth decay—or a fluoride rinse.

- Have regular dental checkups and cleanings to spot small problems early.

- Avoid eating too many sweets—they contribute to tooth decay.

- Wear a mouth guard if you play contact sports.

- Avoid using your teeth as tools and don't chew on hard objects such as pens, pencils, and hard candies.

LESSON 1 REVIEW Write the answers to these questions on a separate sheet of paper, using complete sentences.

1) Describe one action you can take to protect your sight.

2) What is the purpose of wax in your ears?

3) Why is wearing a sunscreen important when you are in the sun?

4) What are the two basic rules of good skin care?

5) What is one action that can prevent tooth decay?

Exercise and Rest for Fitness

Endurance
Ability to stay with an activity for a long time

Flexibility
Ability to twist, turn, bend, and stretch easily

Physical fitness is your body's ability to meet the demands of daily living. That means having enough energy to do all the things you want to do. Physical fitness is a key part of your overall good health. It affects your emotional, social, and physical well-being.

What Are Three Elements of Health-Related Fitness?

Three elements of health-related fitness are heart and lung **endurance**, muscular fitness, and **flexibility**. Endurance is the ability to stay with an activity for a long time. Heart and lung endurance is the fitness of your heart, blood vessels, and lungs. It is the ability of your heart and blood vessels to move oxygen efficiently through your blood to your lungs. Your energy depends mainly on your body's ability to take in and use oxygen. For this you need a strong heart, clear lungs, and blood vessels free of fat deposits.

Muscular fitness is the strength and endurance of your body's muscles. Muscular strength is the amount of force that your muscles put out to overcome a resistance. Muscular endurance allows you to lift, push, and pull objects without unusual muscle fatigue.

Flexibility is the ability to twist, turn, bend, and stretch easily. Flexibility helps to prevent muscle pulls and strains and increases range of motion in your joints.

What Are the Benefits of Exercise?

Regular exercise can improve your health-related fitness. It increases your heart and lung endurance. It firms and strengthens your muscles. It improves your flexibility. Exercise gives you more energy. It helps you feel better and look better.

Table 5.2. Types of Exercise

Aerobic exercise
Activity that increases a person's heart rate

Anaerobic exercise
Activity that quickly uses up oxygen in the body

Calorie
A unit that measures the amount of energy in food

Isokinetic exercise
Activity that builds muscle strength when muscles resist tension through a full range of slow motions

Isometric exercise
Activity that uses muscle tension to build strength

Isotonic exercise
Activity that builds muscle strength with repeated movements while using weights

Table 5.2. Types of Exercise

Exercise Type	Purpose	Examples
Aerobic exercise (steady, continuous activity)	Helps heart and lungs work more efficiently	Walking, running, bicycling, swimming, cross-country skiing
Anaerobic exercise (short spurts of activity)	Improves body's ability to operate at peak performance	Sprinting, tennis
Isometric exercise	Builds muscle strength through muscle tension	Pushing against a wall
Isotonic exercise	Builds muscle strength with weights	Any body movement, push-ups, pull-ups
Isokinetic exercise	Builds muscle strength with tension resistance through slow motions	Workout with machines that control force of pushing and pulling

Exercise can also reduce the chance for illness. For example, regular exercise reduces the risk of heart disease. Regular exercise also can shorten the time it takes to get well if you do become sick.

Another benefit of exercise is weight control. Exercise burns up extra **calories**. A calorie is a measure of the amount of energy in food. Besides burning up extra calories, exercise speeds up the rate at which your body burns calories.

Finally, exercise helps you to reduce anxiety and relieve stress. Exercise can be fun, and it's a good way to make friends.

What Are Some Kinds of Exercise?

Different types of exercise have different purposes. Look at Table 5.2 to see some types of exercise and their purpose. In all, exercise is one of the best ways of keeping your mind and body healthy.

What Are the Parts of an Exercise Program?
A good exercise workout includes these five parts:

- A Warm-Up Period
- An Aerobic Exercise to Improve Heart and Lung Endurance
- Exercises to Improve Muscular Fitness
- Exercises to Improve Flexibility
- A Cool-Down Period

Maximum heart rate *Heartbeats per minute when exercising as hard, fast, and long as possible*

Warm-Up
Always begin your exercise workout with a warm-up. Warming up increases blood flow to your muscles and prepares your body for extended exercise. It allows your heart rate to increase gradually rather than suddenly. A warm-up reduces risk of injury that can happen if you push your body into brisk exercise too fast. A warm-up should take about five minutes. You can warm up by walking and doing stretching exercises to improve your flexibility.

Exercises to Improve Heart and Lung Endurance
Your **maximum heart rate** is heartbeats per minute when you exercise as hard, fast, and long as you can. Although maximum heart rate differs among people, it is about 220 minus your age. For example, if you are 16, your maximum heart rate is about 204 beats per minute.

To determine your pulse rate . . .

Your pulse rate, or heart rate, is the number of times your heart pumps blood each minute. To take your pulse:

- Place two right fingers on the side of your neck just below your jawbone (see illustration).

- You can also place two right fingers on the thumb side of your left wrist.

- **Caution:** Do not take your pulse with your thumb because it has its own pulse.

- To locate your pulse, feel the thump against your fingers.

- Count each thump as one heartbeat.

- Use a watch with a second hand to count the number of heartbeats in ten seconds.

- Multiply this number by six to get your heart rate for one minute.

- The number of thumps each minute is your pulse rate.

To find out how long you should exercise to improve your heart and lung endurance, do this test:

1. Figure out your rough maximum heart rate by subtracting your age from 220.

Why do many people avoid exercising?

2. Do an aerobic exercise for at least ten minutes.

3. Immediately take your pulse for ten seconds.

4. Multiply this number by six to get your exercising pulse rate per minute.

5. Divide your exercising pulse rate by your maximum heart rate.

6. Multiply the result by 100 to determine the percent of maximum heart rate used.

7. Look at Chart 5.1 on page 110 to find the number of minutes of exercise you need to do three times a week.

Chart 5.1. Heart Rate and Exercise Times

If your maximum heart rate is:	You can exercise for:
50 percent	45–52 minutes
55 percent	37–45 minutes
60 percent	30–37 minutes
65 percent	25–30 minutes
70 percent	20–25 minutes
75 percent	15–20 minutes

Here is an example for a 15-year-old with a pulse rate of 123 after walking briskly for 10 minutes:

$$220 - 15 = 205$$
$$123 \div 205 = 0.60$$
$$0.60 \times 100 = 60 \text{ percent}$$

The person must walk at this pace for 30 to 37 minutes three times a week to improve heart and lung endurance.

If you want to decrease your exercising heart rate, slow down. If you want to increase it, pick up your pace. A rule when exercising is not to push yourself beyond being able to have a conversation with someone next to you.

When you exercise to improve heart and lung endurance, you need to do two things:

1. Run, swim, bicycle, walk, or exercise at a steady pace without stopping. Sports such as baseball and softball are not aerobic, since the activity is not steady.

2. At least three times a week, exercise at a level that is 50 to 75 percent of your maximum heart rate for the number of minutes shown in Chart 5.1.

Exercises to Improve Muscular Fitness
Improving muscular fitness involves resistance. Your muscles need to overcome some sort of resistance to become stronger. Exercises like push-ups, sit-ups, and pull-ups improve muscle strength and endurance. Weight lifting and isometric exercises also improve muscle strength and endurance.

Fitness Tip

Do some flexibility and strength exercises two to three times a week—stretching, push-ups, curl-ups, weight lifting.

Exercises to Improve Flexibility

Slow stretching exercises can improve your flexibility. Stretching causes your muscles to relax and lengthen. Slow, gradual movements are best for building flexibility. Avoid fast, bouncy movements, which cause your muscles to contract instead of lengthen.

Cool-Down

End your workout with a cool-down. Your body needs a chance to slow down gradually. If you stop suddenly, you could become light-headed or even faint. Your blood flow needs time to adjust itself. To cool down, continue to exercise, but at a slower pace. Also, stretch to improve your flexibility. A cool-down should take about five minutes.

Why Are Rest and Sleep Important to Fitness?

Rest is basic to the body's well-being. When you are tired, your body is not able to function properly. You have a harder time paying attention and often feel more stressed. Your body also is at greater risk of disease and injury when you are tired. Sleep and rest are necessary to feel better and to stay healthy.

Careers

FITNESS INSTRUCTOR

If you like staying fit, you might think about becoming a fitness instructor. Many companies support health and wellness programs because healthy habits are good for workers. This healthy trend has created a need for fitness instructors. Fitness instructors work with companies to design health programs for their workers. They show workers the correct way to exercise. Fitness instructors also explain how proper exercise helps the body. They may work with doctors and therapists to help workers recover from medical problems. This career requires at least a college degree. The training is similar to that for physical therapists, exercise physiologists, or therapeutic recreation specialists.

Most teens need between eight and nine hours of sleep each night. Depending on your level of activity, you might need additional rest. Rest does not always have to involve sleep. Reducing your level of activity or relaxing is a good way to rest during the day.

Nutrition Tip

Keep three things in mind for healthy eating—balance, variety, and moderation.

LESSON 2 REVIEW Write the answers to these questions on a separate sheet of paper, using complete sentences.

1) What are three major elements of health-related fitness?

2) Name four benefits of exercise.

3) What are two types of exercise?

4) List three examples of exercise that improve heart and lung endurance.

5) Why are rest and sleep important for your body?

WOMEN IN SPORTS

Around 1900, American women were allowed to play only a few sports, like croquet and archery. When playing, they had to wear long dresses with long sleeves. Such clothing made play difficult.

In the years that followed, women started playing volleyball, basketball, and baseball. Today, women have the same opportunities as men. They can play everything from soccer to hockey. They can play on the same teams with men. Many women have become champions in figure skating, running, tennis, gymnastics, and water sports. Women now wear clothes to fit their sport.

Then and Now

■ Hygiene refers to things you do to promote good health. It involves caring for your eyes, ears, skin, hair, nails, and teeth.

■ Your body protects your eyes and sight with bones, eyebrows and eyelashes, blinking, and tears. You can protect your eyes in several ways, including having regular eye exams.

■ Your skull protects the most delicate parts of your ears, and wax keeps dirt out of the ears. You can protect your ears by avoiding loud noise and music, and keeping objects out of them.

■ Loud noise is the most common reason for hearing loss. Hearing loss from loud noise is almost completely preventable.

■ The two basic rules of good skin care are to keep your skin clean and to avoid severe winds, cold, and sun.

■ You can take care of your teeth with daily brushing and flossing and with regular dental checkups.

■ Physical fitness is your body's ability to meet the demands of daily life.

■ Some major elements of health-related fitness are heart and lung endurance, muscular fitness, and flexibility.

■ Regular exercise improves fitness, increases energy, reduces chances of illness, helps maintain weight, and reduces stress symptoms.

■ Some types of exercise are aerobic, anaerobic, isometric, isotonic, and isokinetic exercise.

■ A good exercise program includes a warm-up, aerobic activity, exercises to improve muscular fitness and flexibility, and a cool-down.

■ Rest and sleep are basic to fitness. The body does not function properly without enough sleep. Rest also improves the body's ability to fight disease and injury.

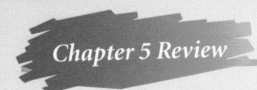

Comprehension: Identifying Facts

On a separate sheet of paper, write the correct word or words from the Word Bank to complete each sentence.

WORD BANK		
acne	infection	oils
bacteria	loud noise	tooth decay
endurance	maximum	warm-up
fungus	normal	wax
hygiene		

1) Things you do to promote good health are _____.

2) In an eye exam, if you stand 20 feet from the chart and can read the 20/20 row, you have _____ vision.

3) _____ in the outer part of the ear keeps dirt out of inner parts of the ear.

4) The most common cause of hearing loss is _____.

5) Other causes of hearing loss are _____, heredity, allergy, wax buildup, or injury.

6) Odor results when perspiration contacts _____ on the skin.

7) _____ is clogged skin pores.

8) A _____ causes athlete's foot.

9) Shampooing and brushing hair help to distribute _____ that make hair shiny and soft.

10) Fluoride is a chemical that prevents _____.

11) Heart and lung _____ is the ability of the heart and blood vessels to move oxygen through the blood to the lungs.

12) Doing a _____ increases blood flow and prepares the body for exercise.

13) _____ heart rate is heartbeats per minute when you exercise as hard, fast, and long as you can.

Comprehension: Understanding Main Ideas

On a separate sheet of paper, write the answers to the following questions using complete sentences.

14) List two ways to protect your eyes.

15) What are two ways you can protect your ears?

16) Describe two things you can do to take care of your teeth.

17) Name two advantages of regular exercise.

18) Why does your body need sleep?

Critical Thinking: Write Your Opinion

19) Why do you think some people play music so loud that it makes their ears ring?

20) Why do you think physical fitness needs to be a lifetime undertaking?

Test Taking Tip | When taking a test where you must write your answer, read the question twice to make sure you understand what is being asked.

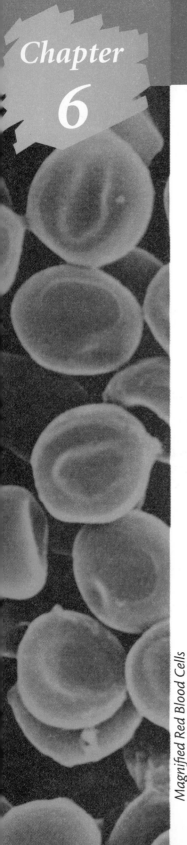

Magnified Red Blood Cells

Chapter

6

The Life Cycle and Human Development

People pass through many stages during their lifetime. When you were younger, your life was very different. You have grown and developed, and have moved through many stages since you were born. Even before you were born, you passed through many stages. At one time, you were just two tiny cells. One of life's most remarkable events is how those cells developed into the person you are today.

In this chapter, you will learn about the stages in the life cycle. You will learn about the physical changes that happen during adolescence. You will learn about how new life forms and develops and about events surrounding birth. Finally, you will learn about how families pass characteristics from parents to their children.

Goals for Learning

▶ To identify the stages in the life cycle

▶ To explain the changes that take place as young people mature into adults

▶ To describe the male and female reproductive systems

▶ To describe how new life forms and develops and the process of birth

▶ To explain how characteristics are passed from parents to their children

The Life Cycle and Adolescence

Many years ago, psychologist Erik Erikson studied the different stages of life. He determined that people usually go through eight stages of life. Erikson's ideas are called a model of social and psychological development.

Erikson believed that a person could overcome an unpleasant experience in one stage by being successful in a later stage. Look at the overview of these stages in Table 6.1 as you read.

Table 6.1. Stages of Social and Psychological Development

Stage	Ages	Psychological Task	Description of Task
1	0–1	Trust versus mistrust	Baby whose needs are met by caretaker develops a sense of trust in others
2	2–3	Independence versus doubt	Older baby tries to learn independence and self-confidence
3	3–6	Enterprise versus guilt	Young child learns to start his or her own activities
4	6–12	Ability versus inability	Child tries to develop skill in physical, mental, and social areas
5	12–19	Identity versus role confusion	Adolescent tries out several roles and forms a connected, single identity
6	20–40	Closeness versus loneliness	Young adult tries to form close, permanent relationships and to make career commitments
7	41–64	Caring for children versus self-absorbtion	Middle-aged person tries to contribute to the world through family relationships, work productivity, and artistry
8	65 on	Meaning and purpose versus despair	Older person thinks back on life, experiencing satisfaction or disappointment

What Are the Early Stages of Development?

The first stage is from birth to 18 months. If infants learn that their basic needs will be met during this time, they learn to trust. If the infant is not well cared for, the infant may learn to mistrust others.

During the second stage from 18 months to age 3, children begin to do things on their own. They begin to be less dependent on others. If they are not allowed to learn some independence, they may start to doubt their abilities or feel shame.

Children between age 3 and up to age 6 are in the third stage of development. Here they learn to explore their world within safe limits. They begin to ask "Why?" They begin to use their imagination and to initiate, or begin, activities instead of simply following someone else. If children are encouraged at this time, they begin to feel capable. If not, they may develop feelings of guilt.

Children usually enter stage four between ages 6 and 12. This is when they begin to make things. This is called having a sense of industry. If children hear positive comments about their efforts, they feel good about their abilities. If they are scolded or discouraged with negative comments, they may feel inferior. Children who feel **inferior** may feel they are not as good as others or as good as they should be.

What Happens From Adolescence to Early Adulthood?

Stage five begins at **adolescence**—ages 12 to 19. This is when many young people are trying to discover things about themselves. They are asking themselves questions such as "Who am I?" and "What do I believe in?" At this stage, teens are involved with many groups of people the same age, or peer groups. They sometimes think about themselves as others do. They are trying to determine their own identity—a sense of who they are and where they are going.

Writing About Health

Some adolescents begin their growth spurts later than others. Sometimes this bothers teenagers. Write about ways teenagers can focus on the importance of self-esteem instead of on being different from others.

Adolescence is a time of determining your identity in relation to others.

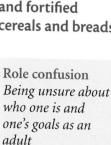
Role confusion
Being unsure about who one is and one's goals as an adult

If a person had trouble with any of the earlier stages of development, that person may have difficulty dealing with stage five. If they have feelings of mistrust, guilt, or inferiority, they may become confused about their role in life. **Role confusion** is being unclear about a person's sense of identity.

Stage six is early adulthood. This stage usually includes ages 20 to 40. This is often the point in life when people leave their parents' home and decide how they feel about a close relationship with another person. Again, if they have had problems during earlier stages, this time can be difficult. If a person at this stage does not feel good about forming close relationships, he or she may feel isolated, or alone.

What Are the Later Stages of Development?

Stage seven represents middle adulthood. During this stage, adults often turn their attention to their families, or to the well-being of their young. If they do not, they may become too concerned with their personal needs. This is called being self-absorbed. Self-absorbed people may have a difficult time finding satisfaction in life.

Stage eight is older adulthood. This last stage of life is a time of reflection and evaluation. It is a time when people look back and think about what they have accomplished. If they feel good about what they have done, they experience a sense of completeness. If not, they may feel despair.

Why Is Adolescence an Important Time in Life?

Each stage of life is important. Yet stage five, or adolescence, has some special challenges. Adolescence is a time of many changes. In this stage, teens ask themselves difficult questions. At the same time, the body changes in many ways. The beginning of adolescence is called **puberty**. Puberty is the time in life when children begin adult development and reach sexual maturity.

What Changes Occur During Puberty?

During puberty, the body changes size and shape. These changes, called growth spurts, occur at different rates and at different times for each individual. Growth spurts can be emotionally disturbing. For example, hands and feet often grow first. Until the arms and legs catch up, a person may feel awkward.

The first growth spurt in males usually happens between the ages of 11 and 15. During this time, boys can grow five inches taller and gain twelve pounds. Girls begin their growth spurt between the ages of 9 and 14. They do not usually grow as large as boys.

The endocrine system in your body includes glands that produce hormones. The pituitary gland produces hormones that signal many changes during puberty. Some hormones control the amount and timing of growth. Some hormones control the development of the **reproductive organs**. Reproductive organs are the organs that allow humans to mature sexually and have children.

Hormones signal changes in both males and females. Oil and sweat glands become more active. Hair begins to grow in other areas of the body and around the **genitals**, or sex organs.

Health Tip

Get at least eight hours of sleep to help your growing body.

Estrogen
Female sex hormone

Progesterone
Female sex hormone

Secondary sex characteristics
Traits that signal the beginning of adulthood such as facial hair for males

Testosterone
Male sex hormone

Hormones also signal the body to develop **secondary sex characteristics**, or traits that signal the beginning of adulthood. Some examples for males are the growth of facial hair, voice change, and broadening shoulders. Examples for females are breast development, widening hips, and narrowing waist.

Three hormones signal the body's reproductive system to develop during puberty. These are **testosterone, estrogen,** and **progesterone**. Testosterone is the hormone that signals the development of secondary sex characteristics in males. Estrogen and progesterone control reproductive development in females.

These hormones play an important role in developing the body's ability to reproduce. You will learn about the reproductive system in Lesson 2.

LESSON 1 REVIEW Write the answers to these questions on a separate sheet of paper, using complete sentences.

1) What might children feel if they don't feel good about their abilities?

2) During stage five of development, what questions might adolescents ask themselves?

3) What do adults usually turn their attention to during stage seven of development?

4) What is a growth spurt?

5) What three hormones signal the body's reproductive system to develop?

Lesson 2

Reproduction

Reproduction
The process through which living beings produce or conceive other living beings

Sperm
Male sex cells produced by the testes

Testes
Two glands in males that produce sperm cells

The ability to reproduce is one of the most amazing features of the body. **Reproduction** is the process through which two human beings produce, or conceive, a child. The reproductive system is the only body system that differs between males and females.

What Changes in the Male During Puberty?

At puberty, the male hormone testosterone begins to be released into a young man's body. Testosterone is produced in the **testes**, the main glands in the male reproductive system. Figure 6.1 shows the male reproductive system. Another function of the testes is to make **sperm**, or male sex cells. Beginning at puberty, the testes make more than 200 million sperm cells every day. Males are usually able to produce sperm from puberty throughout the rest of their life.

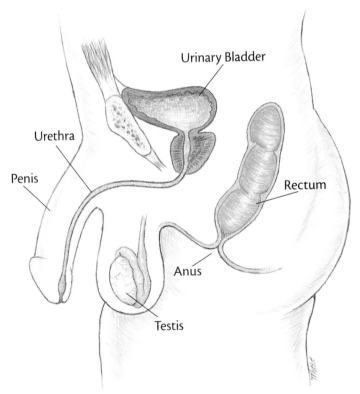

Figure 6.1. The male reproductive system

Fallopian tubes
Passages through which mature egg cells pass from the ovaries to the uterus

Ovaries
Two glands in females that produce egg cells

Ovulation
The release of a mature egg cell

Uterus
Female body part that holds a fertilized egg while it grows

Vagina
Canal in females from the uterus to the outside of the body; birth canal

What Changes in the Female During Puberty?

When girls reach puberty, hormones begin to act on the **ovaries**. Ovaries are the two organs in a woman's body that hold egg cells. Females are born with over a million egg cells already present in the body. Hormones cause the egg cells to mature. As they mature, the ovaries release egg cells. This is called **ovulation**. Once a woman begins to ovulate, she is able to conceive or have child. Each ovary usually releases one egg every other month. Figure 6.2 shows the female reproductive system.

The released egg then travels into one of the two **fallopian tubes**. The egg cell moves in these tubes to the **uterus**. The uterus is where an egg will grow if it is to become a baby. Otherwise, the egg cell leaves the body through the **vagina**.

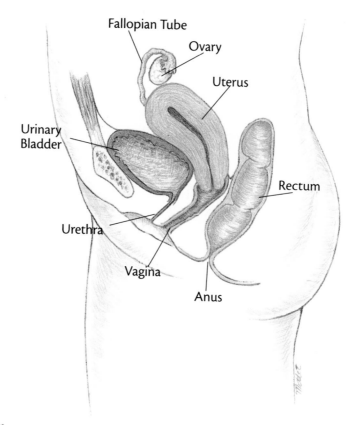

Figure 6.2. The female reproductive system

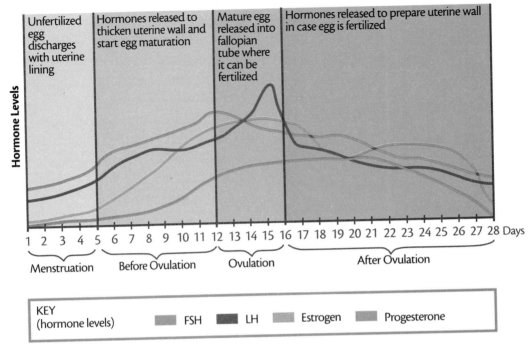

Figure 6.3. The menstrual cycle

The process of releasing an egg is one step in a monthly cycle in women. This cycle is called **menstruation**. When the ovary releases an egg cell, the lining of the uterus begins to thicken with blood tissue. If the egg is to become a baby, it attaches to the wall of the uterus. It stays there for nine months to grow. The blood tissue is the source of nourishment, or food, for a developing baby. Figure 6.3 shows the menstrual cycle.

If the egg does not attach to the wall of the uterus, it leaves the body and the blood tissue is not needed. During menstruation, this blood tissue also leaves the body through the vagina. It usually takes four to six days for the blood tissue to leave the body.

The entire menstrual cycle is usually about 28 days long, although it differs from woman to woman. When one cycle ends, the next cycle begins. This process usually continues until a woman is between 45 and 55 years old. Then, the body slows its production of estrogen and progesterone and the menstrual cycle stops.

Erection
Condition in which the penis becomes hard and larger

Fertilization
The union of an egg cell and a sperm

Penis
Male reproductive organ

Pregnant
Carrying a developing baby in the female body

Sexual intercourse
Inserting the penis into the vagina

How Does New Life Form?

Once both a male and female reach puberty, it is possible for them to reproduce or to conceive a new life. **Sexual intercourse** is nature's way to join a male sperm and a female egg cell to form a new life.

During intercourse, sperm pass through tubes that lead to the penis. The **penis** is the male reproductive organ. It has many small blood vessels. When these vessels fill with blood, the male has an **erection**. That means the penis becomes hard and larger. During this time, sperm can travel through the penis to enter the female body through the vagina.

During intercourse, millions of sperm are released into the female. It takes only one sperm cell to fertilize the female's egg cell. If the female is in the proper stage of the menstrual cycle, an egg may become **fertilized**, or joined by the sperm. If not, the sperm cells die and leave the female's body.

If the sperm and egg unite, the woman becomes **pregnant**, or is going to have a baby.

LESSON 2 REVIEW On a separate sheet of paper, write the word or words in parentheses that correctly complete each sentence.

1) The male hormone is (estrogen, progesterone, testosterone).

2) Males produce (testes, sperm, egg cells) from puberty throughout adult life.

3) The glands that produce eggs are (ovaries, testes, fallopian tubes).

4) The entire menstrual cycle usually lasts about (five, twelve, twenty-eight) days.

5) If an egg cell is fertilized, it stays in the wall of the (vagina, uterus, ovary).

Pregnancy and Childbirth

Gestation
The period of development in the uterus from fertilization until birth; pregnancy

Ultrasound
The use of high-frequency sound waves to show pictures of structures inside the body

*A*s you learned in Lesson 2, when an egg cell and sperm join, the egg becomes fertilized. This begins the process called pregnancy, or **gestation**. Gestation lasts about nine months. This is the period of time needed to allow the fertilized egg to grow and develop.

How Does a Woman Know She Is Pregnant?

There are several signs of pregnancy. A woman may feel sick or very tired. She has probably missed a menstrual cycle, since menstruation stops during pregnancy. Her breasts may feel sore as well.

If a woman believes she might be pregnant, she should find out for sure. A blood test at a doctor's office can check for pregnancy as early as ten days after fertilization. A different test can check a woman's urine for a certain hormone that is released only during pregnancy.

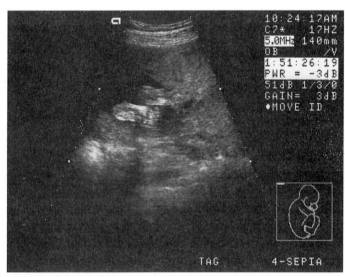

This ultrasound picture shows a baby developing in the uterus.

Some kits can be used to test for pregnancy at home. However, these tests could tell a woman she is not pregnant when she actually is. False results could be a problem since the woman may not get medical care early in the pregnancy.

A doctor can determine if a woman is pregnant for sure in three ways: 1) The doctor can hear the fetal heartbeat. 2) The fetus shows signs of movement. 3) An **ultrasound** picture shows a developing baby. Ultrasound is the use of sound waves to show structures inside the body.

Embryo
Fertilized egg after implantation

Implantation
Process during which the fertilized egg plants itself in the lining of the uterus

Placenta
An organ lining the uterus that surrounds the embryo or fetus

Trimester
A period of three months

Umbilical cord
Structure that joins the embryo or fetus with the placenta

If a woman is pregnant, her doctor will give her important information. A pregnant woman needs to take special care of her body. She needs to pay attention to what she eats and drinks and to what medicines she takes. Her doctor will tell her that smoking and drinking alcohol are harmful for the baby growing inside her. The doctor may also talk about exercise and other concerns, and may suggest other tests. The doctor also will ask the woman to come in for regular checkups during pregnancy.

What Happens As the Fertilized Egg Grows?

In the early stages of pregnancy, many things happen quickly. It takes about four days for the tiny fertilized egg to travel from the fallopian tube to the uterus. While it travels, its cells divide many times. It becomes a ball of cells that plants itself in the lining of the uterus. This process, called **implantation**, happens about six to eight days after fertilization. The uterus is normally small enough to fit into the palm of your hand. Yet, as the tiny cells grow, the uterus expands to hold the fully developed baby.

At this time, the fertilized egg becomes an **embryo**. An embryo is about the size of the dot on the letter i. Figure 6.4 on page 128 shows the steps from ovulation to implantation.

A special organ called the **placenta** develops from the embryo along the lining of the uterus. The placenta surrounds the embryo. The **umbilical cord** joins the embryo with the placenta. The cord transports nutrients to the embryo and removes its wastes.

A special fluid protects the embryo in the uterus. The embryo floats in this liquid, which protects the embryo against temperature changes and injury.

How Does the Embryo Develop?

While each pregnancy is different, Figure 6.5 on page 129 shows the major events that usually occur during each month. The nine months of pregnancy are divided into three **trimesters**. Trimesters are each three months long.

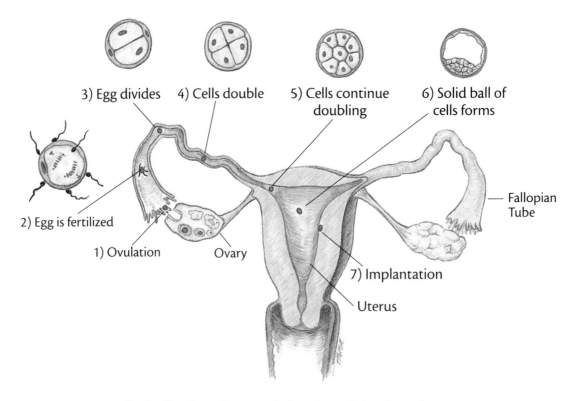

Figure 6.4. Journey of a fertilized egg from ovulation through implantation

Cervix
Narrow outer end of the uterus

Fetus
Unborn baby from eight weeks after fertilization until birth

What do you think is the importance of medical care for a pregnant woman?

After eight weeks or about two months, all the vital organs have started to develop. By this time, the embryo is called a **fetus**. The fetus continues to develop during the rest of the gestation period. At the end of this time, the fetus is considered full term and is ready to be born.

What Happens During Childbirth?

Childbirth has three stages. Figure 6.6 on page 130 shows the first two stages. The process of birth begins with labor pains that happen when the uterus contracts. These contractions begin to pull the **cervix** open. The cervix is the narrow outer end of the uterus. The cervix has been closed to hold the growing baby inside the uterus. It must open, or dilate, to a diameter of about 4 inches.

CHANGES DURING PREGNANCY

Trimester/Month	Embryo/Fetus	Mother
First Trimester		
First Month	Embryo 1/4 inch long; heart is obvious; eyes, nose, and brain appear; arms andlegs are small bumps	Menstruation stops; breasts are tender; fatigue; frequent urination; positive pregnancy test
Second Month	Embryo 1 inch long; head quite large; fingers, toes appear; nervous system and brain coordinate body functions; mouth opens and closes	Possible nausea and vomiting lasting into third or fourth month
Third Month	Embryo becomes a fetus; 3 inches long; weighs about 1/2 ounce	Breasts possibly swollen; thickened waist; uterus well rounded
Second Trimester		
Fourth Month	Fetus 6 inches long; weighs 3 1/2 ounces; sex may be determined; body covered with soft hair	Breasts may discharge liquid; uterus wall more stretched; larger midsection
Fifth Month	Fetus 9 1/2 inches long; weighs 10 ounces; skin less transparent	Feels stronger fetal movements; uterus higher; breasts not much larger; midpoint of pregnancy
Sixth Month	Fetus 12 inches long; weighs 1 1/2 pounds; eyebrows, eyelashes showing; sucks thumb; hiccups; if born at this time, usually dies	Uterus increases in size; fetal movements may feel sharp
Third Trimester		
Seventh Month	Fetus 14 inches long; weighs 2 1/2 pounds; covered with a greasy substance to protect it; responsive to sound and taste; if born at this time, moves actively, cries weakly; can live with expert care	Still feels fetal movements; size of uterus increases; weight gain continues
Eighth Month	Fetus 15 1/2 inches long; weighs 3 1/2 pounds; hair on head; skin red and wrinkled; if born, can survive with proper care	Gains some additional weight; uterus extends; fetal movements continue
Ninth Month	Fetus 18 inches long; weighs 5 1/2 pounds; gestation period ends; body fat makes figure more round, less wrinkled in face	Top of uterus nears breastbone; possible frequent urination because of pressure on bladder; possible difficulty in walking

9 weeks

11 weeks

15 weeks

36 weeks

Figure 6.5. Events in pregnancy. Drawings top to bottom show development of the fetus at 9, 11, 15, and 36 weeks.

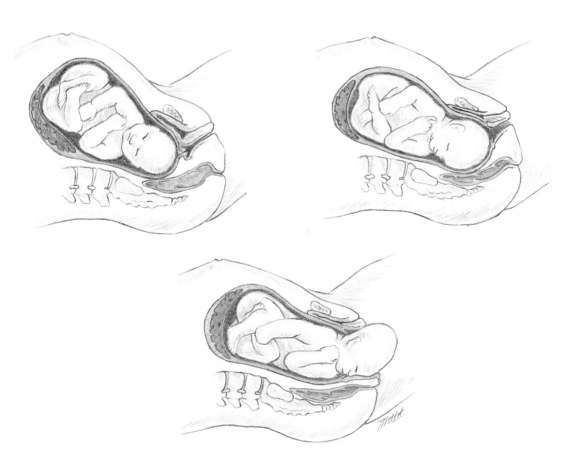

Figure 6.6. Top left: Cervix dilates in first stage of labor. Top right and bottom: Baby is pushed through the cervix and out the vagina in second stage of labor.

Dilation of the cervix is the first, and usually the longest, stage of birth. During this time, the woman feels labor pains that happen more and more often as the contractions continue. Also at this stage, the protective fluid surrounding the fetus breaks and flows out of the woman's body.

When the cervix is dilated, the second stage begins. During this stage, the baby is pushed, usually head first, out from the uterus. The baby is then able to breathe on its own. This stage of birth usually takes from twenty to fifty minutes.

The third stage is called the afterbirth. At this time the uterus contracts to release the placenta, which leaves the woman's body. This stage usually lasts just a few minutes.

CHILDBIRTH

Through history, most women had their babies at home. Sometimes relatives or people with experience delivering babies helped them. As time passed, pregnant women began seeing doctors. Still, as recently as the early 1900s, doctors delivered babies at home. Because of problems, the baby or mother sometimes died during the birth.

Today most American women have babies in hospitals. Many problems can be predicted using ultrasound and other tests. Sometimes, unexpected problems still occur. Maybe an operation or emergency treatment is needed. Then, doctors and nurses are there to help. In a hospital, both mother and child are more likely to remain healthy and safe.

Postpartum
Following birth

How Does the Body Adjust After Childbirth?

The new life has begun, and it is usually a happy, exciting time for the new parents. The woman's body must adjust after birth. It may take several months to return to normal. The changes in her body may cause some emotional ups and downs as a result of changing hormone levels. Sometimes women have **postpartum** depression, which usually lasts a day or two. If it lasts longer or is severe, a woman may need to ask her doctor for help.

LESSON 3 REVIEW Write the answers to these questions on a separate sheet of paper, using complete sentences.

1) How long is gestation?

2) What happens to the fertilized egg cell as it travels through the fallopian tube to the uterus?

3) What does the umbilical cord do?

4) When is an embryo called a fetus?

5) Which stage of birth is usually the longest?

Heredity and Genetics

Chromosomes
Tiny bodies in the center of cells that carry hereditary information

Gender
The condition of being male or female; sex

Gene
A tiny structure in chromosomes that controls the transfer of hereditary characteristics

Genetics
The science that deals with heredity and inherited characteristics

Heredity
The passage of physical characteristics from parents to children

Sometimes children look very much like their parents, and sometimes they don't. This is a result of **heredity**, the passage of characteristics from parents to their children.

What Is Genetics?

Genetics is the science that studies heredity. Genetics, the process of heredity, begins in tiny structures called **chromosomes**. Chromosomes are found in the center of each cell. Most cells contain forty-six chromosomes. The sperm and egg cells, however, each have twenty-three chromosomes. When a sperm and egg unite, the fertilized cell receives twenty-three chromosomes from each parent. The fertilized cell then contains forty-six chromosomes.

As this fertilized egg cell divides, each chromosome in the cell copies itself. The two sets of forty-six chromosomes separate. Each new cell then contains forty-six chromosomes. This process in the cells continues throughout life.

Each chromosome is made up of thousands of **genes**. Genes contain chemical codes that determine a person's characteristics. Through the genes, special characteristics of each parent are given to the children. For example, your father may have given you a certain gene that determines your eye color. Genes influence your hair and skin color, your size and weight, and even the tone of your voice. Genes can also be the cause of inherited diseases.

What Determines Gender?

Of the forty-six chromosomes in a fertilized egg cell, two are special. They determine the **gender**, or sex, of the baby. In females, these two chromosomes look exactly alike and are called X chromosomes. In males, one of the chromosomes is smaller than the other. This is called the Y chromosome. Each egg cell from the woman has an X chromosome. Each sperm cell from the man may have either an X or a Y chromosome. When the two cells join, the chromosome in the sperm determines the sex of the baby. An XX combination results in a girl. An XY combination results in a boy. Look at this simple example.

Figure 6.7 shows the chromosomes for a male.

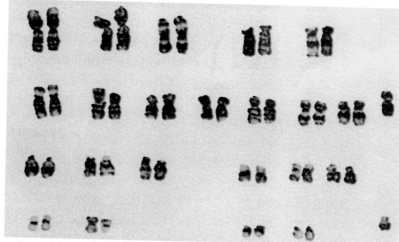

Figure 6.7. A male's chromosomes

How Are Traits Determined?

The chromosomes from each parent determine the characteristics, or traits, of a child. All the chromosomes from the mother line up with the chromosomes from the father. The genes for each trait are next to each other in pairs. Each gene pair controls a trait. For example, you may have received a gene for curly hair from your mother. You may have received a gene for a small nose from your father.

In most pairs of genes, one is **dominant**, or has control. That gene determines which trait a child will inherit. The other gene is called **recessive**, or hidden. That gene does not determine the trait. For example, a girl received a gene for brown eyes from her father. She received a gene for blue eyes from her mother. The gene for brown eyes is dominant, so she has brown eyes. The gene for blue eyes is recessive.

Another example of a dominant gene is hair color. The gene for dark hair is dominant. The gene for blond hair is recessive. You would have to inherit a gene for blond hair from both parents to have blond hair.

The Y chromosome is shorter than the X chromosome. The Y chromosome does not have as many genes. Sometimes this can result in health problems for the male. With fewer genes, the male may not have a dominant gene to link with the X chromosome. That way, a male could receive a gene for an inherited disease that could be a recessive gene. Without the dominant gene to link to it, that trait then appears in the male. The gene and the trait it produces is called **sex-linked**, because the sex chromosome carries the gene.

One example of a sex-linked trait is red-green color blindness. With color blindness a person cannot tell the difference between these two colors. Color blindness rarely affects women.

This girl received a gene for red hair from her mother.

Table 6.2. Genetic Disorders

Disorder	Description	Cause
Hemophilia	Blood does not clot, or clump, normally	Recessive abnormal gene
Dwarfism	Long bones do not develop properly	Dominant abnormal gene
Cystic fibrosis	Abnormally thick mucus, constant respiratory infections	Two recessive genes
Sickle cell anemia	Crescent-shaped red blood cells, weakness, irregular heart action	Two recessive genes
Down syndrome	Mental slowness, slanting eyes, broad skull, broad hands, short fingers	Extra chromosome
Spina bifida	Open spine	Multiple factor inheritance
Cleft palate	Roof of the mouth does not grow together during development	Multiple factor inheritance

Genetic counselor
Someone who helps people determine the likelihood of passing inherited disorders to their children

Is Genetics Important to Health?

Genes cause many health traits that tend to run in families. That is why doctors often ask about family health histories. Knowing about your family's health background can help your doctor understand your medical needs. Problems or diseases that are passed from parents to children are called genetic disorders. Table 6.2 shows some genetic disorders and their causes.

What Is Genetic Counseling?

Sometimes parents with a family history of a genetic disorder wonder about passing the problem to their children. These parents may ask for help from a **genetic counselor**. This person can perform tests and advise parents about the chances of passing on an inherited disease or disorder. In some cases, if the risk is great, the couple may choose not to have children. They may decide to adopt children instead.

MEDICAL TECHNOLOGIST

Medical technologists are like detectives, because they observe and discover things. They collect and store samples for medical tests. They observe chemical reactions. Then they record what they find. Technologists may work in many areas. Sometimes medical technologists study blood or chemicals in the blood. Sometimes they study cells, viruses, and disease-producing organisms. Medical technologists work with microscopes, slides, and automatic analyzers. At least two years of college are usually required for a person to become a medical technologist.

LESSON 4 REVIEW On a separate sheet of paper, write *True* if the statement is true or *False* if it is not true.

1) Genes determine which traits children inherit.

2) Chromosomes contain only a small number of genes.

3) The Y chromosome is shorter than the X chromosome.

4) A recessive gene controls which trait a child will inherit.

5) Color blindness is common in women.

■ Erik Erikson believed life has eight stages. The first four stages happen during childhood. Stages five and six involve young adults. Stage seven happens in middle age, and stage eight happens in older adults. During each stage, people develop socially and within themselves.

■ Adolescence is a time of many changes. Puberty is the beginning of adolescence. It is the time when children develop into adults and reach sexual maturity.

■ During puberty, teens usually experience growth spurts. Their glands are producing more hormones.

■ Three hormones signal the body's reproductive system to develop during puberty.

■ The male hormone is testosterone. The female hormones are estrogen and progesterone.

■ The reproductive system differs for males and females. The male produces sperm cells and the female produces egg cells. If these two cells join during sexual intercourse, they form a new life.

■ The female's ovaries release egg cells. If the egg cell is not fertilized, it passes out of the body along with the blood tissue in the uterus. This monthly process is called menstruation.

■ If the egg cell is fertilized, it begins to grow and divide and implants itself in the uterus. The uterus expands to hold the growing embryo or fetus. The period of growth, or gestation, is about nine months.

■ During childbirth, the cervix must open, or dilate, to allow the baby to pass through. There are three stages of birth: labor, the delivery, and the afterbirth.

■ Heredity is the passage on of characteristics from parents to children. Genetics is the science that studies heredity.

■ Most cells contain forty-six chromosomes. Each chromosome is made up of thousands of genes. Genes contain chemical codes that determine a person's characteristics.

■ The dominant gene controls a pair of genes. A recessive gene is present but does not control whether a child receives a trait. Some inherited traits are hair color, body size, and body shape.

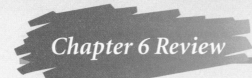

Comprehension: Identifying Facts

On a separate sheet of paper, write the correct word or words from the Word Bank to complete each sentence.

WORD BANK		
cervix	fertilized	ovulation
chemical	fifth	pregnant
chromosomes	gender	testosterone
color blindness	genetics	ultrasound
embryo	gestation	umbilical

1) During the _____ stage of social and psychological development, adolescents ask the question, "Who am I?"

2) _____ is the hormone that signals the development of secondary sex characteristics in males.

3) The process of releasing one egg cell every month is _____.

4) A _____ egg cell is one that has been joined by a sperm cell.

5) If a sperm cell and an egg cell unite, a woman becomes _____.

6) Pregnancy, or _____, usually lasts nine months.

7) The use of sound waves to show a picture of a structure inside the body is _____.

8) After implantation, a fertilized egg is called an _____.

9) The _____ cord joins the embryo with the placenta.

10) Labor pains that pull the _____ open are called contractions.

11) _____ is the science of heredity.

12) Every cell except sperm and egg cells contains forty-six _____.

13) Genes are _____ codes in chromosomes.

14) The _____ of a child is determined by the chromosome that comes from the male.

15) _____ is an example of a sex-linked trait.

Comprehension: Understanding Main Ideas

On a separate sheet of paper, write the answers to the following questions using complete sentences.

16) Why it is important for children to learn to do things on their own?

17) How can a woman tell for sure whether she is pregnant?

18) Why is knowing about your relatives' health important to you?

Critical Thinking: Write Your Opinion

19) Some day you may have children. Which of your physical characteristics and personality traits would you want your children to have? Explain your answer.

20) You have a friend who is troubled because his or her physical development is slower than for others. What could you say to your friend?

Test Taking Tip To prepare for a test, study in short sessions rather than one long session. In the week before the test, spend time each day reviewing your notes.

Magnified Red Blood Cells

The Family

The family is the basic unit of society. Most people belong to a family and depend on the support they gain from their family. There are many different types of family systems.

In this chapter, you will learn about the family life cycle and how new families are formed through marriage. You will learn about parenting and the responsibilities parents have. You will also learn about several family systems and what makes a family healthy. Finally, you will learn about problems in families and where to get help with the problems.

Goals for Learning

▶ To explain the place of dating and marriage in the family life cycle

▶ To identify some characteristics of a healthy marriage

▶ To describe parenting and responsibilities parents have

▶ To identify several family systems

▶ To describe some characteristics of a healthy family

▶ To identify where families can get help for problems

The Family Life Cycle, Dating, and Marriage

Just as individuals have a life cycle, families also have a life cycle. The family life cycle usually includes events such as marriage and the birth of children.

A new family life cycle begins when two people decide to marry. The decision to marry is one of the most important decisions a person makes in life. Many events lead up to the decision to begin a new family life cycle.

What Is Socializing?

Throughout your life, you have grown physically and socially. During adolescence, teens grow to maturity and are usually ready to experience many new things. They are ready to meet and spend time with a variety of people. They are forming ideas about themselves and are ready to form ideas about others.

Socializing is getting together with others to enjoy free-time activities. Socializing includes learning about many male and female friends. By socializing, people learn which traits or qualities they like and dislike in others. They learn more about themselves and the kind of future they hope to have.

One part of socializing is dating. Dating is a good way to get to know other people of the opposite sex better. People learn about others' qualities by doing things together. They learn about interests they have in common. For example, they may learn they enjoy skiing. They also learn interests that differ. Some may enjoy seeing movies while others would rather go to dances. Dating as a group or in couples can be a good experience.

Fitness Tip

Go for a walk or a run when you feel unhappy.

If two people enjoy being with each other, they may decide to date only each other, or go steady. This can help the couple become closer and learn more about each other. However, when they go steady, they give up the chance to get to know other people.

What Are Some Challenges of Dating?

One of the most important challenges in all relationships with others is communication. Open and honest discussion helps you understand each other. It prevents misunderstandings or arguments. While it can be difficult to express your feelings or thoughts, this is an important part of a relationship. Carefully listening to your partner is also an important part of communication.

Another challenge in dating is the decision about your physical relationship. A healthy relationship is based on many elements. Sometimes relationships are based mainly on physical attraction. This attraction may cause people to begin a sexual relationship. If this happens too early in a relationship, the couple may experience problems. For example, the sexual relationship may result in an unwanted pregnancy. Or, it could result in spreading an infection that is transmitted sexually.

Many couples who are dating or going steady choose **abstinence**. Abstinence is choosing to avoid a sexual relationship. It allows a couple to get to know each other in many ways before beginning a sexual relationship. It allows them time to become more mature, to make better decisions, and to avoid unwanted problems. It allows them time to find other meaningful ways of being close, such as sharing deep personal thoughts. Abstinence is the best choice for avoiding an unwanted pregnancy and a sexually transmitted infection.

Another challenge of dating is breaking up. You may decide the person you are dating is not right for you. Or, the person you are dating decides you are not right for him or her. Sometimes the decision to break up is difficult because it is a loss and may involve grief. It may leave a person feeling unhappy or depressed. When this happens, a person can think about his or her self-esteem and look for support from others.

Why Do People Marry?

In our society, most people decide to get married at some time. There are many healthy and unhealthy reasons to get married. Some healthy reasons include knowing and loving a person and wanting to have a family with that person. If two people understand themselves and each other, they have a good chance for a healthy marriage. Their marriage can help make them happy and fulfilled.

Marriage has benefits for couples. The partners give one another companionship. They enjoy communicating with one another and working together on their home and family. They enjoy developing a social life together with other couples and families. Staying together as marriage partners takes effort, which is usually worthwhile. Communication and division of chores help a couple to stay together.

Some people decide to marry because other people strongly encourage them. Some people get married because they are trying to avoid an unpleasant home life. They think if they marry, they will solve their problems.

Sometimes people decide to marry because of an unexpected pregnancy. This usually puts a strain on a marriage from the start. The decision to have children is an important one. The couple can best make it when they are ready to handle the responsibility.

Being a parent involves many responsibilities.

Divorce
Legally ending a marriage

When Do People Marry?

In the past, people often married when they were quite young. This is changing for many reasons. One reason is that people usually live longer now. They do not need to marry young. Also, people have found that they need more education to get the jobs they want. They spend more time in school or in training, and wait to get married. Some people wait to marry because they want to earn enough money to support themselves and their family.

Today, the average age at which men marry is 26. For women, the average age is 24. Studies show that marriages are more healthy and last longer if the couple is older. For example, for every four teenage marriages, three end in **divorce**. Divorce is the legal end of a marriage.

Some people choose not to marry. Some people choose a career or close friendships over married life. This does not mean that their lives are less happy or healthy.

What Are Some Characteristics of a Healthy Marriage?

Many studies have been done on elements that usually lead to a successful marriage. There is no one answer or combination of answers that guarantees a marriage will work. The following are some elements that have been identified as important.

- Agreeing on money matters
- Having similar interests
- Knowing each other well before marriage
- Accepting and supporting each other
- Agreeing about having children and about how to discipline children
- Having common goals
- Sharing household tasks
- Having similar family backgrounds and good relationships with parents

At sometime or another, good and bad things affect a marriage. Moving to a new home or a new job are exciting events. Losing a job or facing an illness are difficult. Couples who are supportive of each other are more able to cope with these changes.

A successful marriage usually requires more than just love. Couples have to be able to communicate, trust each other, and agree on many issues. They have to be willing to work out problems. Some common problems in marriage include money issues, getting along with relatives, and how to raise children. Some couples also have trouble working out a fair way to divide household tasks.

Marriages are more successful when the two people know and understand themselves. Then they are better able to understand their partner and to have a stronger relationship.

LESSON 1 REVIEW On a separate sheet of paper, write *True* if the statement is true or *False* if it is not true.

1) Going steady is always a good decision.

2) Communication is not important in a relationship.

3) Abstinence is the best way to avoid pregnancy.

4) Most people in our society get married at some time during their life.

5) Most teenage marriages end in divorce.

Parenting and Family Systems

A major event in the family life cycle is having children. The decision to have children is an important one that can be healthy or unhealthy.

Why Do Couples Decide to Have a Baby?

When couples decide to expand their family, they are likely to feel good about their decision. Sometimes, couples have a baby for other reasons. They may give in to pressure from friends or parents. They may simply want to pass on the family name. Some couples have children because they believe it will make their marriage stronger. Often, the opposite happens. If a marriage already has problems, the stress of having a baby makes the problems worse.

Some couples have a baby that they didn't plan to have. This also causes stress because parenting includes many responsibilities.

Why would parenting be more challenging for a teen?

What Responsibilities Do Parents Have?

Parents are responsible for the health, safety, and well-being of their children. When a baby is born, the parents' lives change. They plan for the care of their child. They pay the expenses of having a child, including food, clothing, and medical care. Couples find it important to talk with each other even more to work out plans to care for the child.

Parents need to learn parenting skills. They may attend classes or read books or articles on child care. Parents need to learn how to take care of the physical health of their child. They also need to learn how to help their child grow emotionally. They need to help and encourage their children to begin to do things for themselves.

Parents need to set fair limits. Children learn at an early age that they must follow certain rules. If children break the rules, parents need to provide a consequence. A consequence is what happens as a result of something. For example, if a child misbehaves, the consequence may be to sit alone for a few

Adoptive family
Family that includes parents and an adopted child or children

Blended family
Family made when parents live with children from an earlier marriage or marriages

Extended family
Family that includes parents, children, and other relatives

Foster family
Family that cares for children who are in need of short-term parenting from people other than their birth parents

Nuclear family
Family made up of a mother and father and their children

Single-parent family
Family that includes a child or children and one adult

minutes. Providing a consequence is one way to discipline children. Discipline is a way to teach children acceptable behaviors. Discipline should be fair and never harmful.

Finally, parents are important teachers for their children. Children learn from their parents in many ways. They may learn from stories the parents read or tell. They learn life skills. Children also learn by watching their parents. They copy the things their parents do. Parents set an example so their children learn healthy behaviors.

When a couple decides to take on the responsibilities of having a child, they form what is called a **nuclear family**. This is one of many different family systems.

What Are Some Family Types?

The most common type of family today is a family with only two people—a married couple without children. The second most common type is the nuclear family.

Another family type is the **blended family**. In this family, one or both parents have been married before. When children from an earlier marriage live with the new couple, they become a blended family.

In a **single-parent family**, just one adult raises the children. This family type often results from a divorce or the death of a partner. Sometimes the adult has never married. Mothers are most often the head of these families. Sometimes the father, a grandparent, an aunt, or an uncle heads a single-parent family.

A fourth family type is the **extended family**. An extended family is a nuclear family plus other relatives, such as grandparents, aunts, uncles, and cousins.

Families may form and change in other ways. For example, when children are adopted, they become part of an **adoptive family**. Other children may join a **foster family** for a while. A foster family is one that cares for children who are in need of short-term parenting from people other than their birth parents.

An extended family includes a nuclear family and other relatives who represent several generations.

Sometimes children have two families. The parent who is responsible for children after a divorce is the **custodial parent**. In blended and some single-parent families, children live with the custodial parent. They may spend time with the noncustodial parent in another home. This is true when parents have joint **custody** of children. This means that both parents share the responsibilities of raising and caring for the children.

Custodial parent
The parent who is responsible for a child after a divorce

Custody
The legal right and responsibility given to a parent to care for a child after a divorce

Any of these family systems can be healthy or unhealthy. What is important is how the family members work together.

How Is the Family Changing?
The family lifestyle is changing. Many families are smaller today than they were many years ago. Parents may decide to have fewer children because of the cost or because of their jobs. They may believe that they can provide a healthy home for only two rather than four or five children.

Many families want or need extra money. To help support the family, both parents have jobs outside the home. This change in families may be difficult in some ways. For example, with both parents working, it may be harder for parents to decide how to divide the household chores. Many parents must leave their children in day care centers while they work.

What special challenges exist for children growing up in the different family structures?

The number of single-parent families is increasing in the United States. A single-parent family may have some problems because parenting responsibilities fall on just one adult.

What Are the Characteristics of a Healthy Family?
Any family structure can be healthy or unhealthy. Two people who have studied the family structure are Nick Stinnet and

John DeFrain. They found that healthy families have these six important qualities:

1. *Commitment*—Family members support and encourage each other.

2. *Appreciation*—Family members show appreciation for each other.

3. *Communication*—Everyone talks with and listens to everyone else.

4. *Time*—Family members spend time together either working or having fun.

5. *Beliefs*—Family members use their common beliefs to give them strength and purpose.

6. *Coping Ability*—Everyone is better able to handle problems because they get help and support from each other.

LESSON 2 REVIEW Write the answers to these questions on a separate sheet of paper, using complete sentences.

1) Name two ways parents are responsible for their children.

2) What are four types of families?

3) What is a blended family?

4) How has the size of families changed in recent years?

5) What are three characteristics of healthy families?

ORPHANAGES AND ADOPTION

Since the 1400s, European orphans were often placed in orphanages. Orphans are children whose parents have died. Orphanages were special buildings where orphans could live. In 1740, the first American orphanage opened in Georgia. As America grew, so did the number of orphanages.

In the 1900s, adoptions of children into families began to replace orphanages. Often, orphans live with a foster family while waiting for adoption. U.S. adoption figures show that the number of adopted children has increased since the 1960s. About 50,000 American children were adopted during the 1990s. In 1997, there were 13,620 adoptions of children from foreign countries.

Then and Now

Problems in Families

Separation
A couple's agreement, or a court decision made for the couple, to stop living together

*F*amilies change for many reasons. Some changes are difficult for families, such as divorce, illness, and death. However, troubled families can get help.

How Do Separation and Divorce Affect a Family?

Sometimes when a couple decides they cannot live together, they separate. **Separation** may be an agreement between the two people, or it may be a court decision. During the separation, couples usually think about their marriage. They decide if they can improve their marriage. If they believe the marriage is not healthy, they may decide to divorce.

Separation and divorce can be difficult for children. They may worry or feel depressed. They miss the parent who is gone or feel they are losing a parent. They may believe that they were the cause of their parents' problems, but children usually are not the cause.

Children may feel torn if one parent tries to convince them that the other parent is at fault. Children are put in the middle of the adults' problems. A child cannot solve this kind of problem. A child can try to stay out of the conflict and get along with both parents.

How Does Aging Affect a Family?

People are living longer than ever before. Most older people remain independent. Sometimes, however, a family may have aging members with special needs. For example, as people age they may have difficulty getting around. They may need to use a cane, a walker, or a wheelchair. They may have vision or hearing loss. Sometimes older adults begin to lose their memory. They become confused and can't remember simple things. They may have a harder time taking care of their basic needs. They may have to give up driving.

Sometimes these age-related problems cause changes in a family. A home may have to be adapted to meet the needs of an older adult. Some family members may need to spend more time taking care of an older adult. A grandparent may need to live with a family since he or she needs more support.

How Do Illness and Death Affect a Family?

When any family member becomes ill, other members must adjust. They may have to help by taking a greater share of household chores. They may have to provide more support or get support from others. If an adult is ill for a long time, he or she may not be able to work. That may mean less income and high medical bills for the family.

Another difficult change is the death of a family member. For most people, an unexpected death is harder to deal with than one that is expected. For example, it is sometimes easier to accept the death of an older person who has been ill for a long time. When a young person dies unexpectedly, that death may be hard to accept. Each person must deal with death in his or her own way. People usually go through the five stages of grief—denial, anger, bargaining, depression, and acceptance.

As with other changes, family members adjust to their loss in time. They may seek support from others or talk with one another about their grief.

When a family member becomes ill or dies, others help by sharing household chores.

How Do Violence and Abuse Affect a Family?

Problems in a family such as illness and death cannot be avoided. Violence is a problem that can be avoided. **Violence** is actions or words that hurt people or things they care about. It can destroy relationships and result in physical and emotional pain. Violence is never acceptable.

Violence in families has many causes. Sometimes members become angry and hit others. Sometimes people who use alcohol or drugs become violent. Violence can also result from stress or be a learned behavior.

Abuse is a form of violence. Many kinds of abuse can affect families and be a serious problem. **Child abuse** is the physical or emotional mistreatment of children. Physical abuse can be so severe that it results in bruises, broken bones, or even death. **Emotional abuse** also may cause many problems. Most often people do not show any outward signs of emotional abuse such as bruises. Victims of emotional abuse often are depressed, are afraid, avoid others, and have low self-esteem. Harsh words and threats can affect a person inwardly for a lifetime.

Abuse usually is not just one incident. It happens over and over again. A child who is abused often is afraid to ask for help. The abuser may threaten the child. The child believes that something even worse will happen if he or she tries to get help.

Another form of abuse is **neglect**—failing to care for a person's needs. It may include leaving a young child alone for long periods. It may mean the adult does not provide food, clothing, or a safe place to live. A child who is neglected may become ill or die.

Sexual abuse is any sexual contact that is forced on someone. This abuse affects many children and teens. Victims may be afraid to report sexual abuse because they feel shame or fear.

Adults may also be victims of abuse. In an unhealthy marriage, one partner may hurt or abuse the other. Sometimes older adults are abused or neglected.

Abuse
Physical or emotional mistreatment; actions that harm someone

Child abuse
The physical or emotional mistreatment of children

Emotional abuse
Mistreatment of a person through words, gestures, or denying affection

Neglect
Failure to take care of basic needs; regular lack of care

Sexual abuse
Any sexual contact that is forced on a person

Violence
Actions or words that hurt people or things they care about

GOOD WILL HUNTING

The 1998 film *Good Will Hunting* tells about Will, a young man who lives in Boston. Will works as a university janitor. He solves a difficult math problem that students cannot solve. A math professor discovers that Will is a genius. He wants to work with Will, who has been a victim of abuse. Will can work with the professor only if he has counseling. With the help of a psychologist, Will learns about himself. Then Will faces a choice. Should he pursue the "safe" work life familiar to him? Or should he take the challenge of following his high potential?

Marriage counselor

A person trained in helping couples work on marriage relationships

In any abuse, the victims, abusers, and other family members need to get help. Victims of abuse need to know that the abuse is not their fault. The victim is not wrong—the abuser's behavior is wrong.

How Can a Troubled Family Find Help?

Problems in a family can affect the health of each member. A family may need help to solve a problem. Dealing with a problem is better than trying to avoid it. For example, a teenager may run away to avoid a problem. That usually causes more problems. Some problems are so severe that a person may attempt suicide.

Family members can do several things to get help. Families can go to special counseling centers in many cities for little or no cost. People at the center give advice on how to begin dealing with the problem.

A couple whose marriage is in trouble can talk with a **marriage counselor**. Marriage counselors are trained to help couples improve or save their marriage.

Family counselors work with problems in families. They talk with family members and offer suggestions to help solve conflicts.

Careers

ADOLESCENT COUNSELOR

Many teens today face problems such as alcohol and drug abuse, eating disorders, depression, violence, and AIDS. Adolescent counselors help teens with these problems. They may also be asked to find safe places for runaway and homeless teens. Crisis intervention may be necessary if there is substance or physical abuse. Sometimes counselors can help teens with job readiness skills. Adolescent counselors must be able to understand how teenagers feel. They must be able to form trusting, caring relationships with young people. Requirements vary from on-the-job experience to two-year college programs. Never before has the need for adolescent counselors been so great.

Many communities have several kinds of support groups. These are groups of people who share a common problem and offer each other encouragement in dealing with it. Many support groups help people who have had a death in the family. Other support groups help people deal with alcohol or drug problems.

Sometimes just talking with a friend or a trusted person helps a person handle a problem.

LESSON 3 REVIEW Write the answers to these questions on a separate sheet of paper, using complete sentences.

1) What feelings may children have about a divorce in their family?

2) How can aging affect a family?

3) What is neglect?

4) What is one kind of family problem that can be avoided?

5) What is a support group?

■ A new family life cycle begins with marriage. Socializing and dating lead up to marriage.

■ Communication is an important element in relationships.

■ Dating couples must agree on several issues, including their physical or sexual relationship. A sexual relationship can lead to an unwanted pregnancy or a sexual disease.

■ Often couple who are dating decide to stop dating. This can leave a person feeling unhappy or depressed.

■ Most people in the United States marry at some time. People get married for both healthy and unhealthy reasons.

■ People today are waiting longer to get married.

■ Some elements that usually lead to a healthy marriage include having similar family backgrounds, more education, and secure jobs.

■ People have a baby for both healthy and unhealthy reasons.

■ Parents are responsible for the health, safety, and well-being of their children. They pay the expenses of having children.

■ Parents need to learn certain skills to help their children grow physically and emotionally. They must set rules and provide discipline.

■ There are several family systems. These are nuclear, blended, single-parent, extended, adoptive, and foster families.

■ Any family system may be healthy or unhealthy.

■ Some qualities of healthy families are commitment, appreciation, time, communication, beliefs, and coping ability.

■ Separation, divorce, aging, illness, and death can affect families.

■ Abuse may be physical or emotional. It may be directed at children or adults. Violence and abuse are never acceptable. Victims of any kind of violence or abuse need to get help.

■ Many organizations help married couples and families with problems.

Comprehension: Identifying Facts

On a separate sheet of paper, write the correct word or words from the Word Bank to complete each sentence.

WORD BANK		
abstinence	consequence	nuclear family
abused	custodial parent	pressure
aging	healthy	separation
appreciation	marriage counselor	single-parent
communication	medical	socializing

1) _____ is getting together with others to enjoy free time.

2) One important element in a relationship is _____.

3) _____, or avoiding a sexual relationship, prevents an unwanted pregnancy.

4) Some people decide to marry because of social _____.

5) Parents need to set fair rules and provide a _____ if children break the rules.

6) A married couple living with their own children is a _____.

7) One adult raising children alone has a _____ family.

8) A _____ is the parent responsible for children after a divorce.

9) Any family system can be _____ or unhealthy.

10) When family members are thankful for the help they receive, they show _____.

11) _____ is when one spouse moves away from the family.

12) Problems with walking, vision, hearing, and memory come with _____.

13) An illness in the family may mean high _____ bills.

14) A child who often has bruises or marks on his or her body may be _____.

15) A _____ often can help couples who have trouble with their relationship.

Comprehension: Understanding Main Ideas

On a separate sheet of paper, write the answers to the following questions using complete sentences.

16) Why is socializing important?

17) What are some reasons couples decide to have a baby?

18) List three ways families are changing.

Critical Thinking: Write Your Opinion

19) Age-related problems can be difficult for older adults. How could you help an older adult?

20) Do you think it is better for a family to solve problems rather than avoid them? Explain your answer.

Test Taking Tip | Before you begin a test, look it over quickly. Try to set aside enough time to complete each section.

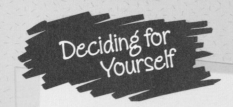
Cloning Technology

On February 24, 1997, Dolly the Sheep became the world's most famous animal. Dolly is a clone, which is a plant or animal grown from a single cell of a parent. Its genes are the same as the parent's genes. This cloning technology shocked the world. As this new technology was announced, people wondered whether humans will ever be cloned.

Human cloning seems unrealistic because it appears so complicated. Yet, researchers easily clone other organisms from single cells. Cloning and genetic engineering are creating cows and sheep that produce healing proteins.

An American medical researcher wants to clone human beings. Some state and U.S. lawmakers, however, are considering laws to make cloning illegal. Several states have already passed such laws.

Here are some opinions that have been expressed about cloning:

- "Cloned cells could repair damaged tissues that would help sick people."

- "What's so bad about cloning? People don't object to identical twins, which are a kind of clone."

- "Why do we have a brain to make new discoveries if we are not to use it?"

- "If we are not careful, we may end up with something we can't control."

Questions

1) How would you respond to each of the above opinions about cloning?

2) What is your personal opinion about cloning human beings?

3) What would be the advantages or disadvantages of using cloning to get rid of genetically transmitted diseases?

4) If personalities could be cloned, how would you like having everyone be the same without individual differences?

■ The body systems are the skeletal, muscular, nervous, endocrine, circulatory, respiratory, digestive, and excretory systems. Skin, hair, and nails form another system.

■ Protecting the eyes includes regular eye exams.

■ Protecting the ears includes avoiding loud noise and music to prevent hearing loss.

■ Skin care involves keeping the skin clean and avoiding severe wind, cold, and sun.

■ Dental care includes daily brushing, flossing, and regular checkups.

■ Major elements of health-related fitness are heart and lung endurance, muscular fitness, and flexibility.

■ Regular exercise improves fitness, increases energy, reduces illness, maintains weight, and reduces stress.

■ Sleep and rest permit the body to function properly and improve its ability to fight disease and injury.

■ Puberty is the time when children develop into adults, reach sexual maturity, and have increased hormone production.

■ If a male sperm cell fertilizes a female egg cell, a child is conceived.

■ The embryo or fetus grows in the uterus during the nine-month gestation period.

■ If the female egg cell is not fertilized, it passes out of the body during menstruation.

■ The three stages of childbirth are labor, delivery, and afterbirth.

■ Heredity is the passage of characteristics from parents to children.

■ Dating couples must agree on their sexual relationship, which can lead to unwanted pregnancy or sexual diseases.

■ Elements that usually lead to a healthy marriage are similar family backgrounds, more education, and secure jobs.

■ Parents are responsible for the health, safety, and well-being of their children.

■ Some family systems are nuclear, blended, single-parent, extended, adoptive, and foster families.

■ Some qualities of healthy families are commitment, appreciation, communication, beliefs, and coping ability.

■ Separation, divorce, aging, illness, death, violence, and abuse are problems that affect families. Many organizations help couples and families with problems.

> We are indeed much more than we eat, but what we eat can nevertheless help us to be much more than what we are.
>
> —Adele Davis, *Let's Get Well*

Nutrition

D id you have breakfast this morning? Research tells us that students who do not eat breakfast tend to score lower on tests than those who have had a nourishing morning meal. Consider food as fuel for your body. Consider how a radio sounds when the batteries are low. If your body is without food, it fades like the sounds on a radio with low batteries.

People are becoming more concerned about the importance of eating properly. Poor diets can contribute to heart attacks, strokes, and some types of cancer. Yet despite all the warnings, many Americans still consume unhealthy foods. In this unit, you will learn how to make healthy choices when deciding what to eat.

▶ Chapter 8 The Role of Diet in Health

▶ Chapter 9 Making Healthy Food Choices

☑ Self-Assessment

1. When you chew your gum, do you swallow it?

2. About how many days a week do you eat at a fast food restaurant?

3. How many glasses of water do you drink each day?

4. Do you add salt to your food?

5. How much sugar do you think you eat and drink each day?

6. How many servings of fruits do you eat each day?

7. How many servings of vegetables do you eat each day?

8. Generally, how many servings of meat, poultry, fish, dry beans, eggs, and nuts do you eat each day?

9. About how many servings of bread do you eat each day?

10. About how many servings of dairy products do you eat or drink each day?

The Role of Diet in Health

Food is fuel. Food provides the nutrients that your body's systems need to function properly. Deciding what food to eat is important. Good food choices help a person stay healthy. Poor food choices can cause problems. Eating too much or not enough food also can cause problems. The food you eat affects your health, and can also affect the quality of your life.

In this chapter, you will learn what a healthy diet is. You will learn how certain guidelines help people choose a healthy diet. You will learn about the nutrients the body needs. You will learn about special dietary needs and how diet relates to some health problems.

Goals for Learning

▶ To describe the effect of healthy eating on the body

▶ To explain how food provides calories and nutrients

▶ To explain the importance of the six essential nutrients and which foods contain them

▶ To identify special dietary needs

▶ To predict how diet relates to some diseases

Magnified Vitamin C Crystal

A Healthy Diet

Diet
Food and drink regularly eaten

Diet consists of the foods that a person eats and drinks. It is not losing or gaining weight. Diet can affect the way you look, feel, and perform. A well-balanced diet gives you a healthy appearance. It makes your hair shine and helps to keep your skin clear. It gives you energy to do everything you need or want to do. Eating healthy food also contributes to your emotional health. It gives you energy to deal with stress. Your diet affects your general health. Therefore, making healthy food choices is important to your overall health.

One goal of a healthy diet is to maintain an ideal weight for a person's age and height (see Tables C.2 and C.3 in Appendix C). Some people, however, think diet only means losing weight. A healthy diet can help people lose or gain weight if their doctor recommends it. Usually a healthy diet helps people to maintain an appropriate weight for their age and height.

What Is a Healthy Diet?

A healthy diet includes a variety of foods. The United States government has set up guidelines to help people choose a healthy diet. These guidelines are listed here.

Dietary Guidelines

- Eat a variety of foods.
- Balance the food you eat with physical activity.
- Choose a diet with plenty of grain products, vegetables, and fruits.
- Choose a diet low in fat, saturated fat, and cholesterol.
- Choose a diet low in sugars.
- Choose a diet low in salt and sodium.

The U. S. government developed the Food Guide Pyramid (see Figure 8.1) to help people decide how much and what kinds of food to eat. It groups food according to the number of servings a person should eat daily.

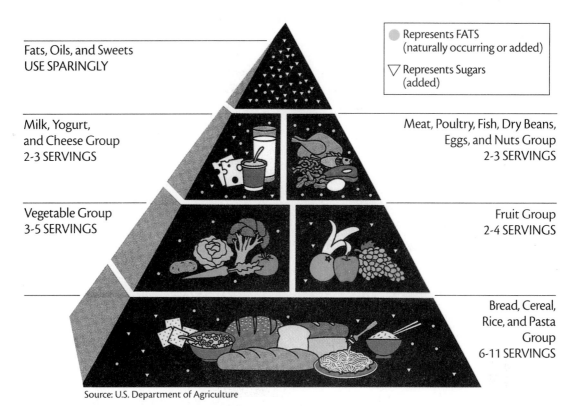

Fats, Oils, and Sweets
USE SPARINGLY

Represents FATS
(naturally occurring or added)

▽ Represents Sugars
(added)

Milk, Yogurt,
and Cheese Group
2-3 SERVINGS

Meat, Poultry, Fish, Dry Beans,
Eggs, and Nuts Group
2-3 SERVINGS

Vegetable Group
3-5 SERVINGS

Fruit Group
2-4 SERVINGS

Bread, Cereal,
Rice, and Pasta
Group
6-11 SERVINGS

Source: U.S. Department of Agriculture

Figure 8.1. The Food Guide Pyramid

Think of everything you ate yesterday. How well did you meet the pyramid guidelines?

The foods you should eat the most are in the bottom layer, or foundation, of the pyramid. These are breads, cereals, and other grains. The next layer of the pyramid includes vegetables and fruits. Among the foods in the third layer are dairy products, meat, poultry, and fish. Fats, oils, and sweets—in the top layer of the pyramid—should be eaten the least. Choosing foods from the pyramid puts variety in your diet and meets other dietary guidelines.

How Does Food Provide What Your Body Needs?

Food provides the calories and nutrients your body needs. A calorie is a unit that measures the amount of energy in food. Your body uses the calories or energy from food for heat, movement, growth, and repair. Gender, individual growth patterns, and activity levels all determine the number of calories a person needs. For example, a person who is tall, muscular, and active needs more calories than a small person who is less active. Table 8.1 on page 166 shows the average calorie needs for certain ages, weights, and heights.

Table 8.1. Average Calorie Needs by Age, Weight, and Height

	Age (years)	Weight (lb)	Height (inches)	Average Energy Requirement (kcal per day)
Males	11–14	99	62	2,500
	15–18	145	69	3,000
	19–24	160	70	2,900
	25–50	174	70	2,900
	51+	170	68	2,300
Females	11–14	101	62	2,200
	15–18	120	64	2,200
	19–24	128	65	2,200
	25–50	138	64	2,200
	50+	143	63	1,900

Source: *Recommended Dietary Allowances,* 10th ed., ©1989 by the National Academy of Sciences, National Academy Press, Washington, D.C.

Essential nutrients
Chemical substances in foods that the body cannot make

Foods also contain nutrients. Nutrients that the body gets from food are called **essential nutrients**. There are six nutrients that the body cannot make or cannot make enough of to satisfy its needs. Scientists have discovered about fifty of these nutrients. They are divided into six essential nutrient classes that you will read about later in this chapter. No one food contains all the nutrients your body needs. A healthy diet must include a variety of foods. Some food sources for the six essential nutrient classes can be found in Table B.1 of Appendix B.

Foods vary in the calories and nutrients they provide. Some foods are high in calories, but low in nutrients. For example, a teaspoon of sugar has about 15 calories, while a teaspoon of green beans has 2 calories. Green beans have more nutrients and fewer calories than sugar. This is important for two reasons. First, because the body needs nutrients to stay healthy, it is important to know which foods contain the most nutrients. Second, the body also needs a certain number of calories. Foods that are good sources of nutrients but low in calories are called nutrient dense. A healthy diet consists of nutrient-dense foods.

It is important to know how many calories your body needs, and how many calories are in the foods you eat. If people often eat food with more calories than they need, they will gain weight. A healthy diet includes a balance of foods high in nutrients with enough calories to maintain an ideal body weight. Ideal body weight is based on height and age.

How Can You Plan a Healthy Diet?

The Food Guide Pyramid is a help in planning your diet. It shows the six food groups and the servings you need each day. Table 8.2 shows the serving sizes for the food groups.

Table 8.2. Serving Sizes for the Food Groups

Food Group	Suggested Daily Servings	What Counts as One Serving?
Bread, cereal, rice, and pasta	6–11	1 slice of bread $1/2$ hamburger bun or English muffin Small roll, biscuit, or muffin 3–4 small or 2 large crackers $1/2$ cup cooked cereal, rice, or pasta 1 ounce cold breakfast cereal
Vegetable	3–5	$1/2$ cup cooked vegetables $1/2$ cup chopped raw vegetables 1 cup leafy raw vegetables such as lettuce or spinach
Fruit	2–4	1 whole fruit such as a medium apple, banana, or orange $1/2$ grapefruit 1 melon wedge $3/4$ cup juice $1/2$ cup berries $1/2$ cup cooked or canned fruit $1/4$ cup dried fruit
Milk, yogurt, and cheese	2–3	1 cup milk 8 ounces yogurt $1^{1}/2$ ounces natural cheese 2 ounces process cheese
Meat, poultry, fish, dry beans, eggs, and nuts	2–3	Amounts should total 5 to 7 ounces of cooked lean meat, poultry, or fish a day.
Fats, sweets	Use sparingly	Count 1 egg, $1/2$ cup cooked beans, or 2 tablespoons peanut butter as 1 ounce of meat.

For example, you need two to four servings of fruit each day. Each serving could be one apple, or ¾ cup of orange juice, or ½ cup of strawberries. The number of servings that is right for you depends mainly on your calorie needs.

To adjust your diet to your needs, you need to know how many calories and nutrients are in the foods you eat. Often food labels list the number of calories and nutrients in foods. Learning about the calories and nutrients in food will help you choose a healthy diet.

LESSON 1 REVIEW On a separate sheet of paper, write the word or words from the Word Bank that match each description.

1) _____ is the usual food that a person eats and drinks.

2) The _____ is a way to see how much and what kind of food to eat.

3) Food provides calories and _____ for your energy needs.

4) One guideline for a healthy diet is to eat a _____ of foods.

5) An orange would count as one _____ of fruit.

Carbohydrates, Fats, and Protein

Carbohydrate
Chemical substance in foods that provides starches and sugars

Protein
A substance in food needed for growth and repair of body tissues

A person's diet must provide the body with the six essential nutrients. The three nutrients that provide energy in the form of calories are **carbohydrates**, fat, and **protein**. Carbohydrate, fat, and protein are all nutrients that your body needs. Not enough or too much of these nutrients may result in health problems. Eating the right amount of many foods to provide your body with the nutrients it needs means a healthy, balanced diet.

What Are Carbohydrates?

Carbohydrates are starches and sugars that come mainly from plant food. They give your body much of the energy it needs each day. There are two kinds of carbohydrates—complex and simple. Complex carbohydrates are in foods such as potatoes, pasta, and bread. Table 8.3 on page 170 lists some foods with high amounts of complex carbohydrates. Simple carbohydrates are in sugar, foods such as jelly and syrup, and many soft drinks.

Complex carbohydrates are important to the body. They are the best source of dietary carbohydrates. Foods with complex carbohydrates make you feel satisfied and full. They also contain other nutrients that add fiber to the diet. Fiber is not a nutrient, but it is important in helping move foods through the digestive tract. Table B.2 in Appendix B lists the fiber content of some foods. Studies show that some types of fiber in the diet help protect against certain diseases, including some cancers.

Simple carbohydrates, or sugars, have many different names. For example, sucrose is table sugar, fructose is sugar in fruit, and lactose is sugar in milk. The body uses sugar for quick energy.

Carbohydrates give the body much of the daily energy it needs.

Table 8.3. Foods High in Complex Carbohydrates

	Total Carbohydrates (grams)	Simple Carbohydrates (grams)	Complex Carbohydrates (grams)
Bread, 1 slice	13	1	12
Corn flakes, 1 oz (low sugar)	24	2	22
Pasta or rice, 1/2 cup, cooked	20	0	20
Beans, 1 cup cooked	40	0	40
Potatoes, corn, or peas, 1 cup	30	6	24
Carrots or beets, 1 cup	12	6	6
Broccoli, 1 cup cut up	7	0	7

Sugar requires little digestion and enters the bloodstream quickly. However, the energy boost a person receives from sugar wears off quickly. The person then feels tired or slow moving. This is because sugar has no other nutrients.

Sugars found in foods are either added sugar or natural sugar. For example, an apple contains the natural sugar fructose and a candy bar contains added sugar. Some foods with added sugar provide no nutrients. For example, a 12-ounce can of sweetened cola contains 9 teaspoons of sugar and no nutrients.

Many foods that provide a source of sugar also provide other nutrients. Fruits, vegetables, and bread provide enough sugar from carbohydrates for your body. Too much added sugar in your diet can cause such problems as tooth decay.

Fitness Tip

Go for a run or swim to burn off extra calories.

Glucose
The main sugar in blood; the major energy source of the body

Glycogen
Glucose that is stored in the body

Dietary guidelines recommend that most calories come from complex carbohydrates. Look at the Food Guide Pyramid on page 165 again. Foods containing carbohydrates are found in the bottom two layers, which make up over half of the pyramid. The pyramid recommends six to eleven daily servings of bread, cereal, rice, and pasta. It recommends three to five daily servings of vegetables. Those two groups contain complex carbohydrates. The pyramid recommends two to four daily servings of fruits, which contain simple carbohydrates.

How Does the Body Use Carbohydrates?

Carbohydrates are chemical compounds. The body changes carbohydrates into **glucose**, the main sugar in blood. Glucose circulates through the body to provide a source of fuel for cells. Extra glucose is stored in the liver and muscle tissue as **glycogen**, or starch. When your body needs more glucose, glycogen can be changed back into glucose. Glucose is the main nutrient the brain requires to help you think clearly and concentrate.

Skipping meals can rob your brain of the glucose it needs. Eating at least three meals a day at fairly regular times can help ensure that your brain has enough glucose.

Then and Now

FOODS IN AND OUT OF SEASON

Since the 1800s, experts have suggested we eat fruits and vegetables for a healthy diet. Gardeners and shoppers could only eat fresh fruits and vegetables during summer. These foods were dried and stored for winter use.

After 1900, canned foods became available. Since 1930, we have been able to buy frozen fruits and vegetables. Because of better transportation, more countries can sell fresh produce. Now we can buy apples from New Zealand, pineapples from Hawaii, and cabbages from China. Even when some fruits and vegetables are out of season in the United States, our stores import and sell them.

Fats provide the body with energy but should be eaten sparingly.

You sometimes may eat too many carbohydrates and not get enough physical activity to use the energy they provide. Then the body stores the extra sugar and starch as fat.

What Are Fats?

Like carbohydrates, fats also supply the body with energy. The difference is that fats are stored energy. Fats are part of all body cells. Fat helps protect internal organs from temperature changes. They protect your body from outside blows and are part of the protective covering of nerves.

Fats in your diet are broken down in your body into fatty acids, which are either **saturated** or **unsaturated**. Examples of foods high in saturated fats are butter, meat, ice cream, and chocolate.

A diet high in saturated fats can be unhealthy. Too many fats can cause high levels of **cholesterol**. Cholesterol is a waxy, fatlike substance that is important in making hormones. It also helps digestion. This kind of cholesterol, called blood cholesterol, is carried in the bloodstream. A high level of certain kinds of cholesterol in the blood can cause health problems. Cholesterol can build up in blood vessels and clog them. The blood cannot flow freely, which may cause strokes and heart attacks.

Another kind of cholesterol, called dietary cholesterol, is found in some foods. One way to reduce the risk of high blood cholesterol is to avoid foods high in saturated fats. Saturated fats can be replaced with foods containing unsaturated fats. For example, you can eat less red meat and more fish. Fish contains unsaturated fat. You can also use vegetable oils instead of animal fats and butter. You can drink skim milk instead of whole milk.

Cholesterol
A waxy, fatlike substance in body cells that helps with certain body functions; some kinds can clog blood vessels

Saturated fat
Substance in food from animal products that may lead to high cholesterol in blood

Unsaturated fat
Substance in food from vegetable and fish oils that help lower the amount of cholesterol in blood

Amino acid
A small chemical unit that makes up protein

While fats are important to your body, too many fats lead to a higher risk of certain diseases, as clogged arteries. Eating too many fats can also cause people to gain weight. Table C.1 in Appendix C shows some exercises to maintain body weight.

Fats are in the top layer of the Food Guide Pyramid, which includes foods to be eaten sparingly. It is recommended that not more than 30 percent of your daily calories comes from fat.

What Is Protein?

Protein is a nutrient that helps build muscle and repair all body tissues. It is part of every cell in the body. Muscles, bones, blood, and skin all contain protein. Since cells are always being replaced, the body needs protein throughout life.

Some protein foods are fish, meat, eggs, milk, poultry, peanuts, seeds, peas, and beans.

Carbohydrates, fats, and proteins are all sources of energy. However, the body only uses protein for energy if it does not get enough calories from carbohydrates and fats.

Proteins are made up of chains of building blocks called **amino acids**. There are many kinds of amino acids. Your body is able to make proteins except for nine that are called essential amino acids. You must get these amino acids from your diet. Your body can make new proteins from these nine essential amino acids.

Foods such as fish, meat, eggs, milk, and poultry usually contain all nine essential amino acids. Some foods provide only a few of the essential amino acids. These are plant foods such as grains, seeds, peas, and beans. Combining certain foods will provide all nine amino acids. For example, eating both peanut butter and wheat bread or macaroni and cheese can provide all the essential amino acids.

Nutrition Tip

Eat 2–3 servings from the milk and meat groups on the Food Pyramid to get your daily protein.

The amount of protein the body needs depends on your age and body size. As with other nutrients, the body needs only a certain amount of protein. If the body receives more than it needs, the protein becomes a source of extra calories. Foods provide different levels of nutrients. A food high in protein may also be high in fat. For example, eggs provide a high level of protein but an equal amount of fat. It is important, therefore, to choose protein foods carefully and not to eat too much protein.

Look at the Food Guide Pyramid on page 165. It suggests two to three servings of milk products each day. It suggests two to three daily servings of meat, chicken, fish, eggs, dry beans, or nuts. These servings provide the needed nutrients but not too much in order to avoid health problems.

LESSON 2 REVIEW Write the answers to these questions on a separate sheet of paper, using complete sentences.

1) How are carbohydrate, fat, and protein alike?

2) How does glucose help the body?

3) List two foods that contain saturated fat and two that contain unsaturated fat.

4) What nutrient helps protect internal organs and nerves?

5) What are essential amino acids?

Careers

FOOD TECHNOLOGIST

Eating right can be a challenge. Food technologists help people choose nutritious foods to eat. Most food technologists work in hospitals or nursing homes. Registered dietitians supervise them. Technologists may train and supervise food service staff and create their work schedules. Some food technologists change recipes to fit the special food needs of people in hospitals or nursing homes. Technologists understand nutrition and enjoy helping people make good food choices. Training varies from on-the-job training to two-year college programs.

Vitamins, Minerals, and Water

Vitamin
A substance needed in small amounts for growth and activity

Mineral
A natural substance needed for fluid balance, digestion, and other bodily functions

Carbohydrates, fats, and proteins are the three essential nutrients that provide the body with energy. The other three essential nutrients are **vitamins**, **minerals**, and water. While these nutrients do not provide energy, they help the body change food into energy. Compared with carbohydrate, fat, and protein, your body needs small amounts of vitamins and minerals. Your body needs enough water to replace the amount it loses every day.

Why Are Vitamins Important?

Vitamins are substances that the body needs for normal growth and to maintain life. Vitamins combine with enzymes to increase the rate of reactions of chemical changes that take place in the body. Table 8.4 on page 176 shows the purposes and sources of some vitamins.

Some vitamins can be lost during food preparation. For example, the B vitamins and vitamin C dissolve in water. When cooking vegetables that contain these vitamins, many of the vitamins are released into the water. When you pour off the water, you lose the vitamins. To prevent this, use a small amount of water to cook vegetables, and avoid cooking them too long. You get more vitamins from uncooked vegetables than from cooked vegetables. To stay healthy, a person must eat foods with vitamins every day because the body does not store them.

People spend millions of dollars on vitamin supplements. Do you think people should take these? Why?

The body needs foods high in vitamins for normal growth.

Table 8.4. Essential Vitamins

Vitamin	Purpose	Sources
Vitamin A	Helps skin, hair, eyes, lining of nose and throat	Milk, egg yolk, beef liver, carrots, sweet potatoes, yellow squash, spinach, other greens
B Vitamins Niacin	Protects skin and nerves, aids digestion	Beef, chicken, turkey, liver, whole wheat, milk, cereals, mushrooms
Thiamin	Protects nervous system, aids appetite and digestion	Pork, sunflower seeds, whole grains, cereal, green beans, peanuts, organ meats
Riboflavin	Increases resistance to infection, prevents eye problems	Milk, milk products, pork, liver, eggs, bread, rolls, crackers, green leafy vegetables
Vitamin C	Helps to form bones and teeth, increase iron absorption, resist infection and stress	Tomatoes, most citrus fruits, kiwi, potatoes, fruit juices, green pepper
Vitamin D	Needed for strong bones and teeth	Fish oils, milk, sunlight
Vitamin E	Helps maintain cell health, has possible role in reproduction	Vegetable oils, margarine, peaches
Vitamin K	Aids in blood clotting	Green leafy vegetables, soybeans, bran, peas, green beans, liver

Vitamins A, D, E, and K dissolve in fat. These vitamins can build up and be stored in the body's fatty tissue. These vitamins are found in meat, milk, eggs, and other foods.

As with other nutrients, vitamins are important in maintaining a healthy body. It is possible, however, to have too many vitamins. Extra vitamins such as vitamins A and E could be harmful to the body and even poison the system. People need vitamins in small amounts. Most people are able to get all the vitamins they need from their diet.

Calcium
Mineral important for maintaining strong bones and teeth

Phosphorus
Mineral that works with calcium to maintain strong bones and teeth

Why Are Minerals Important?

Minerals are substances formed in the earth. The body needs small amounts of many minerals to stay healthy. Minerals are important for some body functions, including digestion and keeping fluids balanced.

One important mineral is **calcium**. Calcium is found in dairy products and leafy vegetables. Calcium is important for controlling certain body functions and for maintaining strong bones and teeth. Another important mineral is **phosphorus**, which combines with calcium to keep bones firm. Phosphorus is found in peas, beans, milk, meat, and other foods. The body needs larger amounts of calcium and phosphorus than other minerals.

The body uses only small amounts of the minerals iron and sodium. Iron is found in liver, beef, dried fruits, whole grain foods, and leafy green vegetables.

Sodium, or salt, another mineral, is essential for controlling the amount of fluids in your body. You need only a small amount of salt in your diet. Too much sodium may cause high blood pressure. Sodium is found in many foods. Therefore, you probably don't have to add salt to your foods.

Minerals cannot be stored in the body. It is important to get enough minerals every day to maintain the body systems. A balanced diet will include the minerals your body needs.

Why Is Water Important?

Water helps each cell in the body to do its work. About 60 percent of your body's weight is water. Water carries nutrients, hormones, and waste products to and from the body's organs. It helps you digest and absorb food. Water also helps control the body's temperature.

Foods high in minerals are important for digestion and fluid balance.

Water does not contain calories, but it is an important nutrient. Each day the average body loses eight glasses of water. For this reason, you should drink at least eight glasses of water every day. You can drink plain water or get water in juices, soups, and other drinks.

LESSON 3 REVIEW On a separate sheet of paper, write *True* if the statement is true or *False* if it is not true.

1) Vitamins, minerals, and water provide energy.

2) The body needs small amounts of vitamins.

3) Minerals are often lost during food preparation.

4) Calcium and phosphorus work together to maintain firm bones.

5) People should drink at least eight glasses of water every day.

Drink at least eight glasses of water daily to replace what the body loses.

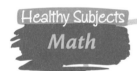

Math

BODY MASS INDEX

Have you ever wondered if your weight is right for your height and build? Find out by figuring out your body mass index. Let's say you weigh 145 pounds and are 6 feet tall.

(1) Multiply your weight in pounds by 0.45 (145 lb. x 0.45 = 65.25).

(2) Multiply your height in inches by 0.025 (72 in. x 0.025 = 1.8).

(3) Multiply this number times itself (1.8 x 1.8 = 3.24).

(4) Divide the answer in step 1 by the answer in step 3 (65.25 ÷ 3.24 = 20.1).

Your index number should fall between 19 and 25. If it is below 19 or over 27, check with your doctor.

Special Dietary Needs

The Food Guide Pyramid provides general guidelines for people to follow to choose a healthy diet. Yet people must adjust their diet to their own specific needs. For example, you must know how many calories you need each day based on your gender, body size, and activity level. You also must know which foods give you the nutrients you need. As you age, your calorie needs will change.

What Special Dietary Needs Do Teenagers Have?

Because teens are growing and changing, they need more calories, calcium, and iron. Since boys are usually larger and grow more than girls do, they need more calories.

Calcium is an important mineral in teenagers' diets. Calcium is needed for bone growth. If your diet does not contain enough calcium, the body takes calcium from your bones. Over time, loss of calcium from bones can cause them to break easily. The best sources of calcium are milk, yogurt, cheese, and ice cream (see Table B.3 in Appendix B). The body is able to absorb calcium from dairy products because they contain vitamin D.

Writing About Health

Think about how your eating pattern compares with the suggestions in the Food Guide Pyramid. Write how you might change your eating pattern to make it more healthful.

Iron is important for getting oxygen into the blood and cells. It is found in liver and other meats, dried fruits, whole grain foods, and leafy green vegetables. Foods containing vitamin C help the body absorb iron. For example, a meal with meat and potatoes provides iron and vitamin C to help the body absorb the iron. Teenage girls need more iron to make blood cells to replace cells that are lost during menstruation.

What Special Dietary Needs Do Athletes Have?

People who are very active require more calories. They get the extra energy they need from more calories. Studies show that athletes do not need extra protein, vitamins, or minerals as long as they have a balanced diet.

KEEPING A FOOD RECORD

Use the Food Guide Pyramid to plan a menu for yourself for the next week. At the end of each day, check to see how many of the planned foods you actually ate. Monitor your energy level. Think about how you feel as you follow the suggested daily servings for each food group. Do you notice any difference in your ability to keep going without feeling tired or hungry between meals?

Athletes should eat at least three hours before a competition. That way, the stomach has time to digest the food. The meal should be low in fat and easy to digest, and should include three glasses of liquid. Athletes need to replace the water they lose through perspiration before, during, and after strenuous activity.

Over the years, athletes have tried many different diets to try to improve their performance. Sometimes these diets can be harmful. It is safest for athletes to eat a healthy, balanced diet with enough calories to match their increased level of activity.

How Is Diet Important in Weight Control?

Eating foods with too many calories can cause a person to gain extra weight. Not getting enough calories can cause a person to become too thin. A healthy diet with an appropriate level of physical activity can help a person maintain proper weight.

It is important to discuss any plans you have for weight change with a doctor. Some plans can be unhealthy and cause other problems. A healthy and balanced diet is the best way to maintain a proper weight level.

Very active people and athletes require more calories for energy.

How Does a Poor Diet Affect Health?

If the six essential nutrients are lacking in the diet, a person may have **malnutrition**. Malnutrition results from a diet that lacks one or more of the essential nutrients. Some people eat enough food but still do not get enough nutrients.

Some signs of malnutrition are feeling tired, frequent headaches, stomachaches, or depression. Malnutrition may lead to serious health problems such as softened bones.

Another problem that results from a poor diet is a **deficiency**. A deficiency is a lack of something. For example, people who do not have enough iron in their diet may have iron deficiency. Deficiencies also may lead to more serious health problems such as damage to the nervous system or heart.

Both malnutrition and deficiencies usually can be prevented by eating a balanced diet.

You have a friend who vomits often. Your teacher calls this bulimia. How might this behavior contribute to malnutrition?

technology

COMPUTER PROGRAMS FOR DIET MANAGEMENT

Did you know that computer programs can help people improve their food choices? Some programs use the Food Guide Pyramid to make sure one's diet is healthful and well balanced. A glycemic index shows people how different foods affect blood sugar levels. This is especially useful in controlling obesity or diabetes. Daily menus can be automatically created. Sports, activities, and exercises are suggested. "Quizzes" rate how well a person is doing. Some computer games help create healthy eating habits. As healthy food shoots down junk food, health suggestions seep into the player's awareness. These computer programs also include a healthy eating guide, body weight logs, body mass index, and a calorie tracking system.

Eating the recommended number of servings from all six food groups helps prevent certain diseases.

How Are Diet and Disease Related?

Several diseases are related to diet. If a person's diet is unhealthy, the risk is greater for certain diseases. Some of these diseases are high blood pressure, heart disease, and cancer. For example, a person may have too much salt in the diet. This extra salt causes the body to hold extra fluid. This affects the blood vessels, and can result in higher blood pressure.

The systems of your body need the variety of nutrients that certain foods provide. If your diet does not include those foods, your systems may not function as well. As a result, you may get a disease. Your diet can also include too much of certain nutrients such as salt, sugar, or fat. In that case, you also may have a high risk for health problems.

While a proper diet cannot prevent people from getting certain diseases, it can often lower the risk of getting them. Nutrition is one risk factor people can control.

LESSON 4 REVIEW On a separate sheet of paper, write the word or words in parentheses that correctly complete each sentence.

1) Teenage boys usually need more (water, calories, iron) than girls.

2) Teenagers usually need more (salt, calcium, iron) in their diets for bone growth.

3) Athletes need to replace (water, protein, calcium) lost through perspiration.

4) Malnutrition is a result of a diet that lacks (oxygen, calories, nutrients).

5) Too much salt in the diet may lead to (deficiency, high blood pressure, depression).

■ The U.S. government offers guidelines for a healthy diet. It also developed the Food Guide Pyramid to show how much and what kinds of food to eat.

■ Foods provide calories and essential nutrients. Foods vary in how many calories and nutrients they provide.

■ The body needs six essential nutrients. Carbohydrate, fat, and protein are three nutrients that give the body energy. Vitamins, minerals, and water are three nutrients that help the body convert food into energy.

■ Carbohydrates are starches and sugars that come mainly from plant food. They provide much of the energy the body needs.

■ Carbohydrates break down into glucose, the body's main source of energy. Glycogen is stored glucose.

■ Fats are stored energy. Fats protect internal organs and nerves. Too many saturated fats can lead to high levels of cholesterol in the blood. Some kinds of cholesterol can clog blood vessels.

■ Protein builds muscle and repairs tissue. Animal products and some plants provide protein. Protein is made of amino acids. Certain foods provide the body with the nine necessary amino acids.

■ The body needs vitamins in small amounts for normal growth and activity. Some vitamins dissolve in water and are not stored in the body. Vitamins that dissolve in fat can be stored in the body.

■ Minerals are important in small amounts for fluid balance and digestion. Calcium, phosphorus, and iron are especially important minerals.

■ Water carries nutrients, hormones, and waste products to and from the cells. People generally need eight glasses of water every day.

■ Teenagers have special dietary needs, including more calcium and iron.

■ Athletes need more calories and must replace the water they use during increased physical activity.

■ A healthy diet is important in weight control. A doctor can help decide what special dietary needs a person might have.

■ A healthy diet includes foods with all six essential nutrients. Not enough or too much of these nutrients can lead to health problems.

■ Some diseases are related to diet. A healthy diet can lower the risk of getting certain diseases.

Comprehension: Identifying Facts

On a separate sheet of paper, write the correct word or words from the Word Bank to complete each sentence.

WORD BANK		
amino acids	digest	glucose
balanced	disease	protein
blood pressure	essential	saturated
calcium	Food Guide Pyramid	vitamins
carbohydrates		water

1) The _____ helps determine how much and what kind of food to eat.

2) _____ nutrients are food substances that your body cannot manufacture.

3) Potatoes, pasta, and bread are good sources of _____.

4) Carbohydrates are broken down into blood sugar, or _____.

5) Sugar is easy to _____ and enters the bloodstream quickly.

6) _____ fat may lead to a high level of cholesterol.

7) Muscles, bones, blood, and skin all contain _____.

8) The body needs nine _____ that are the building blocks of protein.

9) Some _____ dissolve in water.

10) An important mineral found in dairy products is _____.

11) A _____ diet will include the vitamins and minerals your body needs.

12) _____ is a nutrient that does not contain calories.

13) A diet high in salt could result in high _____.

14) A balanced diet can lower the risk of getting some kinds of _____.

Comprehension: Understanding Main Ideas

On a separate sheet of paper, write the answers to the following questions using complete sentences.

15) Which food groups in the Food Guide Pyramid provide complex carbohydrates and which provide simple carbohydrates?

16) What does the body do with extra sugar and starch?

17) What is malnutrition?

18) How is diet related to disease?

Critical Thinking: Write Your Opinion

19) Do your favorite foods contain many nutrients? Explain your answer.

20) In what ways could people change their diet to make it healthier?

Test Taking Tip | Always read directions more than once. Underline the words that tell how many examples or items you must provide.

Making Healthy Food Choices

*F*ood is an important part of our lives. For most people, mealtimes are a time to enjoy conversations with family members or friends. People enjoy social events that include food—dinners, parties, banquets, festivals, and picnics. Many things influence the food choices people make for meals and special events. It is important to realize why you choose certain foods in your diet. It is also important to develop an eating pattern that helps maintain a healthy diet.

In this chapter, you will learn about healthy eating patterns and about factors that influence our food choices, such as advertising. You will learn about how the government helps make sure foods are safe. Finally, you will learn about reading food labels and about substances that are added to foods.

Goals for Learning

▶ To identify healthy eating patterns

▶ To describe what influences food choices

▶ To describe how government agencies ensure food safety

▶ To explain how to read food labels in order to make healthy food choices

▶ To explain the purpose of food additives

Magnified Vitamin C Crystal

Healthy Eating Patterns and Food Choices

A person's lifestyle affects his or her diet. Sometimes a busy lifestyle results in a poor diet. Knowing more about what influences food choices can help people improve their diets.

How Does Your Eating Pattern Affect Your Diet?

People usually have a schedule for when they eat. For example, their normal lunch time may be noon. A schedule, or pattern, is helpful. It provides your body with food for energy at regular times each day. Sitting down to a balanced meal each morning, afternoon, and evening will help set a healthy eating pattern.

Sometimes it is difficult for people to follow a healthy eating pattern. In the United States today, many people eat on the run. That is, they have to eat something quickly. Their work, school, or activity schedules are busy. They don't have time to prepare and eat a meal at home. They may rely on fast-food restaurants for meals. Often, fast foods are high in fats and salt and may not provide the nutrients the body needs.

Setting a healthy eating pattern is important. For example, eating a balanced breakfast every morning helps give you the energy you need for the day's activities. In some ways, breakfast is more important than an evening meal. People are usually more active in the earlier part of the day. They use up more calories and energy during that time, so they need a good breakfast. In the evening, they may be less active and need fewer calories. So the evening meal could be smaller. Breakfast foods should include complex carbohydrates to give your body the energy it needs. Avoid foods high in sugar. They provide an energy burst that is used up quickly and leaves you feeling tired.

Writing About Health

Think about the food choices you have made. Compare one influence that resulted in a healthy meal with one that resulted in poor food choices.

Snacks can be a part of a healthy eating pattern. Nutritious snacks can add protein, vitamins, and minerals to your diet. For example, you can add vitamin C by eating pineapple or oranges. You can add vitamin A by eating carrots or green peppers. You may also try eating whole-grain bread or raisins as snacks. Combining nutritious snacks with balanced meals will help you set a healthy eating pattern.

What Influences Food Choices?

Nutritious snacks can be part of a healthy diet. Be careful to avoid snacking in place of regular meals. Late night snacking can disturb your sleep and affect your weight.

Many things influence the foods you choose to include in your diet. These may include where you live, the time of year, your religion, or your cultural background. Your family's eating habits and your peers may influence your food choices. The location of your home may affect some of your food choices. For example, if you live close to a source of fresh fish or seafood, your diet is more likely to include those items. The time of the year can influence your choices, since some foods are in season at certain times during the year. For example, you may find fresh strawberries at the grocery store during early June but not during December.

Often cultural background or religion affects the food choices people make. For example, some cultural groups include more rice, beans, or spicy foods in their diets than others do. Some religions have rules about certain foods. For example, they may have rules about eating meat.

Healthy Subjects
Geography

FISH FOR LIFE

A study was done of 1,800 Greenland natives during a twenty-five-year period. In that time, only three people had heart attacks. There have been similar findings in Japan and other Asian countries. This rate seems to be due to the large amount of fish that people in those places eat. The rate of heart attacks in North America is more than ten times higher than in these other countries. Many Americans eat more meat, which has "bad" cholesterol that clogs blood veins. The oils in fish, on the other hand, contain "good" cholesterol, which helps blood flow quickly. Many experts recommend eating fish at least twice a week.

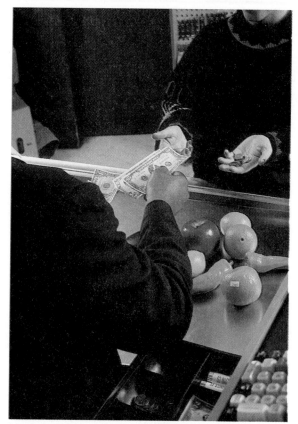
How much a person can afford to spend influences food buying choices.

Several other things can influence the foods people choose to eat. Sometimes people cannot afford the cost of some foods. They buy foods that are the least costly to get the most for their money. Another influence is friends. For example, you may have dinner at a friend's house and discover a food that you've never tried before.

Association also influences food choices. Association means that the food reminds you of something else. You may strongly like or strongly dislike certain foods because of association. For example, you may enjoy toasted marshmallows because they remind you of a picnic that you enjoyed with friends. Or, you may dislike marshmallows because you once got sick eating them.

The many things that affect your choice of foods can be positive, negative, or both. If you think about why a certain food is a part of your diet, you may decide to make some changes. For example, you may realize that you eat a certain breakfast cereal because another family member does. You notice it is high in sugar, so you decide to eat whole-grain toast instead.

How Does Stress Affect Food Choices?

Think about a time when you were stressed and didn't want to eat. How do you think not eating affected your stress?

Stress often affects food choices. People who are feeling a great deal of mental stress may forget about their diet. They don't realize they are using more energy and need more nutrients. They may ignore feelings of hunger and not eat enough. Then, by not getting the nutrients they need, they experience more physical stress as well.

The feelings of stress sometimes cause people to eat too much. They may choose foods high in sugar or salt, which could also be harmful. It's important to remember that a healthy diet combined with exercise may help reduce the effects of "bad" stress.

How Does Advertising Affect Food Choices?

Many foods and beverages are promoted on TV and the radio and in newspapers and magazines. Often, people choose foods simply because they have heard them advertised. Companies spend large amounts of money to encourage people to buy their products.

Some techniques, or methods, advertisers use to convince you to buy their products are described here.

New product—Packages may include the words *new* or *improved*. Advertisers use these words to appeal to your desire to be different and try something you haven't tried before. Sometimes the product may be the same, but the packaging is new.

Old-Fashioned—Some products say the food is prepared the same way it was prepared many years ago. People may associate old-fashioned foods with happy memories. They may buy the food because it reminds them of a relative or longtime friend. For example, a company advertises its mashed potatoes as being "just like mom used to make."

Expensive and superior—This makes people feel that they should buy only the best. Advertisers are hoping that people will feel this product is better than others. Usually products that are advertised as "superior" cost more. For example, advertisers say their mustard "costs a little bit more but it's worth it."

Inexpensive and a bargain—This technique is used to convince people they are getting the most for their money. The buyer must look at price and number of servings to determine if this is true.

Recommended by someone famous—These advertisements use an athlete or a TV or movie star to encourage people to buy a certain product. They want people to believe that if someone famous uses the product, it must be good.

Contains no cholesterol—This can be a confusing claim. Many people are trying to lower cholesterol levels in their diets. They may buy a product simply because it states that it has no cholesterol. For example, an ad for peanut butter may state, "This product has no cholesterol." Yet, no peanut butter contains cholesterol, since peanuts are plants and cholesterol is found in animal products. A product can be low in cholesterol but still be high in saturated fats from coconut or palm oils.

All these techniques are used to encourage people to buy products. The products may or may not be good ones. They may be inexpensive, or they may be costly. People must look closely at the foods they buy to be sure they are choosing foods that are nutritious and priced fairly.

How Do Fads Affect Your Diet?

A fad is something that becomes popular for a short time. When people believe in a food fad, they may change their diet. For example, they may have heard that they should eat grapefruit six times daily for two weeks. Grapefruit can be a healthy food, but eating too much of it is not healthy.

EXAMINE FOOD ADVERTISING

Learning to examine food ads takes practice. For a few days, look for food and beverage ads in the media—TV, radio, magazines, newspapers, billboards. Then walk through your local market. Find two or three products for which you saw ads. Carefully read the list of ingredients on the packages. A food contains the most of the ingredients that are listed first. It contains the least of the ingredients that are listed last. What are the main ingredients in the products? How healthy do you think these products are? Do you think the advertising that you saw was true?

The body needs nutrients from a variety of foods. Food fads usually focus on one food or on an unhealthy eating pattern. They can cause serious health problems.

There are many things to think about when choosing foods for your diet. Choosing good food and setting a healthy eating pattern will help your body get the nutrients it needs.

LESSON 1 REVIEW Write the answers to these questions on a separate sheet of paper, using complete sentences.

1) Why is it difficult for some people to set a healthy eating pattern?

2) What are three things that influence a person's choice of foods?

3) How does stress affect food choices?

4) Why do advertisers use famous people to promote their products?

5) How can a food fad be harmful to your health?

Careers

DIETARY AIDE

Hospitals and nursing homes always need good dietary aides. These workers help to prepare food for residents. Many dietary aides work on a tray assembly line. They follow directions about what should go on each person's tray. Then they deliver the trays. After a meal, they pick up the trays and return them to the kitchen. They record the amount of food patients eat. Aides may help sort recyclables and trash, wash dishes, and do other clean-up tasks. Dietary aides are sometimes called food service workers. Dietary aides usually receive on-the-job training.

Food Labels and Food Additives

You know which nutrients your body needs, but you also need to know which foods contain these nutrients. To adjust your diet to your needs, you need to know how many calories are in one serving of the foods you eat. This information is provided on food labels. Food labels also list additional substances that are added to the foods you eat.

How Does the Government Ensure Food Safety?

The United States government has agencies to make sure the foods people buy are labeled correctly and are safe to eat. These agencies set rules for food producers to follow. The agencies control food safety, cleanliness, advertising, labeling, and packaging.

The U.S. Department of Agriculture (USDA) is in charge of all programs dealing with the production of food. It conducts national food surveys to determine eating patterns in the United States. It is responsible for inspecting and grading meat and poultry.

The Food and Drug Administration (FDA) controls food and drug safety. It determines which ingredients are safe. The FDA also controls food labeling.

The Food and Nutrition Board of the National Research Council conducts studies on the nutrients people need. It also recommends standards and guidelines to help people meet those needs.

What Does a Food Label Tell You?

The government has set guidelines for what information must appear on a food label. The information includes what is in the package and how to store the food. Labels give the weight and lot number of the product. Some labels say the product should be used by a certain date to ensure freshness. Figure 9.1 on page 194 shows a sample food label.

Daily Value
Section of a food label that provides information about the percent of nutrients in the product

Nutrition Facts
Section of a food label that provides information about the product

Food labels also must include information about the nutrients and ingredients in the product. These appear under the heading **Nutrition Facts**. Nutrition Facts tell the size of one serving and how many servings are in the package. They also list the number of calories per serving as well as the number of calories from fat.

An important part of the Nutrition Facts label is the percent of the **Daily Value** for each nutrient found in the food. This percent tells how much of that nutrient is found in the food compared with the total amount needed each day. It is based on a diet of 2,000 calories per day. For example, the Daily Value for sodium is 2,400 milligrams (mg). The label in Figure 9.1 shows that the product has 250 mg of sodium per serving. Then it shows that the food has 10 percent of the Daily Value for sodium. The Daily Value information helps you determine how many nutrients you are getting in one serving of that food.

Under Daily Values, a food label must give the amounts of total fat, cholesterol, sodium, total carbohydrate, and protein. Amounts are given in grams or milligrams. Next to the amount in milligrams the label shows you the actual percent of Daily Value.

Look at Figure 9.1. A serving of tuna is about 3 percent of the Daily Value for calories. What helpful nutrients are provided in tuna that are over 3 percent?

CHUNK LIGHT TUNA IN WATER

Nutrition Facts	**Amount/Serving**	**%DV***	**Amount/Serving**	**%DV***
Serv. Size 2 oz. drained (56g / about 1/4 cup)	**Total Fat** 0.5g	1%	**Total Carb.** 0g	0%
Servings about 2.5	Sat. Fat 0g	0%	Fiber 0g	0%
Calories 60	**Cholest.** 30mg	10%	Sugars 0g	
Fat Cal. 5	**Sodium** 250mg	10%	**Protein** 13g	23%

* Percent Daily Values (DV) are based on a 2,000 calorie diet.

Vitamin A 0% • Vitamin C 0% • Calcium 0% • Iron 2%
Niacin 20% • Vitamin B-6 8% • Vitamin B-12 20% • Phosphorus 8%

INGREDIENTS: LIGHT TUNA, WATER, VEGETABLE BROTH, HYDROLYZED CASEIN, HYDROLYZED SOY PROTEIN, SALT.

Figure 9.1. Food label

Additive
A substance added to foods in small amounts

Preservative
A substance added to food to prevent spoiling

Why is it important to be able to read and interpret a food label?

Fitness Tip

Wait an hour after a heavy meal before exercising.

The Nutrition Facts label also must include the amount of vitamin A, vitamin C, calcium, and iron in the product. The label may list other vitamins and minerals as well. This information also is listed as a percent.

Finally, the label must list all the ingredients in the product. The ingredients are listed in order by weight, from the most to the least. For example, on a can of soup, the first ingredient listed is water. The weight of the water in the soup is more than the weight of any other ingredient. Some people must check the list of ingredients carefully. If they have an allergy to a food, they can tell from the list of ingredients whether that food is included.

All the information on the food label can be helpful in choosing food. If you are trying to limit a substance in your diet such as salt, the label tells you what percent of sodium, or salt, is in one serving. By using the information on the label, you can tell if the product is priced fairly. You can look at the price and the number of servings and decide how much each serving costs. You can then compare that amount with other packages to see which product is the best value.

What Are Food Additives?

A food **additive** is a substance added to food to change it in some way. Additives change color, flavor, or texture. Additives such as sugars or salt are sometimes added to help prevent the food from spoiling. Sometimes nutrients are added to foods. For example, vitamin C is added to some fruit drinks, and calcium is added to some fruit juices.

Food additives have been the subject of much discussion. Some people question whether additives are safe. The U.S. government has passed laws about food additives. The laws state that additives must be tested and must not be found to cause cancer in animals or humans. Food producers must test the additives and give their results to the FDA. The FDA decides whether the additive is safe.

Preservatives are substances that often are added to food. They prevent bacteria from growing and spoiling the food.

Eat sweets sparingly.

Preservatives such as sugar and salt are necessary since many foods spoil quickly. Preservatives help by keeping canned, packaged, or frozen foods safe to eat.

In general, the substances added to foods are added in very small amounts. A person would have to eat a large amount of a food with additives to reach a dangerous level. Because foods are being processed more, it is a good idea to find out which additives are in the foods you eat often. You may decide to try to add more fresh or natural foods to your diet.

LESSON 2 REVIEW On a separate sheet of paper, write *True* if the statement is true or *False* if it is not true.

1) The Food and Drug Administration controls food labeling.

2) The ingredient list on a food label shows only the main ingredients in that product.

3) Percent Daily Values are based on a diet of 2,000 calories per day.

4) Nutrition Facts do not list minerals.

5) Additives are usually found in foods in large amounts.

RECIPES OLD AND NEW

When our grandparents cooked, they didn't worry as much about nutrition as today's cooks do. Compare the two recipes for plum pudding. One is from 1903, the other from 1990.

Plum Pudding (1903)	*Plum Pudding (1990)*
3 cups beef fat	1 1/2 cups vegetable oil
3 cups raisins	6 cups raisins and chopped fruit
3 cups water	4 cups whole wheat bread crumbs
1 tsp. salt	1 3/4 cups fruit juice
3/4 cup sugar	1 cup brown sugar
3 cups flour	2 cups whole wheat flour
4 eggs	6 eggs
3 tsp. spices	3 tsp. spices
	3 tbsp. lemon rind

Then and Now

The new recipe has less fat and more vitamins from fruit. It also has fiber from whole wheat. Today, many recipes can be made healthier.

■ A healthy eating pattern includes regular, balanced meals and nutritious snacks. A healthy eating pattern is important.

■ Many things affect food choices. These include where a person lives, the season of the year, cost of food, and a person's cultural background. Association and stress also influence food choice.

■ Advertisers use several techniques to encourage people to buy their products.

■ Fad diets are diets that usually focus on a certain food. These diets can cause serious health problems.

■ The U.S. government has set up agencies to make sure foods are labeled correctly and are safe to eat. They are the USDA, the Food and Nutrition Board of the National Research Council, and the FDA. The FDA is responsible for food labeling.

■ Food labels provide information about the product. Labels include Nutrition Facts, Daily Value information, and a list of all ingredients in the product. Nutrition Facts tell serving sizes, number of servings in the package, and number of calories per serving. Food labels are helpful in choosing foods for your diet.

■ Additives are substances that are added to foods to change them in some way. Some additives are preservatives that help prevent the food from spoiling. Additives are included in very small amounts.

Comprehension: Identifying Facts

On a separate sheet of paper, write the correct word or words from the Word Bank to complete each sentence.

WORD BANK		
additive	Daily Value	preservatives
animal	first	serving
associate	food fad	snacks
breakfast	labeling	stress
cost	natural	sugar

1) _____ is an important meal. It provides energy for the early part of the day.

2) _____ provides quick energy that is used up quickly.

3) Nutritious _____ can add protein, vitamins, and minerals to your diet.

4) Some people may think about popcorn when they see a movie. They _____ popcorn with movies.

5) A person who feels a great deal of _____ may forget to eat a healthy diet.

6) Products that are advertised as "superior" may _____ more.

7) A _____ food comes from nature and has not been processed.

8) Cholesterol is found in _____ products.

9) A diet that promotes eating one fruit many times each day for weeks is probably a _____.

10) The FDA controls the _____ of foods.

11) Nutrition Facts on a food label give the amount of nutrients in one _____ of the product.

12) The _____ of a food is based on a diet of 2,000 calories per day.

13) On an ingredient list, the main ingredient is listed _____.

14) A substance that changes the color of a food is an _____.

15) _____ are substances added to foods to prevent the growth of bacteria.

Comprehension: Understanding Main Ideas

On a separate sheet of paper, write the answers to the following questions using complete sentences.

16) What do advertisers want people to believe when they use a famous athlete or entertainer to promote their product?

17) How does the U.S. Department of Agriculture help make sure foods are safe?

18) What are some reasons foods contain additives?

Critical Thinking: Write Your Opinion

19) What things influence your choices of food? Do you need to make any changes in your diet to make it healthier?

20) How can reading the information on food labels help you plan a healthy diet?

| Test Taking Tip | When you read test directions, try to restate them in your own words. Tell yourself what you are expected to do. That way, you can make sure your answer will be complete and correct. |

Loaded Words

Think of all the foods that are available that are advertised as "light," "low fat," "nonfat," or "fat free." These words in ads and on food labels can be loaded. The message seems to be that any fat in foods is bad.

Advertisers use loaded words like *low fat, no fat, fat free, light,* or *low calorie* to make us think their foods will keep us healthy. Many people believe they are making healthy food choices when buying these products.

It is true that taking in too much fat is unhealthy. But it is important to remember that the body needs a certain amount of fat to function properly. It is just as important to read all of the information on food labels. For example, it is important to notice the amount of salt or sugar in a product and the total calories.

Combining regular exercise with a balanced diet of foods from all six food groups is the best way to be healthy and fit. That means keeping daily fat intake at 30% of total daily calories.

Questions

1) Look for food ads in print or on the radio or TV. List any loaded words that hint that choosing the foods will improve your health. What positive feelings do you associate with the words?

2) List any negative words that hint you could hurt your health by choosing other foods. What negative feelings go with these words?

3) Why is reading the food label the best way to tell how healthy a food is?

4) Why is it important to exercise a little more on days when more than 30 percent of your total daily calories comes from fat?

■ The Food Guide Pyramid shows how much and what kinds of food to eat each day.

■ The six essential nutrients are carbohydrates, fats, protein, vitamins, minerals, and water.

■ Carbohydrates break down into glucose—the body's main source of energy.

■ Fats are stored energy. They protect internal organs and nerves. Too many saturated fats can lead to high levels of cholesterol in the blood.

■ Protein provides energy, builds muscle, and repairs tissue. Animal products and some plants provide protein.

■ The body needs vitamins for normal growth and activity. Minerals are important for fluid balance and digestion. Water carries nutrients, hormones, and waste products to and from the cells. People generally need eight glasses of water every day.

■ Teenagers have special dietary needs, including more calcium and iron. Athletes need more calories and must replace the water they use during increased physical activity.

■ A doctor can help decide what special dietary needs a person might have.

■ A healthy diet includes foods with all six essential nutrients. Not enough or too much of these nutrients can lead to health problems.

■ A healthy diet can lower the risk of getting certain diseases.

■ A healthy eating pattern includes regular, balanced meals and nutritious snacks.

■ Where a person lives, the season of the year, cost of food, a person's cultural background, association, and stress can influence food choices. Advertisers use several techniques to influence people to buy their products.

■ Fad diets, which usually focus on a certain food, can cause serious health problems.

■ The USDA, the Food and Nutrition Board of the National Research Council, and the FDA control food labeling and safety.

■ Food labels include Nutrition Facts, Daily Value information, and a list of all ingredients in the product. Labels are helpful in choosing foods.

■ Additives are added to foods to change them in some way. Preservatives help prevent food from spoiling.

I have met a lot of people in my life who were brave and courageous. But when I met Ryan, he gave new meaning to these words ... Ryan White was a miracle of humanity.

—Elton John

Unit 4

Preventing and Controlling Diseases and Disorders

When was the last time you were sick? If it has been so long ago that you can't remember, it could be because you make wise decisions about your health. Young adulthood is usually a time of excellent health, when your body is in peak physical form. However, this does not happen automatically.

Diseases affect how you feel in many ways. You can prevent yourself from getting many diseases by taking certain precautions. In this unit, you will learn about symptoms, causes, and what you can do to prevent yourself from becoming infected or sick.

Ryan White, 1972–1990

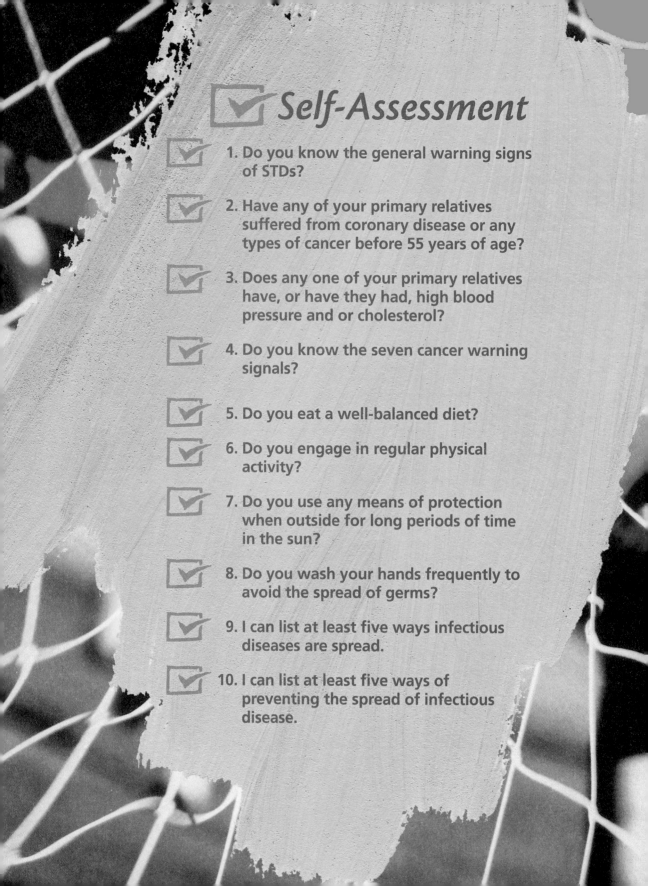

Self-Assessment

1. Do you know the general warning signs of STDs?

2. Have any of your primary relatives suffered from coronary disease or any types of cancer before 55 years of age?

3. Does any one of your primary relatives have, or have they had, high blood pressure and or cholesterol?

4. Do you know the seven cancer warning signals?

5. Do you eat a well-balanced diet?

6. Do you engage in regular physical activity?

7. Do you use any means of protection when outside for long periods of time in the sun?

8. Do you wash your hands frequently to avoid the spread of germs?

9. I can list at least five ways infectious diseases are spread.

10. I can list at least five ways of preventing the spread of infectious disease.

Disease—Causes and Protection

Have you ever wondered how you came down with the flu or got a cold? Have you wondered what your body does when you get sick? Your body has an amazing line of defenses that keep you from getting a disease or infection. Those same defenses help you if you do become sick. When you know how diseases spread, you can take action to prevent getting or giving them.

In this chapter, you will learn the causes of diseases. You will learn about the body's physical and chemical barriers to infection and how the immune system works.

Goals for Learning

▶ To explain the causes of acquired diseases

▶ To describe the causes of inherited diseases

▶ To identify some of the body's barriers to infection

▶ To explain how the immune system works

Magnified HIV Virus

Causes of Disease

Communicable
Something that can be passed from one person to another

Disease is the interruption or disorder of normal body function. A person can either acquire or inherit a disease.

What Are Some Causes of Acquired Diseases?

Many diseases are acquired. An acquired disease is caused by infection, human behaviors, or environmental conditions that affect health.

Why do you think people often get a cold or the flu within a couple days after flying on an airplane?

When infection causes an acquired disease, the disease is called **communicable**. That means one individual can pass the disease to another individual. You sometimes hear the word *contagious*, which also means communicable. Germs that cause communicable diseases are passed from person to person. For example, you can get a cold or flu germ from another person.

An acquired disease can also result from a person's behaviors. For example, healthy food choices and regular exercise may help to prevent heart disease. People who don't make healthy choices about food and exercise are more likely to have heart disease. People may also inherit a tendency toward heart disease. For these people, choosing a healthy lifestyle is especially important.

WAYS THAT GERMS ARE SPREAD

- Through direct physical contact with an infected person
- By droplets that an infected person coughs into the air
- By contact with an object that an infected person has used
- By contact with food or water with a pathogen in it
- Through the bites of infected animals, including insects

An acquired disease can also come from the environment. For example, small children living in older homes who eat chips of lead-based paint can get lead poisoning. Nonsmokers who breathe others' cigarette smoke may get lung diseases, including cancer.

Immune
Resistant to infection

Incubation
Time between the initial infection and the appearance of symptoms of a disease

Pathogen
An agent that causes disease

What Are the Stages of Infectious Disease?

When a person acquires a communicable infection, the disease usually passes through certain stages. Germs that cause communicable diseases are called **pathogens**. Pathogens include bacteria, viruses, fungi, or one-celled organisms. For example, viral pathogens cause the common cold, chicken pox, measles, and influenza or flu.

After a person is infected with a disease-causing pathogen, the disease passes through several stages. Figure 10.1 shows these stages of infectious disease. The first stage is **incubation**. This is the time it takes after a person is infected for symptoms of the disease to appear. This period may be days, weeks, months, or even years.

If the body's defenses are effective in fighting off the pathogen during incubation, a person may never become ill. It is the body's **immune** system that resists infection.

Fitness Tip

Exercise to increase your resistance to communicable diseases.

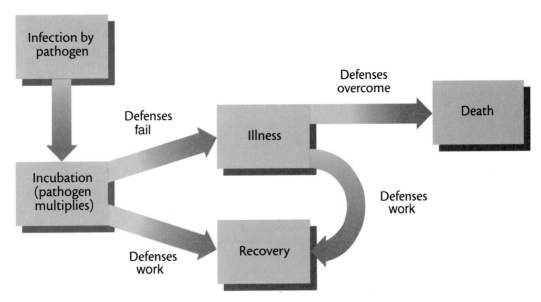

Figure 10.1. Stages of infectious disease

Deformity
Abnormally formed structure

Health Tip

Wash your hands often to prevent some infectious diseases.

If the body's defenses are not effective in fighting off the pathogen during incubation, a person becomes ill. When a person is ill, usually the immune system is effective in fighting the illness. The person recovers in a few days. For example, if you get a cold, you are usually well again in about ten days.

Sometimes conditions that lower the effectiveness of the immune system reduce the body's ability to protect itself from pathogens. Some conditions such as AIDS can be so serious that a person's defenses against disease are no longer effective. People can die from infections when the body is not able to protect itself from pathogens that are part of the normal environment.

Fortunately, the immune system successfully fights most infectious diseases.

What Are Some Causes of Inherited Diseases?

An inherited disease is passed through the genes from parents to children. You can't get an inherited disease any other way. There are three main causes for inherited diseases.

Some inherited diseases can be passed from parents to children through a single abnormal gene. For example, hemophilia, a blood clotting disorder, is passed through a single gene. Sometimes an abnormal gene combined with other conditions may result in an inherited problem. **Deformities**, or abnormally formed structures such as cleft (split) lip and clubfoot, are caused this way. The third main cause of a genetic disorder is an abnormal chromosome. When a chromosome breaks or fails to divide properly, a genetic disorder may result from it. A genetic disorder can also happen if the genes become positioned incorrectly on the chromosomes. An example of this kind of genetic disorder is Down syndrome.

HEALTH UNIT COORDINATOR

Health unit coordinators perform non-nursing duties. They may handle forms when patients enter or leave health care facilities. They give health-related information to nurses, doctors, and other health care workers. Other duties include entering doctors' orders on computer. They order special diets, drugs, equipment, supplies, laboratory tests, and X-ray exams. Health unit coordinators may be called unit managers, ward/unit secretaries, ward clerks, or hospital service coordinators. They may be called clinic station assistants, receptionists, or transcription, admission, or communications clerks. Two to four years of training are required. Health unit coordinators also must know basic medical terms, nursing and testing procedures, basic science, and general therapy requirements.

LESSON 1 REVIEW On a separate sheet of paper, write the word in parentheses that correctly completes each sentence.

1) Disease is an interruption or disorder of (abnormal, immune, normal) body function.

2) A disease that one individual passes to another is (communicable, inherited, acquired).

3) An abnormal gene combined with other conditions can cause a (deformity, pathogen, incubation).

4) A germ that causes a communicable disease is called a (deformity, gene, pathogen).

5) The body system that resists infection is the (nervous, muscular, immune) system.

How the Body Protects Itself From Disease

Mucous membrane
The moist lining of all body passages

Mucus
Secretion of the mucous membranes

The human body has many ways to protect itself from disease and infection. Germs that are washed off the skin never enter the body. The body's physical and chemical barriers, or defenses, protect it from infection. Its immune system also defends the body from disease.

How Does the Body Fight Infection?

Physical and chemical barriers are the first way your body protects itself from infection. The skin and mucous membranes are physical barriers to infection. **Mucous membranes** are the moist linings of your mouth and other body passages. The tiny hairs in your respiratory passages are another physical barrier. These hairs whip rapidly back and forth to sweep pathogens and dust out of your body. These barriers prevent pathogens from getting through your body's surface.

Your body also has chemical barriers to infection. Saliva, tears, and sweat clear pathogens from your body's surface. Urine carries pathogens out of your body. **Mucus**, the fluid that the mucous membranes secrete, clears pathogens from your respiratory system. The strong acids produced in your stomach kill pathogens that enter the digestive system.

Your body's physical and chemical barriers prevent pathogens from getting into your bloodstream. When pathogens enter the bloodstream, they travel to different organs. Infection occurs when a pathogen enters the organs and interferes with their normal function.

In spite of your body's physical and chemical barriers to infection, pathogens sometimes do enter the bloodstream. This can happen because of a break in the skin such as an open sore or a wound. Your body's immune system then fights pathogens that enter your body.

Writing About Health

Think about your personal health practices. List the things you could do to prevent getting an infectious disease such as a cold. Then list the things you could do when you have a cold to avoid spreading it to others.

TONSILS

Tonsils are pieces of tissue on both sides of the human throat. Sometimes tonsils have an infection called tonsillitis. Tonsillitis can cause a sore throat, fever, and difficulty swallowing. For many years, doctors simply removed diseased tonsils.

Recently, however, researchers have learned that tonsils are useful. Tonsils are part of the body's immune system. They trap bacteria and viruses entering the body. Also, the tonsils produce chemicals that help fight infections. Today the common treatment for tonsillitis is medicine. Tonsils are sometimes still removed. But that happens only when the infection doesn't go away with medical treatment.

Antibody
A protein that kills a specific pathogen

How Does the Immune System Work?

The immune system is the body's final line of defense against infection. When a foreign substance enters the bloodstream, the blood makes **antibodies**. Antibodies are proteins that kill specific pathogens. If the correct antibodies are in the blood when an infection occurs, they can begin to fight it. They may knock out the infection during the incubation stage. You may never actually become sick.

Antibodies form in the blood in a number of ways. If you do become sick, antibodies to a pathogen develop during the course of the illness. Then the antibodies help to fight the illness so that recovery is speeded up.

Some antibodies remain in the body after a disease is over. These antibodies give you immunity so you won't get the disease again. For example, once you have mumps, you will probably not get the disease again. You are immune.

THE BUBONIC PLAGUE

An epidemic is a widespread disease. And the bubonic plague has been one of the world's worst epidemics. Fleas from infected rats carry the plague. It causes fever, pain, and open sores. It is usually deadly. The first recorded plague was in 435 B.C. The worst known outbreak occurred in Europe from 1347 to 1351. Known as the Black Death, it killed millions of people. In the early 1900s, over ten million people in India died of the plague. Today, there are medicines to fight this disease. The U.S. Public Health Service isolates people and cleans up infected areas. This has helped stop the disease whenever it has appeared in the United States.

Vaccination
An injection of dead or weakened viruses to make the body immune to the viruses

Immunization
Means of making the body immune from a disease

Antibodies may also be in the blood as a result of a **vaccination**, or **immunization**. A vaccination is an injection, or shot, of dead or weakened viruses into your body. Enough virus is injected to make you immune to but not sick from the disease. When you get a vaccination, your body manufactures antibodies against that disease. For example, when you get a measles vaccination, your body makes antibodies to the measles virus. Then you are immune to measles.

You may already have antibodies when you are born. That is to say you are born immune to some diseases. For example, humans cannot get certain diseases that animals get. Humans are naturally immune to such diseases.

Some immunities are acquired naturally. Babies are protected from certain diseases because of antibodies in their mother's milk. This immunity works in babies until their own immune system takes over.

Without the immune system, people would have many more diseases and infections. Your immune system is an important defense against disease.

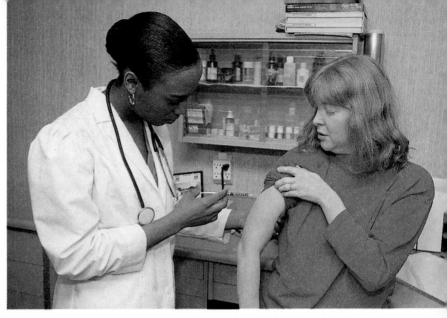

Vaccinations help the body build immunity to some diseases.

Action for Health

KEEPING TRACK OF YOUR VACCINATIONS

Ask your family to help you make a list of all your vaccinations and the dates when you had them. This chart shows some usual types of vaccinations and the ages when they are recommended. If your vaccinations are not up to date, see your doctor.

Vaccine	Recommended Age
Diphtheria-whooping cough-tetanus	2, 4, 6, and 15 months; 4 to 6 years
Oral polio vaccine	2, 4, and 15 months; 4 to 6 years
Measles	15 months; 4 to 6 years
Mumps	15 months; 4 to 6 years
German measles	15 months; 4 to 6 years
Tetanus-diphtheria	14 to 16 years; every 10 years thereafter
Chickenpox	12 to 18 months; adults who've never had the disease

LESSON 2 REVIEW On a separate sheet of paper, write the word from the Word Bank that matches each description.

WORD BANK

antibodies

barriers

chemical

physical

vaccination

1) Physical and chemical _____ are the first way the body protects itself from infection.

2) The skin is a _____ barrier to infection.

3) Mucus is a _____ barrier to infection.

4) When a foreign substance enters the bloodstream, the blood makes _____.

5) A _____ is one way a person becomes immune to a disease.

■ Diseases can either be acquired or inherited.

■ Infection, human behaviors, or environmental conditions cause acquired diseases. An acquired disease is communicable when infection causes it.

■ Pathogens are the germs that cause communicable diseases.

■ The first stage of infectious disease is incubation, which can last days, weeks, months, or years.

■ If the body's immune system effectively fights off a pathogen, a person may never become ill.

■ If the body's immune system cannot effectively fight off a pathogen, a person becomes ill. The immune system then fights the illness, and a person usually recovers.

■ If a condition lowers the effectiveness of the immune system, the body's ability to fight the condition is lowered. A person may not recover.

■ The body has physical and chemical barriers to infection. Some physical barriers are the skin and mucous membranes. Some chemical barriers are saliva, tears, stomach acids, and urine.

■ The immune system fights foreign substances that enter the bloodstream by producing antibodies.

■ Antibodies get in the blood in a number of ways. Earlier infections or vaccinations build antibodies in the blood to fight infections. You may be born with certain antibodies. A baby gets them through its mother's milk.

■ A person gets an inherited disease through a single abnormal gene, an abnormal gene along with other conditions, or an abnormal chromosome.

Comprehension: Identifying Facts

On a separate sheet of paper, write the correct word or words from the Word Bank to complete each sentence.

WORD BANK		
antibodies	illness	pathogens
chemical	immune	physical
communicable	incubation	prevent
environment	mother's milk	resistance
genes	mucous	vaccination

1) An acquired disease is _____ when infection causes it.

2) Acquired diseases that are not communicable can result from a person's behaviors or _____.

3) Inherited diseases are only passed through the _____ from parents to child.

4) _____ are germs that cause communicable disease.

5) The first stage of infectious disease is _____.

6) The body's _____ system resists infections.

7) When _____ to infection is lowered, a person is more likely to become infected with a pathogen.

8) The body has _____ and chemical barriers to disease and infection.

9) The skin and _____ membranes are physical barriers to infection.

10) Saliva, tears, urine, and mucus are examples of _____ barriers to infection.

11) When a foreign substance enters the bloodstream, the immune system works by forming _____.

12) Antibodies to a pathogen can form during the course of an _____.

13) Antibodies that remain in the body after an illness _____ you from getting the disease again.

14) A _____ is a shot of weakened viruses into the body.

15) Babies are protected from certain disease because of antibodies in their _____.

Comprehension: Understanding Main Ideas

On a separate sheet of paper, write the answers to the following questions using complete sentences.

16) What are four causes of acquired diseases or infections?

17) What are three causes of inherited diseases?

18) What are two possible results when a person becomes ill with an infectious disease?

Critical Thinking: Write Your Opinion

19) What do you think you could do to protect yourself from getting a cold from another person?

20) Why do you think it is important to make sure you get vaccinations?

Test Taking Tip Be sure you understand what the test question is asking. Reread it if necessary.

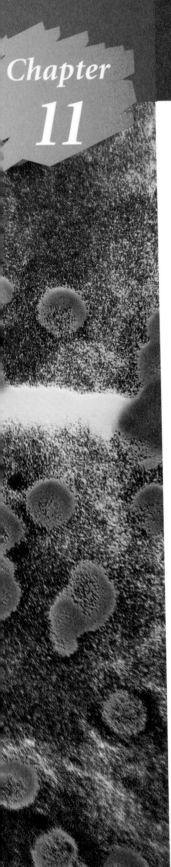

Magnified HIV Virus

Preventing AIDS and Sexually Transmitted Diseases

Communicable diseases that are passed through sexual contact can be very serious. A pregnant mother who is infected with a sexual disease can pass the disease to her baby. Some of these diseases can be cured or treated with medicine. While some of these diseases cannot be cured, all of them can be prevented.

In this chapter, you will learn what causes AIDS, how it is acquired, and its symptoms. You will learn about infections that result when the immune system is weakened. You will learn about symptoms, treatments, and prevention of four common communicable sexual diseases.

Goals for Learning

▶ To describe the causes of AIDS and how it is acquired

▶ To identify symptoms of AIDS and infections it causes

▶ To describe the symptoms and treatment of four common sexually transmitted diseases

▶ To identify help or resources for people with sexually transmitted diseases

▶ To explain how sexually transmitted diseases can be prevented

Acquired immunodeficiency syndrome (AIDS)
A disorder of the immune system

Human immunodeficiency virus (HIV)
The pathogen that causes AIDS

Opportunistic
Caused by a usually harmless germ that can infect a person whose immune system is greatly weakened

A very serious communicable disease is **acquired immunodeficiency syndrome (AIDS)**. AIDS is a disorder of the immune system. The first cases of AIDS in the United States were identified in 1981. Since then, the disease has spread at an alarming rate not only in the United States but throughout the world. Many people have died from it. Figure 11.1 shows the number of reported AIDS cases in the United States.

What Causes AIDS?

Human immunodeficiency virus (HIV) causes AIDS. HIV infects body cells and cripples the human immune system. As a result, the body becomes open to **opportunistic** pathogens. These are normally harmless pathogens that cause infection when a person's immune system is greatly weakened.

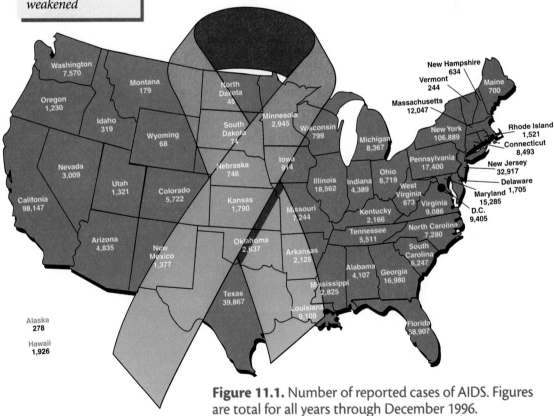

Figure 11.1. Number of reported cases of AIDS. Figures are total for all years through December 1996.

AIDS UPDATE

Scientists are searching for an AIDS cure. In 1984, about 3,450 people died from AIDS. The number of deaths increased each year until 1996. That year, 50,140 people thirteen years old and older died. Recently, new drugs and some cancer-fighting therapies have limited the virus in some people. In 1997, the number who died was down to 38,780. Because of research and greater health precautions, fewer people are dying of AIDS. Although AIDS has no cure yet, many people with AIDS are living longer with fewer painful symptoms.

How Is AIDS Acquired?

Like all illnesses caused by a virus, AIDS is a contagious disease. Therefore, it is important to know how this communicable disease is acquired. HIV is spread in these ways:

1. *Body fluids*—HIV is known to be transmitted through blood, semen, vaginal secretions, and breast milk of infected persons. It is spread through exchange of these fluids from one person to another. It has not been transmitted through fluids such as saliva, sweat, and urine.

2. *Sexual activity*—AIDS can be spread through sexual activity with an infected partner. Each new partner in turn can infect others.

3. *Sharing needles among drug users*—Any needle that is used for injection of a drug or medicine into the body has blood on it. Drug users who share needles risk getting HIV.

4. *Mother to child*—HIV can be passed from a mother to a baby before, during, or after birth. It can also be passed to a baby when the baby drinks its mother's breast milk.

A blood test often shows whether a person is infected with HIV or has AIDS. If people aren't aware that they are infected with HIV, they don't realize that they may get or already have AIDS.

How Is AIDS Not Acquired?

AIDS is a serious disease that cannot be cured. Because of this, some people have irrational fears about how it is acquired. These people are afraid to be around people with AIDS. It is important to know that AIDS is not acquired by casual social contact. This is because HIV cannot survive outside of the body. For that reason, merely touching, holding, or hugging a person with HIV or AIDS will not spread the disease. Contact such as shaking hands, hugging, kissing, crying, coughing, and sneezing does not spread AIDS.

Some other ways that AIDS is not spread are sharing cups, dishes, and other eating utensils. Bathing in the same pool or hot tub has not been shown to spread AIDS. No evidence shows that bites from sucking insects such as mosquitoes spread HIV.

Another student has tested positive for HIV. The counselors have said other students need not be concerned. Why do you think there is no reason to worry?

What Are the Symptoms of AIDS?

AIDS is an illness that can have a long incubation period. A person infected with HIV may not show outward signs of AIDS for six to ten years or longer. During that time, however, HIV is weakening the person's immune system.

Then and Now

A SMALLPOX VACCINE

In America, the smallpox disease had been deadly, especially among American Indians. In 1796, English doctor Edward Jenner discovered a way to prevent smallpox. He injected people with a vaccine made of dead smallpox virus. This helped the body fight the disease. Jenner called his treatment "vaccination." The first U.S. vaccinations came less than a year after Jenner's discovery. The first public vaccinations against smallpox were begun in Boston in 1802. Most children today are vaccinated before starting school.

Today, smallpox has been wiped out in the United States. Medical researchers also have developed other vaccines. These protect against diseases such as measles, mumps, and chickenpox. Researchers are working on a vaccine to combat HIV and AIDS.

When symptoms of AIDS appear, they are like symptoms of infection with HIV. Some of these symptoms are a feeling of weakness, chills and fever, night sweats, dry cough, and shortness of breath. Other symptoms are fatigue, stiff neck, headache, weight loss, skin rashes, diarrhea, and swollen lymph glands. A person may also have sores in the mouth. The entire body may be swelled with fluid.

Because HIV weakens the immune system, people who are infected with it also can have other serious diseases. These are caused by the opportunistic pathogens that the body cannot resist. For example, a person can have a certain kind of **pneumonia**. Pneumonia is a lung infection. Another serious disease can be **Kaposi's sarcoma**, a rare type of cancer. Still other serious problems can result from the attack of AIDS on the nervous system. The disease can also cause brain damage.

How Safe Is the Blood Supply?

AIDS can be acquired through infected blood. For this reason, it is important to know that the American blood supply is most always safe for **transfusions**. A transfusion is the transfer of blood from one individual to another.

In 1985, a test was developed to detect HIV in blood. Since that time, all blood given for transfusions is tested. Blood can be released for transfusions only when the test for HIV is negative. Sadly, some people who had blood transfusions before 1985 have been infected with HIV. These infections are now prevented because of the blood test.

People who need a transfusion can give their own blood. Then the blood is set aside until the person needs it.

Are Health Care Workers Safe From HIV?

Doctors, dentists, and other health care workers can be at risk for acquiring AIDS because they work with body fluids.

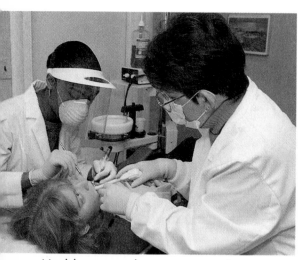

Health care workers use preventive measures such as wearing gloves and a mask to protect themselves and patients.

A hospice is a nontraditional setting for health care. It is a place where individuals with illnesses like AIDS can receive the care they need. The atmosphere in a hospice is home-like. People who receive hospice care are well enough to be safely cared for outside of a hospital. Hospice patients also may be people who no longer can be helped in a hospital.

Family, friends, and volunteers who have no formal medical training are often the people who provide hospice care. A hospice volunteer may help by feeding or dressing a patient or by talking and reading to the person.

These people may care for patients infected with HIV. They may not always know if a person has HIV. Small cuts on the skin can provide a pathway for HIV to enter a health care worker's bloodstream.

Health care workers protect themselves through preventive measures such as wearing gloves and masks when working with body fluids. They treat every patient as though he or she may carry HIV or other pathogens.

What Is the Future for People With AIDS?

At this time, AIDS is a disease with no vaccine and no cure. Some treatments increase the quality and length of life for people with AIDS. Eventually, however, all people with AIDS will die of the disease unless a cure is found. Scientists are researching many possible cures, but it may be years before they find one that works. For now, prevention is the only choice. AIDS can be prevented by avoiding contact with HIV-infected blood or other body fluids. Abstinence from sexual activity is one way to avoid this contact.

Evidence shows that people in the United States have taken preventive measures against the spread of AIDS. In 1996, the number of reported cases of AIDS fell for the first time in the history of the disease.

LESSON 1 REVIEW Write the answers to these questions on a separate sheet of paper, using complete sentences.

1) What causes AIDS?

2) What are four ways that AIDS is acquired?

3) Why is AIDS not acquired by casual social contact?

4) What are two opportunistic diseases that a person with AIDS can get?

5) How can AIDS be prevented?

Sexually Transmitted Diseases

Antibiotic
A substance that can destroy the growth of certain germs

Chlamydia
A sexually transmitted disease

Genital herpes
A sexually transmitted chronic infection

Gonorrhea
A sexually transmitted disease

Sexually transmitted disease
Any disease that is spread through sexual activity

Syphilis
A sexually transmitted infectious disease

*I*n theUnited States, one in four people under age 21 have had a **sexually transmitted disease**. Any disease that is spread through sexual activity is a sexually transmitted disease. For example, AIDS is a sexually transmitted disease because it can be spread through sexual activity. These diseases can be serious because they cause other diseases if they aren't treated. Besides AIDS, some sexually transmitted diseases are **gonorrhea**, **chlamydia**, **syphilis**, and **genital herpes**.

What Is Gonorrhea?

Gonorrhea is a sexually transmitted disease. One quarter of the people who have this infectious disease are between 10 and 19 years of age. It can also be transmitted to babies as they pass through the birth canal of an infected mother. Gonorrhea can cause an eye infection in babies that can lead to blindness.

In males, symptoms are a white discharge from the urethra and burning while urinating. From 20 to 40 percent of males, however, have no symptoms and don't know they are infected. Females may have a discharge from the vagina and some swelling and redness in the genital area. Most females, however, also have no symptoms and don't know they are infected. The gonorrhea bacteria can also infect the rectum and throat.

Fortunately, gonorrhea can be treated successfully with a shot or pill of the **antibiotic** penicillin. An antibiotic is a substance that can destroy the growth of certain germs. If a person thinks he or she may have been infected, many clinics can quickly diagnose and treat gonorrhea. All newborn babies are treated with a special eye medicine immediately after birth to prevent the eye infection.

If gonorrhea is not treated in males, it can lead to sterility, which is the inability to produce a child. If it is not treated in females, it can spread throughout the reproductive system. Untreated gonorrhea and other sexually transmitted diseases can cause an advanced infection that can lead to sterility in females.

Gonorrhea can also spread to the bloodstream. Once in the bloodstream, the bacteria can infect other parts of the body. This can lead to heart valve problems and other diseases. For example, gonorrhea in the joints can cause arthritis, a painful inflammation.

Chancre
A painless, hard sore that is the first sign of syphilis

Gonorrhea is an important public health concern. Because many people don't have symptoms, they do not know they are infected and can spread the disease.

What Is Chlamydia?

The symptoms of chlamydia, another sexually transmitted disease, are similar to those for gonorrhea. For some females, symptoms may be a discharge from the vagina and pelvic pain. Usually, however, females have no symptoms. Males may have a discharge from the urethra and pain when they urinate.

Like gonorrhea, chlamydia can infect a baby as it passes through the birth canal. It can cause an eye infection that results in blindness.

Chlamydia can be treated with an antibiotic.

What Is Syphilis?

Syphilis is a sexually transmitted disease that progresses in three stages if left untreated. The first stage of syphilis is a **chancre**, a painless, hard sore with a small amount of yellow discharge. The chancre is usually on the penis, anus, or rectum in men. It appears on the cervix and genital areas in women. It can also appear on the lips, tongue, tonsils, fingers, and mucous membranes. In this stage, the lymph glands may be swollen but not painful.

Health Tip

Avoiding sexual contact is the best way to prevent a sexually transmitted disease.

Part of staying healthy is avoiding contact with pathogens that cause diseases, including sexually transmitted diseases.

The second stage of syphilis appears six to eight weeks later, often as a rash that doesn't itch. A person has a vague feeling of discomfort, headache, aching bones, loss of appetite, and other symptoms.

During the third stage of syphilis, the symptoms disappear for many years. In 40 percent of people with the disease, it progresses and affects the heart and brain.

Most people with syphilis become infected by sexual contact. Syphilis can also be passed from mother to baby through the placenta.

Many states require people to have a blood test for syphilis before issuing them a marriage license. The test identifies individuals with the disease so that they can be treated with penicillin or another antibiotic. Treatment also prevents the spread of infection to babies at birth.

What Is Genital Herpes?

Genital herpes is a **chronic**, or lasting, infection. The main symptom of genital herpes is clusters of painful small blisters in the genital area. The blisters break, heal, and come back.

Health Tip

Reserve sexual activity for marriage.

Herpes is spread by contact with the broken blisters. Avoiding contact with the pathogen that causes herpes can prevent this communicable disease.

Genital herpes can cause other problems. Sometimes the repeated infections in females involve the cervix, which may lead to cancer of the cervix. Genital herpes can infect a baby passing through the birth canal, and can cause brain damage in the baby.

The disease has no cure. A pill controls the symptoms. It speeds up healing but doesn't get rid of the infection. Over time, the infections tend to be less severe, but genital herpes never goes away.

What Help Is Available?

Except for genital herpes and AIDS, most sexually transmitted diseases are easily cured when they are detected early. For diseases without a cure, medical treatment may make people more comfortable.

Many clinics concentrate on diagnosing and treating individuals and their partners who suspect they have a sexually transmitted disease. The staff at these clinics know that the possibility of having a sexually transmitted disease can be difficult and embarrassing. They appreciate a person's strength and good judgment in seeking medical advice. They protect the identity of their patients.

Action for Health

PRACTICE SAYING "NO"

When you communicate effectively, people around you have a clear understanding of what you mean. When you decide to abstain from something, you need to express that decision in a way others clearly understand. Make a list of different ways you can communicate a "no" answer.

How Are Sexually Transmitted Diseases Prevented?

There are no vaccines for sexually transmitted diseases, and the body doesn't build up immunity to them. Like all communicable diseases, they can be prevented by avoiding contact with the pathogens that cause them. Therefore, the best prevention for sexually transmitted diseases is choosing abstinence from sexual activity.

LESSON 2 REVIEW On a separate sheet of paper, write the word from the Word Bank that matches each description.

<table>
<tr><td>

WORD BANK

abstinence

chronic

gonorrhea

sterility

syphilis

</td><td>

1) Gonorrhea can lead to _____.

2) The symptoms for chlamydia are similar to the symptoms for _____.

3) The first stage of _____ is a chancre, a painless, hard sore.

4) Genital herpes is _____, meaning it is lasting and never goes away.

5) The best way to prevent sexually transmitted diseases is _____.

</td></tr>
</table>

Careers

LABORATORY ASSISTANT

Would you like to help detect diseases? Then you might choose to become a laboratory assistant. Laboratory assistants work with medical technicians. Assistants look for disease-producing organisms in specimens of human urine, blood, and saliva. They report all organisms that are not normal. Laboratory assistants usually work in hospitals, clinics, and doctors' offices. In addition to working with specimens, they help to maintain equipment. If anything is not working correctly, they report the problem to their supervisor. They also must keep themselves safe. This involves wearing rubber gloves or disposing of needles safely. Some one-year programs are available, but a two-year or associate's degree is usually needed.

CHAPTER SUMMARY

■ Acquired immunodeficiency syndrome (AIDS) is a contagious disorder of the immune system caused by human immunodeficiency virus (HIV). HIV weakens the immune system, leaving it open to other opportunistic infections.

■ AIDS is spread through contact with certain body fluids, through sexual activity, by drug users sharing needles, and from mother to child.

■ AIDS is not spread through casual social contact.

■ First symptoms of AIDS reflect symptoms of infection with HIV. As the disease progresses, more serious diseases such as pneumonia and Kaposi's sarcoma can follow.

■ The blood supply in the United States is safe because of a test for HIV. The test is used on all blood that is given for transfusions.

■ Health care workers who are around body fluids and needles use preventive measures to protect themselves and patients.

■ No cure is now available for AIDS. It can be prevented by avoiding contact with body fluids that may be infected with HIV.

■ Any disease spread through sexual contact is a sexually transmitted disease.

■ Gonorrhea has almost no symptoms in males or females. Penicillin cures it, but untreated gonorrhea can lead to sterility.

■ Chlamydia has symptoms similar to gonorrhea. It can be treated with antibiotics.

■ Syphilis can progress in three stages if it is not treated. A chancre is the first stage of syphilis. Penicillin is used to treat syphilis.

■ Genital herpes is chronic and has no cure.

■ An infected mother can pass AIDS or any of the other four sexual diseases to her baby.

■ People with sexually transmitted diseases can get treatment at clinics that protect their identity.

■ All sexually transmitted diseases can be prevented by avoiding contact with the pathogen.

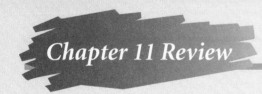

Chapter 11 Review

Comprehension: Identifying Facts

On a separate sheet of paper, write the correct word or words from the Word Bank to complete each sentence.

WORD BANK		
abstinence	Kaposi's sarcoma	social contact
chlamydia	opportunistic	sterility
chronic	penicillin	symptoms
immune	sexually transmitted	syphilis
incubation		virus

1) AIDS is a disorder of the _____ system.

2) The cause of AIDS is human immunodeficiency _____, or HIV.

3) When a person's immune system is weakened, it is open to _____ pathogens.

4) AIDS has an _____ period that can last six to ten years.

5) AIDS is not acquired through casual _____.

6) Weakness, chills and fever, dry cough, and weight loss are some _____ of AIDS.

7) Two opportunistic infections that can appear as AIDS progress are pneumonia and _____.

8) One in four people under age 21 in the United States have had a _____ disease.

9) Untreated gonorrhea can lead to _____, or the inability to have children.

10) Gonorrhea and syphilis can both be treated with _____.

11) _____ progresses in three stages.

12) Females with _____ have almost no symptoms.

13) Genital herpes is a _____ infection because it never goes away.

14) The best prevention for sexually transmitted diseases is _____ from sexual activity.

Comprehension: Understanding Main Ideas

On a separate sheet of paper, write the answers to the following questions using complete sentences.

15) What are the four main ways that AIDS is spread?

16) Why is the blood supply in the United States safe for transfusions?

17) What is the first symptom of syphilis?

18) How are the symptoms of gonorrhea and chlamydia similar?

Critical Thinking: Write Your Opinion

19) How do you think you could show caring and concern for a person infected with AIDS?

20) Besides the other diseases they can cause, why do you think sexually transmitted diseases are so dangerous?

Test Taking Tip   If you don't know the answer to a question, put a check beside it and go on. Then when you are finished, go back to any checked questions and try to answer them.

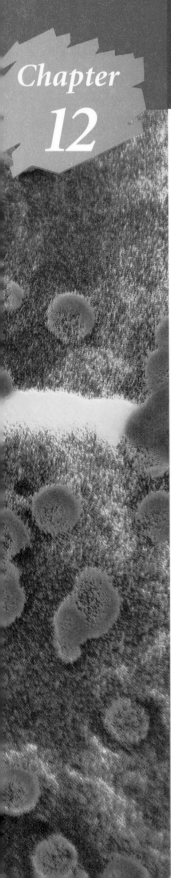

Magnified HIV Virus

Chapter

12

Common Diseases

When your body is in good health, you could compare it to a band. Each system is like an instrument that plays a certain part. Each system contributes to the harmony that the band as a whole produces. Occasionally, however, a body system hits a "bad note." When a body system is affected with a disease, the body's harmony is disrupted. These diseases can affect the body's overall health.

In this chapter, you will learn about heart and blood vessel diseases and their risk factors. You will learn what causes cancer, its warning signs, its risk factors, and how it is treated. Finally you will learn about diabetes, arthritis, epilepsy, and asthma and how they are treated.

Goals for Learning

▶ To describe some cardiovascular diseases and their risk factors

▶ To explain the causes, symptoms, warning signs, risk factors, and treatments of cancer

▶ To explain the types of diabetes and its treatment

▶ To describe arthritis, epilepsy, and asthma and their treatments

Cardiovascular Diseases and Problems

Cardiovascular
Relating to the heart and blood vessels

Hypertension
High blood pressure

Cardiovascular disease is a group of disorders that affects the heart and blood vessels. It is the leading cause of death in the United States. Appendix C lists some figures on deaths from cardiovascular disease. Some common cardiovascular diseases are high blood pressure and arterial diseases. Fortunately, many technologic advances have improved the treatment of cardiovascular diseases and problems. Preventive measures such as low-fat, low-sodium diets, exercise, and not smoking have reduced these diseases and problems.

What Is High Blood Pressure?

Blood pressure is the force of blood against the walls of the arteries when the heart pumps. Blood pressure normally goes up during exercise and goes down during sleep or relaxation. When a person's blood pressure regularly remains above 140/90, that person has **hypertension**, or high blood pressure.

Artery walls thicken in response to higher blood pressure. Hypertension, therefore, contributes to heart disease by causing the heart to pump harder than normal against increased pressure in the arteries. If hypertension is not treated, it leads to other kinds of cardiovascular disease.

The exact cause of most hypertension is unknown. It can affect both adults and children. For adults, some contributing factors may be stress, tobacco use, and a high-salt or high-fat diet. Heredity is another contributing factor. For example, if one of your parents has high blood pressure, you could have it, too. For children, the cause of hypertension is usually different. It might be a kidney disease or abnormality of the blood vessels present from birth.

Most people do not know they have hypertension. Its symptoms are not obvious. The only way to find out if you have hypertension is to have your blood pressure measured. A doctor can tell you if you have hypertension and how to control it.

Arteriosclerosis
A chronic disease in which arterial walls thicken, harden, and lose flexibility, resulting in impaired blood circulation

Atherosclerosis
A form of arteriosclerosis in which large- and medium-sized arteries become narrow from a buildup of fat along their walls

Research shows many children already have atherosclerosis. Why do you think that is so?

High blood pressure cannot be cured. Usually, however, it can be controlled with medicine and diet. The medicines help to lower blood pressure. A diet that is low in salt, sugar, cholesterol, and saturated fats can also help control blood pressure. Regular exercise also helps to lower blood pressure.

What Are Some Diseases of the Arteries?

When a person is born, the lining of the arteries is smooth. Over many years, fat can build up along the lining of the arteries. Usually this results from a person's dietary choices or from heredity. Eventually this fat buildup can harden like cement. This process is called **arteriosclerosis**, or hardening of the arteries. It is a chronic disease in which the arterial walls thicken and lose their flexibility. This results in impaired blood circulation.

Arteriosclerosis can result in many other diseases, including a condition called **atherosclerosis**. In atherosclerosis, large- and medium-sized arteries become narrow from a buildup of fat along their walls. Figure 12.1 shows this buildup. These narrowed arteries slow the flow of blood to the heart. The blood then thickens. This may result in a blood clot. The fat deposits or a clot can block a blood vessel. If this happens, the heart doesn't get enough oxygen and a heart attack can result. Often this buildup can be prevented with diet.

What Is a Heart Attack?

Like every muscle in the body, the heart muscle requires nutrients and oxygen. A heart attack occurs when the supply of blood and nutrients to the heart is severely reduced or stopped. If the blood supply is cut off for a critical amount of time, the muscle tissues are injured and die. How serious a heart attack is depends on how much tissue dies.

If a heart attack is mild, the heart can still function. Other arteries will do the work that the blocked arteries did. Scar tissue may form where the damage occurred. This tissue is not flexible and does not contract when the heart contracts. That means the heart may never function at its highest capacity again.

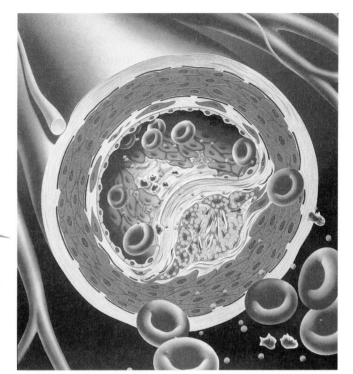

Figure 12.1. Cross section of an artery showing fat buildup and blockage

Nutrition Tip

Watch your salt—you only need 2,400 milligrams of sodium each day.

Angina pectoris
Severe pain associated with an inadequate supply of blood to the heart

Fortunately, new technology helps in treating people who've had a heart attack. For example, machines can monitor the sounds and electrical activity of the heart. Equipment can determine the amount of disease or damage to the heart. Operations can open or bypass blocked arteries. Doctors sometimes replace a diseased heart with the healthy heart of a person who has died. Sometimes artificial heart valves replace diseased valves or implanted devices regulate the heart.

In addition to these technological treatments, many medicines help people who've had a heart attack. Changes in diet, exercise, and smoking are critical to the success of both treatments.

What Is Angina Pectoris?

People with atherosclerosis may have a condition called **angina pectoris**, or angina for short. Angina is a severe pain that results from an inadequate supply of oxygen-rich blood to the heart. Often angina occurs before a heart attack.

A person can have angina pain without actually having a heart attack. The pains, however, can seem like those of a heart attack. A person with angina can take medicine to relieve the pain when it starts. The pain is also relieved with rest and relaxation. People with angina may need to reduce their activity at times or have an operation to improve circulation.

What Is a Stroke?

A **stroke** occurs when the blood supply to the brain is suddenly stopped. Arterial disease or a clot that blocks an artery because of atherosclerosis can stop the supply. Because high blood pressure leads to atherosclerosis, hypertension may be an underlying cause of stroke.

When the blood supply to the brain is stopped, some brain cells cannot function. If these cells cannot get the blood and nutrients they need, they die. After a stroke, the part of the body that the dead brain cells controlled loses its ability to function. For example, if the part of the brain that controls speech is affected, a person may not be able to speak. A stroke affects every individual differently, depending on the part of the brain that is injured. Some people notice little difference, while others may never be able to function well again. It can take a person years to learn ways to make up for the damage that a stroke has done.

Careers

OCCUPATIONAL THERAPY ASSISTANT

Occupational therapy assistants help people with mental, physical, developmental, or emotional problems. These problems may make independent living or everyday tasks difficult. Assistants work with occupational therapists to help patients learn or relearn how to dress, cook, eat, or clean. They may teach work skills or how to interview for a job. They help patients to cope with stress. They must watch how well patients do with therapy. If patients have more problems at home or at work, occupational therapy assistants may suggest therapy changes. Some one-year training programs are available, but a two-year or associate's degree is usually required.

Some new medicines can help to decrease or eliminate the effects of a stroke if a person gets them within six hours.

What Are Some Cardiovascular Risk Factors?

A risk factor is a habit or trait that is known to increase a person's risk of having a disease. Serious diseases, such as cardiovascular disease, have many risk factors. Some risk factors cannot be changed. Risk factors for cardiovascular problems that usually cannot be changed are:

■ *Family medical history*—A person may inherit a tendency to cardiovascular disease. You cannot change your genetic makeup. Knowing your family's medical history, however, can help you and your doctor evaluate your risk.

■ *Being male*—Men have a greater risk of heart attacks before middle age than women do. After middle age, women's risk increases.

■ *Aging*—With increasing age, everyone's risk of heart attack increases. More than half of all heart attacks occur in people who are age 65 or older.

■ *Race*—Some races have a high risk of cardiovascular disease. For example, African Americans have an unusually high rate of hypertension.

How Can Cardiovascular Problems Be Prevented?

The following risk factors can be changed to reduce the chances of having cardiovascular problems:

■ *Smoking*—A person can lower the risk for cardiovascular problems by choosing not to smoke. Smoking can lead to hypertension and other cardiovascular diseases. A smoker is twice as likely to have a heart attack, and even to die from it, as a nonsmoker is. When people quit smoking, their risk of cardiovascular disease rapidly decreases.

■ *Cholesterol*—High blood cholesterol is another major risk factor for cardiovascular problems. Keeping intake of saturated fats low helps lower blood cholesterol levels. That means eating small amounts of animal fat, such as eggs, butter, and meat.

Fitness Tip

Exercise regularly, especially if cardiovascular disease runs in your family.

Eating healthy foods that are low in saturated fat and sodium helps to prevent cardiovascular problems.

■ **Being overweight**—Excess weight strains the heart and contributes to cardiovascular problems. Also, it can increase blood cholesterol levels and blood pressure. Planning a balanced diet helps to maintain a safe body weight.

■ **Physical inactivity**—Being inactive can limit the ability to withstand a sudden change in blood pressure. Physical activity helps a person to withstand these changes. For example, aerobic activities such as walking, running, swimming, or bicycling for just 20 minutes daily can help. These activities help to increase blood flow to the heart and strengthen it. Physical activity can also reduce mental stress, which may contribute to cardiovascular problems.

LESSON 1 REVIEW Write the answers to these questions on a separate sheet of paper, using complete sentences.

1) When does a person have high blood pressure?

2) What are two diseases of the arteries?

3) When does a heart attack occur?

4) What happens when brains cells die as a result of stroke?

5) What are two risk factors for cardiovascular disease that can be changed?

Cancer

Cancer is the second leading cause of death in the United States. For that reason, it can seem frightening to many people. Knowing about the causes and risk factors for cancer can help reduce fears about it.

Benign
Not harmful to health

Malignant
Harmful to health

Tumor
A mass of tissue formed from the abnormal growth of cells

What Causes Cancer?

An abnormal and harmful growth of cells in the body causes cancer. There are more than 100 different types of cancers. Some cancers are more harmful than others.

Cancer cells grow in the body in a more disorderly and uncontrolled way than normal cells do. Cancer may invade normal tissues and spread to other parts of the body. When cancer invades normal tissues, those organs cannot function properly. Sometimes the abnormal growth of cells forms a mass of tissue called a **tumor**.

If the growth of cells is uncontrolled, the tumor is called **malignant**. That means it is harmful to health. The more cancer invades normal tissues and spreads to other organs, the more harmful a cancer is. Some tumors are not malignant. They do not spread, and are not harmful to health. These are called **benign** tumors. More than 90% of tumors are benign. For example, some tumors in the breast are benign. They are actually collections of cells filled with fluid that are not cancerous and are usually harmless.

Where Does Cancer Develop?

Cancer can develop in any tissue of the body, but it tends to occur in some areas more than others. Table C.4 in Appendix C shows the most common places for cancer in men and in women.

Once a person has cancer, the disease can spread to other parts of the body. It can spread to places in the body far from the original tumor. Cells from a malignant tumor can break away and get into the lymphatic system and the bloodstream.

These loose cancer cells reach other sites in the body where they can grow without control into other tumors. Some cancers do not travel through the bloodstream. They spread by attaching to nearby organs and invading those organs.

What Are the Symptoms of Cancer?

The symptoms of cancer depend on where the disease is located in the body. For example, someone with lung cancer may have a cough that doesn't improve with treatment. Or, a woman with breast cancer may feel a lump in her breast. If the cancer has spread to her bones, a woman with breast cancer may have back pain.

If cancer has moved into the blood, it may cause unusual bleeding. When cancer involves the blood and lymph tissues, immune system deficiencies can lead to other infections.

Some symptoms for a particular cancer are not specific. Instead, a person may not feel well but not have specific symptoms. Unusual weight loss and a poor appetite may occur as a result of cancer.

Sometimes changes in skin and body functions are warning signs of cancer. For example, blood in the feces may be a sign of cancer in the intestines. If that cancer grows, it may cause a change in bowel habits.

THE SEVEN WARNING SIGNS OF CANCER

C hange in bowel or bladder habits

A sore that will not heal

U nusual bleeding or discharge

T hickening or lump in the breast or elsewhere

I ndigestion or difficulty in swallowing

O bvious change in a wart or mole

N agging cough or hoarseness

What Are the Warning Signs of Cancer?

Usually cancer has some warning signs that help to detect the disease early. These seven early warnings may signal the presence of cancer. They are listed in the box.

Early detection is the most important factor for long-term survival. People who talk with a doctor about these warning signs are more likely to be cured.

How Is Cancer Treated?

Now more than ever before scientists are finding cures for cancer. For example, **Hodgkin's disease** is a cancer of the lymph glands that often affects adolescents and young adults. With treatment, up to 90 percent of Hodgkin's disease can be cured.

There are as many treatments for cancer are there are types of cancers. Usually one or more of three treatments is used to treat cancer. One common treatment for many forms of cancers involves taking drugs that destroy the cancer cells. This form of treatment is called **chemotherapy**. Each kind of cancer may require a different kind of drug.

A second kind of treatment for cancer is surgery, or an operation, to remove the abnormal growth of cells. The third kind of treatment for cancer is **radiation**, or the transmission of energy in the form of waves. Radiation destroys cancerous tissue.

Often the treatments for cancer produce side effects that make people very sick. For example, a person receiving chemotherapy may lose his or her appetite and experience an upset stomach. Even so, these treatments allow people with cancer to live longer with the disease than they would without treatment. Many people survive cancer because of treatment.

What Are the Risk Factors for Cancer?

Just as with cardiovascular disease, there are some major risk factors that may cause cancer. If you know what the risk factors are, you can avoid some of them.

A health care plan decides to charge double for treating smoking-related illnesses. How might this influence whether plan members continue to smoke?

- **Cigarette smoke**—Substances or agents that cause cancer are called **carcinogens**. The carcinogens that cause the greatest number of deaths in America are those found in cigarette smoke. In fact, it contains forty-three known carcinogens. As a result, smokers have a much higher risk for cancer than nonsmokers do.

- **Toxic chemicals**—**Toxic** chemicals are substances that are harmful to human health or to the environment. Many chemicals used in industry, on farms, and in the home have been found to be carcinogenic.

■ *Radiation*—While radiation is used to treat cancer, too much radiation can cause it. It is important to have only the X rays you need.

■ *Sunlight*—Sunlight is a source of natural radiation that can cause skin cancer. For example, people who sunbathe or use tanning booths expose themselves to harmful radiation. That gives them a high risk for **malignant melanoma**, the most common form of skin cancer. See Appendix C.

■ *Heredity*—The same genes that control heredity control the reproduction and day-to-day function of cells. A strong hereditary tendency toward cancer may run in many families. For example, daughters of women who have breast cancer have a higher risk of getting breast cancer.

■ *Viruses*—Viruses can cause cancer in almost every living creature. A virus can insert its genes into human chromosomes. This causes a **mutation**, or change, that leads to cancer. No cancer caused by a virus, however, can be spread from person to person. Also, not everyone is open to cancers caused by viruses. People who have a weakened immune system from AIDS, which is caused by HIV, are more open to cancer.

How Can You Avoid the Risk Factors for Cancer?

You can prevent many forms of cancer by avoiding the agents and behaviors that are known to cause it. For example, you can avoid cigarette smoke and exposing yourself to the sun without protection. Applying sunblock lotions before you go outdoors can help protect your skin. Protective clothing such as long-sleeved shirts, wide-brimmed hats, and sunglasses also offer protection. You should try to avoid toxic chemicals and exposure to X rays. If you have an inherited tendency to certain kinds of cancer, you should see your doctor regularly.

Smoking cigarettes is a risk factor for cancer.

LESSON 2 REVIEW Write the answers to these questions on a separate sheet of paper, using complete sentences.

1) What causes cancer?

2) What do the symptoms of cancer depend on?

3) What are three of the seven warning signs of cancer?

4) What are the three treatments for cancer?

5) How can cancer be prevented?

Action for Health

SELF-EXAMINATIONS

You can learn to examine yourself for changes that may be early warning signs of cancer.

For Females: Doing a Self-Exam of the Breasts

Females with mature breasts should learn to do a self-examination regularly after each menstrual period. The three ways to examine breasts are before a mirror, in the shower, or lying down.

Stand before a mirror and look at your breasts for any unusual shapes, depressions, or lumps. Look for unusual changes.

In the shower or lying down, use the left hand to examine the right breast and the right hand to examine the left breast. Use the pads of your first three fingers. Examine each breast in a widening circle around the nipple until you cover the entire breast. Also, check the nipple, beneath the nipple, and the area between the armpit and the breast.

For Males: Doing a Self-Exam of the Testes

Cancer of the testes is one of the most common cancers in males between the ages of 20 and 35. Most testicular cancers are first discovered during self-examination. Self-examination of the testicles should be done once a month. The best time for males to do self-examination of the testes is immediately after a bath or shower. A male can gently roll each testicle between the thumb and fingers, noting any abnormal lumps.

Diabetes

Diabetes is usually a chronic disease that results from too little insulin, or from the body's inability to use insulin. Insulin is a hormone produced in the pancreas. Insulin is important for growth because it is essential for the storage and release of energy.

The digestive system breaks carbohydrates down into glucose. With the help of insulin, the body's cells use glucose for the energy they need. Without insulin, body cells cannot use glucose. Then the sugar that a person eats stays in the bloodstream.

As diabetes progresses, it produces changes in the blood vessels. Because of these changes, people with diabetes may lose their vision. The disease can damage their kidneys and cause cardiovascular disease, stroke, or decreased circulation in their hands and feet.

The two most common types of diabetes are type I and type II.

What Is Type I Diabetes?

Type I diabetes, or **insulin-dependent diabetes**, causes a person to depend on insulin for survival. This kind of diabetes usually starts in childhood. It may cause extreme abnormalities in the body's ability to use glucose. This problem results in high levels of glucose in the blood. When a person's high blood glucose level is not controlled, it can lead to a **diabetic coma**. When this happens, the person loses consciousness and must be treated at once.

Type I diabetes seems to result from a defect in the immune system. The body's immune system destroys the cells of the pancreas that produce insulin. Besides frequent urination and extreme thirst, symptoms of type I diabetes are rapid weight loss, fatigue, and extreme hunger.

What Is Type II Diabetes?

Type II diabetes, or **non-insulin–dependent diabetes**, usually occurs in adulthood after age 40. This is the most common type of diabetes. In type II diabetes, the pancreas produces insulin, but the body cells cannot use it effectively. Type II diabetes is milder than type I diabetes is. Type II diabetes has been linked to heredity, inactivity, and obesity.

Often people with type II diabetes don't know their blood glucose level is higher than normal. Their symptoms may be blurry vision, slow-healing sores, sleepiness, and tingling in the hands or feet.

How Do You Know if You Have Diabetes?

There are two ways to check for diabetes. During a regular medical checkup, your doctor can test your blood for glucose. If someone's blood glucose level is high, the person may have diabetes. Your doctor can also check for glucose in your urine to determine if you have diabetes. Normally, urine has no glucose in it.

Non-insulin–dependent diabetes
Diabetes that usually does not cause a person to depend on insulin; type II diabetes

If you know someone with diabetes, how has the person's life been affected by it?

DIABETES

Diabetes is a disease in which a person's body does not produce enough insulin. As a result, the blood carries an unsafe amount of sugar. Infections and poor blood flow once were common side effects. Until the early 1900s, most people with diabetes did not live long.

In 1921, Canadian doctor Frederick Banting began to research diabetes. The following year, he perfected an insulin injection for diabetes patients. Since then, millions of people with diabetes have been able to live longer by using insulin. Today, researchers are working on a pill that will stimulate the pancreas to make insulin. Perhaps in the future, insulin injections may not be needed.

People with diabetes can lead otherwise normal lives.

What Is the Treatment for Diabetes?

Many people with diabetes are treated with insulin. They learn to measure the proper amount and give themselves a shot of insulin.

Some people with diabetes do not need to take insulin. A simple change in the foods they eat may keep their blood glucose at a safe level. For people who are overweight, weight loss and exercise may return their blood glucose to a normal level.

An important part of treatment for people with diabetes is learning which foods are safe to eat. Sugary foods such as candy and soda can cause dangerously high levels of glucose in a person's blood. People with diabetes also must eat regularly, especially after taking insulin. They may need to eat nutritious snacks throughout the day. Insulin causes the blood sugar level to decrease. When a person has an empty stomach, a shot of insulin could cause dangerously low levels of glucose. Sugar found in orange juice or hard candy quickly restores the person's blood glucose level.

LESSON 3 REVIEW On a separate sheet of paper, write the word from the Word Bank that matches each description.

1) Diabetes results from too little _____, or the body's inability to use it.

2) _____ diabetes causes a person to be dependent on insulin.

3) A _____ is a life-threatening state resulting from inadequate control of blood glucose levels.

4) Type II, or non-insulin–dependent, diabetes usually occurs in _____.

5) A doctor can test the blood or _____ for glucose.

WORD BANK
adulthood
diabetic coma
insulin
type I
urine

Arthritis, Epilepsy, and Asthma

Arthritis
A group of diseases that result in swelling of the joints and rubbing on the bones

Cartilage
A cushion in the joints

Osteoarthritis
A condition in which the cartilage in joints wears away

Rheumatoid arthritis
A destructive inflammation of the joints

You have read about diabetes, which is a chronic disease. Most chronic diseases have no cure. With medical care, however, a chronic disease can be controlled. This lesson describes three common chronic diseases.

What Is Arthritis and How Is It Treated?

Arthritis is a group of very painful diseases that result in swelling of the joints and rubbing on the bones. Sometimes a person loses the function in the joints that are affected with arthritis. There are two main types of arthritis, which together affect about forty million Americans.

The first and most serious type of arthritis is **rheumatoid arthritis**. It is a destructive inflammation of the joints. In rheumatoid arthritis, the joints become stiff, swollen, and tender. A person with this disease may not be able to move the joints and may feel weak and tired. Rheumatoid arthritis can involve other tissues throughout the body and may result in deformity. Usually, the treatment for rheumatoid arthritis includes drugs to relieve the inflammation and pain.

The second and most common type of arthritis is **osteoarthritis**. In this kind of arthritis, the cartilage in the joints usually wears away. When **cartilage**, a cushion in the joints, wears away, the bones rub on one another. This wear and tear can change the structure and shape of a person's joints, making them ache and feel sore. It can also cause loss of movement. The same drugs that have been used to treat rheumatoid arthritis have been used for osteoarthritis. New studies, however, show that these drugs may hinder the body's natural process of fighting osteoarthritis.

When arthritis severely damages the joints, a person may be able to have a joint replacement. This is an operation to replace the worn-out joint with an artificial joint. Artificial joints works just like the body's own joints.

Writing About Health

Make a list of the things you have learned in this chapter that might change the way you interact with someone with a chronic disease. What would you do now that you might not have done before?

What Is Epilepsy and How Is It Treated?

Epilepsy is a chronic disease affecting 2.5 million Americans that is caused by disordered brain activity. Epilepsy is characterized by **seizures**, which are a physical reaction to the disordered brain activity. There are two main kinds of epileptic seizures.

The most common kind of seizure is a **grand mal** seizure. A person having a grand mal seizure usually loses consciousness and falls down. The person's muscles stiffen, and the body shakes uncontrollably. During a grand mal seizure, a person may lose control of body functions. A seizure lasts about 2 to 5 minutes. Afterward, a person may act strangely or be sleepy for a while. Often the person does not remember the seizure.

The other kind of seizure is a **petit mal** seizure. A person having a petit mal seizure does not lose consciousness but may simply stare for a moment. The person might drop an object he or she is holding or act confused. A petit mal seizure lasts less than 30 seconds, and others may not notice anything different. Only a person's thought processes are affected during a petit mal seizure.

Not all seizures are the result of epilepsy. In fact, a person is said to have epilepsy only after he or she has had two seizures of unknown cause. While seizures may have many other causes, most seizures have no known cause.

Epilepsy is usually treated with a medicine that controls the seizures. For many years, epilepsy was misunderstood. People who had epilepsy were avoided. When a person with epilepsy has proper medical care and takes the medicine as directed, the seizures can be controlled. In all other ways, a person with epilepsy can live a normal, active life.

Epilepsy
A chronic disease caused by disordered brain activity and characterized by seizures

Grand mal
An epileptic seizure in which a person loses consciousness

Petit mal
An epileptic seizure in which a person does not lose consciousness

Seizure
A physical reaction to the disordered brain activity that causes epilepsy

---

If someone is having a seizure:

- **Move nearby objects to protect the person**
- **Loosen clothing**
- **Place a cushion under the head**
- **Turn the head to the side**
- **Do not put an object in the mouth**
- **Call for help if the seizure lasts more than a few minutes**

Most people with chronic diseases lead normal lives with proper treatment.

What Is Asthma and How Is It Treated?

Asthma
A respiratory disease that causes breathing difficulty

Asthma is a respiratory disease that causes difficulty in breathing. Many things trigger asthma. Often it results from an allergy to mold, pollen (a powdery material from plants), animal fur, or dust. Asthma affects some people during certain seasons of the year more than other seasons. Strong emotional responses may also trigger asthma.

During an attack of asthma, a person may cough, wheeze, and be short of breath. The linings of the bronchioles may produce a great deal of mucus. Then the bronchioles contract, and the person has difficulty breathing. The fear of not being able to breathe can cause emotional stress. A person may have an attack of asthma once every few hours to only once every few years.

A person can get asthma at any age, but it often affects children. About 12.4 million Americans have asthma, and 4.8 million of those are under age 18. The number of people generally who have asthma is increasing.

Without treatment, asthma can be life threatening. Many different medicines are used to treat asthma. Usually a person breathes the asthma medicine directly into the air passages.

The medicine can quickly relieve the person's breathing difficulty. Sometimes stronger drugs are needed.

LESSON 4 REVIEW On a separate sheet of paper, write *True* if the statement is true or *False* if it is not true.

1) Arthritis is a disease that inflames joints and may change their structure.

2) In osteoarthritis, bones rub on one another after the cartilage is worn away.

3) A seizure is the orderly brain activity that characterizes asthma.

4) A person with epilepsy who has a grand mal seizure loses consciousness.

5) Allergies to cartilage cause asthma.

Action for Health

PLANNING YOUR NEXT DOCTOR'S APPOINTMENT

You can develop your own health-promoting skills, including regular visits to your doctor. These regular visits are an important part of maintaining good health. You can plan your next doctor's appointment. Keep the following points in mind:

- See your doctor once a year, or follow his or her recommendations about when to schedule appointments.
- If you need to find a doctor, ask a trusted person to recommend one.
- Bring a list of questions with you to your doctor's office. Ask any questions you have about your own health or about tests that are done on your body.
- Read the information in your doctor's office to be better informed about health issues.

CHAPTER SUMMARY

■ Cardiovascular disease affects the heart and blood vessels and is a leading cause of death in the United States.

■ Hypertension, or high blood pressure, happens when a person's blood pressure regularly stays above 140/90. Most people do not know they have hypertension.

■ Arteriosclerosis and atherosclerosis are the result of a buildup of fat along the lining of the arteries. These diseases narrow the arteries.

■ A heart attack happens when the narrowed arteries don't deliver enough oxygen and nutrients to the heart. A damaged heart cannot function at full capacity.

■ People with atherosclerosis may have angina pectoris, a severe pain that results from inadequate oxygen to the heart.

■ A stroke happens when the blood supply to the brain is cut off. Some brain cells may die, affecting the function of the part of the body that they control.

■ Some risk factors for cardiovascular disease and problems cannot be changed; others can be prevented.

■ An abnormal, harmful growth of cells causes cancer, usually forming a tumor. Some tumors are malignant, or harmful; others are benign, or not harmful.

■ Cancer can affect any body part. Its symptoms depend on the body part that is involved. There are seven warning signs for cancer. Most treatment involves chemotherapy, surgery, or radiation. Some risk factors for cancer can be avoided.

■ In Type I diabetes, a person depends on insulin. In Type II diabetes, the pancreas produces insulin, but the body cells cannot use it effectively.

■ Rheumatoid arthritis is a destructive inflammation of the joints. In osteoarthritis, cartilage wears away, causing bones to rub on one another. Treatments for arthritis may include medicine and joint replacements.

■ Epilepsy results from disordered brain activity. It is characterized by seizures, which can be controlled with medicine.

■ Asthma causes breathing difficulty. An allergy usually causes asthma, which can be controlled with medicine that is inhaled.

Chapter 12 Review

Comprehension: Identifying Facts

On a separate sheet of paper, write the correct word or words from the Word Bank to complete each sentence.

WORD BANK		
arteriosclerosis	grand mal	oxygen
asthma	insulin-dependent	pressure
cancer		rheumatoid
chemotherapy	malignant	stroke
glucose	melanoma	

1) Hypertension causes the heart to pump harder than normal against increased _____ in the arteries.

2) _____ is hardening of the arteries.

3) A heart attack results from a reduced supply of _____ and nutrients to the heart.

4) When the supply of blood to the brain is cut off, a _____ can happen.

5) An abnormal growth of cells that is harmful is called a _____ tumor.

6) Symptoms of _____ depend on the part of the body that it affects.

7) _____ is treatment that destroys cancer cells.

8) The most common form of skin cancer is malignant _____.

9) Type I diabetes is also called _____ diabetes.

10) Getting a shot of insulin when a person has an empty stomach can cause dangerously low levels of _____ in the blood.

11) _____ arthritis is a destructive inflammation of the joints.

12) A _____ seizure causes a person with epilepsy to lose consciousness.

13) An allergy to mold, pollen, animal fur, or dust may trigger an attack of _____.

Comprehension: Understanding Main Ideas

On a separate sheet of paper, write the answers to the following questions using complete sentences.

14) Name one risk factor for cardiovascular disease than can be controlled and one that cannot be controlled.

15) What are two of the seven warning signs of cancer?

16) What are two risk factors for cancer and how can you avoid them?

17) Why is diet important in controlling diabetes?

18) How does medicine help a person who has epilepsy?

Critical Thinking: Write Your Opinion

19) Did you learn something new about the importance of a person's diet as you read this chapter? Explain your answer.

20) How important do you think it is to know your family's medical history?

Test Taking Tip Look for specifics in each question that tell you in what form your answer is to be. For example, some questions ask for a paragraph, and others may require only one sentence.

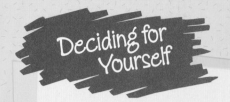

Deciding for Yourself

What's the Truth About Caffeine?

Some people believe that caffeine is a drug that has positive effects on the body. Others believe it has negative effects. Caffeine is found in chocolate and some coffees, teas, and colas. It is also in some headache and cold medicines.

It is possible to sort out facts from myths about caffeine. You can:

- **Check original sources.** Look at the original studies quoted in newspapers, in magazines, and on television to see their true context.

- **Look for generalizations.** Stories in the media may claim more than the research evidence supports. Sound research studies clearly indicate the conditions such as who was involved and the size of the study.

Now look at the following statements.

- **Since it is a drug, caffeine addiction is similar to serious drugs.** "Absolutely not," says Charles O'Brien, M.D., professor of psychiatry at the University of Pennsylvania School of Medicine. O'Brien emphasizes that cocaine and heroin are highly addictive drugs that lead to serious health risks. He says no evidence shows that caffeine produces similar outcomes.

- **Caffeine in cola drinks causes too much activity in children.** Judith Rapoport, M.D., chief of the Child Psychiatry Branch of the National Institute of Mental Health, says this isn't so. She says, "With our studies, the majority of children had little response to caffeine."

- **Caffeine causes breast cancer.** Both the American Medical Association and the National Cancer Institute have concluded that caffeine intake and breast disease have no link.

Questions

1) How might you check original sources for the above information?

2) Are any of the responses to the statements generalizations? Which ones?

3) Do you think caffeine has a positive or negative effect on the body? Explain your answer.

4) If you drink coffee or cola with caffeine, what effects have you noticed on your body?

■ An acquired disease is communicable when infection from a pathogen causes it. How the immune system fights a pathogen determines whether people become ill or how well they recover. The body has physical and chemical barriers to infection. The immune system fights foreign substances by producing antibodies.

■ Inherited diseases come through a single abnormal gene, an abnormal gene along with other conditions, or an abnormal chromosome.

■ Acquired immunodeficiency syndrome (AIDS) is a contagious disorder of the immune system caused by human immunodeficiency virus (HIV). HIV weakens the immune system.

■ AIDS is spread through contact with certain body fluids, through sexual activity, by drug users sharing needles, and from mother to child. It is not spread through casual social contact.

■ All blood for transfusions in the United States is tested for HIV.

■ No cure is yet available for AIDS. It can be prevented by avoiding contact with body fluids that may be infected with HIV.

■ Gonorrhea, chlamydia, and syphilis are sexually transmitted diseases that can be treated with penicillin or other antibiotics. Genital herpes is chronic and has no cure.

■ An infected mother can pass AIDS or other sexual diseases to her baby.

■ People with sexually transmitted diseases can get treatment at clinics. Avoiding contact with the pathogen can prevent sexually transmitted diseases.

■ Cardiovascular disease and problems are a leading cause of death in the United States. Some risk factors for them cannot be changed; others can be prevented.

■ Hypertension (high blood pressure), arteriosclerosis, atherosclerosis, heart attacks, angina pectoris, and strokes are types of cardiovascular disease and problems.

■ An abnormal, harmful growth of cells causes cancer, usually forming a tumor. Some tumors are malignant; others are benign. Cancer can affect any body part.

■ Diabetes, arthritis, epilepsy, and asthma are some other common diseases.

Drug misuse is not a disease, it is a decision, like the decision to step out in front of a moving car. You would call that not a disease but an error of judgment.

—Phillip K. Dick, *A Scanner Darkly*

Use and Misuse of Substances

What do you think of when you hear the term *drug use*? Most people think only of illegal drugs. However, tobacco, alcohol, and caffeine are also drugs—drugs that are legal for adults. Legal drugs such as nicotine and alcohol cause twenty to thirty times as many deaths as illegal drugs.

Medicines prescribed by doctors or over-the-counter medicines can help us fight and prevent some illnesses. It is important to learn how to use medicines wisely and safely. In this unit, you will learn about drugs that help people and drugs that cause harm. It is important to learn the facts about different drugs so you can make wise decisions about staying healthy.

Self-Assessment

1. Which drug causes the greatest number of proven birth defects?

2. Have you had friends and/or family members express concern about your use of a substance?

3. What kind of people do you hang out with?

4. What would you do if you knew that your friend or family member had been exposed to alcohol abuse?

5. What would you do if a friend showed signs of using drugs?

6. Which would you be more likely to do on a weekend – go to a party where there will be drinking or stay home?

7. Do you give in to peer pressure easily when substances are involved?

8. One or both of my parents/guardian had or currently has a problem with substance abuse.

9. I know the immediate and long-term effects of drugs.

10. I can avoid peer pressure about drug use.

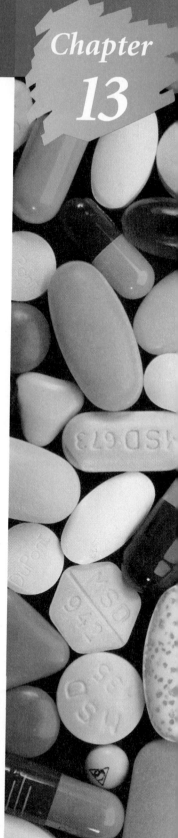

Medicines and Drugs

Have you ever played a word association game? Someone says a word and you say the first word that comes to your mind. Each person might respond differently to the same word. For example, when you hear the word *drugs*, you might say "medicines." Someone else might say "illegal." Whether a drug is a medicine or an illegal substance, taking it involves health risks. To avoid health risks, it is important to know whether a drug is safe. You must know how it can affect your mind and body.

In this chapter, you will learn about drugs that can help to prevent illness and maintain or recover health. You will learn about the effects of drugs that can harm the body and mind. You also will learn which drugs are legal and which drugs are not legal.

Goals for Learning

▶ To explain the types and purposes of medicines

▶ To describe how medicines are taken and possible problems

▶ To identify some cautions to follow when taking medicines

▶ To describe the effects of using tobacco and alcohol

▶ To explain the effects of psychoactive and other dangerous drugs

Assorted Medicines

Medicines

Drug
A chemical substance other than food that changes the way the mind and body work

Medicine
A drug that is used to relieve, treat, cure, prevent, or identify a disease or problem

Pharmacist
Druggist

Prescription
A written order from a medical person for a medicine or other treatment

From time to time, everyone has problems that may range from simple aches and pains to major illnesses. Sometimes, a **drug** or **medicine** is necessary to relieve pain and restore health. A drug is a chemical substance other than food that changes the way the mind and body work. A medicine is a drug that is used to treat, prevent, or identify a disease or problem. All medicines are drugs, but not all drugs are used for medical purposes. This lesson describes drugs that are used for medical purposes. While some drugs described in Lessons 2–4 are used for medical purposes, most of them are not.

What Are the Types of Medicines?

The Food and Drug Administration (FDA) divides medicines into two types according to how they are bought. The first type is available only with a **prescription**, or a written order from a medical doctor. These are called prescription medicines. Only a doctor can write a prescription, and only a **pharmacist**, or druggist, can fill one.

The second type is over-the-counter (OTC) medicines. These medicines are available for anyone to buy in drugstores and other stores without a prescription.

Prescription medicines are generally stronger than OTC medicines. Because prescription medicines are strong, they can have some unwanted side effects. That is why only a doctor can prescribe stronger medicines. Even so, OTC medicines also can have unwanted side effects. Because of these possible side effects, it is important to read the labels on both prescription and OTC medicines. It is especially important to read the label so you know the purpose of a medicine.

What Are Some Purposes of Medicines?

Both prescription and OTC medicines are available for many purposes. Usually, medicines are grouped according to the purpose for which they are used. Some of the major reasons for the use of medicines are:

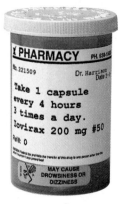

Labels give instructions for use of prescriptions.

To relieve pain—Medicines that a person takes to relieve pain are called **analgesics**. Some analgesics are mild; they work for minor pains like a sore muscle. Most mild analgesics, such as aspirin or an aspirin substitute, are OTC medicines. Other analgesics are very powerful; they control severe pain such as after an operation. Powerful analgesics such as morphine are prescription medicines.

To reduce or destroy pathogens—Antibiotics are a kind of medicine that controls infection by destroying bacteria and other pathogens. Sulfa drugs also reduce or destroy pathogens. Most antibiotics and sulfa drugs are prescription medicines. Some OTC medicines that can be rubbed on minor wounds may contain a small amount of an antibiotic.

To restore normal cardiovascular functions—Many different medicines are used to treat problems of the heart and blood vessels. These medicines may slow heartbeat, control blood pressure, dilate veins and arteries, or control the rhythm of the heart. These are all prescription medicines. New studies, however, show that aspirin, an OTC medicine, can help to prevent a heart attack in some adults.

To prevent a disease—Medicines such as vaccines prevent different diseases by giving a person immunity. For example, vaccinations prevent diseases like measles, mumps, or chicken pox. Vaccines are a prescription medicine that you get in a doctor's office or at a health clinic.

To relieve symptoms of a disease—Examples of medicines that relieve symptoms are preparations for the common cold. These medicines relieve a sore throat or cough, dry up a runny nose and eyes, or reduce mucus. Most cold medicines are mild and can be purchased over the counter. Some cold preparations are strong, and a doctor must prescribe them.

To replace body chemicals—Some prescription medicines replace chemicals that the body cannot produce. Insulin, for example, is a prescription medicine. People with type I diabetes take insulin because their pancreas cannot produce it.

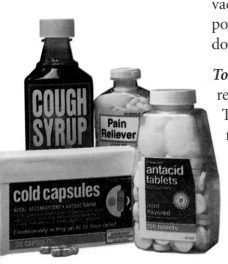

Labels on OTC medicines also give instructions for use.

Writing About Health

Some people take medicines that aren't necessary and may be harmful. Write why you think it is important to take only necessary medicines.

To reduce anxiety—Many medicines can reduce depression, nervousness, and other mental health problems. Strong forms of these medicines are only available with a doctor's prescription. Milder forms, such as mild sleep aid, can be purchased over the counter.

How Are Medicines Taken?

It is important to know the purpose of a medicine and how you should take it. Usually a medicine is taken in the way that it will start working the fastest. For example, you may be instructed to swallow a medicine after a meal. That might be because the medicine can get into your system quicker when your stomach is full. It may also prevent you from having an upset stomach from the medicine. You may be instructed to take other medicines before meals. These medicines may work better when your stomach is empty.

Sometimes medicines, such as vaccinations, are given to you as a shot. The medicine goes directly into a blood vein or a muscle. Other medicines are breathed in and go through the lungs first. For example, medicines for asthma are breathed in to help the respiratory passages. Creams, lotions, and patches are applied to the skin. The medicine is then absorbed into the body through the skin.

How Does a Medicine Affect the Body?

A person's size, weight, age, and body chemistry make a difference in how a medicine affects the body. For example, a short, thin adolescent may experience unwanted side effects from a dose of medicine; a tall, heavy adult, may experience no side effects from the same dose. Your doctor determines the amount of a medicine that is right for you. Sometimes the doctor might have to increase or decrease the amount so that it works properly and does not cause unwanted side effects.

Because each person's body chemistry is different, a medicine may affect each person somewhat differently. For example, most people can take penicillin for a bacterial infection. Some

PATENT MEDICINES

Around 1900, newspapers were full of ads for "patent medicines." These medicines were said to cure one or more illnesses or problems. But the medicines were often fifty percent or more alcohol. Also, manufacturers never tested them for safety or the accuracy of the claims. People wanted to feel better. So they believed the claims and ordered the medicines. Sellers became rich, but the medicines didn't help the buyers.

Today the Food and Drug Administration (FDA) regulates medicines. Researchers must prove a medicine does what it claims. No medicine can be sold without FDA approval.

people, however, are allergic to penicillin and cannot take it. Other drugs can be taken in place of penicillin.

What Are Some Problems With Taking Medicines?

In taking any medicine, the effects of the medicine on the body can cause problems. For this reason, a person always needs to know the specific purpose of a medicine and how it should be taken. A person also should know which medicines he or she cannot take in order to avoid problems. Four possible problems with taking medicines are unwanted side effects, dependence, mixing medicines, and misusing medicines.

Many medicines cause unwanted side effects. For example, a person may get a rash or a headache from taking a medicine. Some of these unintended effects are minor and only cause discomfort. Other side effects such as hypertension or irregular heartbeat can be serious.

A person can become dependent on a medicine. For example, a person may take a medicine to sleep. In time, the person may not be able to sleep without taking the medicine.

Mixing one or more medicines can cause problems. A person who takes one medicine may also need to take another medicine. Sometimes two different medicines cause a bad chemical reaction in the body.

PHARMACY CLERK

Pharmacy clerks usually work in hospitals. Under a pharmacist's direction, they measure out or mix prescriptions. They deliver these prescriptions to each nursing unit. They then pick up pharmacy charge sheets from each unit. Often they are responsible for figuring out the cost of various drugs. Checking on the pharmacy's stock of drugs is another duty. If the pharmacy is short on items, pharmacy clerks order supplies. They keep accurate records of all drugs and supplies. They also may type and file reports and answer phones. Some five- to ten-month programs are available. Most states require licensing. Two-year programs at community colleges can lead to getting a license.

Misusing medicines is a serious problem. A person can misuse a medicine by taking more or less than the recommended amount. Taking two pills instead of one for a cold, for example, could cause a person to fall asleep while driving. Someone can misuse a medicine by taking it for a longer or shorter time than it should be taken. For example, if you stop taking an antibiotic too soon, the infection may flare up because it is not completely gone. Another misuse of a medicine is taking it for a purpose other than the intended one. Although drugs are usually not misused on purpose, accidental misuse may result in damaging consequences.

How Does the Government Keep Medicines Safe?

The U.S. government has many laws and agencies that control the safety of medicines. Before a company can sell any medicine, the FDA requires the medicine to be tested carefully to prove its intended effect. The company must submit the test results to the FDA. It must also submit papers stating the purpose, ingredients, possible side effects, and other information about the medicine. The FDA then decides whether the medicine can be made available to the public. It also decides whether the medicine must be sold with a doctor's prescription.

The FDA determines how medicines must be labeled. Labels must give the purpose of the medicine, the recommended amount, possible unwanted side effects, and cautions. Reading a label tells you whether it is safe to take the medicine and how to avoid problems.

What Are Some Cautions for Taking Medicines?

The appropriate use of drugs can improve a person's health and life. The inappropriate use of drugs can involve serious risks. To avoid problems with any medicine, you can follow these simple guidelines:

All drugs have some side effects. Discuss with your doctor alternatives to treatment with medicines.

- Tell your doctor about any other health problems you have. Tell the doctor about any other medicines you are taking before you get a new prescription.

- Follow the directions for taking a medicine exactly as they are given. Take the full prescription unless your doctor tells you to do otherwise.

- Tell your doctor immediately if you have any unwanted side effects from a medicine.

- Take only medicines that are prescribed for you. Be careful not to confuse one medicine with another, and don't take someone else's prescription medicine.

- Store medicines properly; throw away outdated medicines.

- Never mix medicines, and never mix medicines and alcohol.

LESSON 1 REVIEW Write the answers to these questions on a separate sheet of paper, using complete sentences.

1) What is the difference between a medicine and a drug?

2) What is the difference between prescription and OTC medicines?

3) List three purposes of medicines.

4) What factors influence how a medicine affects the body?

5) What are four possible problems involved with taking medicines?

Tobacco and Alcohol

Addiction
A need for a habit-forming substance

Emphysema
A serious respiratory disease that causes difficulty in breathing

Nicotine
A chemical in tobacco to which people become addicted

Stimulant
A drug that speeds up the central nervous system

Why do cigarette companies target teenage smokers?

A drug is a chemical substance other than food that changes the way the mind and body work. Some drugs change the way the body works in harmful rather than helpful ways. Two drugs that have harmful physical and mental effects are tobacco and alcohol.

Why Do People Use Tobacco?

People may use tobacco for similar reasons. Many teens and adults smoke tobacco to feel comfortable in social situations. Some people say smoking relaxes them. Teens may smoke because of pressure from peers or because advertisements persuade them to smoke. They believe that they can quit smoking before it has any harmful effects on their body. In reality, however, research suggests that the younger people are when they start to smoke, the harder the habit is to break.

The main reason people continue to smoke is because of **nicotine**, a chemical in tobacco. People develop an **addiction** to nicotine, which means they have a need for a habit-forming substance. Nicotine is in all forms of tobacco. That includes cigarettes, cigars, pipe tobacco, and smokeless tobacco, which is put between the cheek and gums and chewed.

What Are the Physical Effects of Tobacco?

The nicotine in tobacco is a **stimulant**. It speeds up the central nervous system despite people's belief that tobacco relaxes them. Nicotine increases the heart rate and blood pressure and narrows the blood vessels. Long-term tobacco use causes a buildup of material in the blood vessels that can result in a heart attack, stroke, and lung and other cancers. The buildup can also cause chronic bronchitis and **emphysema**, a serious respiratory disease that causes difficulty in breathing.

Besides nicotine, burning tobacco produces more than 2,000 other harmful chemicals. These chemicals include tars and other compounds that form a thick, brown, sticky substance in the lungs. Tars cripple and destroy the tiny structures that line the bronchial tubes and help keep the lungs clean.

Tobacco smoke also produces gases, including carbon monoxide, which replaces the oxygen in red blood cells. This lack of oxygen makes physical activity difficult. Other smoke-produced gases contain poisonous chemicals that can cause tumor growth and cancer.

Smokeless tobacco also can cause immediate and long-term health problems. For example, it can wear away tooth enamel, cause tooth decay, and cause gums to shrink so teeth loosen and fall out. Smokeless tobacco can cause white, leathery patches in the mouth that may turn into cancer.

People who do not smoke but who breathe in others' tobacco smoke also can be harmed.

All forms of tobacco contain nicotine, an addicting substance.

How Does Smoke Affect Nonsmokers?

Many studies have shown that healthy nonsmokers can get respiratory diseases and cancers by inhaling smoke from burning cigarettes. This is called passive or second-hand smoke. Nonsmokers get these diseases because they inhale into their lungs slightly smaller amounts of the same harmful gases that smokers inhale.

Nonsmokers can get many of the same physical effects that smokers get. For example, they can also have heart and lung problems. Their eyes become irritated, they get headaches, and they cough from the passive smoke. Passive smoke can make existing illnesses worse for nonsmokers. For example, if a nonsmoker has an existing heart condition, breathing passive smoke can worsen it.

Because of the harm that passive smoke can do, many laws forbid smoking in public places and on public transportation. For example, nonsmokers have the right to be seated in nonsmoking areas of restaurants. Also, many workplaces have become smoke free.

How Can People Stop Smoking?

Fortunately, as more people realize the problems that smoking causes, they are choosing to quit smoking. The addiction to nicotine is powerful. Therefore, people who stop smoking should know they will probably go through a period of **withdrawal**. This is a physical reaction to the absence of a drug in the body. During withdrawal from nicotine, people may have a headache, be unable to sleep, and have difficulty concentrating. They may feel crabby and have some anxiety.

Help is available for people who choose to quit smoking. They can get skin patches or a special gum as prescriptions from their doctor. These aids allow people to ease away gradually from their addiction to nicotine. Classes, support groups, and professionals also are available to help people quit smoking.

Why Do People Use Alcohol?

The reasons that some people use alcohol are like the reasons that people use tobacco—to feel comfortable in social situations. People drink to give themselves more self-confidence, to relax, or to escape uncomfortable emotions. In reality, however, alcohol doesn't help any of these emotions. Many teens may try alcohol because of peer pressure or because they have seen their parents drink. Some try it because of the influence of advertising.

People can become both physically and psychologically addicted to ethyl alcohol, the kind of alcohol found in wine, beer, and hard liquor. Alcohol is a **depressant**, a type of drug that slows down the central nervous system. It is also a **psychoactive** drug, meaning it affects the mind or mental processes.

All of these drinks contain about the same amount of pure alcohol.

It is a mistake to think that some forms of alcohol, such as beer or wine coolers, are safer than others. A 12-ounce can of beer, a 4-ounce glass of wine, or 1.5 ounces of hard liquor all contain about the same amount of pure alcohol. That means people can become just as addicted to beer as they can to whiskey. Such addiction can cause serious problems in the body.

How Does Alcohol Affect the Body?

Alcohol has a negative effect on every major system in the body. Alcohol is not digested, but is absorbed directly from the stomach into the blood and then is carried throughout the body. How alcohol affects the body depends on the amount a person drinks, body size, and whether the stomach is empty or full.

After entering the body, alcohol combines with oxygen, mainly in the liver, in a process called oxidation. The liver can oxidize only about ½ ounce of alcohol per hour. When people drink any amount of alcohol, their judgment, vision, reaction time, and muscle control are affected. Their blood-alcohol (BAC) level begins to rise. Some short-term effects of alcohol are impaired driving ability, dizziness, flushed skin, dulled senses and memory, and a relaxed feeling.

Long-term use of alcohol can cause serious diseases such as cancer of the liver, stomach, colon, and mouth. It can also damage the brain, pancreas, and kidneys. Long-term alcohol use can cause high blood pressure, heart attacks, strokes, diseases of the liver, and birth defects. These health problems have costs to society.

With just one drink, people can rapidly lose muscle coordination and cannot perform simple activities like walking a straight line. People cannot speak or think clearly, their mind is confused, and their hearing and vision become less sharp. When people are affected physically in these ways, serious accidents such as car crashes can result.

How Does Alcohol Affect Driving?

When a person's BAC level rises to the point of **intoxication**, it can affect many things, including the ability to drive. Intoxication is excitement or stimulation caused by use of a chemical substance. In most states, a person over 21 with a BAC level of .08 to .10 percent is considered legally intoxicated. At these levels, it is against the law to drive a car.

Even if the BAC level is under .08 percent, it is still not safe to drive. Driving is not safe for anyone who has been drinking. The risk of harm to one's self and others is great. Even in small amounts, alcohol affects judgment and reduces attention and the ability to withstand light. It causes a person to be drowsy, to have a slower reaction time than normal, and to underestimate speed and distance.

What is the BAC at which your state considers a person legally intoxicated?

Most states have a "zero tolerance law" for drunk driving. This law has reduced the BAC for people under 21 to .02 percent. This law and the legal drinking age of 21 in all states have helped to reduce the percent of fatal car crashes.

technology

SOFTWARE FOR ALCOHOL TESTING

People who drink and drive are dangerous to themselves and others. Breath analyzers help police keep drunk drivers off the roads. These analyzers measure blood alcohol levels. One analyzer is called "ignition interlock." It is put on the cars of people who have had problems with drinking and driving. The device is wired to the car's starter. Before starting the car, the driver blows into the device. Sensors check for alcohol in the breath. If they sense alcohol, the car will not start. The computer records the number of failed tests. It can even tell if the system has been tampered with. Such technology keeps everyone safer.

Alcoholism
A disease characterized by dependence on alcoholic beverages

Driving drunk involves many consequences, including heavy fines and having a driver's license taken away. People who are stopped for driving drunk may have to spend time in jail and be evaluated for **alcoholism**. Alcoholism is a disease characterized by dependence on alcoholic beverages and lack of control in drinking.

When Is a Person an Alcoholic?

The main characteristic of an alcoholic is not being able to control his or her drinking. These people are physically and mentally dependent on alcohol. They cannot manage stress without alcohol, and they cannot stop drinking each time they start.

Alcoholism is classified as a disease. A tendency for alcoholism runs in families, just as the tendency for heart disease runs in families. If a member of a family is an alcoholic, other family members have an increased risk for the disease.

People can recover from alcoholism by abstinence from drinking. Often medical and psychological help is also needed.

WORD BANK

depressant

drinking

intoxicated

nicotine

passive

LESSON 2 REVIEW On a separate sheet of paper, write the word or words in the Word Bank that correctly complete each sentence.

1) The chemical in tobacco to which people become addicted is _____.

2) _____ smoke can cause heart and lung problems in nonsmokers.

3) Alcohol is a central nervous system _____.

4) A person is considered legally _____ with a blood alcohol level of .08–.10 percent.

5) The main characteristic of an alcoholic is not being able to control his or her _____.

Stimulants, Depressants, Narcotics, and Hallucinogens

Amphetamine
A central nervous system stimulant

*L*ike medicines, drugs are grouped according to their purpose. One group of drugs is called psychoactive drugs because they produce behavioral or mental changes. Some psychoactive drugs can be used as prescription medicines under a doctor's direction. Sometimes, however, these drugs are bought illegally without a doctor's prescription and direction. Other psychoactive drugs have no medical use and are made and bought illegally.

What Are the Effects of Stimulants?

One kind of psychoactive drugs is stimulants, which speed up the body's central nervous system. They increase respiratory, heart, and metabolic rates and cause high blood pressure. People become dizzy and lose their appetite. People also may have headaches, blurred vision, sweating, and sleeplessness. In large amounts, stimulants cause irregular heartbeat and other problems. Inhaling or injecting stimulants can raise blood pressure so high that people have a stroke or high fever. Heart failure and even death can result. People can become physically dependent on stimulants.

Stimulants change the way the mind works. They provide a feeling of energy and fool people into thinking they're not tired. These feelings can cause people to become psychologically and physically dependent on stimulants. The dependence begins when the effect of the drug wears off and the user feels tired and depressed. The user then craves the drug in order to achieve the same feeling of energy again.

The nicotine in tobacco is a stimulant. Two other stimulants are described below.

Amphetamines

Amphetamines are synthetic stimulants, which means they are produced from chemicals in a laboratory. These drugs speed up the heart and breathing. They cause anxiety and reduce the desire to eat or sleep. Doctors do not prescribe amphetamines as much as they once did. Doctors may still prescribe them, however, for a disease that causes people to fall suddenly into deep sleep.

People use illegal amphetamines to lose weight, to stay awake and alert, or to improve their athletic ability. They also use them to cancel the effects of depressants. As the effects of amphetamines lessen, people may be depressed.

"Speed," "ice," and "crystal" are other names for an illegal amphetamine called methamphetamine. Ice, a form of speed that is smoked, can cause permanent mental illness. Ice and crystal cause very high blood pressure, which can lead to heart failure or a stroke. Repeated use causes physical dependence.

Health Tip

Use physical exercise to relax your body and relieve anxiety.

Cocaine

Cocaine is a stimulant that is made into a white powder from the leaves of the coca plant. This highly addictive drug is now illegal, but at one time it was used for medical purposes. Like other stimulants, cocaine creates a feeling of energy in the user. The feeling of energy is actually increased heart rate, blood pressure, and breathing. In large amounts, it may cause shaking, seizures, and heart and respiratory failure. These problems can be life threatening.

Dependence on cocaine occurs rapidly—sometimes with first use. Cocaine dependence can cause enormous damage to physical and mental health. Usually cocaine is inhaled, or snorted, through the nasal passages. It is absorbed through the mucous membranes and enters the bloodstream. The drug contracts the blood vessels in the nose, causing it to be dry. Constant use can destroy the wall that separates the nasal passages. People who use cocaine all the time stop eating properly, and malnutrition may result. The drug can make existing heart problems worse and can increase the risk of a fatal heart attack in any user. People who inject cocaine risk getting AIDS if they share needles.

Cocaine also affects mental health. Use of cocaine gives a false feeling of confidence for the first few minutes. Severe depression and an intense desire for more cocaine follow the feeling of confidence. To avoid the depression, people use more and more of the drug to get the same feeling of confidence. Consequently, a user quickly builds up **tolerance** to cocaine. Tolerance is the ability to withstand increasing amounts of a drug without reacting to it and to achieve the desired effect. Some mental effects of cocaine are a sensation of insects crawling under the skin, confusion, and hallucinations.

Crack is a smokable form of cocaine. It is made when cocaine is mixed with baking soda to form lumps that look like rocks. "Freebase" is another name for this kind of cocaine. The rocks are mixed with ether and then lit so the drug can be smoked. This dangerous process may produce an explosion and fire.

Like other forms of cocaine, the effects of crack last only a few minutes. A terrible depression follows the first effects. Because of the intense desire to use the drug again, people can become extremely addicted to it. The same health problems that cocaine causes are even more extreme with crack.

What Are the Effects of Depressants?

A second kind of psychoactive drugs is depressants. Depressants produce sedation, or calming, because they slow down the central nervous system. They lower blood pressure, heart rate, and metabolic rate. High amounts of depressants can cause sleepiness, confused thinking, loss of muscle control, and nausea. An overdose, or too much, of a depressant may cause heart, lung, and kidney failure. It can even result in coma and death. Depressants can create both physical and psychological dependence.

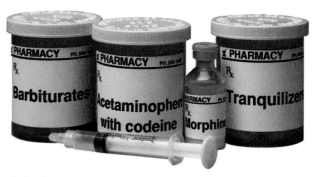

While depressants have been prescribed and used legally, many people who abuse them get them illegally.

Barbiturates
A category of sedative-hypnotic drugs

Narcotic
An analgesic made from the opium poppy

Sedative-hypnotic drug
A prescribed depressant that reduces anxiety or promotes sleep

Tranquilizers
A category of sedative-hypnotic drugs

If people use alcohol and depressants together, their health risks are increased. This combination can depress the central nervous system, causing death.

When a woman uses depressants during pregnancy, her baby may be born dependent on the drugs. The baby also may have symptoms of withdrawal from the depressants at birth. Birth defects and long-term behavioral problems may result.

Some people use depressants to handle stress, but that is very dangerous. Tolerance to depressants builds up quickly. Within a few weeks of regular use, depressants lose their effectiveness and no longer work. By that time, however, users may be dependent on the drugs and need more of them. People may feel worse than when they started using the depressants. Increased use of depressants can result in death, depending on the amount and the manner in which they are used.

Sedative-hypnotic drugs are depressants prescribed by a doctor to reduce anxiety (sedatives) or promote sleep (hypnotics). Table 13.1 shows the purposes and dangers of three categories of sedative-hypnotic drugs—**barbiturates**, minor **tranquilizers**, and major tranquilizers.

What Are the Effects of Narcotics?

A third kind of psychoactive drugs is **narcotics**. Used as analgesics to relieve pain, narcotics are made from the opium poppy. Some common medicines that are narcotics are morphine and codeine.

Table 13.1. The Sedative-Hypnotics

Category	Prescribed for	Dangers
Barbiturates	Relaxation (rarely for sleep)	Produce negative side effects Overdose can lead to death Produce rapid dependence
Minor tranquilizers	Anxiety, sleeplessness, muscle spasms	Produce dependence Withdrawal causes severe shaking
Major tranquilizers	Serious mental disorders	Strong, unpleasant side effects

Morphine relieves severe pain experienced after an operation or during the late stages of cancer. Codeine is used to relieve pain and to control coughing.

Narcotics act as a strong depressant on the central nervous system. At first, narcotics produce a feeling of well-being. After that, they cause drowsiness, nausea, and sometimes vomiting. An overdose of narcotics results in shallow breathing, cold and damp skin, seizures, coma, and even death. Narcotics produce strong physical dependence and tolerance. The symptoms of withdrawal are so painful that people continue to use narcotics to avoid the pain of withdrawal.

Heroin, which is illegal in the United States, is a narcotic made from the opium poppy. Babies of mothers who use heroin may be born dead or prematurely. Babies who are born addicted to heroin may go through severe withdrawal pain. People who inject heroin with a dirty needle can get blood poisoning and many serious infections, including AIDS. An overdose can cause death.

What Are the Effects of Hallucinogens?

A fourth kind of psychoactive drugs is **hallucinogens**, which confuse the central nervous system. They change the way the brain processes information from the sense organs, including information about sight, hearing, smell, and touch. Because they change thoughts and moods, hallucinogens make things appear to be what they are not. Physically, they can cause pupils to dilate and can increase body temperature, blood pressure, and heart rate. A person who uses hallucinogens may feel weak and sick.

Health Tip

Use your refusal skills—don't go to a party where there will be drugs.

The mental dangers of hallucinogens are worse than their physical effects. Users may experience anxiety, confusion, terror, and panic attacks. Because hallucinogens distort a person's thinking, the user may do something that causes accidental injury or death.

Hallucinogens can cause permanent brain damage. For example, users may have flashbacks, which is experiencing the

LSD
A synthetic hallucinogen

PCP
A synthetic hallucinogen

Despite the problems associated with drugs, people continue to use and abuse them. Why do you think this happens?

effects of the drug without using it again. Because the drug remains stored in the body, flashbacks can occur at any time for the rest of a person's life.

Hallucinogens are illegal and have no current accepted medical uses. Some hallucinogens are synthetic drugs that are known as street drugs. These dangerous drugs leave poisonous substances in the brain and may damage its chemistry.

LSD, perhaps the best-known synthetic hallucinogen, was originally used in research to treat mental illnesses. LSD didn't cure any mental problems, however, and often caused additional ones. LSD is both illegal and dangerous.

PCP may be the most dangerous synthetic hallucinogen because its effects vary greatly. It may cause memory problems, depression, and violent behavior. A person who takes a large dose of PCP may have seizures, a coma, and heart and lung failure.

LESSON 3 REVIEW On a separate sheet of paper, write the word from the Word Bank that matches each description.

WORD BANK

dependent

depressant

flashbacks

stimulants

tolerance

1) _____ speed up the central nervous system.

2) A person who uses cocaine quickly builds up _____ to it.

3) If a woman uses depressants during pregnancy, her baby may be born _____ on them.

4) Narcotics act as a strong _____ on the central nervous system.

5) LSD or PCP can cause _____ without using the drug again.

Other Dangerous Drugs

Some drugs are dangerous because of the effects they have on the body and mind.

What Is Marijuana?

Marijuana
A drug from the hemp plant Cannabis sativa

THC
The psychoactive chemical in marijuana and hashish

Marijuana is an illegal drug that is taken from the hemp plant called Cannabis sativa. Because hemp leaves and buds have an intoxicating effect, some people smoke, drink, or eat them. Marijuana contains more than 400 chemicals, one of which is called **THC**. THC has a strong psychoactive effect that can produce drug dependence.

THC is harmful because it may be stored in the body's fatty tissues for up to thirty days. It is stored mainly in the brain, kidneys, liver, lungs, and reproductive organs. All these organs have high numbers of fat cells. Long-term use of marijuana may harm all of these organs. In addition, THC harms proper growth and division of cells.

Marijuana affects each person differently. It can act like a central nervous system depressant, a pain reliever, or an hallucinogen. Marijuana can lower body temperature and increase blood pressure and heart and pulse rates. It makes the eyes red and increases the appetite. A person's driving and movement skills can decrease after using marijuana.

Marijuana affects a person's mental functioning by impairing memory, concentration, and judgment. As a result, a person's performance in school or at work may decrease. People can experience mood changes with their first use of marijuana. Users may become indifferent and lose their ambition.

Studies show that using marijuana has serious health risks, including chronic lung disease. For example, marijuana smokers inhale deeply and try to hold the smoke in their lungs for a long time. This does as much damage to the lungs as up to twenty regular cigarettes. In addition, marijuana smoke can cause cancer and may interfere with the immune system's effectiveness in fighting infections and diseases.

What Are Inhalants?

Inhalants are chemicals that people breathe into their body. Some inhalants may be used for an analgesic or pain-relieving effect. Other inhalants are used for an hallucinogenic effect. Chemicals with an hallucinogenic effect are generally found in products that are not used as drugs. Some examples of these products are glues, gasoline, spray paints, and other sprays. Using an inhalant for a different purpose than it was intended is considered illegal drug use.

Using paint thinner, polish remover, glue, or spray paint as an inhalant is illegal drug use.

Designer drug
A substance with a slightly different chemical makeup from a legal drug

Inhalant
A chemical that is breathed in

Look-alike drug
A substance made from legal chemicals to look like a common illegal drug

Why are marijuana, inhalants, and designer drugs so appealing to teenagers and young adults?

Using inhalants can harm the mind and body first of all by depressing the central nervous system. Users may have slurred speech, poor judgment, confusion, dizziness, headaches, and hallucinations. They may even become unconscious. Some physical effects of using inhalants are sneezing, coughing, sniffing, and nosebleeds. Inhalants can cause more serious damage, including permanent brain damage. A person who uses high amounts of inhalants can die immediately by suffocation, or smothering.

What Are Designer and Look-Alike Drugs?

A **designer drug** has a chemical makeup that is like the chemical makeup of a legal drug. Drug dealers, however, make designer drugs to be slightly different from the original drug and usually many times stronger. Many designer drugs imitate narcotics. An example of a designer drug is "China White," which imitates the narcotic heroin.

Look-alike drugs are made from legal chemicals to look like common illegal drugs. Actually, however, they may contain any kind of substance. For example, people who think they are buying an amphetamine may be getting LSD.

Anabolic steroid
A synthetic drug that closely resembles the natural male sex hormone testosterone

Some people suggest that all drugs should be legal. What are the advantages and disadvantages of such an action?

All designer and look-alike drugs are illegal. Because users really don't know what is in these drugs, an overdose could result. Even modest doses can raise blood pressure and heart rate. These drugs can be toxic in the body. Therefore, a person who combines look-alike drugs with other drugs risks death.

What Are Anabolic Steroids?

Anabolic steroids are synthetic drugs that resemble the natural male sex hormone testosterone. They are used both medically and illegally. When used medically, anabolic steroids help people who do not produce enough testosterone naturally. Athletes sometimes use anabolic steroids illegally to improve their performance. When athletes use these drugs with muscle-building exercise and diet, their body weight and muscle strength may increase.

Anabolic steroids can produce both physical and mental effects on the body. They can cause high blood pressure, heart and kidney disease, or life-threatening liver cancer. In adolescents, their bones may stop growing prematurely so they do not reach normal adult height. Males may have baldness, shrunken testes, and decreased sperm production. Females may have breast shrinkage, increased facial hair, a deepened voice, and male-pattern baldness. Both sexes may become sterile from using steroids.

Although steroids generally are not used to alter mood or consciousness, they have negative mental effects. In both sexes, steroids can cause aggressive behavior, sometimes called "'roid rages." Other mental effects are anxiety, depression, sudden mood swings, and hallucinations.

LESSON 4 REVIEW Write the answers to these questions on a separate sheet of paper, using complete sentences.

1) For how long can THC remain stored in the body?

2) Why is it harmful to inhale and hold marijuana in the lungs?

3) What are some sources of illegal inhalants?

4) How are designer drugs different from the drugs they copy?

5) What can happen to adolescents who use steroids?

■ A drug is a substance that changes the way the mind and body work. All medicines are drugs but not all drugs are medicines.

■ Medicines are bought with a doctor's prescription or over the counter without a prescription. Differences between the two depend on their strength and possible side effects.

■ Medicines are grouped according to their purpose or use.

■ Usually medicines are taken in the way they will start working the fastest.

■ Body size, weight, age, and body chemistry influence how a drug affects an individual.

■ It is important to take medicines for their intended purpose according to the directions on the label. This can avoid problems such as unwanted side effects, dependence, and mixing or misusing medicines.

■ The U.S. government controls the safety of medicines with strict requirements for drug companies and with drug labels or instructions.

■ Both tobacco and alcohol are addicting drugs. The nicotine in tobacco is a stimulant. Alcohol is a central nervous system depressant and psychoactive drug. Using either drug can result in serious diseases involving the heart, lungs, and other body organs.

■ People who breathe in passive tobacco smoke can have the same health problems that smokers have.

■ Alcoholism, a disease resulting from dependence on alcohol, is curable with medical and psychological help and abstinence from drinking.

■ Stimulants, depressants, narcotics, and hallucinogens are all addictive psychoactive drugs. Stimulants speed up the central nervous system, and depressants and narcotics slow it down. Hallucinogens confuse the central nervous system and have no medical use.

■ Marijuana, inhalants, designer and look-alike drugs, and anabolic steroids are dangerous addicting drugs. Marijuana and designer and look-alike drugs are illegal. Inhalants and steroids have some medical uses, but often are misused.

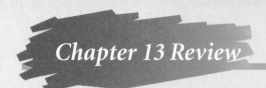

Comprehension: Identifying Facts

On a separate sheet of paper, write the correct word or words from the Word Bank to complete each sentence.

WORD BANK		
alcoholics	depressants	nicotine
anabolic steroids	emphysema	pharmacist
analgesic	FDA	THC
brain damage	flashbacks	withdrawal
depressed	legally intoxicated	

1) Only a _____ can fill a prescription written by a doctor.

2) A medicine that relieves pain is an _____.

3) The _____ requires drug companies to submit test results and information about medicines.

4) _____ is in all forms of tobacco.

5) A serious respiratory disease that can result from smoking is _____.

6) In most states, a blood alcohol level of .08 to .10 percent means a person over 21 is _____.

7) _____ are people who cannot control their drinking.

8) People may become _____ when the effects of amphetamines wear off.

9) Using alcohol and _____ together can depress the central nervous system to the point of death.

10) Babies born addicted to heroin go through severe _____ pain.

11) People who use hallucinogens may have _____ for the rest of their life.

12) The _____ in marijuana is stored in the brain and other organs for up to 30 days.

13) People who inhales glues, spray paints, and other sprays may have permanent _____.

14) Adolescents who use _____ may stop growing prematurely.

Comprehension: Understanding Main Ideas

On a separate sheet of paper, write the answers to the following questions using complete sentences.

15) What are three purposes of medicines?

16) What are four factors that make a difference in how medicine affects the body?

17) What is the zero tolerance law?

18) How do alcohol, tobacco, stimulants, depressants, narcotics, hallucinogens, and inhalants affect the central nervous system?

Critical Thinking: Write Your Opinion

19) Why do you think some people never misuse drugs and others become dependent on them?

20) Why do you think alcoholism or any drug dependence could be considered a family disease?

Test Taking Tip Read test questions carefully to identify those questions that require more than one answer.

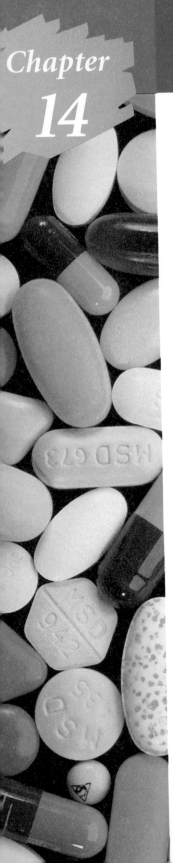

Assorted Medicines

Drug Dependence— Problems and Solutions

*E*veryone is faced with choices and problems in life. People who choose drugs usually are struggling with problems. They may see drug use as a quick solution, but drug use never provides a solution to life's problems. In fact, drug use adds to life's problems.

It is important to understand the problems that drug dependence creates. It is equally important to know about solutions for drug dependence. Perhaps it is most important to know about healthy alternatives to avoiding drug use.

Goals for Learning

▶ To explain physical and mental drug dependence

▶ To identify the pattern and signs of drug dependence

▶ To describe how drug dependence costs the family and society

▶ To explain the steps in recovery from drug dependence

▶ To identify resources for help with drug dependence

▶ To describe healthy alternatives to drug use

Drug Dependence—The Problems

Drug dependence
A need for a drug resulting from occasional or long-term use of that drug

Dependence on alcohol and other drugs is a serious problem not only for the individual but also for families and society. It is important to understand more about this dependence and its costs for individuals, families, and society.

What Is Drug Dependence?

Drug dependence is a need for a drug that results from occasional or long-term use of that drug. Other names for drug dependence are addiction and substance abuse disorder. Drug dependence can be physical, psychological, or both.

Physical Drug Dependence

Physical dependence on a drug occurs when the body develops tolerance for the drug and experiences withdrawal when drug use is stopped. The body begins to develop tolerance as people use more of a drug. Tolerance is the ability to withstand increasing amounts of a drug without reacting to it and to achieve the desired effect. If people develop tolerance for one drug, they may develop tolerance for other drugs as well. Then in order to get the same effect from the drugs, people must increase their use of them. When people who have developed tolerance suddenly stop taking a drug, they go into withdrawal.

Withdrawal is the physical reaction to the sudden absence of a drug in the body. Generally, symptoms of withdrawal are the opposite of the effects of the drug. Take, for example, a person who becomes dependent on a depressant such as alcohol. If the person suddenly stops using the depressant, the central nervous system speeds up. When a person who becomes dependent on a stimulant such as an amphetamine suddenly stops using it, the central nervous system slows down.

Heredity may influence whether people become physically dependent on drugs. For example, a person's tendency to alcoholism may be inherited. If other family members have alcoholism, an individual may have a greater tendency to the disease. Research studies aren't clear whether this tendency is biological or learned.

The drugs that produce the strongest physical dependence are narcotics, barbiturates, and alcohol. Withdrawal from narcotics is extremely painful, and withdrawal from alcohol or barbiturates can be life threatening without medical care.

Psychological Drug Dependence

Psychological dependence on a drug occurs when people believe they need the drug to feel good. Usually psychological drug dependence begins when people have personal problems. For example, people may be having problems with their feelings of self-worth, their parents, or their marriage. They use a drug and notice that its effects deaden the emotional pain that the problem gives them.

When the effect of the drug wears off, the emotional pain comes back. To avoid this pain, people use the drug again to escape their feelings. Users then begin to have a mental desire to use the drug over and over again. Even if they stop using the drug, they may still experience a psychological need for it.

Generally, drugs that produce a psychological dependence are psychoactive drugs such as alcohol, marijuana, cocaine, heroin, and amphetamines. These drugs change the way a person thinks. They can also produce physical dependence.

Healthy Subjects
Literature

"JUNIOR ADDICT"

The African-American writer Langston Hughes wrote many poems and stories about addiction. His poem "Junior Addict," which was published in 1961, describes an African-American boy. Hughes suggests that the boy is sad because of his drug use. His problem may be linked to the way his people have been treated in America. If only he can live to see "the sunrise" far away. Hughes calls to the African sunrise to "come, quickly, come." He indicates that the little boy may find strength and hope if he can feel pride in his heritage. This must happen quickly, for time runs out for addicts—even young ones.

People can be just physically or just psychologically dependent on a drug. Usually, however, they are dependent in both ways to some degree. The specific symptoms of dependence are different for each drug, but dependence-producing drugs all have one thing in common. They create a need that requires increasing use of the drug to produce satisfaction or to avoid pain or discomfort.

What Are the Pattern and Signs of Dependence?

Whether a drug produces physical or psychological dependence, or both, the pattern and signs of use seem to be the same.

The main pattern of drug dependence is that a person's life revolves around the drug. People who are dependent on drugs are just like everyone else until they use their drug of choice. Then their physical behavior and personality changes. They spend their time thinking about the drug, getting a supply and using it, and recovering from its side effects. After they recover, the pattern starts over again. As the pattern becomes more established over time, people become drug dependent.

It is possible to recognize some signs of drug dependence. If people have only one or two of the following signs, they may not have a drug problem. If they show many of these signs, however, they may have a drug problem.

- Changes in appearance
- Major changes in behavior
- Changes in friends
- Sudden mood changes
- Angry, aggressive, or resistant behavior

Recognizing signs of possible drug dependence is important for family members.

SMOKE ALARM

Long before Columbus arrived, American Indians smoked tobacco. Until 1800, much of the world used tobacco as money. In the 1880s, a North Carolina manufacturer used the first cigarette-making machine. Cigarette smoking spread. During and after World War II, films and advertising glamorized smoking.

Research shows, though, that smoking contributes to heart and lung disease and cancer. In 1972, cigarette companies had to print health warnings on advertisements and cigarette packages. Soon, states began to forbid smoking in public places. Airlines banned smoking on many U.S. flights. In the 1980s and 1990s, states and families sued tobacco companies. They said the companies had misled people about the dangers of smoking.

> SURGEON GENERAL'S WARNING: Quitting Smoking Now Greatly Reduces Serious Risks to Your Health.

- Loss of memory and concentration
- Lying, cheating, and stealing
- Reduced energy and ambition
- Loss of interest in favorite activities or hobbies
- Borrowing money
- Trouble with the police
- Drop in performance at school or work
- Many absences and tardiness
- Becoming angry or hostile when discussing drug use

Being able to recognize these signs may be especially important for family members, since they may be affected greatly by a drug user's problem.

How Does Drug Dependence Affect the Family?

Families are affected by changes in the behavior and personality of a family member who is drug dependent. As the person becomes more dependent on a drug, the changes increase. The drug-dependent person's behavior may become hard for the family or anyone to predict, or tell in advance.

Because drug-dependent people's behavior is unpredictable, family members sometimes try to protect them. This is called **enabling**. For example, family members enable drug-dependent people by saying they are sick when they are actually drunk. The family may take care of drug users by making excuses for their actions. This behavior enables the users to continue using. The family keeps drug users from having to face the consequences of their behavior.

Enabling behavior usually happens in an attempt to protect the family image. However, it winds up hurting everyone. Enabling keeps the person from facing the effects of drug use. Then the person continues getting deeper into drug dependence. Enabling also often delays getting help for the drug user. As the problem goes on, the emotional well-being of family members is affected. Children growing up in families with drug dependence often suffer stress and abuse.

Continued drug dependence affects not only the family but also society.

Action for Health

LEARNING ABOUT THE COSTS OF DRUG USE IN YOUR COMMUNITY

Find out about the major costs of drug use in your community. Contact your local or state health department. Ask the professional health workers to provide you with statistics on the costs of drug use in your community.

Other sources to contact for this information include local mental health centers, the American Cancer Society, and the American Lung Association. You might also contact local law enforcement officials for statistics about crimes related to drug use. Many counties have mental health and drug education agencies that are listed in the blue pages of the telephone book.

How Does Drug Dependence Cost Society?

Alcohol and drug dependence is a major problem that costs American society billions of dollars each year. For example, in 1993 the use of alcohol, tobacco, and other drugs cost American society nearly $400 billion. That is about $1,608 for every man, woman, and child. Some of these expenses are lost work time, lost jobs, car crashes, crime, and health problems. As a result, everyone must pay higher taxes as well as higher insurance and health care costs.

Drug dependence costs more than money—it costs lives. For example, alcohol-related car crashes are the leading cause of death among teens. In 1994, alcohol-related car crashes killed 2,222 people between the ages of 16 and 20, according to the Center for Substance Abuse Prevention.

Drug dependence costs not only present lives but also future lives. Pregnant women who use drugs run the risk of giving birth to drug-dependent babies. Women who drink alcohol when they are pregnant may give birth to babies who are smaller than normal. These babies also may have several kinds of defects that cannot be reversed, including loss of mental ability and deformed physical features. Mothers who use cocaine during pregnancy may give birth to babies who are dependent on cocaine. These babies don't like to be held and fail to respond to other humans. They will probably have physical and behavioral problems throughout their lives.

LESSON 1 REVIEW Write the answers to these questions on a separate sheet of paper, using complete sentences.

1) When does physical drug dependence occur?

2) When does psychological drug dependence occur?

3) What are three signs of drug dependence?

4) What is enabling?

5) What are two ways that drug dependence costs society?

Drug Dependence—The Solutions

Detoxification
Removing addictive drugs from the body

People who are drug dependent or who are close to someone who is drug dependent can take positive steps. Recovery from drug dependence is the first step.

How Do People Recover From Drug Dependence?

The process of recovery from drug dependence involves three main steps. The first step requires a person to recognize that he or she has a problem with drugs.

The second step in recovery is **detoxification**, or removing addictive drugs from the body. Detoxification should take place in a hospital under medical care to avoid serious problems.

The third step in recovery is learning to live day to day without drugs. This is a long-term process through which a person regains emotional health and learns new coping skills. With help from professional treatment counselors, people gain new understanding of themselves. They learn to use decision-making and problem-solving skills to handle difficulties in a healthy way.

The process of recovery never stops, because drug dependence cannot be cured. Drug dependence can, however, be treated successfully. Because drug dependence is never cured, abstinence is the goal of recovery. This means that a person never uses drugs again. Sometimes people go back to using drugs again. Even so, a person can still achieve recovery and the goal of abstinence.

Where Can Individuals and Families Get Help?

Successful treatment programs set up a plan to help each individual. Each person who has drug dependence is different and may respond differently to treatment.

For this reason, trained professionals use a combination of approaches that may best help each individual. All programs help people to avoid drug use.

Writing About Health

Think about some healthy choices you have made that kept you from drug use. Write about whether the choices had short- or long-term physical or mental health benefits.

Where people get help may depend on the substance that they used and how long they used it. It also depends on the individual's desire for help. Some types of treatment resources or centers are described here.

Counseling

Most schools have counselors or a student assistance program. Students can use these resources to talk over concerns about their own, a family member's, or a friend's drug use. Counselors at community mental health centers can help by directing people to treatment centers. They also can provide ongoing help and encouragement after treatment or for family members.

Support Groups

A common place for treatment is support groups. These are groups in which members help one another. Alcoholics Anonymous (AA) was the first organization to offer support groups. The goal of treatment for AA members is never to drink again. Believing that alcoholics are responsible for managing their disease day by day, AA groups are based on the "buddy system." That means that each individual in AA has a sponsor. The sponsor is available around the clock to help the individual deal with the desire to drink.

AA has three other groups for family members of alcoholics. Al-Anon is a support group for adult family members who are affected by another adult's alcoholism. Alateen is for 12- to 18-year-olds, and Alatot is for 6- to 12-year-olds. Members of these groups help one another deal with the problems of living in a home in which someone has alcoholism.

Other support groups have formed for treating alcohol and other drug dependencies. Two examples are Cocaine Anonymous and Narcotics Anonymous. The National Council on Alcoholism and Drug Dependence also offers information and referral for help with drug-related problems.

Residential Treatment Centers

An individual can go to a regular hospital, a mental health hospital or center, or other agency that treats drug

SUBSTANCE ABUSE COUNSELOR

Substance abuse counselors work with people who are addicted to alcohol or other drugs. The counselor's goal is to break the addiction. First, addicted people must admit they need help. This can be difficult because often people do not feel they need help. Some counselors are recovering substance abusers themselves. This helps them understand those they are helping. Along with other health professionals, counselors develop treatment plans. Some substance abuse counselors may work only with alcoholics. Others work with people addicted to other drugs. Some work only with children, teenagers, pregnant women, or other groups. Preparation includes a one-year certification program, two-year associate's degree, or four-year college degree.

dependence. The individual lives in such a center, called a residential treatment center, during treatment. There the person receives help from health professionals who are trained in treating drug dependencies. Different centers may focus on certain age groups or phases of treatment. For example, some centers may treat only adolescents.

The doctors, psychologists, social workers, and counselors in these centers use the medical approach to treatment. That means they take the drug-dependent person slowly off a drug. Sometimes the professionals use medicines to help individuals through withdrawal from a drug.

Some treatment centers are run by state or local governments, and others are privately owned. Government-operated centers may be less expensive than privately owned centers. In either case, a person's health insurance plan often covers treatment in these centers.

Halfway Houses

Sometimes when people leave a treatment center, they go to a halfway house. These houses provide shelter and food for recovering individuals as they ease back into society. As long as people stay off drugs, they may stay in a halfway house to adjust to drug-free living.

Outpatient Treatment Centers

Some individuals receive treatment in an outpatient treatment center. These centers are for people who can function in society without drugs while recovering from their drug dependency. Usually people live at home while they get treatment for a few hours each day at the center. This kind of treatment generally lasts longer than residential treatment.

How Can People Avoid Drug Use?

People who don't use drugs never need to go through drug treatment. There are many ways to avoid ever starting to use drugs.

Refusing Drugs

Fitness Tip

Do aerobic exercises to manage stress.

The main reason that adolescents use drugs is peer pressure. Sometimes it helps to practice resisting peer pressure or saying no in a safe setting, such as a classroom. Practice in a safe setting can give a person confidence to say no in a real setting. For example, someone may need to say no at a party where people are using drugs.

One refusal technique for anyone feeling pressure to use drugs is to say no and walk away. If it is hard to walk away from a situation, a person can avoid it in the first place. For example, if you know there will be drugs at a party, you simply do not go.

Here are some other refusal techniques.

- Change the subject. Refuse an offer of drugs and then talk about something else.
- Give honest reasons for not using drugs. For example, you could say you want to be in control of your life rather than having drugs control your life.
- Keep repeating that you don't want to use drugs.
- Give facts about why the drugs will harm you and why you won't use them.
- Choose to associate only with people who don't use drugs.

Teens can pull together in resisting peer pressure to use drugs.

Getting Help

Getting help for stress and other problems can help to avoid drug use. This may be especially important for people who live in a home where there is drug use. Those people need to know that they are not responsible for the drug user's behavior. They also need to realize that they are responsible for their own behavior.

A person can get help to avoid drug use from a trusted, trained person. Sometimes supportive friends can help. Parents, school counselors or nurses, teachers, or other family members may be sources for help.

Many toll-free hotlines also are available. The National Treatment Hotline offered by the Center for Substance Abuse can link people with treatment in their community.

Nutrition Tip

Eat a balanced diet to maintain normal brain chemistry.

Eating Properly

Eating a balanced diet every day increases energy levels and general health and maintains normal brain chemistry. When a person's brain chemistry is normal, it is much easier to cope with stress and other problems.

What Are Some Alternatives to Drug Use?

Using drugs to deal with life's problems is a risky choice that never really solves problems. Activities that help a person develop self-esteem are better alternatives. It is important to find activities that meet the need to be part of a group. It is also important to have fun, share excitement with friends, and get relief from problems. Some of the best activities are those that become part of a lasting healthy lifestyle.

Here are some activities that can increase fitness and energy, reduce stress, and improve moods and feelings about oneself. Best of all, they can be done all through life.

- Do something physically active. It can improve mental and physical fitness, reduce stress, and increase energy, self-esteem, and pride. It also gives a sense of accomplishment. Try a dance class for exercise and energy to cope with stress.

- Get involved in an important cause that helps others and adds purpose to life. For example, you might volunteer at a hospital or for an environmental cleanup. You might help a younger child with a project.

- Join an interest or activity group with people who share common concerns. For example, you might work on the school newspaper or help to organize a walk for charity.

- Work at a part-time job not only for the paycheck but also for the pleasure of doing a job well. A job also can help to increase feelings of self-worth, self-esteem, and self-confidence.

LESSON 2 REVIEW Write the answers to these questions on a separate sheet of paper, using complete sentences.

1) What are the three main steps in recovery from drug dependence?

2) How do support groups work?

3) How are residential treatment centers, halfway houses, and outpatient treatment centers different?

4) What are two techniques for refusing drugs?

5) Name three alternatives to drug use.

■ Drug dependence is a psychological or physical need for a drug resulting from occasional or long-term use of that drug.

■ In physical dependence, the body develops tolerance for a drug and experiences withdrawal when drug use is stopped. A person may inherit a tendency toward physical drug dependence. Narcotics, barbiturates, and alcohol cause the strongest physical dependence.

■ In psychological drug dependence, people believe they need a drug to feel good and deaden the pain of personal problems. Psychoactive drugs produce psychological drug dependence.

■ People usually have some degree of both physical and psychological drug dependence.

■ The main pattern of drug dependence is that a person's life revolves around a drug. The more recognizable signs of drug dependence that a person shows, the greater are the chances of being drug dependent.

■ When family members try to protect a loved one from the results of drug dependence, they enable the person's continued drug use. Enabling delays admitting the problem and getting help. It hurts everyone.

■ Drug dependence costs society in dollars, present lives, and future lives. Babies born to drug-dependent mothers usually have problems throughout life.

■ People can recover from drug dependence, although they are never cured. The three main steps in recovery are admitting the problem, detoxifying, and learning to live every day without drugs.

■ Treatment in support groups involves members helping one another to stay drug free. There are also support groups for people who live with or are close to a drug dependent person.

■ People live in residential treatment centers during treatment. Some people live in halfway houses for a short time after treatment to learn skills for functioning in society. People live at home when going to outpatient treatment centers.

■ Many hotlines provide information, referral, and support to people with or affected by drug dependence.

■ People can avoid or find healthy alternatives to drug use.

Comprehension: Identifying Facts

On a separate sheet of paper, write the correct word or words from the Word Bank to complete each sentence.

WORD BANK		
abstinence	enabling	sign
admitting	halfway houses	support groups
alternative	management	tolerance
bad effects	pattern	withdrawal
detoxification	personal problems	

1) Physical drug dependence occurs when a body has _____ and withdrawal.

2) Tolerance is the ability to withstand increasingly more of a drug without _____.

3) _____ is the physical reaction to the sudden absence of a drug in the body.

4) Psychological drug dependence usually begins when people believe they need a drug to cope with _____.

5) When people think about a drug all the time, they display the main _____ of drug dependence.

6) A drop in performance at school or work is a _____ of drug dependence.

7) Protecting someone from the results of their drug use is called _____.

8) _____ is getting addicting drugs out of the body.

9) The first step in recovery from drug dependence is _____ the problem.

10) The goal of recovery is total _____ from drugs.

11) Alateen and Al-Anon are _____ for family members and people close to alcoholics.

12) In a residential treatment center, a person withdraws from drugs under medical _____.

13) _____ help to ease recovering individuals back into everyday life.

14) Working at a part-time job can be a healthy _____ to drug use.

Comprehension: Understanding Main Ideas

On a separate sheet of paper, write the answers to the following questions using complete sentences.

15) How does drug dependence affect family members?

16) What are two expenses of drug dependence to society?

17) What happens in the third step of recovery from drug dependence?

18) How do activities that are alternatives to drug use help a person?

Critical Thinking: Write Your Opinion

19) What do you think are some benefits of a drug-free lifestyle?

20) Why does it benefit family members to be involved in a loved one's treatment for drug dependence?

Test Taking Tip | Try to answer all questions as completely as possible. When asked to explain your answer, do so in complete sentences.

The Truth About Smoking

Picture this photo. Young people are laughing and having a great time. These "cool" people are eating at the beach, dancing on the sand, and smoking cigarettes. The picture implies that to have fun, people must smoke.

On an average day, four thousand smokers quit smoking or die from smoking-related diseases. But tobacco companies have used carefully planned marketing approaches to attract replacement smokers—often teens. Young people often become addicted to tobacco before they think carefully about the negative health effects of smoking.

Several states have sued tobacco companies for billions of dollars in health care costs. In most cases, settlements have been reached before trial. In Minnesota, part of the settlement was to forbid showing casual smoking in entertainment such as movies. The U.S. government also is trying to protect the public's health. But the tobacco companies have strong lobbies that try to persuade lawmakers not to pass laws against the tobacco industry.

Antismoking groups have begun to show the truth about tobacco ads. One billboard shows a cool camel dressed as Death—cigarettes in one hand, a scythe (symbol of death) in the other. The headline reads: "Smooth Reaper." Another shows a half-open coffin with cigarettes on the satin inside. The headline reads: "New Crush-Proof Box." These pictures make us ask what the truth is about tobacco ads.

Questions

1) Why do tobacco companies target children and young people in their ads?

2) Do you think someone who is dying of lung cancer from smoking should receive a settlement in a suit against a tobacco company? Why?

3) Who do you think should pay the health care costs of smoking-related diseases? Why?

4) Why do you think tobacco lobbies have so much influence on lawmakers?

■ Medicines are bought with a doctor's prescription or over the counter without a prescription. Medicines are grouped according to their purpose. Taking medicines for their intended purpose according to directions avoids problems.

■ The U.S. government controls the safety of medicines and how drugs are labeled.

■ Tobacco and alcohol are addicting. The nicotine in tobacco is a stimulant. Alcohol is a central nervous system depressant and psychoactive drug. Using either drug can result in serious diseases. Breathing passive smoke produces health problems for nonsmokers.

■ Alcoholism results from dependence on alcohol and is curable with medical and psychological help and abstinence from drinking.

■ Stimulants, depressants, narcotics, and hallucinogens are addicting psychoactive drugs. Stimulants speed up the central nervous system, depressants and narcotics slow it down, and hallucinogens confuse it. Marijuana, inhalants, designer and look-alike drugs, and anabolic steroids are other addicting drugs.

■ Drug dependence is a need for a drug resulting from its occasional or long-term use. People usually have some degree of both physical and mental drug dependence.

■ In physical drug dependence, the body has both tolerance for and withdrawal from a drug. Narcotics, barbiturates, and alcohol cause the strongest physical dependence.

■ In mental drug dependence, people believe they need a drug to feel good and deaden the pain of personal problems. Psychoactive drugs produce mental drug dependence.

■ The more recognizable signs of drug dependence that a person shows, the greater are the chances of being drug dependent.

■ Drug dependence costs society money and present and future lives.

■ People can recover from drug dependence, although they are never cured. The three main steps in recovery are admitting the problem, detoxifying, and learning to live every day without drugs. People can avoid or find healthy alternatives to drug use.

■ Treatment in a support group involves members helping one another to stay drug free. There are support groups for people who live with or are close to a drug-dependent person.

Don't go into Mr. McGregor's garden: your Father had an accident there; he was put into a pie by Mrs. McGregor.

—Beatrix Potter, *The Tale of Peter Rabbit*

Injury Prevention and Safety Promotion

When was the last time you rode a bicycle? Did you wear a helmet? In some places you can be ticketed for not wearing a helmet. Do you always wear a seat belt? These are just two examples of things you can do to reduce your risks of injury.

According to a recent opinion poll, four out of five Americans feel that life today is riskier than ever before. Yet our life expectancy continues to rise as we discover new ways to stay safe and live longer. Through laws, education, and technology, communities are working to provide a safe environment. In this unit, you will learn about things you can do to help yourself, your family, and your community. You will learn ways to reduce risks of injuries at home and away.

☑ Self-Assessment

☑ 1. I know what I should do if a severe burn occurs?

☑ 2. Which injures more adolescents—car crashes, burns, or poisoning?

☑ 3. Do you know what CPR stands for?

☑ 4. Do you know how to do CPR in a emergency?

☑ 5. Do you have a smoke detector in your house?

☑ 6. Do you know what you should do if a person has a heart attack?

☑ 7. Do you know what you should do if someone is conscious and choking?

☑ 8. Do you know how to stop serious bleeding?

☑ 9. I know what to do if someone is poisoned.

☑ 10. I know how to remove a bee stinger from the skin.

Reducing Risks of Injury

*E*veryone faces risks of injury every day both at home and away from home. These injuries range from falls to motor vehicle crashes. People today are more aware of risks in their lives than ever before. They are also more aware of the steps they can take to reduce the risks. Laws, education, and technology have all helped to increase the safety of the individual, the family, and the community. Identifying some common risks and learning what can be done to reduce those risks also increases safety. With that knowledge, you can lower both the likelihood and the results of injuries to yourself and others.

In this chapter, you will learn how to reduce common risks at home, away from home, and on the road. You will also learn what you can do to prepare for and stay safe during natural disasters.

Goals for Learning

▶ To describe ways to reduce the risks of falls, fire, poisoning, and electrical shock at home

▶ To identify ways to reduce risks at work and during recreational activities

▶ To explain how to reduce the risks of vehicle crashes and increase bicycle and motorcycle safety

▶ To describe ways to stay safe during common natural disasters

Shattered Auto Glass

Reducing Risks at Home

*E*veryone would like to think that home is a safe place, but accidents and injuries do happen there. In 1994, 19,674,000 injuries occurred in homes. Fortunately, a large number of accidents at home can be avoided.

Most injuries that occur at home are the result of falls. Other causes of injuries at home are fires, poisoning, or electrical shock. Many of these injuries can be prevented. In each case, steps can be taken to reduce the risks involved.

How Can the Risks of Falls Be Reduced?

Everyone can trip and fall, but young children and older people are especially at risk.

Stairs are a dangerous place for falls. To make stairways safe, they should be well lit, in good repair, and free of litter. Tightly secured handrails, carpeting, and nonskid strips all can help to prevent falls on stairs.

Bathtubs and showers are common places where people fall. To make tubs and showers safe, grip bars can be installed to provide a handle. Nonskid mats or stickers on the bottom of bathtubs also can help prevent falls.

Spills or objects scattered on floors cause people to slide or trip and fall. Spills should be cleaned up when they happen. In addition, fastening throw rugs in place can prevent people from tripping and falling. Keeping toys and other objects off floors and all pathways is another preventive measure.

People often fall from unstable chairs, boxes, or piles that they stand on to reach high places. A safe stepladder or step stool is a better choice than a wobbly chair or box.

How Can the Risks of Fire Be Reduced?

Making sure electrical outlets are not overloaded is one way to prevent electrical fires. Another way is to check for bad wiring or damaged electrical cords. A licensed electrician can repair these problems.

Fuel or fire starters should be kept away from sources of heat and out of the reach of children. All flammable liquids should be stored in tightly closed containers away from heat, including a fireplace. Also, matches or lighters should be kept out of the reach of small children.

Fires in fireplaces and chimneys are often the cause of house fires. To prevent this, a screen should be placed over a fireplace when a fire is burning. Also, a fire in a fireplace should be attended at all times. Fires in chimneys can be prevented by having them cleaned each year.

Space heaters and furnaces can cause fires in homes. All heating units should be cleaned regularly and checked to ensure they are operating safely. Only extension cords that match the requirements of a space heater should be used.

Loose-fitting clothing and many lightweight materials can easily catch fire near an open flame. Caution should be taken around burning candles, fireplaces, and grills when people wear such clothing.

What Are Some Fire Safety Devices?

Two devices that can help if a fire does start are a **smoke detector** and a **fire extinguisher**. A smoke detector is a device that sounds loudly when it senses smoke or high amounts of heat. It warns people so they can take action immediately. At least one smoke detector should be installed on every level of a house and outside bedrooms. To make sure the batteries work, smoke detectors should be tested every month. The batteries should be changed yearly.

A fire extinguisher is a portable device containing chemicals that put out small fires. An extinguisher should be kept in the kitchen, since many fires can start from spills on the stove or in the oven. Almost everyone in a family can learn when and how to use a fire extinguisher.

What Can Be Done if a Fire Starts?

A fire extinguisher should only be used to put out small fires. A small fire is one that is confined to the area where it started.

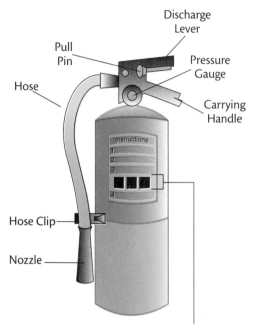

A slash through a symbol means do not use this extinguisher on that type of fire.

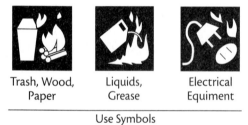

| Trash, Wood, Paper | Liquids, Grease | Electrical Equiment |

Use Symbols

Figure 15.1 The parts of a fire extinguisher

A CALL FOR HELP

The **911** telephone number is for emergencies. The system is available in about half of the United States. Where the system isn't available, calls can be made to an emergency operator, the police, or the fire department. The caller can help the 911 operator by providing information calmly, answering all questions, and following directions until instructed to hang up.

For example, a fire extinguisher can put out a fire in a wastebasket, furniture cushion, or small appliance. A person should know how to use a fire extinguisher correctly. The person's back should always be to an escape route in order to leave quickly.

It is important to be familiar with what a fire extinguisher can and cannot do before having to use it. A fire extinguisher has symbols on it that show the type of fire it can put out. A slash through a symbol on a fire extinguisher means the device should not be used for that kind of fire. Figure 15.1 shows the parts of a fire extinguisher and these labels.

Sometimes small fires can be put out in other ways. For example, baking soda puts out a small grease fire on a stove or in an oven. Putting a tight lid on a pan that has a grease fire in it cuts off oxygen to the fire. Water should not be used on a grease fire, because it makes the fire spread. Burners and ovens should be turned off immediately.

People should not attempt to fight fires that they cannot easily extinguish. In case of a large fire that cannot be extinguished, it is best to be prepared ahead of time. A family can prepare itself before a fire ever starts by taking these actions:

• Have regular fire drills, including a drill as if everyone were asleep in bed.

SAFETY FOR BABY-SITTERS

Baby-sitting or watching young children carries many responsibilities for safety. Here are some guidelines that can help avoid risks when watching young children.

- Know the number where parents can be reached and know when they will return.
- Have emergency and neighbors' phone numbers.
- Learn family rules for playing inside.
- Learn how to raise or lower the sides of the crib.
- Keep full attention on the children.
- Keep children away from appliances, matches, cleansers, soap, medicine, and bodies of water.

- Have a signal that alerts everyone to a fire drill. For example, someone could press the button on the smoke detector.
- Drop to the floor on hands and knees and crawl to a door. Stay close to the floor where there would be less smoke and more oxygen.
- Feel the door and doorknob to check for warmth. If a door is hot, everyone should take a second escape route, such as a window.
- Get out of the house at once without stopping to take belongings, and go to a designated meeting place.
- Call the fire department from a neighbor's home.
- Stop, drop, and roll on the ground if clothing has caught fire.

Safety gates that keep young children away from stairs and other dangerous places can prevent injuries.

How Can the Risks of Poisoning Be Reduced?

A poison causes injury, illness, or even death when it enters the body. Most poisonings happen with babies and young children because they put so many things in their mouth. Sometimes two different medicines or drugs interact and cause poisoning. Drug overdoses are the main cause of poisoning in 15- to 24-year-olds. Most risks of poisoning can be reduced in these ways:

- Store medicines and dangerous chemicals and household products in their original containers out of children's reach or in locked places.
- Never run a vehicle in a closed garage to avoid poisoning from exhaust.
- Use household products with dangerous fumes, or odors, in plenty of fresh air or outdoors.
- Inspect the yard for such plants as poison ivy, poison oak, and poison sumac. Find out how to remove them safely.
- Keep the number of the local poison control center near the telephone.

How Can the Risks of Electrical Shock Be Reduced?

An **electrical shock** is a flow of electric current through the body. Electrical shock may cause serious burns, injuries to internal organs, and even death. These shocks can happen when appliances are wet, don't work properly, or are used with too many other appliances.

Here are some ways to avoid electrical shocks:

- Never use an electric appliance if the floor, your body, or your clothing is wet. Examples of such appliances are hair dryers, power tools, and radios.
- Pull on the plug, not the cord, when disconnecting lamps and appliances.
- Stay away from power lines that are down and do not fly kites near any power lines.
- Cover electrical sockets with safety plugs in houses with small children.

Action for Health

PLANNING ESCAPE ROUTES FROM YOUR HOUSE

Do you know how you would get out of your house in case of a fire? Follow these guidelines to make a plan of escape from every room of your home.

1. Draw a floor plan of your home. Show two or more escape routes from each room to use in case of fire. Include an emergency meeting place that your family has chosen outside your home.

2. Decide who will give assistance to anyone in your family with special needs during the escape.

3. Post the floor plan where every family member can review it once in a while. Make sure each family member is familiar with the routes and the emergency meeting place.

4. Beneath the floor plan, write the names of two neighbors whose homes you can go to in case of emergency.

- Have only a licensed electrician repair appliances and add, replace, or repair wiring in a home.

- Do not put a bare metal object such as a screwdriver into an electrical outlet.

- Unplug electrical appliances that do not seem to be working properly.

LESSON 1 REVIEW Write the answers to these questions on a separate sheet of paper, using complete sentences.

1) Where are two places that people commonly fall in the home?

2) What are two fire safety devices that can help if a fire starts in a home?

3) For what kind of fires should a fire extinguisher be used?

4) What are two actions that can prevent poisoning?

5) What is electrical shock?

Reducing Risks Away From Home

Occupational Safety and Health Administration (OSHA)
U.S. government agency that seeks to protect the safety and health of American workers

*I*njuries occur not only at home but also in the workplace and during recreational activities. These injuries can be reduced.

How Can Injuries at Work Be Reduced?

If you have a job, you may already know about job safety. Every year, about 13.2 million work-related injuries occur, and 6,500 people die from injuries on the job. In addition, millions of workdays are lost every year because of work-related injuries and illnesses. In 1996, all expenses for injuries and lost productivity cost Americans about $121 billion.

Many occupational injuries and illnesses can be prevented. A U.S. government agency that seeks to protect the safety and health of American workers is the **Occupational Safety and Health Administration (OSHA)**. OSHA sets standards for industrial safety and provides education about safety procedures. For example, OSHA sets standards for noise and fire safety, protective clothing and safety gear, and safe levels of certain substances. It then works with employers and employees to ensure that the standards are met.

Employers are responsible to reduce risks of injury to employees by informing them of possible dangers on the job. They also must remove dangers in the workplace, train workers properly, and make employees aware of safety regulations.

Employees also can reduce the risks of injuries on the job. Getting necessary rest helps employees to be alert at work and avoid injuries. Employees need to follow all safety procedures, learn how to use equipment properly, and wear any required protective clothing or devices.

The Occupational Safety and Health Administration sets standards for protective safety gear.

How Can Recreational Injuries Be Reduced?

Everyone enjoys some kind of recreation. Every day, however, people are injured or die while engaging in recreational activity. Water and sports safety are special concerns.

Water Safety

Drowning is the third most common cause of accidental death in the United States. Drowning most often occurs among people between the ages of 15 and 24. It usually results from swimming and boating accidents, often when people have been drinking alcohol.

Knowing how to swim can prevent drowning. Swimming classes usually are offered through schools, at community pools, or through community recreation programs.

A technique that can help prevent drowning is called **survival floating**. This technique helps victims in warm water conserve their energy while they wait to be rescued. Figure 15.3 shows how survival floating works.

Drowning can be prevented in other ways. Before going out in a boat, people should check the weather conditions and make sure the boat is in good repair.

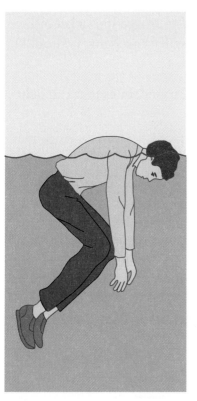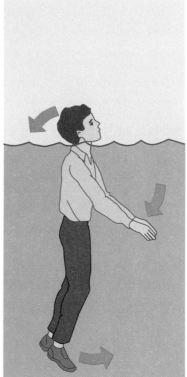

Figure 15.3 Survival floating.
Left: In the float position, rest face down for several seconds. Let arms and legs dangle.
Right: Slowly tilt head back so it clears the water. Exhale and take a new breath while pressing arms down and bringing legs together. Return to the float position.

GREATER SAFETY IN THE WORKPLACE

Since the Industrial Revolution, workers have faced dangers in the workplace. Many people have been seriously injured or killed. In 1970, the U.S. Department of Labor set up the Occupational Safety and Health Administration (OSHA). Improved safety standards cut the workplace death rate in half. Because of OSHA rules, fewer people in the clothing industry get lung diseases. Machine enclosures, better ventilation, and masks limit cotton dust in the air. Mine walls and ceilings are better built, so fewer miners die in cave-ins. In places using dangerous chemicals, workers now wear protective uniforms. As a result of OSHA rules, employers pay less money for insurance claims. Most importantly, fewer people die in work accidents.

Everyone in a boat should wear an approved life jacket or life preserver at all times. If a boat overturns, passengers should stay with the boat until help arrives.

SKATING SAFETY TIPS

- Wear a hard helmet, knee and elbow pads, and light gloves.
- Ride only on smooth surfaces in areas without vehicle traffic.
- Control your speed.
- Ride only where there are few pedestrians, and slow down for them.
- Curl up into a ball and roll if you fall to decrease your chance of injuries.

Here are some other water safety guidelines that can help prevent drowning:

- Swim only in places where a lifeguard is on duty and follow any posted water safety rules.
- Dive only where you know water is a safe depth. Also make sure there are no rocks, floating objects, or other swimmers where you are diving.
- If you get pulled along in a strong current, swim at a 45-degree angle to the shore and try not to panic.
- Don't attempt to rescue someone who is in danger of drowning unless you have had special training.
- Heed any warning signs to stay off thin ice. If no signs are posted, find out if it is safe to walk or skate on the ice.
- If ice begins to crack while you are on it, lie down and crawl away from the crack to safety.

Sports Safety

Injuries to people engaging in sports activities are very common. In fact, a whole group of doctors treat only sports injuries. Many sports accidents can be prevented by following these few simple guidelines:

Does your school have regular fire drills? What else could your school do to ensure safety?

- Know how to use recreational or sports equipment properly and safely as it was intended to be used. Make sure all equipment is working correctly.

- Wear the protective gear that is required or recommended for a sport. For example, a person should wear a helmet, knee pads, and elbow pads when skateboarding or in-line skating. (See Table C.5 in Appendix C.)

- Learn the skills needed to do the activity.

- Learn and follow any recommended safety guidelines, including proper warm-up and cool-down exercises.

- Don't try to do more than you are able or know how to do.

- When camping, always make sure someone knows where you will be, never camp alone, and take plenty of food and water.

LESSON 2 REVIEW Write the answers to these questions on a separate sheet of paper, using complete sentences.

1) How does OSHA protect American workers from injury?

2) What are two ways that employees can reduce injuries on the job?

3) What is survival floating?

4) When and where is it safe to dive into water?

5) What should a person wear during a sports activity?

Careers

INDUSTRIAL SAFETY SPECIALIST

Industrial safety specialists work for the Occupational Safety and Health Administration (OSHA), a government organization. Its mission is to save lives, prevent injuries, and protect American workers' health. Industrial safety specialists make sure companies correct unsafe conditions. They might discover dangerous asbestos materials in a building. They may convince workers to "buy into" industrial safety, since all workers need to understand how to be safe. Industrial safety is challenging because of the many regulations to be followed. Industrial safety specialists must be concerned with waste disposal, environmental safety, pollution, and health hazards. Most employers require a college degree. Continuing education also is necessary to keep up with changes on the job.

Reducing Risks on the Road

Motor vehicle crashes cause the highest number of deaths among 16- to 24-year-olds in the United States. Fortunately, safe driving practices can prevent many of these crashes.

Using seatbelts reduces injuries.

How Can Vehicle Crashes Be Reduced?

The best prevention for vehicle crashes is to take a driver's training course to learn safe driving skills and habits. Students in these courses learn road rules and defensive driving skills. They learn to watch out for drivers who make mistakes or adjust for unsafe road conditions.

A critical safe driving habit is observing and maintaining the speed limit. When road conditions are dangerous, traveling below the posted speed allows safe handling of a vehicle. For example, it is important to reduce speed in fog, rain, snow, or ice. It is also important to reduce speed on dirt roads and when pavement is damaged.

TO AVOID CRASHES:

- Keep the vehicle properly maintained.
- Maintain good vision by clearing moisture and ice from windows and making sure windshield wipers and defrost fans work properly.
- To see and be seen, use headlamps from dusk until just after sunrise and in rain, snow, and fog.
- Leave enough distance between you and the vehicle in front of you so you can stop quickly and safely without a crash.
- Avoid driving when your judgment might be clouded because of frustration, stress, anger, or other strong emotions.

Wearing a seat belt at all times can reduce injuries if an accident does occur. Both drivers and riders should buckle their seat belt securely. Small children should always be buckled into car seats that meet specific state requirements.

A safe decision is never to use alcohol or other drugs and especially never to drive under their influence. It is safest never to ride with a

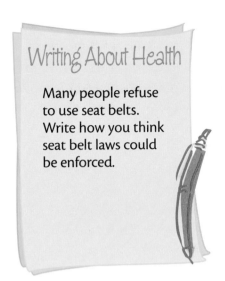
driver who is under the influence of alcohol or other drugs.

Some other tips to help avoid crashes are listed in the box on page 316.

How Can Bicycle and Motorcycle Safety Be Increased?

Bicyclists and motorcyclists are hard to see and are less protected than people riding in closed vehicles. These reasons and human error increase their risk for accidents. Figures show that 600,000 disabling injuries and 900 deaths resulted from bicycle accidents in 1995. In that same year, 55,000 injuries and 2,221 deaths resulted from motorcycle accidents. Following a few safety tips can prevent many of these accidents.

Do you think seat belts should be installed in school buses? How would you ensure they are used?

Both bicyclists and motorcyclists should wear the proper hard safety helmets. They should obey all traffic rules and follow many of the same tips for vehicle drivers. They should never grab onto a moving vehicle and always keep a safe following distance. In addition, bicyclists should:

- Make safe turns and cross intersections with care. Signal all turns with the left arm straight out for a left turn and the forearm up for a right turn.

- Ride single file as far to the right as possible with the flow of traffic, not against it.

- Wear bright clothing to be seen in daylight and reflective clothing to be seen at night.

- Have the right safety equipment and make sure the bike is in good repair.

Motorcyclists should follow the safety tips in the box.

MOTORCYCLE SAFETY TIPS

- Learn to drive their vehicle properly and safely before taking it on the road.
- Ensure that the cycle has working lights, reflectors, and rearview mirrors.
- Make sure the cycle is in good repair and have it inspected regularly.
- Wear proper clothing for protection and to avoid getting it caught in moving parts.
- Be especially careful on wet surfaces.

LESSON 3 REVIEW On a separate sheet of paper, write the word or words in parentheses that correctly complete each sentence.

1) The best prevention for vehicle crashes is a (driving course, reflector, safe distance).

2) It is important to (increase, maintain, reduce) speed with dangerous road conditions.

3) Drivers, bicyclists, and motorcyclists all should maintain a safe (racing, following, signaling) distance from the next vehicle.

4) Bicyclists and motorcyclists are less (frustrated, stressed, protected) than people in closed vehicles.

5) Bicyclists should ride (double, single, triple) file as close to the right as possible.

SAFER CARS

The first automobiles had no doors, roofs, or windshields. They were not as safe as modern cars. Of course, they were not as fast either. At that time, there was little traffic. Over the years, the number of cars increased. So did driving speeds and concerns about safety.

Car manufacturers improved safety. They provided seat belts, antilock brakes, car seats for children, brake and signal lights, and shock-absorbing bumpers. Some models offered safer steering columns and windows. Since the 1970s, cars with front-wheel drive have provided greater control. In the 1990s, air bags became required equipment for new cars.

Then and Now

Safety During Natural Disasters

Hurricane
A severe tropical storm with heavy rains and winds above 75 miles per hour

Tornado
A funnel-shaped column of wind with speeds up to 500 miles per hour

Natural disasters are sudden emergencies that result from causes in nature. Hurricanes, tornadoes, floods, earthquakes, blizzards, and lightning are all natural disasters. Some natural disasters such as hurricanes and tornadoes can be predicted. Others such as earthquakes cannot be predicted. People who have no warning can be injured or killed in natural disasters, which cause millions of dollars in damage. With warning and preparation, however, people can survive these disasters with few or no injuries.

How Can People Prepare for a Hurricane?

A **hurricane** is a severe tropical storm with heavy rains and winds above 75 miles per hour. Most hurricanes can be predicted. They affect the southern and eastern coasts of the United States. When a storm begins to develop, the National Weather Service sends out a hurricane watch or warning. A watch means that a hurricane may occur, but a warning means that one is expected within the next 24 hours. People listen to the radio or television for further instructions and prepare to move quickly if necessary.

To prepare for a hurricane, tape or board windows and bring in items from outside. If advised to leave your home, go to a designated place until conditions are safe again. Before leaving home, shut off gas and electric power. Avoid any downed power lines to prevent being killed by electric shock. If the hurricane is close, it is best not to drive. Stay indoors on the downwind side of the house or building.

How Can People Prepare for a Tornado?

Another natural disaster involving high winds and heavy rain is a **tornado**. A tornado is a funnel-shaped column of wind with speeds up to 500 miles per hour. Usually tornadoes happen in the central and southern parts of the United States. These dangerous storms can be predicted. The National Weather Service issues a watch when a tornado may occur and a warning when one can happen within minutes or hours.

Tornadoes have a characteristic funnel-shaped cloud, or
column of wind.

People who live in the area of an approaching tornado must
take shelter at once. Go to the basement and stay there. If you
don't have a basement, go to the center of the house on the
lowest floor. Crouch or lie flat in a closet or bathtub and cover
your head.

If outside and you have time, move away from a tornado at
right angles to its path. If the tornado is too close, lie face
down in a ditch or the nearest low spot. People in a mobile
home should go to a tornado shelter. If there is no shelter,
they should leave the home and head for low, protected
ground.

Flash flood
*A dangerous event
that occurs
suddenly without
warning because of
heavy rains*

Flood
*An event that
occurs when a body
of water overflows
and covers
normally dry land*

How Can People Prepare for a Flood?

A **flood** is a natural disaster that occurs when a body of water overflows and covers normally dry land. Floods may result from severe rainstorms or when unusually heavy winter snows melt in the spring. Most floods can be predicted hours to days in advance. Occasionally, however, very heavy rains cause dangerous **flash floods** suddenly and without warning.

If people live in flood areas, they need to know where to go if they are ordered to move to high ground. If they have time before leaving, they should turn off gas, electricity, and water. They should also move their belongings to an upper floor.

During a flood, do not try to cross a stream where water is at or above knee level. Do not drive over flooded roads or land. If your car stalls because of flood water, leave it and go to higher ground at once.

After a flood, do not touch electrical equipment in wet areas. Throw away any foods or liquids that the flood water touched. Drink only bottled or boiled water until you are told the water supply is safe again.

Flooding can force people to leave their home for higher ground until the water goes down.

Earthquakes cause tremendous damage.

How Can People Prepare for an Earthquake?

Another natural disaster is an **earthquake**. An earthquake happens when plates—major slabs of rock in the earth's crust—shift and move, causing the earth to shake. Most earthquakes in the United States occur along the West Coast. Scientists cannot yet predict when an earthquake will occur. Even though earthquakes cannot be predicted, individuals in earthquake areas can prepare emergency plans.

To prepare for an earthquake, store emergency supplies such as flashlights, extra batteries, and a first aid kit. Learn where the main gas valve is in a house or building and how to shut it off. Anchor heavy items such as pictures or mirrors so they cannot fall on beds.

During an earthquake, duck under a strong table or desk and cover your face and head if you are indoors. Hold this position until the shaking stops. Stay away from glass and do not use elevators or stairs. If you are driving, move to the shoulder of the road, stop, and stay in the car. Do not stop under bridges, overpasses, or power lines. If outside, stay in a clear space away from buildings, walls, trees, and power lines.

After a quake, turn off the gas valve if you smell gas to avoid a fire from a broken gas line. Stay away from downed power lines and out of damaged buildings.

How Can People Prepare for a Blizzard?

A natural disaster that occurs in winter is a **blizzard**. A blizzard is a violent snowstorm with winds over 35 miles per hour that last for at least three hours. The temperature during a blizzard is at or below 20 degrees, and the visibility is approaching zero. The National Weather Service can predict blizzards, which occur mainly in the northern plains of the United States.

During a blizzard, stay in your home or a warm shelter. Do not travel even short distances. If there is a medical emergency, alert local authorities for help. If the heat goes out in your home, dress in layers of warm clothing and sleep under several light blankets.

Health Tip

Learn the steps to remain safe during natural disasters that happen in your area.

If you live in an area where blizzards occur, carry emergency gear in your vehicle during the winter. Emergency gear includes blankets, a flashlight, snacks, wool mittens and hat, extra socks, and warm boots. If your vehicle becomes stuck during a blizzard, stay in it. Run the vehicle only a few times each hour for heat. Clear snow away from the tailpipe to keep exhaust out of the vehicle. Keep moving and stay awake to keep from freezing.

How Can People Prepare for Lightning?

A natural disaster called **lightning** is an electrical discharge that commonly occurs during thunderstorms. Lightning is dangerous because it can strike and kill people. The National Weather Service can predict lightning storms, which occur in certain seasons in most areas of the United States.

Civil defense
An organized system of emergency measures that volunteers take to help people in disasters

During a lightning storm, stay indoors or in a closed vehicle. Unplug electrical equipment and use the telephone only in an emergency. If you are outdoors, find shelter away from trees, tall objects, and water. That is because lightning usually strikes tall objects or on water. Lie down in the lowest possible place if you cannot get to shelter. Whether indoors or outdoors, stay away from metal objects during a lightning storm.

How Can Communities Prepare for Disasters?

Usually communities have plans to follow in case of natural disasters. For example, if a tornado or severe storms are approaching, sirens sound to alert people to take shelter. People who draw up these plans usually include police, hospital, fire, and public health representatives. The planners may also include local Red Cross, United Way, and **civil defense** representatives. Civil defense is an organized system of emergency measures that volunteers take to help people in disasters.

The agencies that these people represent can teach people how to prevent accidents as well as how to respond in disasters. Many of these agencies offer courses to train people for emergencies. For example, the Red Cross offers courses in first aid and lifesaving.

LESSON 4 REVIEW Write the answers to these questions on a separate sheet of paper, using complete sentences.

1) How are hurricanes and tornadoes alike?

2) What should you do if you are caught outside in a tornado?

3) Why is a flash flood so dangerous?

4) What should you do if you are indoors during an earthquake?

5) Why should you stay away from trees, tall objects, and water during a lightning storm?

■ Serious falls can happen at home on stairs, in tubs and showers, on littered or wet floors, and when standing on unstable objects. Installing simple equipment and using some preventive measures can avoid such falls.

■ Fires caused by electrical problems, fuel and fire starters, space heaters and furnaces, and open flames can all be prevented.

■ Every home should have one or more smoke detectors and fire extinguishers.

■ Small fires in the home can be put out with fire extinguishers or in other ways. A family can prepare a plan ahead of time in case of a large fire, including fire drills.

■ A few simple measures can prevent poisoning or electrical shocks.

■ The Occupational Safety and Health Administration (OSHA) sets standards for safety in the workplace. Employers are responsible to reduce and remove dangers in the workplace. Employees can reduce risks by following procedures and requirements.

■ Learning to swim can prevent drowning. Survival floating and other water safety guidelines also can prevent drowning.

■ Sports injuries can be prevented by using equipment properly, wearing protective gear, and learning necessary skills. Other actions also prevent injuries.

■ Learning safe driving skills and habits, maintaining the speed limit, and driving according to conditions all help to prevent vehicle crashes. Wearing a seat belt can reduce injuries if a crash occurs. Other tips can help to avoid crashes.

■ Bicyclists and motorcyclists can be seriously injured in an accident because they are unprotected. Wearing helmets, following the rules of the road, and taking other preventive actions can reduce risks of accidents.

■ Natural disasters cannot be prevented and may or may not be predictable. People can be prepared and take protective steps in case of hurricanes, tornadoes, floods, earthquakes, blizzards, or lightning.

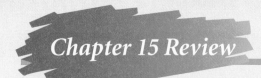

Comprehension: Identifying Facts

On a separate sheet of paper, write the correct word or words from the Word Bank to complete each sentence.

WORD BANK		
civil defense	gear	rest
current	heat	safety helmet
earthquake	OSHA	seat belt
falls	posted speed	survival floating
fire extinguisher	predicted	traffic rules

1) Stairs, tubs, showers, and wet or littered floors are places where _____ can happen.

2) Flammable liquids should be stored in tightly closed containers away from _____.

3) A _____ is a portable device containing chemicals that put out small fires.

4) An electrical shock is a flow of electric _____ through the body.

5) _____ sets standards for industrial safety.

6) Getting enough _____ can keep employees alert on the job.

7) A technique to conserve energy in warm water while waiting to be rescued is _____.

8) A person should wear the protective _____ recommended for a specific sport.

9) Traveling below the _____ is recommended when road conditions are dangerous.

10) Wearing a _____ can reduce injuries in a vehicle crash.

11) Bicyclists and motorcyclists should wear a proper hard
    _____.

12) Vehicle drivers, bicyclists, and motorcyclists all should
    obey _____.

13) Hurricanes, tornadoes, floods, and blizzards can all be
    _____.

14) During an _____, people indoors should
    duck under a strong table or desk.

15) _____ is an organized system of emergency
    measures taken during a disaster.

Comprehension: Understanding Main Ideas

On a separate sheet of paper, write the answers to the
following questions using complete sentences.

16) What does a slash through a symbol on a fire extinguisher
    mean?

17) How should medicines and dangerous chemicals be
    stored to prevent small children from being poisoned?

18) Name one natural disaster and describe one way to stay
    safe during that kind of natural disaster.

Critical Thinking: Write Your Opinion

19) What is one way you could make your own home safer?

20) You may have heard the caution that you shouldn't fool
    with Mother Nature. Why do you think this is especially
    true during a natural disaster?

Test Taking Tip | After you have completed a test, reread each question and answer. Ask yourself: Have I answered the question that was asked? Have I answered it completely?

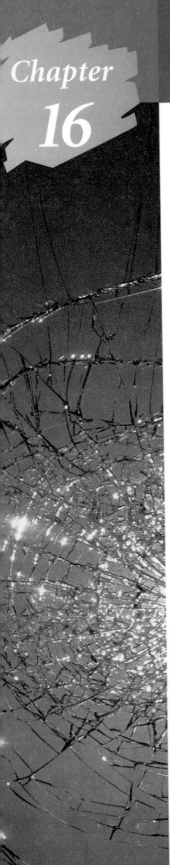

First Aid for Injuries

*I*n emergency situations, closely following specific first aid procedures is critical. In some emergencies, first aid skills can mean the difference between life and death. A person who knows first aid can spot the signs of serious illness or injury and perform the appropriate procedures. Proper first aid can ensure that these illnesses and injuries do not become more serious.

In this chapter, you will learn the basic guidelines for first aid as well as protections for first aid providers. You will learn the signs of choking, respiratory failure, cardiovascular failure, shock, and severe bleeding. You will also learn first aid for these life-threatening emergencies and for poisoning and other common injuries.

Goals for Learning

▶ To identify the basic guidelines for first aid

▶ To describe first aid steps for five life-threatening emergencies

▶ To explain first aid for poisoning and other common injuries

Shattered Auto Glass

First Aid Basics

> **First aid**
> *Immediate emergency care given to a sick or injured person before professional medical care arrives*

*F*irst aid is the immediate emergency care given to a sick or injured person before professional medical care arrives. Proper emergency procedures can reduce the pain of someone's injuries or even save a life.

What Are the Basic Guidelines for First Aid?

The most important thing to do for a victim in an emergency is to remain calm. Then you should follow these guidelines:

1. Survey the immediate surroundings to determine any dangers to the victim and to yourself. Move the victim only in case of danger such as drowning or fire. Make sure you will be safe before you assist the victim.

Emergency Medical Service staff provide first aid for injured people before moving them to a medical facility.

2. Find out if the victim is conscious by tapping on the person's shoulder or loudly asking if he or she is all right. If the person is not conscious, stay with the victim and ask someone to call for emergency help. If you are alone, quickly make the call and return immediately to care for the victim.

3. Check whether the victim is breathing and has a pulse and open airway. If not, try to clear the airway and perform rescue breathing, which is described in Lesson 2 of this chapter.

4. Ask a conscious victim's permission to provide care. Check the person's entire body for any other injuries. Check for emergency medical identification such as a tag, bracelet, or card. These identify medical problems the victim may have such as a heart condition, diabetes, or allergies to medicines.

5. Check for severe bleeding. If you have latex rubber gloves, put them on to protect yourself and apply direct pressure to a wound to stop bleeding.

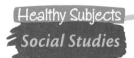

THE AMERICAN RED CROSS

The Red Cross began in Switzerland in 1863. In 1881, Clara Barton helped start the American Red Cross. The organization helps people in wars, natural disasters, or other serious need. Each year, about ten million Americans volunteer for educational programs, hospital duty, or disaster relief work. Red Cross Youth volunteer for hospital work and exchange gifts with needy young people. Volunteers donate much of the blood used by hospitals and during national emergencies. They contribute all of the money that supports Red Cross work. Volunteers are what truly make the Red Cross work.

Good Samaritan Laws
Laws that protect people who assist victims in an emergency

6. Call 911 or 0 for the operator to reach Emergency Medical Service (EMS) for help if this has not already been done. Be prepared to identify yourself and give your location and essential details about the victim. Answer any questions and listen carefully to any instructions. Stay on the line until the call is ended.

After you have done these things, stay with the victim and continue to reassure him or her. Keep the person comfortable and guard against chilling or overheating. Shade the person from the sun, and loosen any tight clothing, taking care not to move the spine or neck. Reassure the person that help is on the way. Use common sense and only the skills you have been trained to use. Make sure your help will not harm the victim.

What Are Good Samaritan Laws?

To protect people who assist victims in an emergency, many states have **Good Samaritan Laws**. The laws only require rescuers to use common sense and skills for which they have training until help arrives. They can get this training in first aid classes through the American Red Cross and the American Heart Association. Rescuers are not expected to risk their own life in providing care.

---

911 SOFTWARE

Every day thousands of people dial 911, seeking emergency help. The system puts callers in touch with police, fire, or medical services. It has computerized dispatching software, caller identification, and radio-transmitting facilities. A vast database contains constantly updated telephone numbers and addresses. The dispatcher's screen shows the caller's number and address even before the call is answered. Computerized maps are connected to the database. With them, a dispatcher can locate a caller simply by entering a telephone number. Deaf and hard-of-hearing persons can also call 911 by using a teletypewriter (TTD). All calls to 911 are recorded. The 911 system has saved many lives.

Universal Precautions
Methods of self-protection that prevent contact with blood or body fluids

What Are Universal Precautions?

To reduce the risk of infectious diseases such as AIDS, medical workers use methods of self-protection called **Universal Precautions**. These precautions prevent contact with blood or body fluids. For example, workers wear latex rubber gloves and other protective barriers such as masks. They carefully dispose of materials like bandages and dressings that have come in contact with body fluids. They thoroughly wash their hands after every procedure. Anyone who provides first aid should use these methods, which protect both the rescuer and the victim.

LESSON 1 REVIEW Write the answers to these questions on a separate sheet of paper, using complete sentences.

1) What is first aid?

2) What is the most important thing to do in an emergency?

3) How can you tell if someone is conscious?

4) What can you learn from emergency medical identification?

5) What is the purpose of Universal Precautions?

First Aid for Life-Threatening Emergencies

Heimlich maneuver
Firm upward thrusts below the rib cage to force a foreign object out of the airway

*I*n first aid, some conditions must be treated before others because they are life threatening. Choking, failure to breathe, cardiovascular failure, shock, and severe bleeding can all be life threatening. Minutes can mean the difference between life and death for people with these conditions. Knowing what to do before help arrives can make that difference.

What Is First Aid for Choking?

Thousands of children and adults choke to death each year because food or a foreign object blocks their airway or throat. It is important to recognize the universal distress signal for choking. A victim who clutches the throat between the thumb and index finger is showing this sign. Other signs of choking are gasping, a weak cough, inability to speak, pale or blue skin, and loss of consciousness.

Because choking is sometimes mistaken for signs of a heart attack, always ask the person if he or she is choking. If a choking victim can still speak or cough, allow the person to try to cough up the foreign object. Never pound on the person's back to try to force out the object because this can make the problem worse.

The universal distress signal for choking

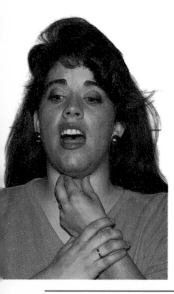

If the choking victim cannot speak, cough, or breathe, perform the **Heimlich maneuver**. These firm upward thrusts just below the rib cage force air from the lungs and the object out of the airway. To do the Heimlich maneuver, which is shown in Figure 16.1A, follow these steps:

1. Stand behind the choking victim and wrap your arms around the person's waist.

2. Make a fist with one hand.

3. Place the thumb side of the fist against the middle of the victim's abdomen above the navel and below the ribs.

4. Use the other hand to grab the fist and give quick, upward thrusts into the abdomen.

5. Repeat this until the object is forced out.

Figure 16.1. First aid for choking

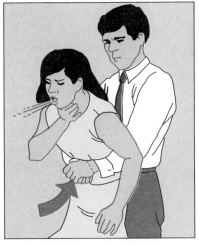
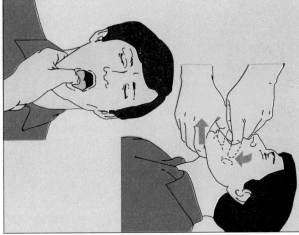

A. The Heimlich maneuver   B. The finger sweep

If the blockage is not removed and the person becomes unconscious, lower the victim to the floor on the back. Open the victim's mouth and check the throat for the blockage using the finger sweep shown in Figure 16.1B. To do the finger sweep, follow these steps:

Health Tip

Be prepared—keep a first aid kit well stocked.

1. Grasp the tongue and lower jaw between your thumb and fingers and lift the jaw.

2. Use your other index finger in a hooking action at the back of the tongue to sweep the object out of the airway.

3. If this doesn't work, begin rescue breathing, which is described below.

If you are alone and happen to choke, you can give yourself abdominal thrusts. Use your hands in the position shown in Figure 16.1A. You also can lean your abdomen over a firm object such as a chair.

What Is First Aid for Respiratory Failure?

Choking is one reason that people stop breathing. Other reasons are electrical shock or drowning. Respiratory failure, or not breathing, is a life-threatening emergency. The signs that a victim isn't breathing are no noticeable breathing movement and blue fingernails, lips, and tongue.

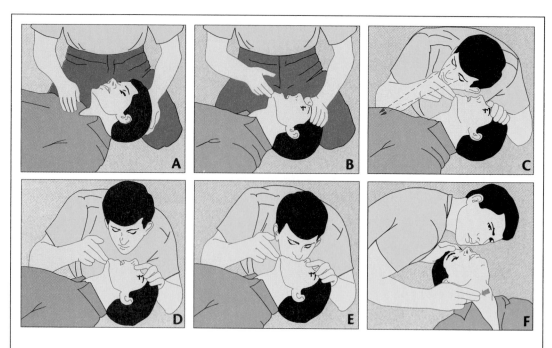

A. Tap on the person's shoulder or loudly ask, "Are you all right?" to find out if the victim is conscious. If the person is unconscious, send someone to call EMS for help.
B. Tilt the head back and lift the chin to open the airway.

C. Look, listen, and feel for breathing for 3 to 5 seconds.
D. Keep the head tilted back and pinch the nose shut.
E. Take a deep breath, seal your lips around the person's mouth, and give the victim two full breaths. For babies, seal your lips

around both the mouth and nose and give gentle breaths once every three seconds.
F. Check for a pulse on the side of the neck for 5 to 10 seconds. If you find a pulse, recheck breathing and continue rescue breathing as necessary.

Figure 16.2. The steps in rescue breathing

Mouth-to-mouth resuscitation
Rescue breathing

Rescue breathing
Putting oxygen from a rescuer's lungs into an unconscious victim's lungs to help the victim breathe

When a victim stops breathing but the circulation and pulse continue, **rescue breathing** is required. This technique is used in a life-threatening emergency to put oxygen from a rescuer's lungs into an unconscious victim's lungs. Figure 16.2 shows the steps of rescue breathing, which is also called **mouth-to-mouth resuscitation.** The best way to learn this technique is in your health class or another training class.

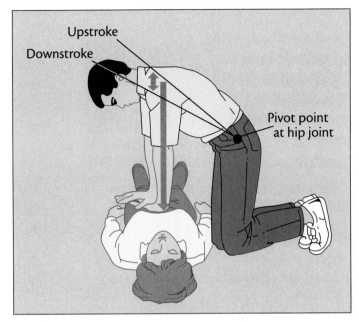

Upstroke

Downstroke

Pivot point
at hip joint

Figure 16.3. Cardiopulmonary resuscitation (CPR)

What Is First Aid for Cardiovascular Failure?

The failure of the heart or circulatory system to function properly is a life-threatening emergency. The cardiovascular system may fail because of electrical shock, poisoning, a drug overdose, or heart disease. It may also fail because a blood vessel is blocked as in a stroke.

Signs of cardiovascular failure include difficulty breathing, irregular pulse, moist face, and pale or blue skin. A person with cardiovascular failure may stop breathing altogether. If a person's heart has stopped beating, the person is in **cardiac arrest** and has no pulse. If a person shows the signs of cardiovascular failure or has a history of heart trouble, call EMS immediately.

Cardiac arrest
A condition in which the heart has stopped beating and there is no pulse

Cardiopulmonary resuscitation (CPR)
An emergency procedure for cardiovascular failure

While waiting for EMS, the victim can be helped with an emergency procedure called **cardiopulmonary resuscitation (CPR)**. This procedure uses both rescue breathing and chest compressions, or presses. The goals of CPR are to open the victim's airway and restore breathing and circulation. To perform CPR, follow these basic steps, which are shown in Figure 16.3.

1. Find the proper hand position.
   - Locate the notch at the lower end of the breastbone.
   - Place the heel of your other hand on the breastbone next to your fingers.
   - Remove your hand from the notch and put it on top of your other hand.
   - Use only the heels of your hands, keeping your fingers off the chest.

Shock
Failure of the circulatory system to provide enough blood to the body

2. Give fifteen compressions.
   - Position your shoulders over your hands.
   - Compress the breastbone 1½ to 2 inches.
   - Do fifteen compressions in about 10 seconds.
   - Compress down and up smoothly, keeping hand contact with the chest at all times.
   - After every fifteen compressions, give two full breaths.

As with rescue breathing, the best way to learn CPR is in your health class or another training class.

What Is First Aid for Shock?

Shock can be a life-threatening emergency resulting from a serious injury or illness such as severe bleeding or a heart attack. Shock is a physical reaction to severe injury in which the circulatory system fails to provide enough blood to the body. Even if an injury is not life threatening, shock can lead to death. Because of that, steps should be taken to treat shock at once.

What would you do if you came upon the scene of a multiple-car accident?

To tell if a person is in shock, you should look for certain signs. Some signs of shock are rapid or slow pulse, fast or slow breathing, and dilated pupils. Other signs are weakness, cold and moist skin, pale or blue skin, thirst, and an upset stomach.

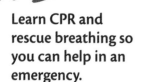

Health Tip

Learn CPR and rescue breathing so you can help in an emergency.

If a person is in shock, have someone call for EMS help at once. Then use these first aid steps for shock until help arrives:

1. Keep the person lying down and elevate the legs about 12 inches to help return blood to the heart. Do not elevate the legs, however, if you suspect injuries to the neck or spine.

2. Maintain the person's normal body temperature, using blankets or other warm covers.

3. Do not give the victim any food or water.

What Is First Aid for Severe Bleeding?

Because severe bleeding can result in shock or death, it must be controlled quickly. The rescuer who helps someone with

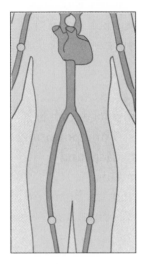

Figure 16.4. Pressure points for the arms and legs

severe bleeding must do four things: (1) stop the bleeding, (2) protect the wound from infection, (3) treat the person for shock, and (4) get EMS help immediately.

A first aid provider helping someone with severe bleeding must first take self-protection measures. Latex rubber gloves or plastic gloves, a sheet of plastic, or several layers of cloth can provide this protection.

After protecting yourself, follow these steps to control severe bleeding:

1. Cover the wound with a sterile bandage or clean cloth.

2. Apply direct pressure to the wound using the palm of your hand. If the blood soaks through the first dressing, leave it in place and add more dressings. Continue doing this until the bleeding stops.

3. Elevate the wound above the level of the person's heart.

Usually bleeding can be stopped with direct pressure and elevation. If bleeding continues, you may need to apply pressure at a **pressure point**. This is a place on the body where an underlying artery can be pressed against a bone to stop bleeding in a limb. To apply pressure to one of these points, use your fingers or the heel of your hand. Press the artery toward the bone, and hold it there until help arrives. Figure 16.4 shows the location of the pressure points for the arms and legs.

LESSON 2 REVIEW On a separate sheet of paper, write the word or words from the Word Bank that match each description.

1) The Heimlich maneuver is for _____.

2) Rescue breathing is for _____.

3) In CPR, the rescuer gives _____ compressions on the breastbone.

4) For _____, maintain normal body temperature.

5) Apply direct _____ to a wound to stop severe bleeding.

WORD BANK

choking

fifteen

pressure

respiratory failure

shock

First Aid for Poisoning and Other Problems

A person trained in first aid can recognize the signs of poisoning, fainting, burns, and other problems and give appropriate help.

What Is First Aid for Poisoning?

Poisons may be swallowed, breathed in, or absorbed through the skin. In any case, medical help should be sought quickly after first aid is given because some poisoning can be life threatening.

Oral Poisoning

Oral poisoning happens when a harmful substance such as a household cleaner is swallowed. Some signs of oral poisoning are sudden severe abdominal pain, upset stomach, and vomiting. The victim may become sleepy and lose consciousness. The person also may have chemical burns on the lips and a chemical odor on the breath. A container containing a poison may be nearby.

If a person has swallowed a poison, call the local poison control center immediately. Give as much information as you can, including the age and estimated weight of the victim. Also give the name of the poison you suspect was swallowed. The poison control expert will give you instructions and send emergency personnel when necessary.

Inhalation Poisoning

Inhalation poisoning happens when someone breathes in harmful fumes, or gases. Signs of inhalation poisoning are headache and dizziness followed by unconsciousness.

A person who has inhaled poison should get fresh air or be moved out of the area at once. If the victim is unconscious, check for a pulse and breathing. Perform rescue breathing or cardiopulmonary resuscitation (CPR) if the victim is not breathing. Take care not to breathe in any harmful fumes when helping a victim. If your own safety is in danger, do not try to help the person but call for help at once.

In case of a drug overdose, call the poison control center and follow their directions. Otherwise, follow these steps.

- Check for breathing, and give CPR if needed.
- Keep the airway open and body temperature normal.
- Reassure and calm the person.
- Keep the person awake.
- Get immediate medical help.

Contact Poisoning

Contact poisoning happens when harmful substances are absorbed through the skin. Poisons may be absorbed from plants such as poison ivy, household cleaning products, or lawn and farm chemicals such as fertilizers. Signs of contact poisoning are a severe rash, swelling, blisters, itching, and burning. Remove clothes that have contacted a poison. Wash skin with soap and large amounts of water. Applying calamine lotion may relieve the itching for a while.

What Other Problems Require First Aid?

Fortunately, most problems requiring first aid are less serious than those described in Lesson 2. First aid can ease the pain of these problems and prevent them from becoming more serious.

Fainting

Fainting is a short-term loss of consciousness caused by too little blood to the brain. Signs that a person is about to faint are pale skin, cold perspiration, and dizziness. Usually the person regains consciousness in a minute or two. Have the individual lie down flat and elevate the feet or bend over so the head is lower than the heart. Loosen any tight clothing and sponge the face with cool water. If the person does not regain consciousness, call EMS or 911.

Bites and Stings

Animal bites—Bites from dogs and other animals can transmit diseases such as **rabies** to humans. Control any bleeding from animal bites, wash the wounds with soap and water, and apply a dressing. If possible, have animal control workers catch the animal so it can be tested for rabies. Do not attempt to catch the animal yourself. Call the local health department to find out if the animal had rabies and if the victim needs treatment for tetanus or rabies.

Snake bites—Only four kinds of snakes in the United States are poisonous: rattlesnake, copperhead, water moccasin, and coral snake. Because serious problems and even death can result from snake bites, they should be treated at once.

Get the victim to a hospital as rapidly as possible or call EMS or 911 immediately. In the meantime, keep the victim calm, still, and lying down. This prevents the venom from circulating throughout the body. Prevent the affected part from moving and keep it lower than the heart.

Insect stings—Some people are allergic to stings from bees, wasps, and hornets and may have a life-threatening reaction. Use the edge of a card or your fingernail to scrape away the stinger. Pulling out the stinger could force the poison under the skin. Wash the sting with cold water or apply a paste of baking soda and water to reduce any swelling and pain. If the person has difficulty breathing, vomiting, upset stomach, or irregular heartbeat, call EMS immediately. If the victim stops breathing, begin rescue breathing.

Bone and Joint Injuries

If you suspect someone has a broken bone, or **fracture**, check for crookedness, swelling, bruising, loss of movement, and severe pain. Keep the body part in the same position in which you found it, and apply a **splint**. A splint is a rigid object that keeps a broken limb in place. If the bone has broken the skin, cover the wound with a sterile dressing without pressing on the bone. If you suspect a broken neck or back, do not move the victim. Call EMS or 911 at once.

A **sprain** is the tearing or stretching of tendons or ligaments connecting joints. Usually sprains occur at wrists, knees, or ankles. A person with a sprain should avoid any movements that cause pain. To reduce swelling, raise the injured part and apply ice or a cold pack. Then get medical attention.

Burns

There are three categories, or degrees, of burns. First-degree burns injure only the outer layer of the skin. These minor burns include some sunburns. Second-degree burns affect the top layers of skin. Severe sunburns may cause second-degree burns. Third-degree burns extend through all the layers of skin to the tissues underneath.

First aid for first- and second-degree burns is the same. First, stop the burn by getting the person away from its source.

Next, cool the burn with large amounts of cool water. Then, without cleaning the burn, cover it with a dry, loose, sterile dressing or a sheet to prevent infection. For third-degree burns, call EMS or 911 immediately, stay with the victim, and watch for shock.

Objects in the Eye

If there is an object in the eye, do not rub the eye. Flushing the eye with water, starting at the corner near the nose, may remove the object. If the object remains, seek medical help.

Nosebleeds

For a minor nosebleed, have the person sit and lean forward. The person should breathe through the mouth and apply direct pressure to the bleeding nostril for ten minutes. A cold cloth across the bridge of the nose may help. If these steps don't stop the bleeding, seek medical care.

Exposure to Heat and Cold

Heat exhaustion usually results from physical exertion in a very hot environment. Signs of heat exhaustion are weakness, heavy sweating, muscle cramps, headache, and dizziness. To give first aid, remove the person from the heat. Loosen the clothing, cool the person with wet cloths, and offer cool water to sip. Call EMS or 911 if the person becomes unconscious.

A **heatstroke** may result when a person remains in high heat too long. The main sign of heatstroke is lack of sweating. Other signs are high body temperature, red skin, vomiting, confusion, rapid pulse, and possible sudden unconsciousness. Call EMS or 911 immediately and follow the same steps for heat exhaustion.

Hypothermia is a serious loss of body heat resulting from being cold too long. It occurs most often in moderately cold, damp weather when an individual is tired and not dressed warmly. Signs are shivering, thick speech, and below-normal body temperature.

Writing About Health

The American Red Cross's motto is "Knowledge replaces fear." Write about how knowledge you gain from training in swimming, boating, CPR, self-defense, or first aid can replace fear.

Frostbite
A tissue injury caused by exposure to extreme cold

Hypothermia can cause death. If the person isn't breathing, perform rescue breathing and have someone call EMS or 911 immediately. Then remove any wet clothing and dry the individual. Slowly warm the person with blankets or other heat sources. Give the person warm liquids to drink. Watch the person until help arrives.

Frostbite is a tissue injury caused by exposure to extreme cold that usually affects the hands, feet, ears, or nose. Skin that has frostbite looks gray or yellowish and feels numb, cold, and doughy. To treat frostbite, slowly rewarm the affected part by placing it in warm water, but don't rub the area. Cover the area with clean, dry bandages and get medical help.

LESSON 3 REVIEW Write the answers to these questions on a separate sheet of paper, using complete sentences.

1) What is the first thing to do if someone has swallowed a poison?

2) What is a disease that can be transmitted to humans through an animal bite?

3) Why should the stinger not be pulled out after an insect sting?

4) What should be done for a fracture?

5) What are first aid steps for heat exhaustion and heatstroke?

Action for Health

APPLYING A SPLINT TO AN INJURED LIMB

Make a splint for a fracture with folded magazines, newspapers, boards, metal strips, or the body. For example, an arm can be splinted to the chest. Follow these rules when applying a splint:

- Splint only if you can do so without causing more pain to the victim.
- Splint the injury in the position you found it.
- Include the joints above and below the injury so they cannot move.
- Check circulation before and after splinting. Loosen the splint if the victim complains of numbness.
- Stay with the person until EMS arrives, and watch for shock.

■ Remaining calm in an emergency is the most important thing to do for a victim. Then determine the dangers in a situation, whether the victim is conscious and breathing, other injuries, and whether bleeding is severe before calling 911.

■ Good Samaritan Laws protect people who assist victims in emergency situations.

■ Following Universal Precautions protects medical workers, first aid providers, and victims from contact with blood and other body fluids.

■ Choking, failure to breathe, cardiovascular failure, shock, and severe bleeding all can be life-threatening emergencies.

■ The Heimlich maneuver is the first aid technique for someone who is choking. It involves upward thrusts just below the rib cage to force an object out of the airway.

■ Rescue breathing puts oxygen from the rescuer's lungs into the lungs of a person who isn't breathing.

■ A person in cardiovascular failure has difficulty breathing, an irregular pulse, and other signs. A person whose heart has stopped beating and has no pulse is in cardiac arrest. Both situations require cardiopulmonary resuscitation (CPR).

■ CPR includes rescue breathing and chest compressions to restore breathing and circulation.

■ Shock happens when the circulatory system fails to provide enough blood to the body. First aid goals are to return blood to the heart and maintain normal body temperature.

■ Direct pressure over a wound is the first measure in first aid for severe bleeding. If bleeding continues, pressure should be applied at pressure points over the underlying artery that supplies blood to an injured limb.

■ The local poison control center can give instructions for oral poisoning. Different measures help inhalation and contact poisoning.

■ First aid steps can be followed for fainting, bites and stings, bone and joint injuries, burns, nosebleeds, and exposure to heat and cold.

Comprehension: Identifying Facts

On a separate sheet of paper, write the correct word or words from the Word Bank to complete each sentence.

WORD BANK		
burns	dangers	insect sting
CPR	elevate	oral poisoning
common sense	fainting	pressure point
contact poisoning	finger sweep	rescue breathing
	frostbite	

1) Surveying the immediate surroundings in an emergency helps determine _____ to the victim and rescuer.

2) If a person is not breathing, the rescuer should perform _____.

3) Good Samaritan Laws require only that rescuers use _____ and skills for which they have training.

4) The _____ is a technique to clear a blockage from a choking victim's airway.

5) _____ uses both rescue breathing and chest compressions to restore breathing and circulation.

6) A rescuer should _____ a shock victim's legs to help return blood to the heart.

7) If direct pressure fails to stop severe bleeding, the rescuer may need to apply pressure at a _____.

8) Chemical burns on the lips may be a sign of _____.

9) Washing the skin with soap and large amounts of water is a first aid measure for _____.

10) Keeping the head lower than the heart is first aid for

_____.

11) A paste of baking soda and water reduces swelling and pain from an _____.

12) Large amounts of cool water should be used for cooling

_____.

13) For _____, it is important to slowly rewarm the affected area.

Comprehension: Understanding Main Ideas

On a separate sheet of paper, write the answers to the following questions using complete sentences.

14) Why should a rescuer check a victim's entire body?

15) Briefly describe the steps of the Heimlich maneuver.

16) What are the four things a rescuer must do for a person with severe bleeding?

17) What is the first thing to do for someone who has inhalation poisoning?

18) What is the first thing to do for heatstroke?

Critical Thinking: Write Your Opinion

19) What are some advantages of being prepared for life-threatening emergencies?

20) Why do you think it is important for rescuers to protect their own safety when trying to help someone in an emergency?

| Test Taking Tip | After you have taken a test, go back and reread the questions and your answers. Ask yourself, "Do my answers show that I understood the question?" |

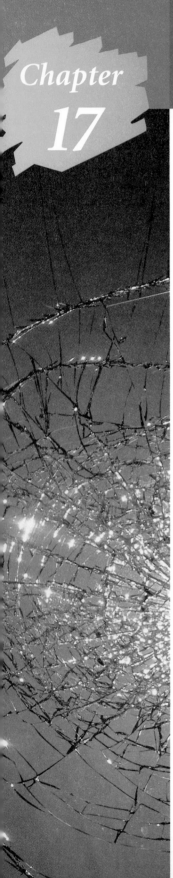

Preventing Violence and Resolving Conflicts

You see violence on television. You read about it in the newspapers. Even the words to some songs are violent. Why, you ask, is it in your health book, too? The answer is simple. Violence has become a health topic. It is a growing threat to the health of young people. We all need to understand violence. Then we can prevent it, preserve our own health, and help protect our friends and loved ones.

In this chapter, you will learn about the many types of violence around us. You will look at its different causes. You will read about the victims and the high costs of violent acts. You will learn that people can avoid violence by respecting one another. They can avoid violence by learning to identify and resolve conflicts in peaceful ways.

Goals for Learning

▶ To define violence and describe its costs

▶ To identify warning signs of conflict

▶ To describe causes of violence

▶ To explain ways to prevent violence and resolve conflicts

Shattered Auto Glass

Defining Violence

What Is Violence?

Violence is actions or words that hurt people or things that people care about. These actions take away people's sense of worth and their right to feel safe.

Violent behavior may be as simple as a push, hitting, or name-calling. Violence can involve damaging someone's property. Or it can be as deadly as using a weapon. Violence never solves problems. It simply creates new ones that usually are even worse than the original problems.

There are different kinds of violence. Media violence is all around us. We read about it in newspapers and see it on television and in films. Many people believe seeing violence on television and in movies teaches children that violence is acceptable.

Often people become the victims of family violence. Problems over money or drug abuse may cause family violence. Parents may become violent toward one another. Children may become victims of a parent's violence. Often parents learned this violent behavior when they were treated this same way as children.

Random violence has no specific target. Property is damaged by spray paint or rock-throwing and even fires. Sometimes people are injured. In some cases, such as drive-by shootings, innocent people are killed.

Gang violence is a growing problem in the United States. Members of gangs sometimes commit random violence. Often, however, they use threats of violence to claim their gang area, or "turf." Those threats may turn into fights that involve weapons.

Most violence occurs among people of the same race. You may believe that most violent acts happen among strangers. Actually, about half the murders in the United States happen among people who know each other.

WEST SIDE STORY

Many films and plays show the effects of hate and gang violence. Leonard Bernstein's musical play *West Side Story* is loosely based on the play *Romeo and Juliet* by William Shakespeare. It is about two enemy gangs. The Sharks are Puerto Ricans. The Jets are whites. Tony, who once was a Jet, falls in love with Maria, the sister of a Shark. The couple struggle but can't get away from the hatred between the two gangs. The play's characters sing, dance, and laugh. Its message, however, is serious: Hating people who are different from you is wrong.

Conflict
A disagreement between two or more people who have different ideas

Health Tip

Compromise to resolve conflicts peacefully.

How Is Conflict Different From Violence?

Conflict is a disagreement between two or more people who have different ideas. Conflict is all around us. It doesn't involve violence, but it can turn into violence. Disagreements among people are normal. Letting conflict turn into violence is not normal.

Conflict may be minor, ongoing, internal, or major. A minor conflict with a family member could be about chores at home. You may have a minor conflict with a friend because you hurt their feelings. Your parents may have a minor conflict with one another about money or how to treat children.

Many conflicts are ongoing. For example, you may have some constant disagreement with a brother or sister. Competing athletic teams have conflict over winning. These conflicts need not become violent.

You may have a conflict within yourself about making a difficult decision. This is an internal conflict. Perhaps someone wants you to go somewhere. You really want to go, but if you go, you will have to give up something else. You may feel confused, tense, or even sad about internal conflicts.

---

348   *Chapter 17   Preventing Violence and Resolving Conflicts*

Disagreements are normal.

Major conflicts can take a long time to resolve. Government leaders face major conflicts. Big companies have major conflicts with other companies or with workers who demand changes. An individual is faced with a major conflict if challenged to a fight. How the conflict is handled will determine whether a violent situation occurs.

Why are teens so prone to violence?

Who Does Violence Affect?

Each year since 1992, an average of 4.3 million Americans over age 12 have been victims of violent crime. Almost half this number were people between the ages of 12 and 24. However, 12- to 24-year-olds make up only 25 percent of the American population. Table 17.1 on page 350 shows how many people in 1994 were victims of robbery, assault or attack, and rape. Appendix C lists some figures on deaths and injuries caused by violence.

Table 17.1. Victims of Violent Crime in 1994

	Robbery	Assault	Rape
Age (all races)			
12–24	12,000	25,000	6,000
25–34	7,000	13,000	3,000
35–49	5,000	9,000	1,000
50 or older	2,000	2,000	*
White			
Age			
12–24	2,000	5,000	1,000
25–34	1,000	3,000	1,000
35–49	1,000	2,000	*
50 or older	*	*	*
African American			
Age			
12–24	4,000	8,000	2,000
25–34	2,000	4,000	1,000
35–49	2,000	3,000	*
50 or older	*	1,000	*
Hispanic			
Age			
12–24	3,000	6,000	1,000
25–34	2,000	3,000	1,000
35–49	1,000	2,000	*
50 or older	*	1,000	*
Other races			
Age			
12–24	3,000	6,000	1,000
25–34	2,000	3,000	*
35–49	1,000	2,000	*
50 or older	*	*	*

* Too few cases to obtain reliable data.

What Are the Costs of Violence?

Violent acts have many different costs. Some of these costs involve money, but many involve physical or emotional injury to people.

The victims of violent acts may have permanent injuries. For example, they may have brain damage. In some cases, victims become paralyzed. When people are paralyzed, they are unable to move their arms or legs.

Another serious injury for victims of violence is mental "scarring," which causes unending fear, anger, or sadness. The costs of treating these mental injuries can add up to thousands of dollars for each victim.

The friends and relatives of victims often feel great sadness and anger. They may be responsible for taking care of the person. In some instances, they may have to help pay medical costs.

People who commit violent acts may feel guilt over what they have done. They often feel worse about themselves than they did before the crime. Someone who is arrested for a violent act may face court and prison time. Once a person has a criminal record, it is hard to get back on track. A violent past may limit future job and housing opportunities.

People who witness violence pay a different kind of price. They may lose their peace of mind and may never feel safe.

All citizens end up paying for crime. The costs of police protection, courts, and prisons are growing all the time. These expenses, as well as the costs of health care and insurance, all increase with crime rates.

No matter how or why violence occurs, we all become its victims.

LESSON 1 REVIEW Write the answers to these questions on a separate sheet of paper, using complete sentences.

1) What is violence?

2) What are some different kinds of violence and of conflict?

3) How often does violence happen among people of different races?

4) Which age group has the highest number of crime victims?

5) Name four groups that are affected by violence.

Causes of Violence

How Can Conflict Be Recognized?

You may think that you can simply avoid conflict, but it is not that easy. We all face situations that involve conflict. If you learn to identify signs of conflict, you will be more able to avoid or resolve a conflict and avoid violence. Here are some warning signs of conflict.

WARNING SIGNS OF CONFLICT

- Shouting
- Name-calling
- Spreading rumors
- The silent treatment
- Insults
- Mean looks
- Making fun of someone
- Getting others to take sides
- Threats or threatening gestures
- Pushing or hitting

What Causes Violence?

The media can have an effect on how people view violence. Young people see violent acts on television and in films. They may well grow up thinking that violence is a way to solve problems.

Do you think the media indirectly causes violence?

Parents sometimes do not set the best examples for their children. If a parent uses violent behavior, the child may think it is acceptable. Many convicted criminals came from homes with violence. They were not able to break a pattern of violence they learned as children.

Many people buy guns as protection for themselves and their families. They usually do not plan to use them. However, just owning a gun increases the likelihood of being involved in violent crime. Unfortunately, the more violence occurs, the more people buy guns and the more violence increases.

The examples that parents set influence their children's behavior patterns.

Alcohol and other drugs make people act in strange and dangerous ways. They also can prevent a person from using good judgment. Half of violent crimes are committed by people under the influence of alcohol or other drugs. People who are addicted to drugs may resort to robbery to get money for those drugs.

Often members of gangs have had troubled lives. A gang may give them a feeling of belonging. Members often wear certain colors or clothes to identify that they are members of a specific gang. Youth groups or organizations that do not depend on violence are better, healthier choices than gangs.

Sometimes having personal problems can lead to violence. For example, you may be having some problems at school, at home, or at your job. When this happens, the stress you feel may affect the way you treat other people. You may feel depressed or hopeless. Physical exercise or talking with a trusted person can help clear your mind and relieve the stress.

How effective are the laws governing availability of guns? Should handguns be made illegal?

Sometimes people participate in violence to show loyalty to a group. Often people will go against their own better judgment because of a group. Doing this is called giving in to peer pressure.

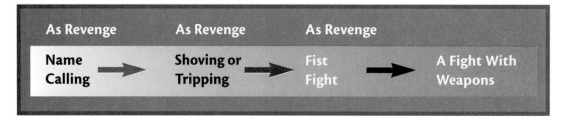

Figure 17.1. Pattern of an insult turning into violence

Prejudice is an opinion that has been formed without enough information or experience. Prejudice means prejudging people based on race, gender, cultural background, or religion. This sometimes leads to hate crimes, which are violent acts against people who belong to a particular group. Individuals who commit hate crimes want to prove they are better, but all they really prove is that they are hateful.

A person who has been insulted or hurt may want revenge. An act of revenge may become more violent than the act that caused it. In an effort to get back at someone, the person may make matters much worse. Figure 17.1 shows how revenge can make an insult grow out of control.

STOPPING VIOLENCE IN THE SKY

Early airports were much simpler than modern airports. There were fewer flights. There were also fewer concerns about violence in the air. In the 1960s and 1970s, however, terrorist activities placed passengers in danger.

In 1973, new security measures were begun. Under these rules, all baggage was X-rayed. Passengers passed through metal detectors. As a result, less terrorism occurred. By the late 1980s, some airports did not enforce these rules well. New terrorism occurred in the 1990s. Again, airports became more careful in examining both passengers and luggage. Such checks keep weapons or bombs from being carried onto planes. The government and airlines do their best to ensure passenger safety.

What Kinds of Crimes Happen to Teens?

Most teenagers are not violent. However, many teenagers become the victims of different kinds of violence. About 49 percent of violent crime victims in the United States are 12 to 24 years old. These crimes include robbery, assault, and rape. Also, about 35 percent of the people killed in the United States each year are under 25.

Age	Numbers
12–21	457,000
22–24	118,000
25–34	319,000
35–49	263,000
50 or older	130,000

Table 17.2. Victims of Robberies in One Year (United States)

Table 17.2 shows that teens make up the largest number of people who are robbery victims.

Rape
The unlawful act of forcing a person to have sexual relations against his or her will

To prevent becoming a victim of an assault, think about some of these ways to avoid assault.

- Do not walk alone at night.
- Walk only in familiar areas.
- Walk quickly and confidently.
- Stay in well-lighted areas.
- If you are being followed, walk quickly to a place where there are other people.
- When driving:
  - park only in well-lighted areas
  - never pick up strangers
  - keep your car doors locked

Sometimes young people become the victims of dating violence. For instance, a date may make fun of you or embarrass you in front of others. He or she may use threats or aggressive behavior to try to control you. Sexual abuse may include making jokes about your body or unwelcome touches or advances with which you are uncomfortable. No one should put up with dating violence.

Rape is the unlawful act of forcing a person to have sexual relations against his or her will. It is a violent crime in which sexual force is used as the weapon. For most people, rape is a crime that can have long-lasting emotional effects. In America, 1 in 89 women between the ages of 12 and 24 are rape victims.

Some young women are the victims of date rape. Warning signs of a possible date rape include threats or unwanted physical moves. A young woman should leave her date if this occurs and call a taxicab, a parent, or a friend.

Reporting a rape is often difficult for the victim. It is estimated that fewer than half of committed rapes are reported. Often victims of rape are embarrassed and may be afraid of being blamed. Sometimes they just don't want to get their date in trouble. Many communities now have female police officers who can support and counsel rape victims.

LESSON 2 REVIEW Write the answers to these questions on a separate sheet of paper, using complete sentences.

1) What are some causes of violence?

2) How much of the violent crime in the United States happens to teens?

3) What are three ways to avoid assault?

4) What are some kinds of dating violence?

5) What is rape?

PHYSICIAN'S ASSISTANT

Even if you don't become a doctor, you might consider becoming a physician's assistant (PA). Under supervision, physician's assistants may do most of a doctor's routine work. They take medical histories, perform physical examinations, and order laboratory tests. In emergencies, PAs treat cuts, scrapes, bruises, and burns. They know how to set broken bones. Sometimes PAs decide what results of lab tests mean. They may make diagnoses or prescribe treatments. PAs may handle tasks before or after surgery. Other responsibilities include office administration. Physician's assistants need experience in health care. They also must attend college and complete a recognized degree program.

Preventing Violence

How Can Anger Be Managed?

You get angry sometimes—we all do. A relative, a friend, or someone you hardly know may offend you. Your body tenses up from anger, your heart beats faster, and your blood pressure rises. You can give yourself time out to avoid saying or doing something you may regret later. During a time out, you can:

- Take a deep breath.
- Wait—count to ten if necessary.
- Exercise, if possible, to reduce your energy level.
- Think of nonviolent solutions.
- Avoid name-calling.
- Ask the other person to talk with you in private.
- Ask a respected adult for advice.
- Identify your own part in the problem.
- Be prepared to apologize if necessary.

How Can Conflict Be Avoided?

Sometimes the best way to deal with a conflict is to walk away. Ask yourself: Is the issue really such a big deal? Is the conflict based on a rumor that may not be true? How will I feel if I just forget about it? Think about what is happening. Maybe the other person is having some serious problems at home or at school. Perhaps the person never intended to cause a conflict. Let it go, and realize that the other person will be easier to get along with at another time.

Go for a run or punch a pillow to reduce anger.

You may want to use a simple hand gesture to end a conflict. This gesture, shown in Figure 17.2 on page 358, means "squash it" or "let's walk away" from a conflict. To make this gesture, bring the palm of one hand down flat onto the vertical clenched fist of the other.

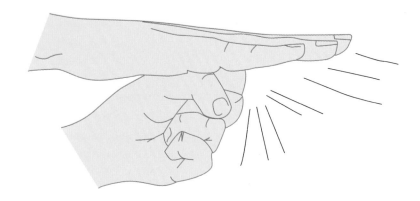

Figure 17.2. "Squash It" gesture to signal walking away from a conflict

How Can Conflicts Be Resolved?

Some conflicts cannot be ignored. When you must resolve a conflict, it is best to talk with the person alone. Having other people around only increases the chance that the situation will get out of control. Don't talk when the other person is under the influence of alcohol or other drugs.

As you explain your feelings, try to remain calm and keep your emotions under control. Insults will not help you to resolve the conflict peacefully. Focus on your feelings rather than the other person's actions. Give the other person a chance to do the same thing. If you have had a part in hurting the other person, don't be afraid to say, "I'm sorry."

How Can You Help Others Avoid Fights?

If other people get into a fight, don't encourage the fight by watching it. Often people in conflict feel they have to follow through when people are watching.

Let people know that you respect them for being able to walk away from a fight. Give respect to someone who is strong enough to apologize.

Writing About Health

In some places, laws have been passed that make concealing guns easier. Write what you think the punishment should be for concealing weapons.

Mediator
Someone who helps people who disagree to talk reasonably

There may be times when you can put pressure on friends not to fight. Let them know you support peaceful solutions to conflict.

You may be able to help as a **mediator**. A mediator is someone who helps others find a solution to a conflict. To mediate:

1. Let both people know that you are not taking sides.

2. Set some rules such as calm, reasonable speech.

3. Let each person state his or her feelings without interruption.

4. Allow them to ask reasonable questions of one another.

5. Encourage them to identify different solutions.

6. Ask them to discuss each solution and to agree on one idea.

7. Work at finding a compromise—don't let them give up without really trying.

What would you do if someone got "in your face"?

Action for Health

STEPS FOR RESOLVING CONFLICT

1. Stay cool. Take a deep breath or go for a walk. Resist acting out in anger.

2. Identify the problem. Take turns listening while the other person talks. Be honest. Avoid insults. Do not interrupt. Ask questions to discover the reasons for the other person's feelings.

3. Find out what people need. Each person says what bothers him or her about the problem. Use "I" messages. Each person says what he or she would like to have happen. Give each person's reasons equal attention.

4. Brainstorm all possible safe solutions. Write down as many solutions as possible. Include even silly solutions— sometimes they work. For each solution, ask if it is fair, respectful, and true to your sense of right and wrong.

5. Agree on a solution that is fair to everyone. Remember, not every conflict must have a winner and a loser.

6. If you can't resolve it together, perhaps you can seek a mediator.

Peer mediation helps to find solutions to conflicts.

Many schools have peer mediation programs. In these programs, students are trained to help peers resolve conflicts. Find out if your school has such a program.

How Can a Person Get Help With a Conflict?

When faced with a serious conflict, you need to get help. Talk with your parents or a peer mediator, teacher, or counselor at school. If they cannot help you, they can probably refer you to someone who can.

You may hear that a friend has plans for a violent act. You may not want to betray your friend's confidence. Nevertheless, it is always okay to break a confidence if a friend plans to do harm. Talk with a parent or other trusted adult who may be able to offer help to your friend.

Lots of people have conflicts. Asking for help does not mean that you are weak. It just means that you care enough about yourself and other people to take control of your life.

How Can Communities Help Fight Crime?

Communities are taking steps to fight crime. One popular method is Neighborhood Crime Watch. In these programs, volunteers are trained to identify possible crimes in progress. Then they report what they see to police. Often, neighbors post signs and stickers that warn potential offenders that neighbors are watching.

Because many crimes occur at night, community leaders in many places are making important changes. For example, they are planning more nighttime activities for young people. They are installing bright lights at nighttime hangouts such as playgrounds and parking lots. Some cities have begun teen curfews that do not allow teenagers on the streets after a certain hour. Additional officers are being added to the police force in some places.

Some other community actions to reduce crime are:

- Set up neighborhood centers where agencies can provide counseling help, recreation, and vocational training.
- Improve or add street lights to aid police and neighborhood watch programs.
- Install security systems in stores to notify police that robbery is in progress.
- Find and train block mothers to provide care for children in danger.
- Provide crime awareness education to reduce an individual's vulnerability to theft and assault.

On a state and national level, governments are passing stricter gun control laws. Many lawmakers are working for tougher punishments for those found guilty of violent crimes. You may wish to write your local lawmakers with your ideas about how your community can better fight crime.

Teens can make a difference by choosing to be peacemakers.

Schools in many cities now have full-time security guards. Some students must pass through metal detectors. Video cameras monitor hall activity. More counselors are being hired to help students in crisis. Perhaps the most positive move that many schools have made is to teach courses in accepting and respecting one another. Teens can choose to be peacemakers rather than troublemakers. You can make a difference.

LESSON 3 REVIEW Write the answers to these questions on a separate sheet of paper, using complete sentences.

1) In your opinion, what is the best way to control anger?

2) What does the gesture for "squash it" mean?

3) What are three steps for resolving a conflict?

4) What is a mediator?

5) Name three things that communities are doing to fight crime.

CHAPTER SUMMARY

■ Violence never solves problems but creates new ones that are usually worse. Some kinds of violence are media, family, random, and gang violence.

■ Conflicts—disagreements between two or more people with different ideas—may be minor, ongoing, internal, or major. A disagreement is normal conflict, but conflict that turns violent is not normal.

■ Nearly half of all violent crimes affect 12- to 24-year-olds. Costs of violence are permanent injuries, mental scarring, hurt to loved ones, lost peace of mind, and money that all citizens must pay.

■ Identifying signs of conflict helps to avoid or resolve conflicts and reduce the likelihood of violence.

■ Causes of violence are the media, parents' poor examples, poverty, owning guns, alcohol and other drugs, and gangs. Other causes are personal problems, group loyalty, prejudice, and the desire for revenge.

■ Robbery, assault, rape, and date rape are crimes that affect teens.

■ Everyone feels anger at times. Some specific techniques can help deal with anger to avoid its turning into conflict and possibly violence.

■ Conflict sometimes can be avoided by letting it go or using the "squash it" gesture as a signal to walk away.

■ Talking alone with the other person is the best way to resolve conflict. Both people must remain calm, avoid insults, and focus on feelings rather than actions.

■ Two ways to help others avoid fights are not to watch their fight and to respect them for walking away from it. Other ways are to pressure others not to fight or to act as a mediator.

■ Talking with a parent, peer mediator, teacher, or school counselor can help with a conflict. Breaking a confidence is acceptable when you know someone plans violence. Social service agencies can help with conflicts and to avoid violence.

■ Neighborhood Crime Watch and other programs help communities fight crime. Local, state, and national lawmakers are making tougher punishments for crime. Schools are taking many actions to fight crime.

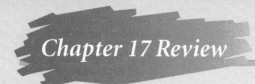

Comprehension: Identifying Facts

On a separate sheet of paper, write the correct word or words from the Word Bank to complete each sentence.

WORD BANK		
alcohol	Crime Watch	same
assault	gun	schools
causes	media	victims
commit	mediator	walk away
conflict	random	

1) _____ violence has no specific target.

2) Most violence occurs among people of the _____ race.

3) _____ is a disagreement between two or more people who have different ideas.

4) Permanent injuries and mental scarring are two costs for _____ of violence.

5) People who _____ violence pay for it with a criminal record and limited future choices.

6) The _____ and parents' poor examples affect how children view violence.

7) Just owning a _____ can lead to violence.

8) Half of violent crimes are committed by people under the influence of _____ or other drugs.

9) Gangs, personal problems, loyalty to a group, prejudice, and desire for revenge can all be _____ of violence.

10) Walking only in familiar areas and with someone are ways to avoid _____.

11) "Squash it" is a hand gesture that signals to _____ from conflict.

12) In being a _____, you may help others work out a conflict.

13) Volunteers in Neighborhood _____ programs identify possible crimes in progress.

14) Courses in accepting and respecting one another is one way that _____ fight crime.

Comprehension: Understanding Main Ideas

On a separate sheet of paper, write the answers to the following questions using complete sentences.

15) What is violence?

16) Name four warning signs of conflict.

17) What are five ways to use a time out in order to manage anger?

18) What are two ways to get help with a conflict?

Critical Thinking: Write Your Opinion

19) What do you think is the most serious cause of violence? Explain your answer.

20) What do you think is fair punishment for a rapist?

Test Taking Tip | Review your corrected tests. You can learn from previous mistakes.

Gun Control to Prevent Violence

As violence increases in America, there is growing concern about gun control. On one side, the National Rifle Association (NRA) supports people's right to keep and bear arms. On the other side, the Center to Prevent Handgun Violence successfully lobbied for the Brady Handgun Violence Prevention Act. This law requires a five-day waiting period before a person can buy a gun. During this time, background checks on the person are conducted.

At one time or another, almost every American has voiced an opinion about gun control. Here are some typical statements.

Against Gun Control

- We should have the right to own a gun without laws to stop us.
- Waiting periods and background checks won't stop someone who wants a gun.
- Gun laws won't decrease violence and crime.
- Every American has the right to self-protection.
- Americans should have the right to use guns for hunting and other recreational purposes.

For Gun Control

- We need gun control laws because guns are hurting and killing more people each year.
- The Brady Bill stops convicted criminals and drug abusers from buying handguns in the United States.
- Violence in the United States gets worse every year. The Brady Bill doesn't go far enough to stop it.
- Without gun control, our schools will only become more violent.
- America is no longer an uncivilized wilderness. Today we have police departments to protect us.

Questions

1) Which of the above statements about guns and violence have you heard?

2) Which ones do you think are believable?

3) Do you think gun laws will help to stop violence? Why?

4) One of the arguments against gun control is "Guns don't kill. People do." How strong do you think this argument is?

■ Fires in homes can be prevented. Smoke detectors, fire extinguishers, and a family plan in case of a fire are important.

■ The Occupational Safety and Health Administration (OSHA) sets standards for safety in the workplace.

■ Learning to swim, survival floating, and following water safety guidelines can prevent drowning.

■ Sports injuries can be prevented by using equipment properly, wearing protective gear, and learning necessary skills.

■ Safe driving skills and habits, maintaining the speed limit, and driving according to conditions help prevent vehicle crashes. Wearing a seat belt can reduce injuries in a crash.

■ Bicyclists and motorcyclists should wear helmets, follow the rules of the road, and take other preventive actions.

■ Remaining calm in an emergency is most important. Then determine other factors before calling 911.

■ The Heimlich maneuver is the first aid technique for someone who is choking.

■ Rescue breathing puts oxygen into the lungs of a person who isn't breathing. A person in cardiovascular failure or whose heart has stopped beating and has no pulse requires cardiopulmonary resuscitation (CPR).

■ First aid for shock is to return blood to the heart and maintain normal body temperature.

■ Pressure over a wound or at pressure points helps stop severe bleeding.

■ The poison control center can give instructions for oral poisoning.

■ A disagreement is normal conflict, but conflict that turns violent is not normal.

■ Nearly half of all violent crimes affect 12- to 24-year-olds.

■ Identifying signs of conflicts helps to avoid or resolve matters before they lead to violence. Dealing with anger can keep it from turning into conflict and possibly violence. Conflict sometimes can be avoided by letting it go or walking away from it. Talking alone with the other person is the best way to resolve conflict.

■ Talking with a parent, peer mediator, teacher, school counselor, or social service agencies can help with conflicts and to avoid violence.

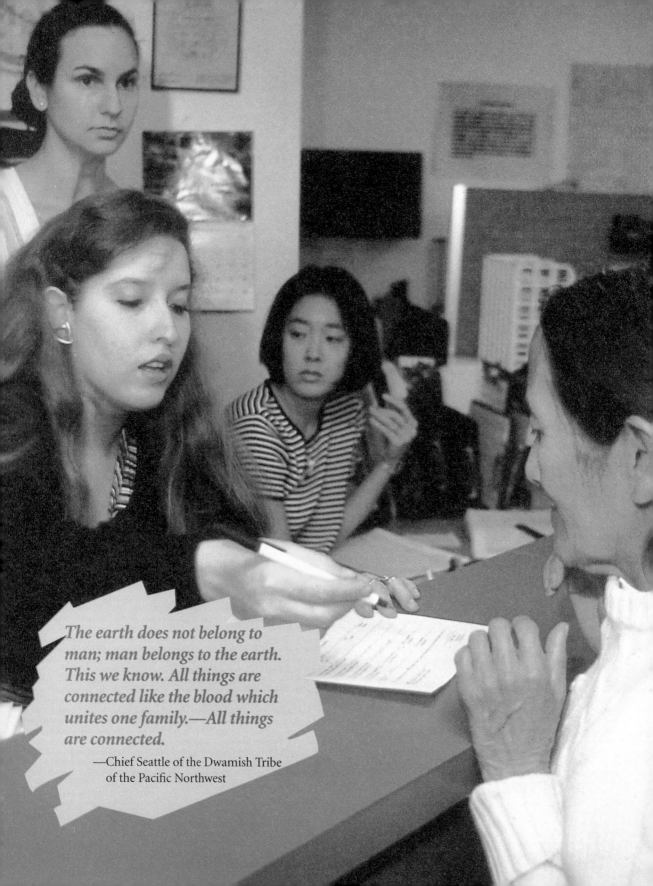

The earth does not belong to man; man belongs to the earth. This we know. All things are connected like the blood which unites one family.—All things are connected.

—Chief Seattle of the Dwamish Tribe
of the Pacific Northwest

Health and Society

D o you buy products with environmentally safe packaging? Do you volunteer for causes that promote public health? Do you recycle on a regular basis? We are all connected in having a responsibility to promote public health and protect our environment. As wise consumers, we can buy products that protect the environment. As members of a community, we can help to promote public health.

As consumers, we are faced with decisions every day that affect us physically, socially, and emotionally. These decisions may range from choosing health care, to helping at the food shelf, to learning how to prevent water pollution. In this unit, you will learn how to be a wise health consumer, promote public health, and protect our global environment.

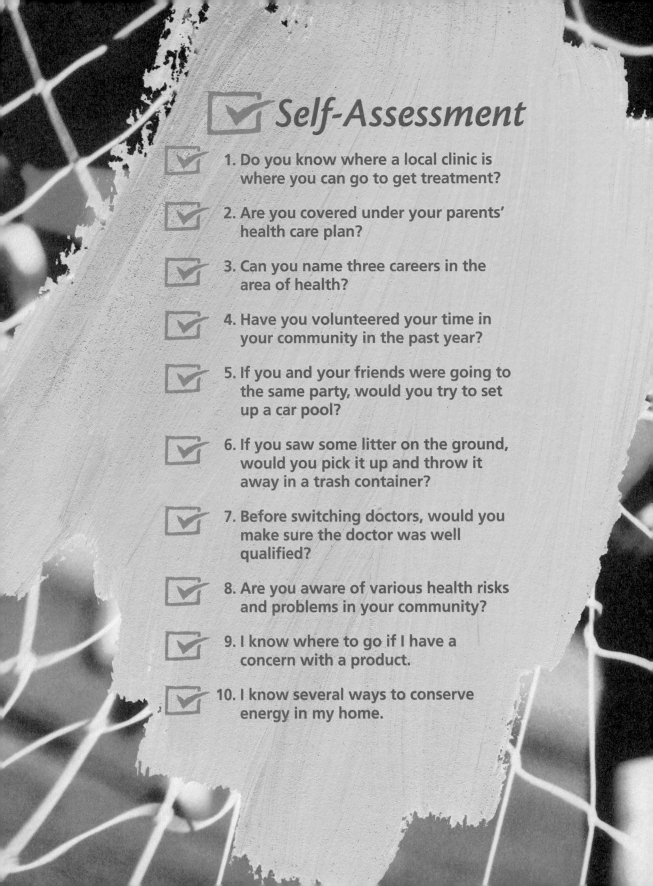

✓ Self-Assessment

1. Do you know where a local clinic is where you can go to get treatment?

2. Are you covered under your parents' health care plan?

3. Can you name three careers in the area of health?

4. Have you volunteered your time in your community in the past year?

5. If you and your friends were going to the same party, would you try to set up a car pool?

6. If you saw some litter on the ground, would you pick it up and throw it away in a trash container?

7. Before switching doctors, would you make sure the doctor was well qualified?

8. Are you aware of various health risks and problems in your community?

9. I know where to go if I have a concern with a product.

10. I know several ways to conserve energy in my home.

Consumer Health

*E*veryone "buys" health products and services every day. You "buy" health care when you use a product or a service that directly affects your physical and emotional well-being. You "buy" health care whenever you see a doctor, dentist, or nurse. From the soap you wash with to the sun screen you use, you "buy" health products and services.

Becoming a wise health "buyer" takes effort. It means learning how to judge the products and services you use. It means knowing when and where to seek health care and ways in which to pay for that care.

In this chapter, you will learn what wise health consumers know and what a consumer's rights are. You will learn what influences people's health choices, how to judge products and services, and how to clear up consumer problems. You will learn when to treat yourself and when and where to seek professional health care. You will learn how health care expenses are paid.

Goals for Learning

▶ To explain the advantages of being a wise health consumer

▶ To describe what influences health consumers

▶ To describe ways to judge products and services and correct problems with them

▶ To analyze when self-care or professional treatment is best

▶ To identify sources for health care

▶ To explain ways to pay for health care

Water

Being a Wise Consumer

Consumer
Someone who buys goods or services

Part of promoting your own health is being a wise **consumer**. A consumer is someone who buys goods or services. For example, you buy goods such as grooming products or over-the-counter medicines. You buy services such as dental or medical care.

What Advantages Does a Wise Consumer Have?

Being a wise consumer has some advantages. First, it can protect and improve your health. This means you avoid buying products that are useless or that may be damaging. It also means you recognize symptoms that signal the need for health care and get the help quickly.

Another advantage of being a wise consumer is saving money. This means getting the best product or service for the least money. Saving money takes some research, but it pays off in the long run. For example, checking consumer and other publications helps you to compare the features, benefits, and prices of different products.

Increased self-confidence is another advantage of being a wise consumer. Speaking up for your rights means taking care of yourself. For example, you can make a complaint to the proper source about a defective product you purchased. Usually this means you can get your money back or have the product replaced. The satisfaction of researching and finding the right product or service also can boost your self-confidence. Knowing and exercising your rights with confidence is part of being a wise consumer.

What Are a Consumer's Rights?

As consumers, everyone has some basic rights. The U.S. government has established the Consumer Bill of Rights, which gives every consumer these rights:

1. *The right to safety*—The consumer has the right to be protected from unhealthy products.

How do you think the Consumer Bill of Rights or the Patient's Bill of Rights can help avoid problems for consumers?

2. *The right to be informed*—People can ask for facts necessary to be protected from misleading advertising and to make wise choices.

3. *The right to choose*—People have the right to make their own choices.

4. *The right to be heard*—When consumers aren't satisfied, they have the right to speak out about it. This often helps to make laws that protect consumers.

5. *The right to redress*—Consumers have the right to get a wrong corrected.

6. *The right to consumer education*—People have the right to be educated about the products and services they buy.

Chart 18.1. Patient's Bill of Rights

1. The right to considerate and respectful care

2. The right to complete current information about your condition in terms you can understand

3. The right to receive all information necessary to give informed consent before any treatment

4. The right to refuse treatment to the extent permitted by law and to be informed of the consequences

5. The right to privacy during examinations and confidentiality concerning your care and records

6. The right to expect a reasonable response when you ask for help

7. The right to be told if your treatment will be part of a research project and to refuse to take part in the project

8. The right to expect good follow-up care

9. The right to an explanation of your bill

10. The right to know hospital rules that apply to your conduct as a patient

If you are a hospital patient, you are protected by another set of rights—the Patient's Bill of Rights. Some of these rights established by the American Hospital Association are shown in Chart 18.1. Many individual hospitals, medical centers, and dental and medical offices have established similar lists of rights. You may have been given a copy of such a list or seen one posted.

What Influences Consumers' Choices?

Many factors influence consumers' choices. Advertisers use techniques that influence people without their realizing it. For example, you may keep singing a catchy tune that you have heard to advertise a product. Without thinking about the reason, you may buy that product. It takes careful thought to consider how accurate advertising claims are.

Many factors influence choices of products such as these.

Another influence on consumers is the advice or opinions of family and friends. For example, if your friend tells you that a shampoo works wonders for his dandruff, you may decide to try it. You also might buy a product because your family has always used it. Word-of-mouth recommendations can be helpful when you consider a purchase. Keep in mind, however, that what is right for another person may not work the same way for you.

Price also influences choices. Well-advertised brand-name products are familiar but usually cost more than less known brands. The size of a product also affects the price. It is important to compare the price with its weight, volume, or count to determine the best value. Where a product is purchased also affects price. For example, the cost of a product in a convenience store may be higher than in a drugstore or discount store.

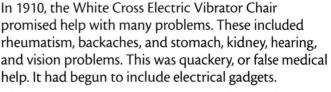

ELECTRICITY AND HEALING

In 1910, the White Cross Electric Vibrator Chair promised help with many problems. These included rheumatism, backaches, and stomach, kidney, hearing, and vision problems. This was quackery, or false medical help. It had begun to include electrical gadgets.

The government began regulating medical devices in 1938. Since then, electricity has been used to treat many illnesses. Small battery-operated devices are placed in the body. They help control the heart or other organs. Larger electrical devices produce healing magnetic or radio waves. Treatments with these devices have helped many people with arthritis and Lyme disease. Researchers believe that in the future, electric waves may help produce cells that fight cancer.

Quackery
The promotion of medical products or services that are unproved or worthless

How Does Quackery Influence Consumers?

Quackery is the promotion of medical products or services that are unproved or worthless. Each year Americans spend billions of dollars on products that claim to cure diseases and reverse conditions for which no cures exist. Persons with chronic diseases such as cancer and arthritis often become victims of quackery. People who are overweight or who are unhappy with the normal process of aging also are targets of quackery.

Quackery can fool even cautious people. People would like to believe that every disease and condition has a cure and that pain and suffering always can be eased. This is not always the case. At worst, people who buy fake treatments or worthless medications delay getting appropriate treatment until the problem is severe. At best, people waste their money on these products and services.

How Can Products and Services Be Judged?

The best way to determine whether a product is worth the cost and right for you is to study its ingredients. This involves making a habit of reading labels. Federal law requires that manufacturers list ingredients on the label of every food, drug, and cosmetic or grooming product. For example, if you were buying an acne medicine, you might look both at brand name and generic, or non-brand name, products. Both have labels listing their ingredients. Food labels usually are easy to read. Labels for cosmetic and grooming products and drugs can be more difficult to read. Reading the label provides important information.

Why might health care providers ask for a large payment in advance?

A doctor or respected agency such as those in Chart 18.2 usually can offer information about a product or treatment. In addition, the wise consumer should keep in mind that if something sounds too good to be true, it probably is.

How Can a Consumer's Problem Be Corrected?

Sometimes people buy a defective product or have a bad experience with a health care provider. When consumers' rights are violated or broken, they can try these actions to correct the problem.

1. The first step is to deal directly with the manufacturer of the product or with the health care provider. Many manufacturers have toll-free numbers. Call and explain your complaint. Ask for your money back or for a fair exchange. Record the names of people you talked with, the dates, and what they said they would do.

2. If you aren't satisfied, contact one of the agencies in Chart 18.2. It is best to submit the complaint in writing. Give the details of your problem, including any lack of cooperation from the manufacturer or caregiver. Send the original letter to the appropriate agency. Send a copy to the company or person the complaint is against. Keep a copy for your records.

3. If you don't get a response within six weeks, send a follow-up letter with a copy of the first letter.

Chart 18.2. Sources of Help for the Consumer

For complaints about a product or service, false advertising, or irresponsible behavior:

Better Business Bureau
Check the phone book for the local bureau

Also for complaints about false advertising:
Federal Trade Commission Office of Public Affairs
6th St. and Pennsylvania Ave. NW
Washington, DC 20580

For complaints about foods, drugs, or cosmetics:
Food and Drug Administration
5600 Fishers Ln.
Rockville, MD 20857

Food Safety and Inspection Service
U.S. Department of Agriculture
1400 Independence Ave. SW
Washington, DC 20250

For complaints about dangerous products:
U.S. Consumer Product Safety Commission
4330 East-West Hwy.
Bethesda, MD 20814

Most of the time, this procedure results in a satisfactory outcome.

LESSON 1 REVIEW Write the answers to these questions on a separate sheet of paper, using complete sentences.

1) What are three advantages of being a wise consumer?

2) List three rights that consumers have.

3) What is quackery?

4) What are two ways you can judge products?

5) Name two agencies that can help consumers.

Seeking Health Care

Wise health consumers know when self-care is appropriate. They also know when it is best not to act as their own doctor.

When Is Self-Care Appropriate?

Prevention is appropriate, ongoing self-care. Good nutrition, regular exercise, and safety practices help to prevent illness or injuries. Not smoking and not breathing in passive smoke are also preventive measures. You practice prevention when you don't use tobacco, alcohol, or other drugs other than those prescribed by a health professional. Maintaining a body weight that's right for your height and age helps to prevent heart and other problems.

Self-care for ordinary colds and other minor illnesses also is appropriate. The key word is *ordinary*. For example, sound self-care for an ordinary cold is to drink plenty of liquids and get extra rest. Minor illnesses and injuries that do not get better within a few days require professional help.

When Should People Seek Professional Help?

Sometimes it is best not to treat your own health problem. As a rule, you should consult a health professional whenever you notice something out of the ordinary about your body, behavior, or thoughts. Here are some examples of situations for which you should seek professional help:

Keep copies of all sales slips, letters, and other papers when trying to correct a consumer problem.

- An injury that is more than a minor cut or bruise or a minor blow to the head
- Any unusual bleeding, such as blood in the urine or feces, or any sharp pain, such as in the abdomen
- A patch of skin or a mole that has changed shape or color
- A minor problem such as a cold, flu, cough, sore throat, vomiting, fever, headache, or body aches that lasts more than a week
- Depression that lasts more than a few days or recurrent thoughts of suicide or harming yourself

Who Are Some Health Care Professionals?

Who to see for professional health care involves many choices. Most often people see a doctor for health care. A **primary care physician** treats people for routine or usual problems. For example, a primary care physician may do preventive checkups and handle easily treated problems. A primary care physician may refer you to a **specialist**—a doctor who works only in a certain branch of medicine. Chart 18.3 lists some medical specialists.

Chart 18.3. Medical Specialists

Allergist Diagnoses and treats allergies such as hay fever and hives	**Obstetrician** Deals with pregnancy and childbirth
Anesthesiologist Delivers drugs that cause loss of sensation to pain during surgery	**Oncologist** Treats cancers
Cardiologist Diagnoses and treats heart diseases	**Ophthalmologist** Diagnoses and treats eye problems
Dermatologist Diagnoses and treats skin problems	**Orthopedic Surgeon** Diagnoses and treats bone and joint problems
Endocrinologist Diagnoses and treats endocrine gland problems	**Otorhinolaryngologist** Diagnoses and treats ear, nose, and throat problems
Gastroenterologist Diagnoses and treats stomach, intestinal, and liver disorders	**Pediatrician** Provides primary care for babies, children, and adolescents
Gynecologist Diagnoses and treats diseases of women	**Psychiatrist** Diagnoses and treats mental and emotional problems
Neurologist Diagnoses and treats nervous system disorders	**Urologist** Diagnoses and treats problems of the urinary tract and male reproductive organs

People often see **nurse practitioners** for minor problems. A nurse practitioner is a registered nurse with special training for providing primary health care. The nurse practitioner does many of the simple things that a doctor does.

At times, doctors refer people to other kinds of health care providers. For example, a doctor might refer someone to a physical therapist or a registered

Today's consumers play a more active role in their health care.

dietitian. A physical therapist helps people to regain their muscle functions. A registered dietitian provides nutritional counseling for people who have special dietary needs, such as those with diabetes.

How Can You Find a Health Care Professional?

Finding a health care professional suited to your needs may be as simple as asking a trusted person for a recommendation. Family members, friends, or other health care professionals such as a school nurse may be able to recommend someone.

Local medical associations can give names and qualifications of physicians in your area. They usually don't recommend a specific person. Directories in the public library list physicians, their specialty, and where and when they received their training.

Once you have a list of names, you can decide whether you prefer a male or female health care provider. You might wish to see a young health professional, or you might prefer someone with more years of experience. If you feel uncomfortable with a health care provider, you may want to choose a different provider.

Look for these qualifications from health care professionals such as doctors, dentists, psychiatrists, and psychologists:

- A certificate from the appropriate board in the person's field.
- An association with a teaching hospital, dental school, or medical center.
- Experience in treating your particular health problems.
- Someone who answers your questions and with whom you feel comfortable. A good doctor-patient relationship is built on mutual respect and trust.

The kinds of places where people see health care professionals differs.

What Are Some Health Care Facilities?

A **health care facility** is a place where people go for medical, dental, and other care. A dental or medical office is one kind of health care facility. Primary health care is provided in these offices, such as routine examinations and tests to diagnose and treat injuries, diseases, and problems.

How can you find out more about a health care professional's qualifications?

Outpatient clinics provide primary health care for people who do not need to stay overnight. Outpatient clinics offer primary care and same-day surgery, meaning the patient has surgery and goes home the same day. Most clinics treat all kinds of medical problems. Others have a specific focus such as adolescent health.

Other facilities provide **inpatient** care, meaning people receive care overnight or longer. Patients can receive nursing care and sometimes **rehabilitation**—therapy needed to recover from surgery or an illness or injury.

A hospital is a facility that is equipped to provide complete health care services. People can receive both outpatient and inpatient care at a hospital. General hospitals provide care for all kinds of sickness and injuries. Teaching hospitals are places where students preparing to be health care professionals receive some of their training. Teaching hospitals may be associated with a medical school.

Research hospitals, which conduct medical studies, offer the advantage of advanced medical care. Specialty hospitals, such as children's hospitals, deal only with certain illnesses or groups.

Hospital emergency rooms and urgent care centers offer walk-in emergency care 24 hours a day. These centers treat people who cannot wait for an appointment at a doctor's office.

Health Tip

Compare ingredients and prices before buying health care products.

Long-term care facilities such as nursing homes offer nursing care around the clock. The elderly or younger people who cannot live independently because of a disability may live there. People who require extended recovery and rehabilitation after surgery may stay in a long-term care facility. A **hospice** is another kind of long-term care facility for people who are dying from diseases such as AIDS or cancer.

LESSON 2 REVIEW Write the answers to these questions on a separate sheet of paper, using complete sentences.

1) List three ways to practice preventive self-care.

2) What is a general rule for seeking professional medical help?

3) What does a primary care physician do?

4) Name three ways to find a health care professional.

5) What are two general kinds of health care facilities?

Action for Health

BECOMING FAMILIAR WITH A HOSPITAL SETTING

Have someone from your class call a local hospital. Ask whether the class can tour the facility. Ask that the tour guide explain how a hospital is run.

If the hospital uses student volunteers, you might ask for information about application procedures, time commitment, and tasks.

Paying for Health Care

Deductible
The first part of each year's medical expenses before the insurance company makes payments

Health insurance
A plan that pays a primary part of medical costs

Health care is expensive. Therefore, it is important to understand some of the ways in which people pay health care expenses.

While people can pay directly for medical expenses, most people cannot afford this out-of-pocket method of payment. **Health insurance** is a less expensive way to pay for health care. The insurance company pays a primary part of people's medical costs. These costs may include medicines, surgery, tests, hospital stays, and doctor's visits. Health insurance covers major medical expenses that people otherwise couldn't afford, such as organ transplants.

Three major kinds of health insurance are private, managed care, and government supported.

How Does Private Health Insurance Work?

With an individual private health insurance plan, people pay for a policy themselves. Individuals regularly pay a premium, or fee, to an insurance company for an insurance policy. In exchange, they have a guarantee that the insurance company will pay part or all of their health care expenses.

Only a four-day stay in the hospital can cost as much as $35,000. What do you think the financial future would be for an uninsured person who had to pay such expenses?

Many employers offer a group plan as a job benefit to workers. Usually the premiums are lower when people join the plan as a group. Employers usually pay the largest amount and workers contribute a smaller amount each month.

In either kind of plan, each individual usually is required to pay a **deductible**. A deductible is the first part of each year's medical expenses before the insurance company makes payments. For example, if you have a $200 deductible, you must pay the first $200 on your medical expenses each year. For all other expenses that year, the insurance company usually pays a certain percentage and the individual pays the rest. For example, if you had a medical expense of $100, the insurance company might pay 80 percent, or $80. You would then pay the remaining 20 percent, or $20.

Some insurance policies only pay a certain amount for some procedures or services. They may not cover other procedures or services. For example, some insurance policies may pay 50 percent for eyeglasses but may pay nothing for a hearing aid. The individual must pay for anything that isn't covered.

How Does Managed Care Work?

Private health insurers have introduced new health care choices for consumers. One such choice is **managed care**. In this arrangement, an organization is the go-between for the patient and the physician. There are two common kinds of managed care.

Health Maintenance Organizations

Health maintenance organizations (HMOs) are corporations made up of member doctors and professional staff who provide complete medical care. The care is provided within certain limits to enrolled members and their families. Members, whether employers or individuals, pay a fixed amount each month.

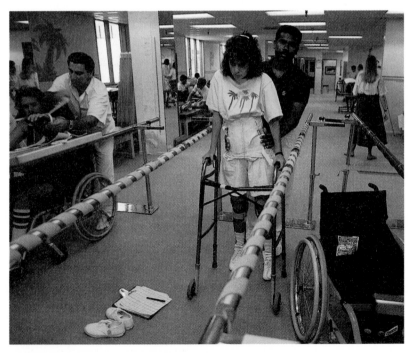

Most health care coverage includes services such as physical therapy.

There are two types of HMOs. Group HMOs require members to go to specific clinics or medical practices for their care. Independent practice associations (IPAs) provide members with a list of participating doctors and hospitals from which to choose.

HMOs emphasize preventive health care such as regular physical exams, well-baby care, and routine vaccinations at no extra charge. Private insurance usually charges for preventive care.

HMOs have some drawbacks. Members are limited in their choice of health care providers, and waiting time for appointments can be long. Also, members must pay all expenses for seeing doctors who are not in the HMO.

Preferred Provider Organizations

Preferred provider organizations (**PPOs**) provide their members more coverage if they choose health care providers in the plan. Members may choose doctors and hospitals outside the PPO network, but they must pay the extra cost. PPOs are generally more expensive than HMOs but less expensive than most private insurance plans.

What Is Government Health Insurance?

Government health insurance includes two kinds of insurance for special groups of people. Both of these programs are run by the Department of Health and Human Services.

Medicare provides insurance for people age 65 or older. It also covers people who receive Social Security disability benefits. Medicare pays for hospital and nursing home care. To cover physician and other expenses, people are expected to purchase additional insurance. The individual also must pay any uncovered expenses.

In 1997, the U.S. Congress passed a new law—Title XXI: State Children's Health Insurance Program. It provides child health care assistance to uninsured, low-income children.

Medicaid provides medical aid for people whose incomes are below an established level. Medicaid is different from Medicare in that it has no age requirement. It is paid for by state and federal taxes. Individual states operate Medicaid and determine the benefits they will offer.

How Else Does Government Pay for Health Care?

Besides Medicare and Medicaid, the U.S. government pays for health care directly or indirectly through tax money. The U.S. Public Health Service (USPHS) runs several agencies that provide this care. The following are five of the eight branches of the USPHS and their functions:

- The National Institutes of Health (NIH) provides grant money for research on health and illness. Universities, hospitals, and private institutes conduct the research. NIH oversees the work of thirteen other agencies, such as the National Cancer Institute.

- The Centers for Disease Control (CDC) is responsible for the control and treatment of communicable diseases. This includes sexually transmitted diseases, such as AIDS.

- The Food and Drug Administration (FDA) enforces laws that ensure the safety, effectiveness, and labeling of food, drugs, and cosmetics.

- The Substance Abuse and Mental Health Administration (SAMHA) oversees programs to prevent and treat alcoholism, drug addiction, and mental illness.

- The Health Resources and Services Administration (HRSA) supports mother and child health programs, community health education, and training programs for health-care workers. It also publishes health information.

How does the saying "An ounce of prevention is worth a pound of cure" relate to paying for health care?

Health departments for state and local governments also pay for public health services through tax money. They inspect restaurants for food safety and cleanliness. They make available at little or no charge health services such as vaccinations, blood pressure screening, and vision tests. They test water to make sure it is pure, oversee waste removal, and license medical workers. State and local health departments also operate centers for people with mental and physical disabilities.

MEDICAL RECORDS TECHNICIAN

If you can keep track of many details, think about a career as a medical records technician. Medical records technicians gather and report patient information. This may include symptoms, medical history, examination results, lab tests, diagnoses, and treatments. All records must be properly arranged. Technicians translate disease names and treatments into coding systems, so being organized and detail oriented is necessary. Most medical records technicians work on computers. They need excellent keyboarding skills. Technicians may work in hospitals, clinics, health agencies, insurance companies, nursing homes, and other health facilities. A high school diploma with on-the-job training is required. Sometimes a medical records course at a community college may be required. The job outlook for medical records technicians is excellent.

How Can Individuals Lower Health Costs?

The most costly medical treatment is inpatient care. Outpatient care, whenever possible, avoids the expense of overnight stays.

People can choose to receive health care from some low-cost alternative places, including the following.

- *Neighborhood health clinics* offer general or specialized medical attention, such as dental or eye care. They charge a relatively low fee to help people who would otherwise not be able to afford health care. Many of these clinics do not require appointments.

- *Alternative Birthing Centers (ABCs)* usually employ certified nurse-midwives to deliver babies. They offer care for low-risk pregnant women before and after giving birth and a real saving on delivery costs.

- *Hospices* provide dying patients with the medical care they need to live out the rest of their life comfortably. The costs for hospice care are lower than for hospital care.

You also can lower health care costs by educating yourself and becoming active in your own health care. Prevention is another way you can keep your own health care costs down.

LESSON 3 REVIEW On a separate sheet of paper, write the word or words from the Word Bank that matches each description.

WORD BANK
deductible
group
managed care
Medicaid
research

1) Two kinds of private health insurance are individual and _____.

2) A _____ is the first part of each year's medical expenses paid for by the individual.

3) HMOs and PPOs are two types of _____.

4) _____ provides medical aid for people with low incomes.

5) The National Institutes of Health provides grant money for _____ on health and illness.

■ Being a wise health consumer has the advantages of protecting and improving health, saving money, and increasing self-confidence.

■ The U.S. government protects consumers with some basic rights. Many health care organizations also set forth rights for patients.

■ Some influences on health consumers' choices are advertising, recommendations of family or friends, and price. Quackery is the promotion of unproved or worthless medical products or services.

■ Reading the label is the best way to judge whether a product is right for you. A doctor or respected agency can offer advice about a product or treatment.

■ Consumers who buy a defective product or have a bad experience with a health care provider can follow some steps to correct the problem.

■ Prevention and taking care of ordinary colds and minor illnesses are wise forms of self-care. You should consult a health care professional for anything out of the ordinary about your body, behavior, or thoughts.

■ Health care professionals include primary care physicians, specialists, nurse practitioners, and providers such as physical therapists.

■ Recommendations from others and checking local medical associations and directories are ways to find a health care professional.

■ Things to look for in a health care professional are board certificates, associations, experience with your health problem, and your comfort with the person.

■ Some health care facilities are dental or medical offices, outpatient clinics, and inpatient facilities for nursing care and rehabilitation. Others are different kinds of hospitals, urgent care centers, and long-term care facilities.

■ Individuals can pay health care costs through private individual or group insurance plans. Health maintenance or preferred provider organizations offer less expensive health care.

■ Government-supported health insurance includes Medicare for people over 65 and Medicaid for poor people. Several government agencies also pay for health care directly or indirectly.

■ Individuals can help to lower health costs by choosing low-cost alternatives when possible, taking part in their own health care, and practicing prevention.

Chapter 18 Review

Comprehension: Identifying Facts

On a separate sheet of paper, write the correct word or words from the Word Bank to complete each sentence.

WORD BANK		
advertising	HMOs	outpatient clinics
Better Business Bureau	ingredients	practitioner
	inpatients	quackery
directly	medical association	rehabilitation
general		routine
group insurance	Medicare	

1) _____ can influence people's health choices without their realizing it.

2) People are influenced by _____ when they buy a product that claims to correct an incurable condition.

3) The best way to judge a product is to study its _____.

4) You can get advice about a product from the _____.

5) The first step in correcting a consumer problem is to deal _____ with the manufacturer or provider.

6) A primary care physician treats people for _____ problems.

7) A registered nurse who provides primary health care is a nurse _____.

8) A local _____ can give you the qualifications of physicians.

9) _____ provide primary health care for people who do not stay overnight.

10) People who stay overnight or longer in health care facilities are _____.

11) Someone recovering from joint replacement surgery may need _____.

12) _____ hospitals provide care for all kinds of sickness and injury.

13) Many employers offer _____ as a job benefit.

14) _____ provide preventive health care at no extra charge.

15) People receiving Social Security disability benefits are qualified for _____.

Comprehension: Understanding Main Ideas

On a separate sheet of paper, write the answers to the following questions using complete sentences.

16) What are the advantages of being a wise health consumer?

17) If you had a painful, swollen foot with some bruising, what should you do about it?

18) What are three major kinds of health insurance?

Critical Thinking: Write Your Opinion

19) If you had an incurable condition, why do you think quackery might appeal to your emotions instead of your ability to reason?

20) Why do you think the cost of health care has become so high?

Test Taking Tip When taking a matching test, match all the items that you know go together for sure. Cross these items out. Then try to match the items that are left.

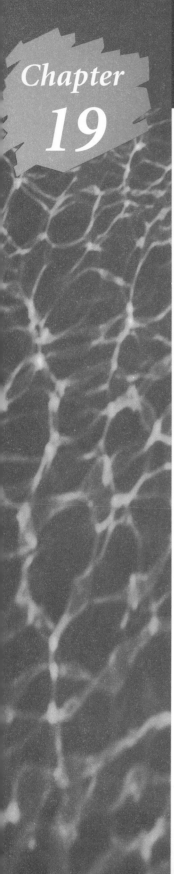

Public Health

*T*he health of a community is important because it can affect each individual's personal health. To promote a community's health and well-being, each individual, family, and neighborhood can help. People do this when they become aware of public health problems and cooperate to solve them. Every effort, no matter how small, can affect the health and well-being of individuals and of the whole community.

In this chapter, you will learn about public health problems in the local, national, and international community. You will learn how the public health system works to solve problems, promote health, and prevent disease. You will learn how you can help to promote public health.

Goals for Learning

▶ To identify public health problems nationally and internationally

▶ To describe community, state, national, voluntary, and international public health services

▶ To explain the role of health promotion and disease prevention in public health

▶ To identify individual opportunities to promote public health

Public Health Problems

Public health
The practice of protecting and improving the health of a community or a nation

Health is more than a personal concern. Health is a concern of whole communities and countries. **Public health** is the practice of protecting and improving the health of a community or a nation. Public health uses such means as preventive medicine, education, and control of communicable diseases to respond to health concerns.

Every ten years the U.S. government sets public health goals on which it works over the coming ten-year period. These include the following general goals.

1. To provide equal health care for all Americans, including children, adolescents, older people, and individuals with disabilities

2. To increase health and quality of life for older Americans

3. To increase the ability of all Americans to obtain the use of preventive health services

These goals are based on several public health problems.

Then and Now

SALK AND THE POLIO VACCINE

A virus causes polio, which is short for poliomyelitis. Polio destroys nerve cells that control muscles. It paralyzes the legs, arms, or body. It makes swallowing, talking, breathing, and heart functions difficult. Polio usually occurs in children. In 1943, the best-known person with polio was President Franklin D. Roosevelt. The same year, polio killed 1,151 people. It handicapped even more.

In 1954, Jonas Salk developed a polio vaccine. After many laboratory tests, he vaccinated Pittsburgh schoolchildren. In 1955, the medicine was tested in forty-four states. Salk said polio would be wiped out before long. He was right. By 1969 no one died from polio. The polio vaccine eliminated an epidemic.

Epidemic
A communicable infectious disease that spreads rapidly and affects large populations

What Are Some National Public Health Problems?

You already know that violence and alcohol and other drug abuse are public health problems in the United States. **Epidemics**, poverty, homelessness, getting health services, and the environment also are public health problems.

Epidemics

When a communicable disease spreads rapidly, affecting large populations at the same time, it is called an epidemic. In the United States, epidemics aren't as common as they once were. For example, polio was an epidemic in the 1940s and 1950s, but the disease was eliminated with the polio vaccine. Nevertheless, epidemics still happen. For example, AIDS has reached epidemic levels.

Poverty

Poverty is a public health concern because it puts people at high risk for serious health problems. Many experts believe that poverty is the foundation for many health problems.

A public health goal of the U.S. government is to provide equal health care for older people.

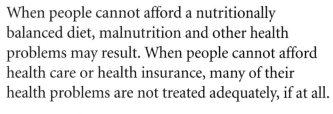

Writing About Health

Which public health problem do you think should be given the highest priority? Write why you think that.

When people cannot afford a nutritionally balanced diet, malnutrition and other health problems may result. When people cannot afford health care or health insurance, many of their health problems are not treated adequately, if at all.

Poverty is the main reason that many children go without vaccinations and other health care. When pregnant women do not get adequate care before a baby is born, both mother and baby can have health problems. These babies may have low birth weight, congenital problems, or slowed mental function.

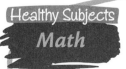

STATISTICS ON EPIDEMICS

Since America's birth, organizations like the Centers for Disease Control have gathered statistics related to national health. Epidemics have killed thousands of people in the United States. The chart below shows how many people died in some of the worst epidemics in America. The far right column shows the total number of Americans at the time.

Date	Disease	Number Who Died	Total U.S. Population at the Time
1832	Cholera	7,340	13,000,000
1878	Yellow fever	20,000	49,000,000
1900–1904	Typhoid	20,520	76,000,000
1900–1904	Tuberculosis	140,600	76,000,000
1916	Polio	7,000	99,000,000
1918	Influenza	550,000	102,000,000
1949–1952	Polio	6,000	151,000,000
1985–1995	AIDS	462,000	248,000,000

Which two epidemics have been the deadliest for the United States? Why do you think so? Why is polio no longer a problem in America?

HOME HEALTH AIDE

Living at home is important for most people, especially when ill. Home health aides help sick people to stay at home by performing routine tasks for them. They might change bed linens, prepare meals, clean, do laundry, and run errands. Aides help bathe and clean people. They may read aloud or play games with them. Under a physician or nurse's direction, aides give medication. They may give massages and other treatments. Usually, health care agencies employ home health aides. Some hospitals run home care programs that employ home health aides. In some cases, individuals hire an aide. Home health aides should know CPR. Many states don't require training for home health aides. However, some states are developing training standards.

Tuberculosis
A communicable lung disease

Homelessness

Homelessness is a community health problem related to poverty. On any given night, 750,000 Americans are without shelter. Of those, 35 percent are families with children. About 25 percent of homeless people are under age 21.

Women often become homeless because of domestic violence. When homeless shelters are overcrowded, women and their children sometimes return to an abusive household. Children cannot attend school regularly and frequently go without any health care.

In some homeless shelters, communicable diseases such as **tuberculosis**—a lung disease—are a growing problem. Poor hygiene also is a problem for homeless people. The other health problems that affect the poor also affect the homeless.

Getting Health Services

High-risk groups of people often are not able to get basic health services. The poor and homeless are two high-risk populations. Teenage mothers and their children, people with mental health problems, and elderly people also are high-risk groups. People with disabilities and recent immigrants to the United States are other high-risk groups.

Lack of transportation may limit basic health services. For example, people living in rural areas often have limited health services available.

Basic health services include vaccinations and medical care for women during pregnancy. Basic health services also include screening for health problems such as breast cancer. Nutritional counseling and exercise and fitness programs for elderly people are other basic health services. In addition, elderly people often need assistance meeting their daily needs. If the population over age 65 increases (as Figure 19.1 projects), even more health resources will be needed for elderly people.

Environment

How is where you live related to the food you eat?

The release of harmful chemicals into the environment is a public health concern. These chemicals pollute, or make harmful, the food people eat, the water they drink, and the air they breathe. Such pollution increases the risk of health problems. Some geographical areas are more polluted than others. In some areas, for example, cancer rates or the number of birth defects are high.

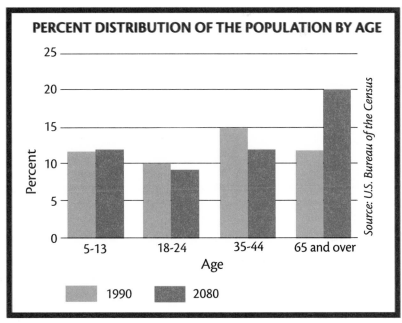

Figure 19.1. Distribution of the population by age

What Are Some Worldwide Health Concerns?

Developing nations often have little money and low standards of living. Often developing nations do not have laws or the resources to protect the environment. When these conditions exist, people cannot meet their basic needs for food, water, and shelter. Then problems such as hunger and malnutrition result. Poverty, AIDS, environmental pollution, and diseases such as malaria are public health concerns in many developing nations. Natural disasters and war also are concerns of worldwide public health.

LESSON 1 REVIEW Write the answers to these questions on a separate sheet of paper, using complete sentences.

1) What are three goals for public health in the United States?

2) Why is poverty a public health concern?

3) Name two high-risk groups that may have trouble getting health services.

4) How does pollution affect health?

5) Name three worldwide public health concerns.

Public Health Solutions

Sanitation
Any measures designed to protect public health

*H*ave you ever gotten a vaccination through a school, neighborhood health center, or local drugstore? What or who made that vaccination possible? Public health agencies, nonprofit groups, and individuals like yourself support organized preventive efforts to ensure the public's health. Most of these health services are provided to individuals at the community level.

What Are Some Community and State Health Services?

All states have public health departments. Most cities and counties have health departments as well. These departments are responsible for ensuring that laws relating to disease and **sanitation** are observed. Sanitation refers to any measures designed to protect public health. Tasks include inspecting restaurants, ensuring water quality, and tracking down sources of communicable diseases.

How well has your community done in providing barrier-free environments for people in wheelchairs?

Community and state health departments also work to provide medical care for low-income individuals. The departments provide vaccination programs, routine tests, and physical examinations. They also may provide visiting nurse and nutrition programs, community clinics, and community education programs. For example, community education programs may target young mothers and their babies, focusing on nutrition and education. Senior centers and aging and nutrition programs assist the elderly. School-based and school-linked clinics and services provide students with health care.

Federal and state governments provide local communities with funds to operate prevention and treatment programs. Most local programs, however, are funded through local taxes and private charities.

Most food shelf programs function through the help of volunteers of all ages.

What Are Some National Health Services?

The Department of Health and Human Services (DHHS) is the U.S. government agency with the largest responsibility for public health. DHHS gathers and analyzes health information, sets health and safety standards, and sponsors education and research. DHHS includes these divisions:

- Health Care Financing Administration—Controls Medicaid and Medicare

- Social Security Administration—Provides income to people who are disabled or retired

- Administration for Children and Families—Oversees programs for low-income families and people with disabilities

- U.S. Public Health Service (USPHS)—Conducts research, promotes disease prevention, and carries out national health policies

The Environmental Protection Agency is another government agency concerned with public health. It sets policy for and monitors the quality of the water and air.

The Occupational Safety and Health Administration and the Consumer Product Safety Commission also are government agencies concerned with public health. They set guidelines for safe exposure to toxic substances for workers and consumers.

Funding for these national health agencies and programs comes from federal income taxes.

What Voluntary Agencies Provide Health Services?

Many nonprofit voluntary health organizations also respond to public health needs. Such organizations are the American Heart Association, the American Cancer Society, and the American Lung Association. These groups provide public health support through education programs. Usually these organizations focus on a single disease such as cancer or heart or respiratory disease. The efforts of these voluntary organizations have helped American citizens learn preventive health measures. Anyone can volunteer to assist the efforts of these groups.

Action for Health

IDENTIFYING HEALTH SERVICES IN YOUR COMMUNITY

Find out about the different disease prevention, health promotion, and treatment programs available in your community. First, list local health agencies and organizations. Check with parents, counselors, librarians, teachers, the newspaper, and the phone book for ideas.

Divide into pairs or teams to gather information about the agencies. Phone each agency and request permission to ask about the items below. Prepare for the interview in advance. Record the answers.

1. Name, address, and phone number of agency
2. Days and hours of operation
3. Types of services and health professionals on staff
4. Who qualifies for services and the fees
5. Whether the services are confidential
6. Languages in which the services are offered

Analyze the information and compare the services. Are there parts of town in which some services are not available? Do several agencies provide the same services?

In many communities, people with common concerns meet together for support and education. Volunteer self-help groups provide support. For example, they support people with organ transplants or those who are recovering from an emotional illness. Sometimes charitable organizations such as the United Way help support these groups.

Voluntary public health agencies are funded by charitable contributions from individuals and businesses.

What Are Some International Health Services?

Eliminating world hunger, providing relief after major disasters, and combating epidemics are shared efforts of the entire human community. One organization that plays a major role in these efforts is the United Nations (UN). Programs of UN agencies such as the World Health Organization (WHO) mainly target developing countries. WHO works to improve living conditions, provide public health services, and prevent disease. Its workers educate people to prevent the spread of HIV, which is at epidemic levels throughout the world.

Health Tip

If you need vaccinations, find out if they will be offered in a neighborhood health center or a school in your community.

Individuals play a significant role in helping to address public health problems.

Other UN agencies provide worldwide health services. The United Nations International Children's Emergency Fund (UNICEF) provides vaccinations, school food programs, and health centers for children. It also helps to train nurses. The Food and Agriculture Organization works in developing countries to improve food production and to distribute food.

The United States also sponsors efforts for international public health. Organizations such as the Peace Corps and the Agency for International Development are two examples of these efforts.

The International Commission of the Red Cross is the world's largest private international public health organization. It provides aid such as food, clothing, medical care, and temporary shelter to victims of natural disasters.

How Do Health Promotion and Prevention Help?

Clearly, a healthy population locally, nationally, and internationally has benefits. Health promotion and disease prevention reduce the demands on the health care system. Preventive health care costs less than treatment of illness. Thus, health promotion and disease prevention are goals of many health professionals and policy makers.

Education for health promotion focuses on sexually transmitted diseases, violence, physical fitness, nutrition, and substance abuse prevention. Those efforts may target specific groups at risk or whole communities. A community-wide nutrition education program, for example, can encourage individuals to lower their fat intake and exercise regularly.

Prevention organizations that work with specific groups are called **advocacy groups**. Advocacy groups may provide health services themselves, or they may help remove health care barriers. They do this by working to change government policies that prevent some people from receiving health care. Advocacy groups may target children, the elderly, the disabled, the mentally ill, or different cultural communities.

Nationally, advocacy groups encourage passage of civil rights laws. For example, laws have been passed that guarantee special education programs in public schools for all children who are disabled. Advocacy also has produced laws that give people who are severely disabled the right to live in the community instead of institutions.

How Can You Promote Public Health?

Health Tip

Check into volunteer opportunities that benefit public health and interest you.

People get involved in health promotion in their community for many reasons. One reason is that disease prevention and health promotion save society money by preventing illness. Another reason is that communities organized to provide mutual support and promote health have fewer problems, including less crime and drug abuse. A third reason is that individuals increase their self-esteem as they work to improve the health of others.

As a first step, you could investigate existing community resources to identify your community's health needs. With this information, you could choose a place to volunteer. For example, you could volunteer to help with a food drive or get people to sponsor you in a benefit walk for the homeless. You could write letters to lawmakers asking for changes or join a health advocacy group.

LESSON 2 REVIEW Write the answers to these questions on a separate sheet of paper, using complete sentences.

1) What services do community and state health departments provide?

2) Name one division of the Department of Health and Human Services.

3) What services do nonprofit voluntary health organizations provide?

4) What does WHO work to do in developing nations?

5) How do advocacy groups foster health promotion and disease prevention?

■ Public health means protecting and improving the health of a community or nation.

■ The United States is committed to providing equal health care for all of its citizens.

■ Epidemics are public health problems because communicable diseases spread rapidly and affect large populations at the same time.

■ Poverty puts people at high risk for health problems. It especially affects children's health.

■ Among people who are homeless are families with children, victims of domestic abuse, and people under 21. Communicable diseases and poor hygiene are problems for the homeless.

■ The poor, the homeless, and teen mothers and their children may have difficulty getting basic health services. The elderly, people with mental health problems or disabilities, and recent immigrants also can have difficulty.

■ Harmful chemicals in the environment that pollute food, water, and air increase the risk of public health problems.

■ Poverty, low standards of living, hunger, malnutrition, AIDS, environmental pollution, diseases, natural disasters, and war are international public health problems.

■ Local and state public health departments ensure that laws on disease and sanitation are observed. They also provide medical care for low-income people.

■ The U.S. Department of Health and Human Services gathers and analyzes health information, sets standards, and sponsors education and research. The U.S. Public Health Service includes many agencies.

■ Nonprofit voluntary health organizations provide education programs in most communities. Voluntary self-help groups also provide support.

■ The United Nations, some U.S. organizations, and the International Red Cross provide public health services internationally.

■ Health promotion and disease prevention through education and advocacy groups reduce costs and relieve demands on the health care system at every level.

■ Individuals can promote public health by volunteering, writing letters to lawmakers, and joining advocacy groups.

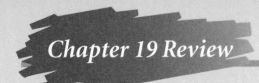

Comprehension: Identifying Facts

On a separate sheet of paper, write the correct word or words from the Word Bank to complete each sentence.

WORD BANK		
advocacy groups	natural disasters	public health
disease prevention	nonprofit voluntary	safety
		sanitation
epidemic	polluted	tuberculosis
health services	poverty	United Nations

1) _____ is the practice of protecting and improving the health of a community or nation.

2) When a communicable infectious disease spreads rapidly and affects large populations, it becomes an _____.

3) _____, a communicable lung disease, is a growing health problem in homeless shelters.

4) _____ puts people at high risk for serious health problems.

5) High-risk groups such as the poor and homeless often cannot get basic _____.

6) _____ air, water, and food increases the risk of health problems.

7) Local and state health departments ensure that laws related to disease and _____ are observed.

8) The Department of Health and Human Services sets health and _____ standards.

9) The U.S. Public Health Service promotes _____.

10) The American Heart Association is a _____ health organization.

11) _____ agencies such as WHO provide health services to developing nations.

12) The International Red Cross helps victims of _____.

13) _____ work to change government policies that prevent people from receiving health care.

Comprehension: Understanding Main Ideas

On a separate sheet of paper, write the answers to the following questions using complete sentences.

14) What is one general public health goal that the U.S. government has set?

15) Name three international public health problems.

16) What kinds of medical care do community and state health departments provide for low-income individuals?

17) What are two benefits of health promotion and disease prevention?

18) How can individuals promote public health?

Critical Thinking: Write Your Opinion

19) What do you think can be done to make sure that people who need health services get them?

20) What kind of real difference do you think individuals can make in cooperating to solve public health problems?

Test Taking Tip When you read true-false questions, the statement must be absolutely correct. Words like *always* and *never* tell you the question is probably false.

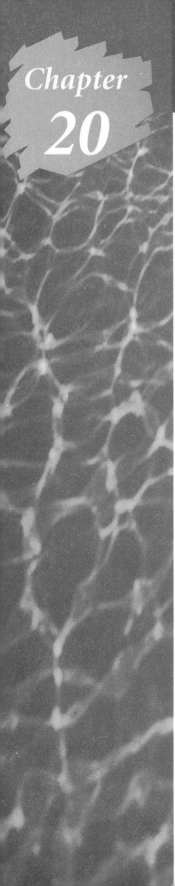

Environmental Health

Newspaper articles or television and radio news programs often feature reports about the environment. More and more we see clear evidence that the earth's air, water, land, and living things are precious and delicate resources. These natural resources must be protected so they are available for future generations.

In this chapter, you will learn about the environment and how it affects your health. You will learn about problems that threaten the environment and what is being done to solve the problems. Each individual can help to protect the environment in specific ways.

Goals for Learning

▶ To explain how the environment affects health

▶ To identify causes of air and water pollution

▶ To describe other environmental problems

▶ To identify actions that protect the environment

Water

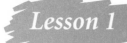

Health and the Environment

All living things depend on their **environment**, or surroundings, for their needs. The environment is a network of interrelated parts, including air, land, water, plants, and animals. Living things depend on air, water, and land for survival.

What Is the Balance of Nature?

Humans contribute to the environment, just as the environment contributes to humans. For example, we breathe out carbon dioxide, which plants need to survive. Plants in turn give off oxygen, which humans need to breathe and survive. When all parts of the environment contribute to one another in this way, a healthy balance of nature is maintained. When any part of the environment is hurt or destroyed, this balance is changed.

A healthy balance of nature . . . is changed through human activity that creates pollution.

What Disturbs the Balance of Nature?

Natural events are constantly disturbing the balance of nature. Earthquakes, volcanoes, and floods sometimes cause extreme damage from which nature eventually recovers. In fact, the changes that natural events produce can renew the environment over time.

Human activity also disturbs the balance of nature. For centuries, humans have changed the environment through settlement, farming, and using the earth's resources. People have removed resources from the environment in the process. As more people inhabit the earth, more demands are made on the earth's resources. For example, metals and minerals are taken from the ground. Coal and oil, which cannot be replaced, have been taken to heat homes and fuel vehicles. Trees are cut to make houses and paper. Less land is available on which to grow crops.

Changes in the environment from human activity may permanently upset the balance of nature. Land that has been mined or stripped of trees may be so damaged that it can no longer grow trees or crops. It may even be unsafe for humans to live on it. As more natural areas are destroyed, many organisms may no longer be able to survive.

How Does Environmental Damage Affect Health?

All this human activity has created wastes that have an immediate effect on health. Wastes from the normal process of life usually don't cause problems because they can be broken down in nature. Industries, however, can give off dangerous chemicals and other harmful wastes. Most of these harmful wastes, which cannot be broken down in nature, are released into the air or water or buried underground. The result is **pollution**—making soil, water, or air impure or unclean by discharging harmful substances into them. For example, an oil spill on water can kill

Writing About Health

When trees or bodies of water are destroyed, what do you think happens to the living things that feed on these sources? Write your thoughts.

fish and waterfowl living there. If that water is used to supply homes, humans are affected as well.

Pollution can be so harmful that it endangers human life. For example, industrial chemicals used to produce products that make life easier also can sicken factory workers. Wastes from factories, power plants, and cars can harm the air and water that humans need to live.

What Is Being Done About Pollution?

Damage to the environment can be reversed. The first step is understanding the problem. People now know that the earth's resources are limited and eventually will run out. They are beginning to understand that the world that sustains our life—the rivers, forests, soil, and atmosphere—is fragile or delicate. The conditions necessary to sustain human life—air, water, animals, and soil—are all interrelated and survive in a delicately balanced existence. Maintaining this fragile existence is one of the most important health issues of the twenty-first century.

Why is the environment described as fragile?

PURIFYING PLANTS

In the 1960s, the National Aeronautics and Space Administration (NASA) was planning to create a life-support system for a moon base. In a study on water and air, plants were found to purify air in sealed test rooms. Also, much of earth's fresh air was found to come from plants. Researchers recently have found that five particular plants are very good at purifying air in homes. They are the Boston fern, the rubber plant, the areca palm, the English ivy, and the dracaena. After years of testing, these plants showed no damage from household air. Do you have plants in your home?

Ecology
The study of the interrelationships of organisms and the physical environment

With this understanding, people have begun to make changes. For example, lakes that were once pronounced dead have been brought back to life. The fish and plants that once dwelled there are making a comeback. The survival of the bald eagle, our national bird, was once threatened. After certain pesticides—chemicals used to kill insects—were banned, the bald eagle is thriving again.

Whole new branches of science concerned with protecting the environment have emerged. **Ecology**, for example, is the study of the interrelationships of organisms and the physical environment. Clinical ecology is a new science that deals with the harmful effects of synthetic and natural substances on humans.

Lesson 5 describes some specific ways individuals can help to protect the environment.

LESSON 1 REVIEW On a separate sheet of paper, write the word or words from the Word Bank that matches each description.

WORD BANK

balance

clinical ecology

environment

flood

pollution

1) All living things depend on their _____ for survival.

2) All parts of the environment contribute to the _____ of nature.

3) A natural event that disturbs the balance of nature is a _____.

4) _____ from human activity produces a threat to human health.

5) _____ deals with the harmful effects of synthetic and natural substances on humans.

Air Pollution and Health

Photochemical
smog
*A form of air
pollution*

*E*very day, you breathe in about 12,000 quarts of air. If the air you breathe is polluted, toxins enter your body. If you breathe in polluted air over months or years, your lungs may be damaged. Air pollution can affect your health whether you are outdoors or indoors.

What Causes Outdoor Air Pollution?

The main cause of outdoor air pollution is burning. Whenever a substance is burned, harmful gases and particles are produced. For example, factories that burn fuels such as oil and coal produce smoke. Motor vehicles that burn gasoline produce exhaust. Other sources of air pollution are tobacco smoke, furnaces that burn waste materials, and leaf burning.

How Does Outdoor Air Pollution Affect Health?

Hydrocarbons are substances made of hydrogen and carbon that are found in motor vehicle exhaust. They are also found in natural gas that escapes into the air and in liquid fuels and solvents that evaporate. Hydrocarbons in the air can irritate, or sting, your nose and throat and make your eyes water. Some can cause cancers.

Photochemical smog forms when sunlight causes hydrocarbons and nitrogen oxides to combine. Photochemical smog forms ozone, a gas that interferes with the body's transfer of oxygen from the lungs to the bloodstream. It irritates the respiratory tract, causing conditions such as asthma, bronchitis, and emphysema. Ozone also can cause eye irritation.

Carbon monoxide is an odorless, colorless gas that is poisonous in high concentrations. It is present in motor vehicle exhaust and tobacco smoke, among other things. Inhaling carbon monoxide affects the red cells in blood, decreasing the oxygen supplied to body cells. The decrease in oxygen can cause headaches, dizziness, blurred vision, and fatigue. Over many years, carbon monoxide can contribute to heart and lung disease.

Sulfur dioxide is a poisonous gas released from factories and power plants that burn **fossil fuels**. Fossil fuels are burnable substances such as coal, oil, and natural gas that form in the earth from plant or animal remains. Sulfur dioxide can irritate the eyes, throat, and lungs, making breathing difficult. It worsens asthma, bronchitis, and emphysema.

Particulates are tiny pieces of solid matter like dust, ash, dirt, and soot that are suspended in the air. Some particulates carry gases and pesticides that can harm the body when inhaled. Particulates may irritate the eyes, nose, throat, and lungs.

Lead is a particulate pollutant. Leaded gasoline increases the level of lead in the air. Only unleaded gasoline can be used in the United States, but leaded gasoline is still used in other countries. Lead enters the bloodstream through the lungs or through absorption of particles into the skin. Too much lead can cause high blood pressure, loss of appetite, and damage to the brain and nervous system.

Outdoor air pollution affects everyone. In some areas, a smog alert is issued when pollution levels are high. People with serious health problems should stay indoors on days when the air quality is poor. Otherwise healthy people should avoid strenuous exercise on such days.

How Does Indoor Air Pollution Affect Health?

Air inside homes and buildings also can affect health. This can happen when homes and buildings are sealed too tightly. This sealing is meant to save energy and prevent air leaks. Sometimes the result is that a building gets too little air circulation, keeping toxins sealed inside and producing air pollution.

Some building materials and household chemicals are toxic. For example, some glues used in wood products such as furniture and paneling release harmful gases. Household chemicals such as paints, drain cleaners, and pesticides release gases that can cause respiratory problems. A building material that releases particulates is **asbestos**, a fibrous material that was used in older homes and buildings. Disturbing asbestos

Greenhouse effect
Gradual warming of the earth's atmosphere

Radon
A colorless, odorless gas that forms from the radioactive decay of radium underground

releases tiny fibers into the air that can severely affect the lungs. Asbestos has been banned in many places, and many places such as schools have been removing it.

There are other indoor air pollutants. Tobacco smoke causes respiratory and other problems for both smokers and nonsmokers. Faulty heaters and appliances can release carbon monoxide and nitrogen dioxide into the air. **Radon** can be a serious indoor air pollutant when it seeps into houses through walls and foundation floors. Radon is a colorless, odorless gas that forms from the radioactive decay of radium underground. It may cause lung cancer.

Indoor air pollution can cause respiratory problems such as shortness of breath, a nagging cough, and nose and throat irritation. Some indoor air pollutants can cause lung and respiratory diseases and certain cancers. Indoor air pollution can also cause eye irritation, upset stomach, headaches, sleeplessness, depression, irritability, dizziness, and fatigue.

How Does Air Pollution Affect the Earth?

Air pollution affects not only people's health but also contributes to long-term changes in the earth's atmosphere. Air pollution causes several kinds of damage.

The Greenhouse Effect

What happens if some countries in the world do not cooperate in efforts to protect the environment?

Many scientists believe that air pollution, especially the increase of carbon dioxide in the air, is causing a **greenhouse effect** on the earth. A greenhouse is warm and humid inside, with a glass ceiling that traps the sun's heat. Similarly, a carbon dioxide cloud caused by air pollution surrounds the earth. This cloud acts like the glass ceiling in a greenhouse, trapping heat and moisture. As a result, the earth's atmosphere may be gradually warming like air inside a greenhouse.

Even slight rises in global temperatures affect rainfall worldwide. Less rainfall in some areas could lead to crop failures and more deserts. More rainfall in other areas could lead to severe floods and erosion. Sea levels could rise, flooding coastal areas and mixing saltwater with freshwater.

The Ozone Layer

Scientists suspect that air pollution has caused a reduction of the **ozone layer**. The ozone layer is a region six to thirty miles above the earth's surface. It shields and protects the earth from the sun's harmful rays. In 1985, scientists discovered a hole the size of the United States in the ozone layer over Antarctica. In addition, the overall ozone layer appears to be thinning.

Scientists know that natural events such as volcanoes can affect the ozone layer. They also believe that chlorofluorocarbons (CFCs) in the atmosphere have an effect. CFCs are chemicals that once were used as cooling agents in refrigerators and air conditioners. CFCs remain in the atmosphere for years, eventually rising up to the ozone layer. They turn ozone molecules into oxygen molecules that cannot protect the earth from the sun's harmful rays. Most CFCs are no longer being used.

How could you change your individual actions to help reduce air pollution?

The increase in the sun's harmful rays may damage crops and marine life, thereby threatening the food supply.

Acid Rain

Acid rain is precipitation—rain, snow, sleet, or hail—that contains large amounts of sulfuric or nitric acids. Sulfur and nitrogen from motor vehicles, factories, and home heating combine with moisture to form sulfuric and nitric acids. These acids spread throughout the atmosphere and return to earth through acid rain. The acids may come back to earth far from where they were produced. For example, factories in the Midwest produce heavy amounts of these acids. The acid rain falls as far away as the Southeast, New England, and eastern Canada.

Acid rain damages rivers, lakes, and marine and plant life. As the water becomes acidic, fish fail to reproduce and may die out. Highly acidic waters draw mercury and lead from the lake beds. When fish absorb this mercury and lead, they become unsafe for humans to eat. In Germany, major forests have been destroyed by acid rain.

These fir trees on top of North Carolina's Mt. Mitchell were killed partly by acid rain.

LESSON 2 REVIEW Write the answers to these questions on a separate sheet of paper, using complete sentences.

1) What is the main cause of outdoor air pollution?

2) If you had asthma, how might photochemical smog and ozone affect you?

3) How do building materials and household chemicals produce air pollution?

4) What is one consequence of the greenhouse effect for the earth?

5) What is effect of acid rain on fish?

Water Pollution and Health

Sewage
Liquid and solid waste from drains and toilets that is carried off in disposal systems

While three-quarters of the earth's surface is covered with water, only a small fraction of that water is freshwater. Most of the earth's water is in oceans, which contain saltwater. Saltwater is unsuitable for drinking or growing crops. Freshwater is as important as air to sustaining human life.

Water beneath the earth's surface is called groundwater, which supplies springs and wells. Groundwater is the largest source of freshwater. As the world becomes more populated, freshwater is becoming harder to find. If people are to have freshwater, groundwater must be kept clean and free of pollution.

What would happen if you could not drink the water available to you now?

What Causes Water Pollution?

For many years, our society has dumped their wastes into oceans, lakes, and rivers. Many of these wastes cannot be broken down. They remain for a long time and do permanent harm. Common sources of water pollution are industrial wastes, **sewage**, oil leaks and spills, agricultural runoff, household chemicals, and acid rain.

Industrial Wastes

Toxic substances from industry produce water pollution when they enter the water supply. Factories and mining operations have been responsible for a great deal of water pollution in the United States. Most industrial wastes such as mercury, lead, and acids cannot be broken down. Often the wastes were dumped into bodies of water or discharged into groundwater. Fortunately, the United States now has laws that prevent most industrial water pollution.

Health Tip

Volunteer to help clean up a roadside or city park.

Sewage

Sewage is waste from drains and toilets that is carried off in disposal systems. Most sewage comes from human body wastes, which contain bacteria and organisms that can cause disease. If raw sewage gets into groundwater and bodies of water, it can kill wildlife and plants. Humans can get diseases such as typhoid fever and cholera from water polluted with sewage.

A 1977 law requires sewage in the United States to be treated before it is released into the environment. Treatment includes adding tiny helpful organisms to break down bacteria and harmful organisms.

Oil Leaks and Spills

The worldwide demand for oil and petroleum is great. To meet the demand, much oil and petroleum are transported across oceans. Sometimes tankers carrying the oil leak, causing oil spills on water. The spills kill wildlife and leave behind carcinogens that can affect humans.

Agricultural Runoff

Growers use chemical fertilizers to encourage plant growth, along with pesticides and herbicides to control bugs and weeds. When it rains, these chemicals run off into streams and bodies of water as well as into groundwater. The fertilizers speed up the growth of **algae**, a wide-ranging group of plants that live in water. These plants quickly use up the oxygen supply in the water so that other plants and fish cannot live. The chemicals in the fertilizers also can get washed into the local water supply when it rains. When these chemicals get into water, they can kill fish in nearby rivers and lakes. They can also contaminate the groundwater that people drink.

Wastes from animal feedlots also produce agricultural runoff that is harmful to the environment and humans.

Many lawmakers are concerned about these two problems from agricultural runoff and are studying what can be done to help.

Household Chemicals

Some household chemicals have ingredients that are harmful to plants and humans if they get into the water supply. Many products now must be sold without these harmful ingredients. For example, laundry detergents must now be sold without phosphorus so that they break down in the environment and do not pollute. Even so, it is important to read labels on household products to learn how to dispose of them safely.

Health Tip

Place your trash in appropriate containers.

How Can Freshwater Be Conserved?

In many areas, freshwater is in short supply. Therefore, protecting it is important. One way to protect freshwater is to conserve it, or use it sparingly.

Here are some ways you can conserve water:

- Use just enough water when you shower or wash your hair to wet the washcloth or lather up. Turn off the tap while you clean and turn it back on just long enough to rinse.

- Fill the tub only halfway when you take a bath.

- Wet the brush when you brush your teeth and turn off the tap until you rinse.

- Wait to run the clothes washer or dishwasher until there is a full load.

LESSON 3 REVIEW On a separate sheet of paper, write the word or words in parentheses that correctly complete each sentence.

1) (Clean water, Groundwater, Saltwater) is the largest source of freshwater.

2) Industrial wastes such as mercury and acid (can, cannot, might) be broken down.

3) Agricultural runoff comes from pesticides, (herbicides, germicides, insecticides), and animal feedlots.

4) (Algae, Pesticides, Oils) use up the oxygen supply in water for other plants and fish.

5) Freshwater can be protected by (conserving, reserving, deserving) it.

Other Environmental Problems and Health

Deforestation
*Cutting and
clearing trees*

Famine
*An extreme food
shortage*

Problems such as the world's growing population, deforestation, solid waste, noise pollution, and radiation can affect the environment. Because these problems affect the environment, they also can affect health.

How Does Population Size Affect Health?

The world's population is nearly 6 billion people. If the population continues to grow at present rates, scientists expect the world population will be 9.4 billion people by 2050. Some experts think the top number of people that the earth can sustain is 12 billion. See Tables C.7 and C.8 in Appendix C.

Growing enough crops to feed so many people is a concern. Many countries have already gone through long periods of **famine**, an extreme food shortage. Famines in Africa, for example, have resulted from long periods of drought without enough rainfall to grow crops.

What would happen if there were a worldwide shortage of wheat?

The more people inhabit the earth, the more automobiles and industry there will be. As automobiles and factories increase, more air pollution will result. As air pollution increases, global warming will increase and the ozone layer will get thinner. As the ozone layer becomes thinner, more harmful rays from the sun will get into the atmosphere. With more harmful rays, skin cancers will increase. You can see that everything in the environment is connected and that many concerns seem to stem from the growing population.

How Does Deforestation Affect Health?

Some people believe that the drought and famine in Africa resulted from **deforestation**, or cutting and clearing trees. Over history, two-thirds of the world's forests have been lost to deforestation. Some African countries lost all of their forests to make room for human settlements, planting crops, and grazing cattle.

The earth needs trees to maintain its delicate balance. When forests are destroyed to help support a growing world population, the fertile topsoil is washed away. The remaining soil can't retain water efficiently. Eventually, the land becomes desert. This results in more famine and also less rain.

Tropical rain forests cover only about 6 percent of the earth's surface yet include half of all the earth's plants. Because of deforestation, only half the earth's original rain forests remain. Each year, millions of acres of tropical rain forest are burned or cleared for crops, cattle ranching, or the lumber.

The destruction of tropical rain forests affects human and environmental health. Plants in the rain forests are the sources for more than one-quarter of the medicines on today's market. In addition, rain forest plants may hold the key to new medicines. Rain forest plants act as the earth's lungs by taking in carbon dioxide. Too much carbon dioxide contributes to global warming.

How Does Solid Waste Affect Health?

Developing nations get rid of few materials because resources are scarce. But in more developed nations, people tend to throw things away after short use and then buy more. In the United States, for example, billions of tons of **solid waste**—garbage or trash—are dumped each year. Disposal of solid waste has an effect on the environment and therefore on human health.

Many communities have dumped solid waste in **landfills**—low-lying ground where waste is buried between layers of earth. One problem, however, is that landfill space is running out in the United States. Another problem is that toxic substances called **hazardous waste** are sometimes dumped. Industries are the largest producers of hazardous waste. Toxic substances released from hazardous waste sometimes leak into nearby ground and pollute the groundwater.

Sometimes the effect of polluted groundwater is noticed immediately. Other times the effect isn't noticed for years. For example, between the late 1930s and early 1940s, an industry

Recycling unwanted household goods can eliminate the landfill problem and eyesores such as this one.

Sensorineural deafness
Permanent hearing loss in which the tiny cells in the inner ear are destroyed

in Love Canal, New York, dumped toxic chemicals into the ground. Later, homes were built there. In 1978, heavy rains flooded basements in those homes. People noticed oily liquids in the floodwater. Hazardous wastes had leaked into the soil and groundwater. The homes were polluted and the people had to move.

Individuals and families can help to reduce hazardous waste. Hazardous waste products such as paint and nail polish can be disposed of separately from the rest of the garbage. Check with your community to learn how this should be done.

How Does Noise Pollution Affect Health?

As the population and industries have increased, so has noise. Noise pollution occurs when sounds in the environment become too great. Too much exposure to loud noise over a long period can cause **sensorineural deafness**. This is a permanent hearing loss in which the tiny cells in the inner ear are destroyed. Many Americans have sensorineural deafness resulting from noise pollution. Too much noise also may cause stress and such related problems as high blood pressure, tension, aggression, and fatigue.

SOFTWARE FOR MONITORING AIR, WATER, NOISE, OR OTHER POLLUTION

We use computer software for many tasks every day. Computer software helps government and private industry perform different kinds of environmental testing. Computers quickly analyze samples of air, water, and soil. In years past, such tests could take days or weeks. Today, computers instantly monitor air quality, detect polluted water or unsafe noise levels, and test soil for harmful particles. Global climate changes and acid rain are being studied in laboratories using computer software. Computer software can detect poisonous radon gases within minutes. Software also helps to manage waste disposal. Our world is cleaner and safer because of help from computers.

Radiation sickness
Illness caused by exposure to high levels of radiation

How Does Radiation Affect Health?

Radiation is the transmission of energy in the form of waves. It occurs naturally in the environment. Usually people are exposed only to low levels of radiation, such as X rays. Industry uses high levels of radiation. Nuclear power plants, for example, use radiation to produce electricity for homes and businesses. People who work in nuclear power plants are exposed to high levels of radiation.

Too much radiation may cause cancer in humans. People who are exposed to very high levels of radiation may experience **radiation sickness**. Some symptoms of radiation sickness are upset stomach, vomiting, headache, diarrhea, hair loss, and fatigue. The sickness can lead to death. The federal government sets exposure safety standards for people who work with or near radiation.

Nuclear power plants are carefully controlled. Still, accidents have occurred at these plants. For example, an accident occurred in 1986 in the nuclear plant at Chernobyl in the former Soviet Union. Many people died immediately. Others died of radiation sickness weeks later. Wind carried radiation across much of Europe, and some scientists predict that many Europeans will die of cancer as a result. Today, the villages and forests around Chernobyl are deserted and considered unsafe. To date, this was the worst nuclear accident.

LESSON 4 REVIEW Write the answers to these questions on a separate sheet of paper, using complete sentences.

1) How are famine and the growing world population related?

2) What do trees do for the environment?

3) How do the rain forests affect human health?

4) How does hazardous waste affect people's health?

5) What are two effects on health from high levels of radiation?

Healthy Subjects

Science   **LEARNING ABOUT WETLANDS**

Wetlands create a rich home for plants and wildlife in our environment. Over time, however, half of all U.S. wetlands have been lost. But scientists are learning to create new wetlands. One research team regularly visits Big Bend National Park in southwestern Texas. The park has a thriving wetland that shelters countless water plants and creatures. The researchers study the insects in this wetland. One kind of fly is especially sensitive to changes in the environment. Researchers count the numbers of this fly and other insects. That helps show which chemicals, water speed, and temperature help the wetland sustain itself. Then researchers can create new wetlands.

Protecting the Environment

*P*rotecting the environment is the responsibility of everyone—governments, the world community, industries, local communities, and individuals.

What Laws Protect the Environment?

The U.S. government has passed several laws to protect the environment. All of these laws are meant to protect human health as well.

The Clean Air Act was first passed in 1970 and has been modified several times since then. It establishes allowable limits on concentrations of air pollutants. It also requires each state to develop a plan to meet its standards.

The National Environmental Policy Act requires federal agencies to consider the impact on the environment of their plans and activities. Before an agency can begin a new project, it must file an "Environmental Impact Statement" explaining how the project will affect the environment. The agency also must hold public hearings about the effect of the project on the environment. Many states have passed similar laws.

Congress has passed other environmental laws. These laws set standards for water safety and control disposal of solid and hazardous wastes. They control cleanup of chemical spills and toxic waste.

What Agencies Protect the Environment?

In the United States, the Environmental Protection Agency (EPA) writes and enforces the environmental laws passed by Congress. Its job is to monitor and protect the environment.

Because so many environmental problems affect the entire world, nations have joined together to try to solve the problems. For example, an international conference in Montreal in 1987 explored solutions to thinning of the ozone layer. The result is that most chlorofluorocarbons (CFCs)are no longer used throughout the world. Nations also have agreed to phase out other substances that may thin the ozone layer.

The United Nations General Assembly established the Conference on Environment and Development. The commission's job is to seek economic development and environmental protection for the purpose of fulfilling everyone's basic needs.

What Are Future Environmental Plans?

If you had to develop new packaging for food, what would you use that wouldn't harm the environment?

Scientists are working on ways to protect the environment from further harm. For example, they are searching for ways to harness solar energy, or energy from the sun. Solar energy is a clean and environmentally safe energy source. Using it to heat and cool homes could reduce the need for oil, gas, and electricity by as much as 70 percent.

Scientists are studying alternative fuels that will reduce motor vehicle exhaust. One possible source is ethanol, or alcohol made from corn—a renewable resource. Some states already use ethanol mixed with regular gasoline. Hydrogen and natural gas are two other alternative fuels that are currently being researched. Even solar energy may one day be used to power motor vehicles.

Many communities provide curbside pickup of materials for recycling.

Action for Health

RECYCLING

Recycling means reusing materials instead of buying new ones. You can make a difference in your community's environment by recycling. It saves natural resources and also reduces solid waste. Newspapers, cardboard, aluminum cans, glass, and some paper and plastics can be recycled. Some communities have curbside pickup of recycled items. Otherwise, you can sort these items and take them to a recycling center.

Motor vehicle manufacturers are investigating alternatives to gas-powered vehicles. One possibility is electric vehicles, which discharge no pollutants.

California has passed a law requiring more fuel-efficient vehicles. Other states also may require less pollution from vehicles.

How Can Individuals Protect the Environment?

Individual actions do make a difference. Each individual can work to protect the environment. Here are some actions you can take to protect the environment.

- Walk, ride a bike, take the bus, or carpool to school or work.
- If you must drive, keep your car tuned up and have the exhaust equipment checked regularly.
- Buy a car that uses not less than 35 miles per gallon of gasoline.
- Turn off lights when you leave a room.
- Keep air conditioning at a constant temperature on the automatic setting and keep windows and doors closed.
- Keep the furnace set at a constant low temperature—perhaps 68 degrees—and wear layers of clothing.
- Take shorter showers.

- Avoid running hot water unnecessarily.

- Use fewer disposables. For example, use a glass instead of a paper or plastic cup, or use cloth towels instead of paper towels.

- Recycle newspapers, cans, bottles, plastic, and paper. Find out what recycling services are available in your community. Reuse items like paper clips, too.

- Buy only what you need.

- In general, select products that contain the least amount of packaging. Purchase consumable items, such as detergent, in refillable containers to use less packaging.

- Look for products with the recycled symbol that indicates recycled materials were used in making them.

- Find alternatives to toxic products for your home. For example, substitute baking soda and water for oven cleaners containing lye. Wash windows with white vinegar and water.

ENVIRONMENTAL PROTECTION WORKER

If you care about the environment, you could become an environmental protection worker. Environmental protection workers support good health and environmental practices. Using computers and other equipment, they check for poisons in samples of the air, water, and soil. They also make sure laws about health standards are followed. Environmental protection workers teach people about poisons. They may take care of equipment like that at underground wastewater treatment plants. This equipment must continually be checked to make sure it cleans the water properly. Environmental protection workers also check the air for dangerous gases. Training and certification vary by state. Specialties such as working with asbestos require training and certification from the Occupational Safety and Health Administration (OSHA).

- If you must buy household products with toxic contents, dispose of them according to instructions on the package.
- Write to lawmakers about your concerns for the environment.
- Plant some trees to take in more carbon dioxide and reduce the greenhouse effect.

LESSON 5 REVIEW Write the answers to these questions on a separate sheet of paper, using complete sentences.

1) What does the National Environmental Policy Act require?

2) What does the Environmental Protection Agency do?

3) What was the result of the 1987 international conference in Montreal?

4) List two things scientists are doing to protect the environment.

5) Name five actions an individual can take to help protect the environment.

- When all parts of the environment contribute to one another, a healthy balance of nature is maintained.

- Much human activity has upset the balance of nature by overusing the earth's resources and producing pollution.

- Because pollution can endanger human health and life, people are finding solutions. Understanding what harms the environment and health is the first step in making changes.

- Burning is the main cause of outdoor air pollution. Motor vehicles and factories produce most air pollution.

- Hydrocarbons, nitrogen oxides, photochemical smog, ozone, carbon monoxide, sulfur dioxide, and particulates are some outdoor air pollutants.

- Some indoor air pollutants are gases and particulates from building materials and household chemicals. Tobacco smoke, faulty heaters and appliances, and radon are other indoor air pollutants.

- Respiratory and lung problems are common health effects of air pollution. There are other health effects as well.

- Results of air pollution on the earth are the greenhouse effect, thinning of the ozone layer, and acid rain.

- Since the supply of freshwater is limited, it is important to conserve and protect it. People need freshwater to sustain human life. Most freshwater comes from groundwater.

- Some causes of water pollution are industrial wastes, sewage, oil leaks and spills, agricultural runoff, and toxic chemicals.

- The growing world population has caused many environmental problems, including deforestation, solid waste, noise pollution, and radiation.

- The United States Congress has passed several laws that protect the environment and therefore human health.

- Nations are working together to protect the environment and still meet people's basic needs.

- Alternative energy and fuel sources provide a means to help protect the environment.

- Individuals can take many actions that help to protect the environment, including conserving energy and water and recycling.

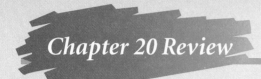

Comprehension: Identifying Facts

On a separate sheet of paper, write the correct word or words from the Word Bank to complete each sentence.

WORD BANK		
agricultural runoff	famine	medicines
burning	greenhouse effect	pollution
carbon monoxide	groundwater	radiation
Clean Air Act	hazardous waste	sewage
ecology	human activity	solar energy

1) Natural events and _____ disturb the balance of nature.

2) Wastes that cannot be broken down in nature produce _____, which harms human health.

3) _____ is a branch of science that is concerned with protecting the environment.

4) The main cause of air pollution is _____.

5) Inhaling _____ decreases the oxygen supply to body cells.

6) The _____ contributes to gradual warming of the earth's atmosphere.

7) If _____ is polluted, the largest source of freshwater is unfit for human use.

8) Typhoid fever and cholera are diseases people get from water polluted with _____.

9) When _____ enters bodies of water, it can kill fish and contaminate groundwater.

10) _____, an extreme shortage of food, results when land cannot produce sufficient food.

11) Plants and trees in tropical rain forests are the source of many _____.

12) Toxic substances dumped in landfills are considered _____.

13) People who are exposed to high levels of _____ may have radiation sickness.

14) The _____ establishes allowable limits on air pollutants.

15) _____ may be an alternative for heating and cooling homes and powering motor vehicles.

Comprehension: Understanding Main Ideas

On a separate sheet of paper, write the answers to the following questions using complete sentences.

16) Describe the health effects of one kind of outdoor air pollution.

17) How can oil leaks and spills on bodies of water affect humans?

18) How does noise pollution affect health?

Critical Thinking: Write Your Opinion

19) Which problem discussed in this chapter do you think could have the most serious effect on the environment and human health?

20) What do you think is the single most important action an individual can take to protect air quality?

| Test Taking Tip | When taking a short-answer test, first answer the questions you know. Then go back to spend time on the questions about which you are less sure. |

Do Air Bags Improve Safety?

Air bags are estimated to have saved 3,000 or more lives. They appear to have prevented many injuries. But they also have caused serious injuries and death to babies, small children, and small adults. Sometimes an air bag on/off switch can be installed.

The Internet has much information about air bag safety, but it is important to evaluate web site information. Separating fact from fiction can be difficult. A fact can be found in reference books. Opinion statements usually are not found in reference books. Opinion statements often come from people or organizations that will profit from stating their own beliefs. You need to sort information before you use it to make a decision.

In looking on the Internet for information about air bags, use these five guidelines to evaluate a web site.

- **Authority:** Who created the web site? What are their qualifications? Can you verify the qualifications?

- **Accuracy:** Are sources of information listed? Can you cross-check the information with other sources?

- **Objectivity:** Are prejudices clearly stated? Are associations with different groups clearly stated?

- **Currency:** Are dates listed on the web site showing when it was first created? when it was last edited or changed?

- **Coverage:** Does the web site have a menu to show what is covered? Can you move around the site easily?

Questions

1) What might be the arguments against tampering with air bags?

2) How accurate would you expect information from safety agencies to be? from car makers?

3) What would you want to know before deciding about installing an on/off switch for an air bag in your car?

4) Whose web sites would be most useful in finding out more about air bags?

■ Being a wise health consumer helps protect and improve health and saves money. The U.S. government gives consumers some basic rights.

■ Reading the label is the best way to judge if a product is right for you.

■ Consumers with a problem can follow some steps to correct it.

■ Names of different types of health care professionals can be gotten through recommendations, local medical associations, and professional directories.

■ Some health care facilities are doctors' or dentists' offices, outpatient clinics, inpatient facilities, hospitals, urgent care centers, and long-term care facilities.

■ Individuals can pay health care costs through private individual or group insurance plans. Several government agencies also pay for health care.

■ Epidemics are public health problems because they spread rapidly and affect large populations at the same time.

■ The poor, the homeless, teen mothers and their children, the elderly, and people with disabilities may have difficulty getting basic health services.

■ Poverty, low standards of living, hunger, malnutrition, AIDS, environmental pollution, diseases, natural disasters, and war are international public health problems.

■ Public health departments, the Department of Health and Human Services, and voluntary health organizations provide public health services in America. The United Nations and the International Red Cross provide international services.

■ Health promotion and disease prevention through education and advocacy groups reduce costs and demands on the health care system.

■ Individuals can promote public health by volunteering, writing letters, and joining advocacy groups.

■ People are finding solutions to environmental health problems, such as reducing air pollution and conserving and protecting freshwater.

■ The growing world population affects many environmental problems, including deforestation, solid waste, noise pollution, and radiation.

■ National and international governments and individuals are taking actions that protect the environment.

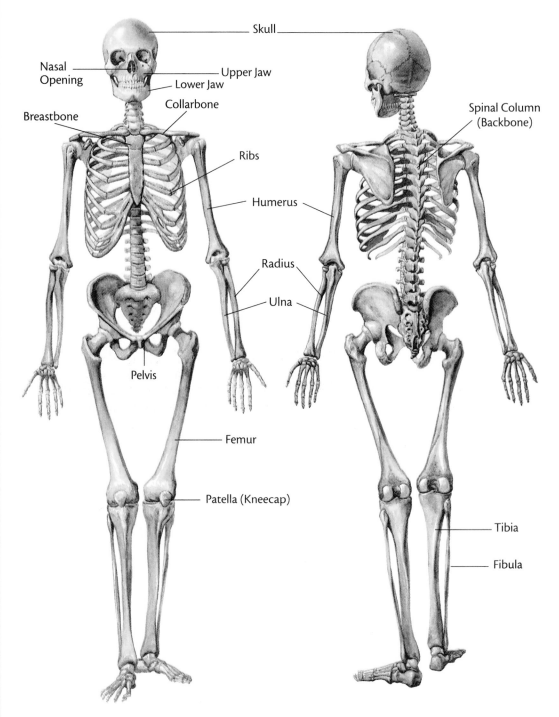

Figure A.1. The skeletal system

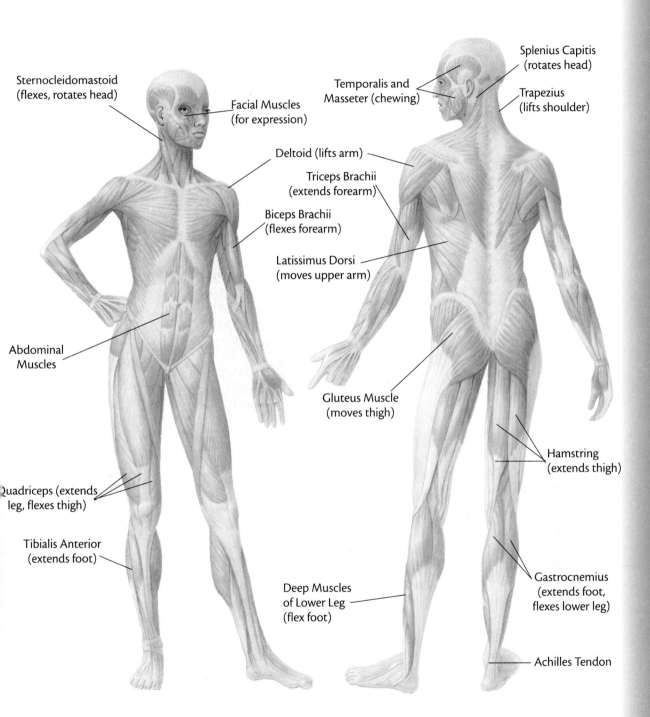

Figure A.2. The muscular system. Left: Female front view. Right: Male back view

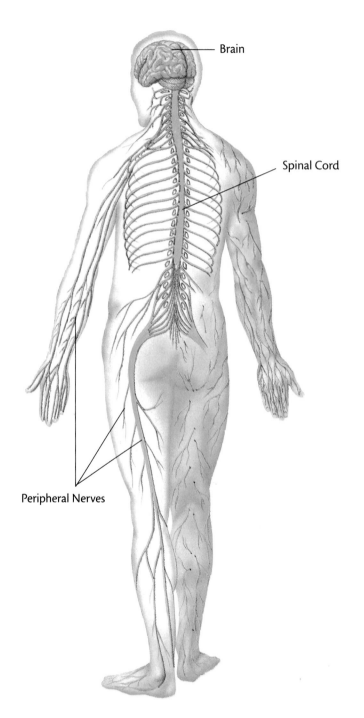

Brain

Spinal Cord

Peripheral Nerves

Figure A.3. The nervous system

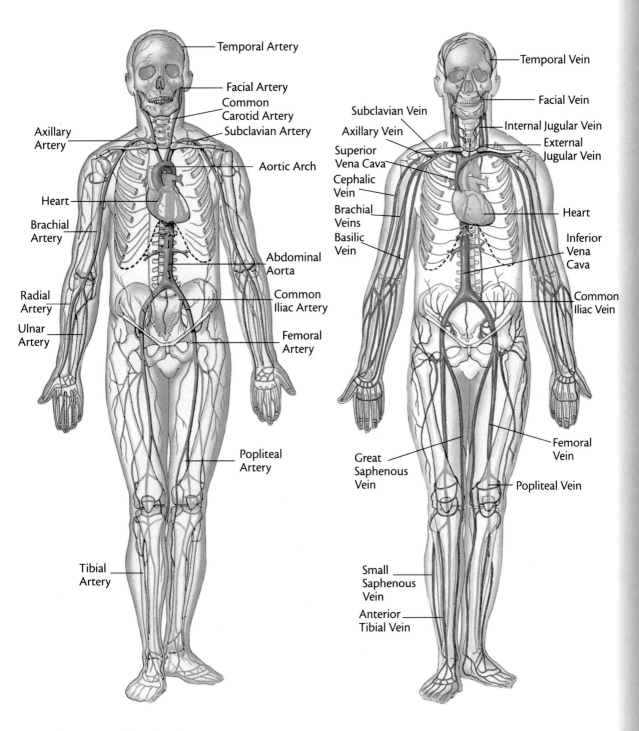

Figure A.4. The circulatory system

Appendix B: Nutrition Tables

Table B.1. The Six Essential Nutrient Classes

NUTRIENT	BEST FOOD SOURCES	WHY THEY ARE NEEDED
Protein	Cheese, eggs, fish, meat, milk, poultry, soybeans, nuts, dry beans, and lentils	To promote body growth; to repair and maintain tissue
Carbohydrate	Bread, cereal, flour, potatoes, rice, sugar, dry beans, fruit	To supply energy; To furnish heat; To save proteins to build and regulate cells
Fat	Butter, margarine, cream, oils, meat, whole milk, nuts, avocado	To supply energy; To furnish heat; To save proteins to build and regulate cells; To supply necessary fat-soluble vitamins and other nutrients
MINERALS		
Calcium	Milk, cheese, leafy green vegetables, oysters, almonds	To give rigidity and hardness to bones and teeth; For clotting of blood, osmosis, action of heart and other muscles, and nerve response
Iron	Meats (especially liver), oysters, leafy green vegetables, legumes, dried apricots or peaches, prunes, raisins	To carry oxygen in the blood
Iodine	Seafood, iodized salt	To help the thyroid gland regulate cell activities for physical and mental health
VITAMINS		
Vitamin A	Whole milk, cream, butter, liver, egg yolk, leafy green vegetables, dark yellow fruits and vegetables	To promote health of epithelial tissues. For health of eyes and development of teeth
Thiamin	Present in many foods, abundant in few; pork, some animal organs, some nuts, whole grains, yeast, dry beans, and peas	To promote healthy nerves, appetite, digestion, and growth; For metabolism of carbohydrates
Riboflavin	Milk, glandular organs, lean meats, cheese, eggs, leafy green vegetables, whole grains	To make for better development, greater vitality, freedom from disease, metabolism of carbohydrates, fats, and protiens
Niacin	Lean meats, liver, poultry, peanuts, legumes, yeasts	To promote good digestion, healthy skin, and a well-functioning nervous system
Vitamin C	Citrus fruits, strawberries, tomatoes, broccoli, cabbage, green peppers	To enhance iron absorption; For deposit of intercellular cement in tissues and bone
Vitamin D	Milk, salmon, tuna, action of sun	To help absorb and use calcium and phosphorus
WATER		
	Drinking water, foods	To supply body fluids, regulate body temperature

Table B.2. Fiber Content of Selected Foods

	Serving size	Dietary Fiber (g)
GRAINS		
Bread, white	1 slice	0.6
Bread, whole wheat	1 slice	1.5
Oat, bran, dry	1/3 cup	4.0
Oatmeal, dry	1/3 cup	2.7
Rice, brown, cooked	1/2 cup	2.4
Rice, white, cooked	1/2 cup	0.8
FRUITS		
Apple, with skin	1 small	2.8
Apricots, with skin	4 fruit	3.5
Banana	1 small	2.2
Blueberries	3/4 cup	1.4
Figs, dried	3 fruit	4.6
Grapefruit	1/2 fruit	1.6
Pear, with skin	1 large	5.8
Prunes, dried	3 medium	1.7
VEGETABLES		
Asparagus, cooked	1/2 cup	1.8
Broccoli, cooked	1/2 cup	2.4
Carrots, cooked, sliced	1/2 cup	2.0
Peas, green, frozen, cooked	1/2 cup	4.3
Potato, with skin, raw	1/2 cup	1.5
Tomato, raw	1 medium	1.0
LEGUMES		
Kidney beans, cooked	1/2 cup	6.9
Lima beans, canned	1/2 cup	4.3
Pinto beans, cooked	1/2 cup	5.9
Beans, white, cooked	1/2 cup	5.0
Lentils, cooked	1/2 cup	4.7
Peas, blackeye, canned	1/2 cup	4.7

Table B.3. Calcium and Fat Content of Dairy Products*

PRODUCT	CALORIES	FAT (grams)	CALCIUM (milligrams)
Skim milk (also called nonfat or fat free)			
Plain	86	0	301
Chocolate	144	1	292
1% milk (also called lowfat or light)			
Plain	102	$2^1/_2$	300
Chocolate	158	$2^1/_2$	288
2% milk (now called reduced fat, not lowfat)			
Plain	121	5	298
Chocolate	179	5	285
Whole milk			
Plain	150	8	290
Chocolate	209	8	280
Buttermilk (lowfat)	100	2	300
Buttermilk (whole)	150	8	300
Sweetened condensed milk	246	7	217

*All nutrition information is based on a one-cup serving except sweetened condensed milk, based on a quarter-cup serving

Appendix C: Fact Bank

FRAME SIZE

To determine your frame size:

1. Extend your arm in front of your body bending your elbow at a ninety degree angle to your body (your arm is parallel to your body).

2. Keep your fingers straight and turn the inside of your wrist to your body.

3. Place your thumb and index finger on the two prominent bones on either side of your elbow, measure the distance between the bones with a tape measure or calipers.

4. Compare to the medium frame chart below. Select your height based on what you are barefoot. If you are below the listed inches, your frame is small. If you are above, your frame is large.

ELBOW MEASUREMENTS FOR MEDIUM FRAME	
Height in 1" Heels	**Elbow Breadth**
Men	
5'2"–5'3"	$2\frac{1}{2}$"–$2\frac{5}{8}$"
5'4"–5'7"	$2\frac{5}{8}$"–$2\frac{7}{8}$"
5'8"–5'11"	$2\frac{3}{4}$"–3"
6'0"–6'3"	$2\frac{3}{4}$"–$3\frac{1}{8}$"
6'4"	$2\frac{7}{8}$"–$3\frac{1}{4}$"
Women	
4'10"–4'11"	$2\frac{1}{4}$"–$2\frac{1}{2}$"
5'0"–5'3"	$2\frac{1}{4}$"–$2\frac{1}{2}$"
5'4"–5'7"	$2\frac{3}{8}$"–$2\frac{5}{8}$"
5'8"–5'11"	$2\frac{3}{8}$"–$2\frac{5}{8}$"
6'0"	$2\frac{1}{2}$"–$2\frac{3}{4}$"

Table C.1. Top 10 Fat-Blasting Exercises

ACTIVITY	CALORIES BURNED (per 30 minutes*)	ACTIVITY	CALORIES BURNED (per 30 minutes*)
Bicycling, vigorous (15 MPH)	340	Spinning class (indoor cycling)	312
Jogging (10- to 12-minute miles)	340 to 272	Jumping rope, slowly	272
Swimming, vigorous	340	Tennis, singles	272
Cross-country ski machine	323	Hiking, uphill	238
		Inline skating	238
		Walking, uphill (3.5 MPH)	204

Table C.2. Recommended Height and Weight for Women

Height Feet Inches	Small Frame	Medium Frame	Large Frame
4'10"	102–111	109–121	118–131
4'11"	103–113	111–123	120–134
5'0"	104–115	113–126	122–137
5'1"	106–118	115–129	125–140
5'2"	108–121	118–132	128-143
5'3"	111–124	121–135	131–147
5'4"	114–127	124–138	134–151
5'5"	117–130	127–141	137–155
5'6"	120–133	130–144	140–159
5'7"	123–136	133–147	143–163
5'8"	126–139	136–150	146–167
5'9"	129–142	139–153	149–170
5'10"	132–145	142–156	152–173
5'11"	135–148	145–159	155–176
6'0"	138–151	148–162	158–179

Table C.3. Recommended Height and Weight for Men

Height Feet Inches	Small Frame	Medium Frame	Large Frame
5'2"	128–134	131–141	138–150
5'3"	130–136	133–143	140–153
5'4"	132–138	135–145	142–156
5'5"	134–140	137–148	144–160
5'6"	136–142	139–151	146–164
5'7"	138–145	142–154	149–168
5'8"	140–148	145–157	152–172
5'9"	142–151	148–160	155–176
5'10"	144–154	151–163	158–180
5'11"	146–157	154–166	161–184
6'0"	149–160	157–170	164–188
6'1"	152–164	160–174	168–192
6'2"	155–168	162–178	172–197
6'3"	158–172	167–182	176–202
6'4"	162–176	171–187	181–207

Weights at ages 25–59 based on lowest mortality.

Weight in pounds according to frame (in indoor clothing weighing 3 lbs.; shoes with 1" heels).

Weights at ages 25–59 based on lowest mortality.

Weight in pounds according to frame (in indoor clothing weighing 5 lbs.; shoes with 1" heels).

Leading Causes of Death

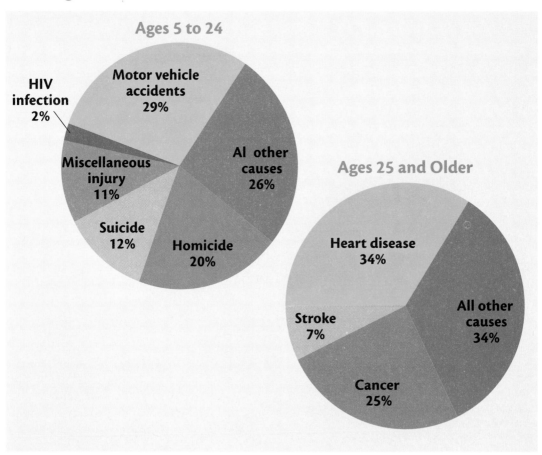

Ages 5 to 24

- HIV infection 2%
- Motor vehicle accidents 29%
- Miscellaneous injury 11%
- Suicide 12%
- Homicide 20%
- All other causes 26%

Ages 25 and Older

- Heart disease 34%
- Stroke 7%
- Cancer 25%
- All other causes 34%

Table C.4. The Most Common Places for Cancer in Men and Women

Men	Women
Prostate Gland 184,500	Breast 178,700
Lung 91,400	Lung 80,100
Colon & Rectum 64,600	Colon & Rectum 67,000
Urinary Bladder 39,500	Uterus 36,100
Non-Hodgkin's Lymphoma 31,100	Ovary 25,400
Skin—Melanoma 24,300	Non-Hodgkin's Lymphoma 24,300
Mouth 20,600	Skin—Melanoma 17,300
Kidney 17,600	Urinary Bladder 14,900
Blood 16,100	Pancreas 14,900
Stomach 14,300	Cervix 13,700
All Sites 627,900	All Sites 600,700

Source: American Cancer Society, Inc., 1998.

The ABCDs of Melanoma

Melanoma is usually curable if you find it early. Follow this A-B-C-D self-examination guide adapted from the American Academy of Dermatology:

■ *A is for asymmetry*—Symmetrical round or oval growths are usually benign. Look for irregular shapes where one half is a different shape than the other half.

■ *B is for border*—Irregular, notched, scalloped, or vaguely defined borders need to be checked out.

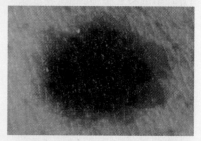

■ *C is for color*—Look for growths that have many colors or an uneven distribution of color. Generally, growths that are the same color all over are usually benign.

■ *D is for diameter*—Have your doctor check out any growths that are larger than 6 millimeters, about the diameter of a pencil eraser.

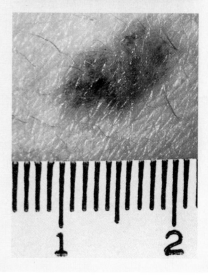

Table C.5. Barriers to Helmet Use

Barrier	Parents	Children	Physician
Lack of perceived need	X	X	X
Lack of recommendation by physician	X	—	X
Don't think child will wear helmet	X	—	—
Cost of helmets	X	—	—
Peer pressure	—	X	—
Lack of "coolness"	—	X	—
Discomfort	—	X	—

Table C.6. State-of-the-Art Care for Five Common Conditions

Condition	Old Thinking	New Thinking
Lower-back pain	Bed rest, stretching exercises	Continuation of normal activities; aspirin, ibuprofen, or acetaminophen for pain
Early-stage breast cancer	Mastectomy	Lumpectomy plus radiation
Ulcers	Drugs to suppress stomach acid secretion	Antibiotics plus drugs that suppress stomach acid secretion
Simple ovarian cysts	Surgery	Depending on age and family history, watchful waiting (periodic pelvic and ultrasound exams)
Type II diabetes	Insulin or sulfonylureas	Diet and exercise; if not effective, insulin, often combined with new oral drugs that prompt insulin, glucophage, or acarbose secretion

Table C.7. World Population Growth and the Food Supply

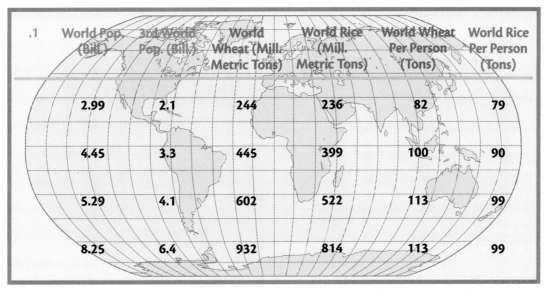

World Pop. (Bill.)	3rd World Pop. (Bill.)	World Wheat (Mill. Metric Tons)	World Rice (Mill. Metric Tons)	World Wheat Per Person (Tons)	World Rice Per Person (Tons)
2.99	2.1	244	236	82	79
4.45	3.3	445	399	100	90
5.29	4.1	602	522	113	99
8.25	6.4	932	814	113	99

Sources: Statistical Abstract of the United States, 1982-1983, p. 855, Table 1513; 1991, p. 830, Table 1434; 1993, p. 839, Table 1372.

Table C.8. Crowding in Five of the World's Largest Urban Areas

Year	Variable	Mexico City (Mill.)	Sao Paulo (Mill.)	Calcutta (Mill.)	Jakarta (Mill.)	Lagos (Mill.)
1960	Pop. (Mill.)	4.9	4.7	5.5	2.7	0.8
	Area (Sq .Ft.)	14.6×10^9	12.6×10^9	5.8×10^9	2.1×10^9	1.6×10^9
	Area/Capita	2980	2681	1054	777	2000
	Area (Sq.Miles)	522	451	209	76	56
	Persons/Sq. Mile	9,387	22,488	26,316	35,526	14,286
1990	Pop. (Mill.)	19.4	18.4	11.8	9.4	7.6
	Area (Sq .Ft.)	14.6×10^9	12.6×10^9	5.8×10^9	2.1×10^9	1.6×10^9
	Area/Capita	753	649	492	223	210
	Area (Sq.Miles)	522	451	209	76	56
	Persons/Sq. Mile	37,165	40,798	56,459	123,684	135,714
2020	Pop. (Mill.)	54.4	52.8	27.0	29.2	49.4
	Area (Sq .Ft.)	14.6×10^9	12.6×10^9	5.8×10^9	2.1×10^9	1.6×10^9
	Area/Capita	268	239	215	72	32
	Area (Sq.Miles)	522	451	209	76	56
	Persons/Sq. Mile	104,215	117,073	129,187	384,211	882,143

Source: Statistical Abstract of the United States, 1993, p. 845, Table 1377.

Glossary

Abnormal—Unusual; different from normal (p. 53)

Abstinence—The willful avoidance of something (p. 142)

Abuse—Physical or emotional mistreatment; actions that harm someone (p. 152)

Acid rain—Rain, snow, sleet, or hail that contains large amounts of sulfuric or nitric acids (p. 416)

Acne—Clogged skin pores that cause pimples and blackheads (p. 103)

Acquired immunodeficiency syndrome (AIDS)—A disorder of the immune system (p. 219)

Addiction—A need for a habit-forming substance (p. 266)

Additive—A substance added to foods in small amounts (p. 195)

Adolescence—Time between ages 12 and 19 when many physical changes take place (p. 118)

Adoptive family—Family that includes parents and an adopted child or children (p. 147)

Adrenal gland—Part of the endocrine system that releases several hormones (p. 84)

Adrenaline—Hormone released into the bloodstream that increases certain body functions (p. 84)

Advocacy group—A prevention organization that helps specific groups get health services (p. 403)

Aerobic exercise—Activity that increases a person's heart rate (p. 107)

Affective disorder—A mental problem characterized by disturbed or uncontrolled emotions (p. 59)

Aggression—Any action that intends harm to someone (p. 20)

Alcoholism—A disease characterized by dependence on alcoholic beverages (p. 271)

Algae—A wide-ranging group of plants that live in water (p. 419)

Allergy—Unusual response of the body to a food or substance in the air (p. 101)

Alveoli—Tiny air sacs at the ends of the bronchioles (p. 88)

Amino acid—A small chemical unit that makes up protein (p. 173)

Amphetamine—A central nervous system stimulant (p. 272)

Anabolic steroid—A synthetic drug that closely resembles the natural male sex hormone testosterone (p. 280)

Anaerobic exercise—Activity that quickly uses up oxygen in the body (p. 107)

Analgesic—A medicine that relieves pain (p. 261)

Anger—Strong feeling of displeasure (p. 20)

Angina pectoris—Severe pain associated with an inadequate supply of blood to the heart (p. 235)

Anorexia—An eating disorder characterized by severe weight loss (p. 63)

Antibiotic—A substance that can destroy the growth of certain germs (p. 224)

Antibody—A protein that kills a specific pathogen (p. 211)

Antiperspirant—Product that helps to control perspiration (p. 103)

Anus—Opening through which feces leave the body; outlet of the digestive tract (p. 91)

Anxiety—A feeling of uneasiness or fearful concern (p. 20)

Anxiety disorder—A mental problem that makes normal life difficult because of intense anxiety (p. 58)

Arteriosclerosis—A chronic disease in which arterial walls thicken, harden, and lose flexibility, resulting in impaired blood circulation (p. 234)

Artery—Vessel that carries blood away from the heart (p. 86)

Arthritis—A group of diseases that result in swelling of the joints and rubbing on the bones (p. 247)

Asbestos—A fibrous material used for fireproofing, brake linings, and building materials (p. 414)

Asthma—A respiratory disease that causes breathing difficulty (p. 249)

Atherosclerosis—A form of arteriosclerosis in which large- and medium-sized arteries become narrow from a buildup of fat along their walls (p. 234)

Athlete's foot—Itching or cracking between the toes caused by a fungus (p. 104)

Attachment—Bond or tie to others (p. 14)

Auditory nerve—Part of the ear that sends sound information to the brain (p. 81)

Bacteria—Tiny structures that cause infection and disease; germs (p. 93)

Barbiturates—A category of sedative-hypnotic drugs (p. 275)

Behavior modification—Form of psychotherapy that teaches a person to replace a less effective behavior pattern with a more effective one (p. 59)

Benign—Not harmful to health (p. 239)

Bile—Substance in the liver that breaks down fats (p. 90)

Bipolar disorder—A mental problem involving an uncontrolled shift from feeling too much energetic emotion to feeling very depressed (p. 61)

Blended family—Family made when parents live with children from an earlier marriage or marriages (p. 147)

Blizzard—A violent snowstorm with winds over 35 miles per hour (p. 322)

Brain stem—Part of the brain that connects the cerebrum with the spinal cord (p. 78)

Bronchi—Air tubes leading into the lungs (p. 87)

Bronchiole—Smallest division of the bronchi (p. 87)

Bulimia—An eating disorder involving bingeing followed by purging (p. 63)

Calcium—Mineral important for maintaining strong bones and teeth (p. 177)

Calorie—A unit that measures the amount of energy in food (p. 107)

Capillary—Tiny blood vessel that connects arteries and veins (p. 86)

Carbohydrate—Chemical substance in foods that provides starches and sugars (p. 169)

Carcinogen—A cancer-causing substance (p. 241)

Cardiac arrest—A condition in which the heart has stopped beating and there is no pulse (p. 335)

Cardiopulmonary resuscitation (CPR)—An emergency procedure for cardiovascular failure (p. 335)

Cardiovascular—Relating to the heart and blood vessels (p. 233)

Cartilage—A cushion in the joints (p. 247)

Cerebellum—Part of the brain that controls balance and muscular activities (p. 78)

Cerebrum—Part of the brain that permits a person to read, think, and remember (p. 78)

Cervix—Narrow outer end of the uterus (p. 128)

Chancre—A painless, hard sore that is the first sign of syphilis (p. 225)

Chemotherapy—Treatment for cancer using certain drugs (p. 241)

Child abuse—The physical or emotional mistreatment of children (p. 152)

Chlamydia—A sexually transmitted disease (p. 224)

Cholesterol—A waxy, fatlike substance in body cells that helps with certain body functions; some kinds can clog blood vessels (p. 172)

Chromosomes—Tiny bodies in the center of cells that carry hereditary information (p. 132)

Chronic—Lasting for a long time (p. 226)

Civil defense—An organized system of emergency measures that volunteers take to help people in disasters (p. 323)

Clinical depression—An affective disorder involving long-lasting, intense sadness (p. 59)

Cocaine—A highly addictive illegal stimulant (p. 273)

Communicable—Something that can be passed from one person to another (p. 206)

Compromise—To come to an agreement by both sides giving a little (p. 35)

Compulsive overeating—An eating disorder involving bingeing but no purging (p. 63)

Conflict—A disagreement between two or more people who have different ideas (p. 348)

Consumer—Someone who buys goods or services (p. 372)

Cope—To deal with or overcome problems and difficulties (p. 23)

Cornea—Part of the eye that light passes through (p. 80)

Crack—A smokable form of cocaine (p. 274)

Custodial parent—The parent who is responsible for a child after a divorce (p. 148)

Custody—The legal right and responsibility given to a parent to care for a child after a divorce (p. 148)

Daily Value—Section of a food label that provides information about the percent of nutrients in the product (p. 194)

Dandruff—Occasional flaking from the scalp (p. 104)

Decibel—A unit that measures sound (p. 101)

Deductible—The first part of each year's medical expenses before the insurance company makes payments (p. 383)

Defense mechanism—A mental device one uses to protect oneself (p. 54)

Deficiency—Lack of a certain nutrient in the diet (p. 181)

Deforestation—Cutting and clearing trees (p. 421)

Deformity—Abnormally formed structure (p. 208)

Delusion—A false belief (p. 61)

Denial—The conscious refusal to take a threat seriously (p. 55)

Deodorant—Product that covers body odor (p. 103)

Depressant—A drug that slows down the central nervous system (p. 268)

Depression—A state of deep sadness (p. 22)

Dermis—Inner layer of skin (p. 93)

Designer drug—A substance with a slightly different chemical makeup from a legal drug (p. 279)

Detoxification—Removing addictive drugs from the body (p. 291)

Diabetes—A disease resulting from too little insulin, or from the body's inability to use insulin effectively (p. 244)

Diabetic coma—A life-threatening condition caused by inadequate control of blood glucose (p. 244)

Diaphragm—A band of muscles that lies beneath the lungs (p. 88)

Diet—Food and drink regularly eaten (p. 164)

Discriminate—To treat differently on the basis of something other than individual worth (p. 45)

Displacement—Shifting an emotion from its real object to a safer or more immediate one (p. 55)

Divorce—Legally ending a marriage (p. 144)

Dominant—Having the most control (p. 133)

Drug—A chemical substance other than food that changes the way the mind and body work (p. 260)

Drug dependence—A need for a drug resulting from occasional or long-term use of that drug (p. 285)

Dysfunctional—Harmed; working abnormally (p. 54)

Earthquake—Shaking that occurs when the earth's plates, or slabs of rock, shift and move (p. 321)

Eating disorder—An attempt to cope with psychological problems through eating habits (p. 62)

Ecology—The study of the interrelationships of organisms and the physical environment (p. 412)

Electrical shock—A flow of electric current through the body (p. 310)

Embryo—Fertilized egg after implantation (p. 127)

Emotional abuse—Mistreatment of a person through words, gestures, or denying affection (p. 152)

Emotions—Feelings (p. 12)

Empathy—Identifying and trying to understand others' feelings (p. 46)

Emphysema—A serious respiratory disease that causes difficulty in breathing (p. 266)

Enabling—Trying to protect someone from the results of abusing drugs (p. 289)

Endurance—Ability to stay with an activity for a long time (p. 106)

Environment—A network of interrelated parts, including air, land, water, plants, and animals (p. 409)

Enzyme—Substance that promotes a chemical reaction in the body (p. 89)

Epidemic—A communicable infectious disease that spreads rapidly and affects large populations (p. 394)

Epidermis—Outer layer of skin (p. 93)

Epilepsy—A chronic disease caused by disordered brain activity and characterized by seizures (p. 248)

Erection—Condition in which the penis becomes hard and larger (p. 125)

Esophagus—Long tube the connects the mouth and the stomach (p. 89)

Essential nutrients—Chemical substances in foods that the body cannot make (p. 166)

Esteem—Value or worth; how one sees oneself or others (p. 14)

Estrogen—Female sex hormone (p. 121)

Extended family—Family that includes parents, children, and other relatives (p. 147)

Fallopian tubes—Passages through which mature egg cells pass from the ovaries to the uterus (p. 123)

Family love—Love based on attachment and support (p. 14)

Famine—An extreme food shortage (p. 421)

Fear—A strong feeling of fright; awareness of danger (p. 20)

Feces—Solid waste material remaining in the large intestine after digestion (p. 91)

Fertilization—The union of an egg cell and a sperm (p. 125)

Fetus—Unborn baby from eight weeks after fertilization until birth (p. 128)

Fire extinguisher—A portable device containing chemicals that put out small fires (p. 307)

First aid—Immediate emergency care given to a sick or injured person before professional medical care arrives (p. 329)

Flash flood—A dangerous event that occurs suddenly without warning because of heavy rains (p. 320)

Flexibility—Ability to twist, turn, bend, and stretch easily (p. 106)

Flood—An event that occurs when a body of water overflows and covers normally dry land (p. 320)

Fossil fuels—Burnable substances formed in the earth from plant or animal remains (p. 414)

Foster family—Family that cares for children who are in need of short-term parenting from people other than their birth parents (p. 147)

Fracture—A broken bone (p. 340)

Friendship—Love based on choice (p. 14)

Frostbite—A tissue injury caused by exposure to extreme cold (p. 342)

Frustration—Being blocked from something (p. 20)

Fungus—An organism that grows in moist places (p. 104)

Gallbladder—Digestive organ attached to the liver that stores bile (p. 90)

Gender—The condition of being male or female; sex (p. 132)

Gene—A tiny structure in chromosomes that controls the transfer of hereditary characteristics (p. 132)

Genetic counselor—Someone who helps people determine the likelihood of passing inherited disorders to their children (p. 135)

Genetics—The science that deals with heredity and inherited characteristics (p. 132)

Genital herpes—A sexually transmitted chronic infection (p. 224)

Genitals—Reproductive, or sex, organs (p. 120)

Gestation—The period of development in the uterus from fertilization until birth; pregnancy (p. 126)

Gland—A structure that secretes a special substance to help the body work (p. 83)

Nutrient—A food substance or ingredient (p. 74)

Nutrition Facts—Section of a food label that provides information about the product (p. 194)

Occupational Safety and Health Administration (OSHA)—U.S. government agency that seeks to protect the safety and health of American workers (p. 312)

Olfactory nerve—Nerve that helps the brain detect smells (p. 81)

Opportunistic—Caused by a usually harmless germ that can infect a person whose immune system is greatly weakened (p. 219)

Optic nerve—Part of the eye that sends light information from the retina to the brain (p. 80)

Optimism—Tending to expect the best possible outcome (p. 35)

Osteoarthritis—A condition in which the cartilage in joints wears away (p. 247)

Outpatient clinic—A place where people receive health care without staying overnight (p. 381)

Ovaries—Two glands in females that produce egg cells (p. 123)

Ovulation—The release of a mature egg cell (p. 123)

Ozone layer—A region above the earth's surface that shields and protects the earth from the sun's harmful rays (p. 416)

Pancreas—A digestive gland that produces insulin and enzymes (p. 90)

Panic attack—A feeling of terror that comes without warning and includes chest pain, rapid heartbeat, sweating, shaking, or shortness of breath (p. 58)

Particulate—Tiny piece of solid matter (p. 414)

Pathogen—An agent that causes disease (p. 207)

PCP—A synthetic hallucinogen (p. 277)

Penis—Male reproductive organ (p. 125)

Peripheral nerves—Nerves that carry all messages sent between the central nervous system and the rest of the body (p. 79)

Personality—All of one's behavioral, mental, and emotional characteristics (p. 29)

Pessimism—Tending to expect the worst possible outcome (p. 35)

Petit mal—An epileptic seizure in which a person does not lose consciousness (p. 248)

Pharmacist—Druggist (p. 260)

Phobia—An irrational or unreasonable fear of something (p. 54)

Phosphorus—Mineral that works with calcium to maintain strong bones and teeth (p. 177)

Photochemical smog—A form of air pollution (p. 413)

Pimple—An inflamed swelling of the skin (p. 103)

Pituitary gland—Part of the endocrine system that controls bodily functions such as growth and development (p. 83)

Placenta—An organ lining the uterus that surrounds the embryo or fetus (p. 127)

Platelet—Element in the blood that helps with clotting (p. 85)

Pneumonia—A lung infection (p. 222)

Pollution—Making soil, water, or air impure or unclean through the discharge of harmful substances (p. 410)

Pore—Tiny opening in the skin (p. 93)

Postpartum—Following birth (p. 131)

Preferred provider organization (PPO)—A form of managed care (p. 385)

Pregnant—Carrying a developing baby in the female body (p. 125)

Prejudice—Negative, or unfavorable, opinions formed about something or someone without enough experience or knowledge (p. 45)

Prescription—A written order from a medical person for a medicine or other treatment (p. 260)

Preservative—A substance added to food to prevent spoiling (p. 195)

Pressure point—A place on the body where an underlying artery can be pressed against a bone to stop bleeding in a limb (p. 337)

Primary care physician—A doctor who treats people for routine problems (p. 379)

Progesterone—Female sex hormone (p.121)

Projection—Accusing another person of having one's own attitudes, feelings, or purposes (p. 55)

Protein—A substance in food needed for growth and repair of body tissues (p. 169)

Psychoactive—Affecting the mind or mental processes (p. 268)

Psychologist—A person who studies mental and behavioral characteristics (p. 53)

Psychotherapy—Psychological treatment for mental or emotional disorders (p. 59)

Puberty—Period at the beginning of adolescence when children develop into adults and reach sexual maturity (p. 120)

Public health—The practice of protecting and improving the health of a community or a nation (p. 393)

Pupil—Dark center part of the eye that adjusts to let in the correct amount of light (p. 80)

Quackery—The promotion of medical products or services that are unproved or worthless (p. 375)

Rabies—A disease transmitted to humans from animal bites (p. 339)

Radiation—The transmission of energy in the form of waves (p. 241)

Radiation sickness—Illness caused by exposure to very high levels of radiation (p. 424)

Radon—A colorless, odorless gas that forms from the radioactive decay of radium underground (p. 415)

Rape—The unlawful act of forcing a person to have sexual relations against his or her will (p. 355)

Rational—Being realistic or reasonable (p. 36)

Reaction—Response (p. 12)

Receptor cells—Cells that receive information (p. 81)

Recessive—Withdrawn; hidden (p. 133)

Rectum—Lower part of the large intestine (p. 91)

Reflex—Automatic response (p. 80)

Rehabilitation—Therapy needed for recovery from surgery or an illness or injury (p. 381)

Relief—A light, pleasant feeling after something painful or distressing is gone (p. 22)

Repression—The unconscious dismissal of painful impulses, desires, or fears from the conscious mind (p. 55)

Reproduction—The process through which living beings produce other living beings (p. 122)

Reproductive organs—Organs in the body that allow humans to mature sexually and to have children (p. 120)

Rescue breathing—Putting oxygen from a rescuer's lungs into an unconscious victim's lungs to help the victim breathe (p. 334)

Respiration—The process of breathing in oxygen and breathing out carbon dioxide (p. 87)

Retina—Part of the eye that receives and sends light information to the optic nerve (p. 80)

Rheumatoid arthritis—A destructive inflammation of the joints (p. 247)

Role confusion—Being unsure about who one is and one's goals as an adult (p. 119)

Romantic love—Strong physical and emotional attraction between two people (p. 14)

Saliva—A liquid in the mouth containing an enzyme that breaks down food (p. 89)

Sanitation—Any measures designed to protect public health (p. 399)

Saturated fat—Substance in food from animal products that may lead to high cholesterol in blood (p. 172)

Secondary sex characteristics—Traits that signal the beginning of adulthood such as facial hair for males (p. 121)

Sedative-hypnotic drug—A prescribed depressant that reduces anxiety or promotes sleep (p. 275)

Seizure—A physical reaction to the disordered brain activity that causes epilepsy (p. 248)

Self-actualization—Achieving one's possibilities (p. 15)

Self-awareness—Understanding oneself as an individual or personality (p. 44)

Self-concept—Ideas one has about oneself (p.15)

Self-defeating behavior—Actions that block a person's efforts to reach goals (p. 53)

Self-esteem—Self-respect; how one feels about oneself (p. 15)

Sensorineural deafness—Permanent hearing loss in which the tiny cells in the inner ear are destroyed (p. 423)

Separation—A couple's agreement, or a court decision made for the couple, to stop living together (p. 150)

Sewage—Liquid and solid waste from drains and toilets that is carried off in disposal systems (p. 418)

Sex-linked—Carried by a sex chromosome (p. 134)

Sexual abuse—Any sexual contact that is forced on a person (p. 152)

Sexual intercourse—Inserting the penis into the vagina (p.125)

Sexually transmitted disease—Any disease that is spread through sexual activity (p. 224)

Shock—Failure of the circulatory system to provide enough blood to the body (p. 336)

Single-parent family—Family that includes a child or children and one adult (p. 147)

Smoke detector—A battery-operated device that sounds loudly when it senses smoke or high amounts of heat (p. 307)

Social comparison—Observing other people to determine how to behave (p. 44)

Social esteem—How others value a person (p. 30)

Solid waste—Garbage; trash (p. 422)

Specialist—A doctor who works only in a certain branch of medicine (p. 379)

Sperm—Male sex cells produced by the testes (p. 122)

Splint—A rigid object that keeps a broken limb in place (p. 340)

Sprain—The tearing or stretching of tendons or ligaments connecting joints (p. 340)

Stimulant—A drug that speeds up the central nervous system (p. 266)

Stress—A state of physical or emotional pressure (p. 17)

Stress response—Automatic physical reactions to stress (p. 17)

Stroke—A cardiovascular disease that occurs when the blood supply to the brain is stopped (p. 236)

Subcutaneous layer—Deepest layer of skin (p. 93)

Substance abuse disorder—An unhealthy dependence on alcohol or other drugs (p. 58)

Suicide—Killing oneself (p. 60)

Survival floating—A technique that someone in danger of drowning uses to conserve energy while waiting to be rescued (p. 313)

Symptom—A bodily reaction that indicates a disease or physical problem (p. 37)

Syphilis—A sexually transmitted infectious disease (p. 244)

Temperament—A person's emotional makeup (p. 29)

Tendon—A strong fiber wound tightly together that joins muscle to bone or muscle to muscle (p. 76)

Testes—Two glands in males that produce sperm cells (p. 122)

Testosterone—Male sex hormone (p. 121)

THC—The psychoactive chemical in marijuana and hashish (p. 278)

Thought disorder—A mental problem characterized by twisted or false ideas and beliefs (p. 61)

Thyroid gland—Part of the endocrine system that releases a hormone that affects metabolism (p. 83)

Tolerance—Ability to withstand increasing amounts of a drug without reacting to it (p. 274)

Tornado—A funnel-shaped column of wind with speeds up to 500 miles per hour (p. 319)

Toxic—Harmful to health; poisonous (p. 241)

Trachea—Long tube running from the nose to the chest; windpipe (p. 87)

Tranquilizers—A category of sedative-hypnotic drugs (p. 275)

Transfusion—The transfer of blood from one individual to another (p. 222)

Trimester—A period of three months (p. 127)

Tuberculosis—A communicable lung disease (p. 396)

Tumor—A mass of tissue formed from the abnormal growth of cells (p. 239)

Ultrasound—The use of high-frequency sound waves to show pictures of structures inside the body (p. 126)

Umbilical cord—Structure that joins the embryo or fetus with the placenta (p. 127)

Universal Precautions—Methods of self-protection that prevent contact with blood or body fluids (p. 331)

Unsaturated fat—Substance in food from vegetable and fish oils that help lower the amount of cholesterol in blood (p. 172)

Ureter—Tube through which urine passes from a kidney to the urinary bladder (p. 92)

Urethra—Tube that takes urine out of the body (p. 92)

Urinary bladder—Bag that stores urine (p. 92)

Urine—Liquid waste product formed in the kidneys (p. 92)

Uterus—Female body part that holds a fertilized egg while it grows (p. 123)

Vaccination—An injection of dead or weakened viruses to make the body immune to the viruses (p. 212)

Vagina—Canal in females from the uterus to the outside of the body; birth canal (p. 123)

Vein—Vessel that carries blood back to the heart (p. 86)

Villi—Tiny fingerlike bulges in the walls of the small intestine that help to absorb nutrients (p. 89)

Violence—Actions or words that hurt people or things they care about (p. 152)

Vitamin—A substance needed in small amounts for growth and activity (p. 175)

Well-being—State of being physically and emotionally healthy; the state of feeling happy, healthy, and content (pp. 20, 30)

Withdrawal—A physical reaction to the absence of a drug in the body (p. 268)

Index

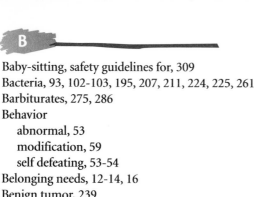

Baby-sitting, safety guidelines for, 309
Bacteria, 93, 102-103, 195, 207, 211, 224, 225, 261
Barbiturates, 275, 286
Behavior
    abnormal, 53
    modification, 59
    self defeating, 53-54
Belonging needs, 12-14, 16
Benign tumor, 239
Bicycle safety, 317
Bile, 90
Biofeedback, 18
Bipolar disorder, 61
Bites, first aid for, 339-340
Bleeding, first aid for, 336-337, 378
Blended family, 147, 148
Blizzard, safety during, 323
Blood, 85-86
    and AIDS, 222
    -alcohol level (BAC), 269-270
    cells, 74, 75, 85, 179
    pressure, 86, 233, 261, 266, 273, 276, 280
    vessels, 86, 89, 172, 266
Body fluids, and AIDS, 220, 222
Body language, 42
Bone injuries, first aid for, 340
Bones, 74-77
    and diet, 177, 179, 181
Brain, 78-81
    and epilepsy, 248
    stem, 78
    and stress reactions, 18-19
    and stroke, 236
Bronchi/bronchioles, 87-88, 249
Bubonic plague, 212
Bulimia, 63
Burns
    degree of, 340
    first aid for, 340-341

Calcium, 119, 177, 179
Calories, 107, 165-168, 174, 179, 180, 193, 194
Cancer, 239-243
    and diet, 169, 182, 195

and environment, 206, 413, 415
    risk factors for, 222, 227, 241-242, 266, 267, 269, 278, 397
    treatment for, 241, 382
    warning signs, 240
Capillaries, 86, 88
Carbohydrates, 169-173, 175, 187, 194, 244
Carbon dioxide
    in the blood, 85-88
    in the environment, 409, 422
Carbon monoxide, 267, 413
Carcinogens, 241
Cardiac arrest, first aid for, 335
Cardiopulmonary resuscitation. *See* CPR
Cardiovascular
    diseases, 233-238, 244
    failure, first aid for, 335
    medicine, 261
Careers, 21, 47, 64, 76, 111, 136, 154, 174, 192, 209, 228, 236, 264, 293, 315, 356, 387, 396, 429
Cartilage, 247
Cells, 74, 85, 92
Centers for Disease Control (CDC), 386, 395
Central nervous system
    effects of drugs on, 266, 268, 272, 274, 276, 278, 285
    parts of, 78
Cerebellum, 78-79
Cerebrum, 78-79
Cervix, 128, 130
Chancre, 225
Chemotherapy, 241
Child abuse, 152
Childbirth, 128, 130-131
    and sexually transmitted diseases, 224-226
Chlamydia, 224, 225
Chlorofluorocarbons (CFCs), 416, 426
Choking, first aid for, 332-333
Cholesterol, 172, 188, 191, 194, 234, 237, 238
Chromosomes, 132-133, 135, 208
Chronic infections, 226
Circulatory system, 85-86
Civil defense, 324
Claustrophobia, 54
Clean Air Act, 426
Clinical depression, 59-61
Cocaine, 273-274, 286, 290, 292
Color blindness, 100, 134

first aid for, 333
reducing risk of, 313
Drugs, 259-283
abuse of, 58, 152, 154, 404
and AIDS, 220, 273, 276
alternatives to, 296
and anxiety, 54
and safety risks, 310, 335
and violence, 353
See also Addiction; Dependency
Dysfunctional relationships, 54, 56-57

E

Ears, 81, 100-102
Earthquake safety, 322-323
Eating disorders, 62-63, 154
Ecology, 412
Egg cells, 123-128, 132
Electrical shock
first aid for, 333, 335
reducing risks of, 310-311
Embryo, 127, 129
Emergency Medical Service (EMS), 329-330, 335-337, 339-342
Emotional abuse, 152
Emotional health/well-being, 5-7, 30-31, 34-39, 44-47, 106, 164
Emotions, 12, 16-23, 31, 32
Empathy, 46-47
Emphysema, 266
Enabling, 289
Endocrine system, 83-84, 120
Endurance, heart and lung, 106, 108-110
Environment, 409
and disease, 206
protecting the, 426-430
and health concerns, 397-398, 409-412, 421-425
See also Pollution
Environmental Protection Agency, 400, 426
Enzymes, 89, 90, 175
Epidemics, 212, 394, 395, 403
Epidermis, 93
Epilepsy, 248
Erection, 125
Erikson, Erik, 117
Esophagus, 89-90

Essential nutrients, 166, 169, 175, 181
Esteem needs, 12, 14-15
Estrogen, 121, 124
Excretory system, 91-93
Exercise, 106-112
and health/fitness, 32, 86, 104, 106-112, 206, 207, 233-235, 237, 238, 246, 273, 378, 403
and muscle tone, 77
and pregnancy, 127
and stress, 18, 24, 60, 190, 238, 296, 353, 357
and weight, 173
Extended family, 147, 148
Eyes, 80
caring for, 99-100
injuries to, 341

F

Fainting, first aid for, 339
Fallopian tubes, 123, 127
Falls, reducing risk of, 306
Family, 141-154
conflict, 348
drug dependency in, 288-289
and genetic traits, 135
love, 14
violence, 347, 352
See also Marriage; Parenting
Famine, 421
Farsightedness, 100
Fat, 169, 172-176, 180, 187, 194, 233, 403
FDA (Food and Drug Administration), 193, 195, 260, 263, 264, 386
Fear, 20, 22
Feces, 91, 240
Fertilization, 125-128, 132
Fetus, 126, 128-129
Fiber, 169
Fight-or-flight impulse, 18
Fire
drills, 308-309
extinguisher, 307-308
and home escape route, 311
putting out a, 308
reducing risks of, 306-308
safety devices, 307
First aid, 328-345
Fitness Tips, 18, 89, 110, 141, 170, 207, 237, 294